Business International's Global Management Desk Reference

Business International's Global Management Desk Reference

Shirley B. Dreifus, Editor
Business International Corporation

McGraw-Hill, Inc.
New York St. Louis San Francisco Auckland Bogotá
Caracas Lisbon London Madrid Mexico Milan
Montreal New Delhi Paris San Juan São Paulo
Singapore Sydney Tokyo Toronto

Library of Congress Cataloging-in-Publication Data

Business International's global management desk reference / Shirley B.
  Dreifus, editor.
     p.   cm.
  ISBN 0-07-009333-4 (cl)
    1. International business enterprises – Management – Handbooks,
manuals, etc. I. Dreifus, Shirley B. II. Business International
Corporation. III. Title: Global management desk reference.
HD62.4.B87 1992
658'.049 – dc20   92-7822
                                                  CIP

1 2 3 4 5 6 7 8 9 0 DOC/DOC 9 8 7 6 5 4 3 2

ISBN   0-07-009333-4

*The sponsoring editor for this book was David Conti, the editing supervisor was
Kimberly A. Goff, and the production supervisor was Suzanne W. Babeuf. This
book was set in Baskerville. It was composed by McGraw-Hill's Professional
Book Group composition unit.*

Printed and bound by R. R. Donnelley & Sons Company.

Contents

v

7. Human Resources   **288**

8. Management   **336**

Preface

You have in your hands a desk reference that holds many of the secrets of global success. Any manager with "international" as his or her mandate can learn from this wealth of information proven ways of doing business anywhere in the world. Readers who will benefit from using this book include the seasoned multinational executive as well as the novice strategic planner whose job it is to consider what new markets to test. Based on the latest findings of *Business International's* consultants and researchers, this book provides success strategies on every aspect of managing international operations, including: how to devise a marketing strategy; organize a global financial management system; implement worldwide quality control; and hire and manage foreign nationals.

In a handy reference form, *Business International's Global Management Desk Reference* provides a step-by-step "how-to" framework for meeting the business challenges of the global decade ahead. Many of the world's most successful, experienced, and well-known companies are found within the pages: Shell, Sony, Kodak, GE, Dow Chemical, and Ford Motor, among hundreds of others. It is easily organized to meet the needs of today's busy international executive. The desk reference is comprised of clearly delineated chapters, headings and corporate examples/solutions for a winning global strategy.

Inside this reference the reader will find how to:

- Update marketing goals to fit changing consumer needs

- Attract and maintain a high-quality staff

- Manage international operations to achieve overall corporate goals

- Improve planning and investment strategies

- Build a global image to stand out in today's competitive marketplace

In today's global environment, managers of any size business need help. This includes planners in marketing, strategic relations, finance, R&D, human resources, legal and public affairs. *Business International's Global Management Desk Reference* is designed to give clear, concise information on a complicated array of global management issues.

Acknowledgments

Business International's Global Management Desk Reference was a project undertaken by BI's Global Services unit in New York. Special thanks to Yasmin Ghahremani, project editor, and Andrea Mackiewicz, contributing editor.

Introduction

In the push to sell their products, companies of all sizes and profit margins will be forced to question current values and develop winning strategies to carry them into the twenty-first century. *Business International's Global Management Desk Reference* highlights ways in which any business can respond to the following *key issues* facing management as the calendar slides through the 1990s.

Organization

• Companies should assess the function of what has been traditionally called the corporate headquarters. At Shell, the basic ownership structure of this diversified firm is built around three holding companies. This way, Shell avoids consolidation of a diversified business by creating a constellation of independent businesses with a three-dimensional matrix that allows the independent operating companies to draw upon global resources.

• Japanese electronics giant, Sony Corporation has developed two management techniques for its global network: zone management and global localization. Sales, manufacturing and product planning are generally decentralized and within the purview of the country headquarters, but all final approvals come from corporate headquarters.

Human Resources

• Companies must search for new ways to transfer knowledge and expertise across the global organization. The emphasis is on team-building and enhanced coordination to cut red tape and shorten the lead time for commercialization of new product ideas. Management layers will continue to shrink: The smallest headquarters staff possible will make strategic decisions, while operational responsibility will be pushed further down into the field. Training will be the keynote in this endeavor. In the US, multinational companies alone will spend approximately $210 billion on employee education and management development programs this year.

• Rewarding and motivating creative employees is becoming an essential adjunct to innovation. Flexible pay and promotion scales are being designed to lessen dependence on such traditional schemes as the Hay Point system. For example, AT&T's Bell Laboratories has replaced Hay with a program that deemphasizes such factors as job descriptions and reporting relationships in favor of experience and record of achievement. Individual scientists now frequently make more in compensation than do their supervisors or even department heads.

• Stung by the rising cost of social welfare systems, governments are pushing more of the benefit burden onto companies. In response, MNCs will replace comprehensive programs with a menu of benefits that will force employees to choose priorities among a range of options.

R&D and Technology

• Cross-functional teams to integrate marketing, manufacturing and finance are succeeding where money, government support and creative manpower have failed. As the time in which an idea becomes commercialized shortens, the need for a business-driven strategy becomes critical. This is particularly so since the application of technology, not the technology itself, is key. Thus, the involvement of manufacturing personnel will begin much earlier in the product development process.

• Finding and retaining good people able to contribute in a variety of work environments is essential to promoting growth within the research and development (R&D) department of the 1990s. Developing new ways to measure the performance of creative workers is a key task.

• Rising costs and demands of customers seeking greater value for their money will require a more targeted approach to the discovery process. A drift away from the basic research will continue and more multinational corporations will pool their scientific resources in consortiums. The number and variety of products in test stages will dwindle as greater focus is placed on true "breakthrough" products rather than on refinements or extensions — the ubiquitous "me too's."

• Protection against technology theft is now a necessary part of any global business strategy. To lessen the risk of leakage in strategic alliances, MNCs are concentrating their serious technological expertise in a few select areas to better monitor the competition and maintain that vital "step-ahead" lead. They will also seek — and in all probability gain — the support of their home governments in the fight against intellectual-property infringements.

Manufacturing

• Manufacturing's role as a strategic offensive weapon — not a cost center — is being challenged by the continuing technological revolution. CAD/CAM systems developed a decade ago are becoming obsolete in the face of AI networks and other breakthrough technologies. Robotics and materials management continue to advance. Together, the pace of change poses a risk to companies anxious about the costs of building new facilities that fail to remain state of the art.

• Multinational corporations are being forced to rethink the concept of the traditional grounded plant in favor of more flexible arrangements, such as time-share plants built in cooperation with other companies and floating equipment packages that are transferable to additional sites. More common are plants with variable configurations that will allow virtually any type and volume of production. The aim is lower cost with a simultaneous improvement in customer service. Product diversification can also take place without significant capital expense.

• Management is increasingly taking the direct initiative in maintaining quality, often surpassing the role of employee quality circles or teams. The emphasis is moving outside the company to involve suppliers and customers in the search for improvements. Quality increasingly stands on its own as a strategic objective for every business function, from human resources to information systems.

Finance

• Continuing fallout from the US Income Tax Reform Act of 1986 will make tax planning a global strategic function. The search for maximization of aftertax profit will induce permanent changes in the ways US-based multinational companies source products and locate plants and facilities. The need for additional low-taxed, foreign-source income to absorb excess US foreign tax credits will impose new responsibilities on affiliates to assume their fair share of the cost of providing a worldwide network of services.

• Intercompany pricing transactions are taking a beating from proposed new super-royalty provisions of the US tax code. With the Treasury Department and the Internal Revenue Service committed to the changes, the prospect is for a buildup in tax tensions with foreign governments and even a possible exposure of income to double taxation as statutes proliferate.

• Cost efficiencies have assumed paramount importance in the management of currency exposures. To be cost effective, MNCs must take a selective hedging approach involving financial and, especially, nonfinancial actions. The latter includes changing sourcing patterns or manufacturing sites to reduce the mismatch between the company's currency profile and that of its competitors.

• Management must consider the financial implications of the single European market. More European companies are reporting that they are being presented with requests from customers and suppliers to handle financial transactions in the European currency unit (ECU). ECU billing and invoicing have several advantages: They reduce the need for price-revision clauses, simplify treasury management and permit the use of a single price list.

• One major Euro-MNC, Saint-Gobain SA, is already striving to negotiate prices in ECUs with its own customers, while a new Paris-based trade group, the Association of the Monetary Union of Europe, has been formed to lobby for greater use of the ECU in private sector transactions. Its members include 100 of the largest industrial companies on the Continent.

Strategic Planning

• Key trends include shorter planning cycles, an emphasis on qualitative judgment, less paperwork and more direct feedback through periodic, on-site meetings. Planners are assuming a major role as communicators, in order to promote companywide awareness of business objectives and how they are going to be achieved.

• Confronted with shorter product cycles and the soaring cost of market entry, MNCs are focusing on ways to accelerate the institutional learning process. One way is to encourage employees to question the rules. Planners see it in the form of demands from top management for more alternative scenarios—the "what ifs."

Marketing/Advertising

• A shakeout in the advertising sector has created new opportunities for companies to get the most bang for the advertising dollar. "Soup to nuts" accounts will dwindle—especially among the large firms as smaller boutiques take their place in the sun.

• Creating one's own market is the key to being first in sales. Niche marketing tactics are outperforming traditional market-share expansion strategies, especially in light of the enormous cost of wresting even a few percentage points from the entrenched industry leaders.

1

Adapting Organizational Structures to a Changing Marketplace

1. Seven Organizational Alternatives for MNCs in the 1990s

While there are no simple recipes for corporate organization, there are seven major options that companies can adapt to create a more effective and responsive organization. Of these seven, it is anticipated that in the 1990s, the two dominant international formats for multinationals will be the mixed structure and matrix overlay. For the most part, considerable drawbacks in worldwide product, pure matrix and international division structures may limit their use in the future. Following is a discussion of the pros and cons of each alternative:

● **Worldwide product structure**.   Domestic businesses are responsible for their own worldwide line and staff, including their own manufacturing plants and sales and marketing forces. Resources may also be shared between businesses.

This structure suits highly diversified MNCs with a need to centrally

1

coordinate upstream activities and integrate R&D, production and marketing. It eases the problems of product know-how and global business focus, but incurs the costs of duplicating resources and discourages the development of functional skills.

• **Worldwide regional.** This mode divides the world into regions, all of which report directly to the corporate executive office. Each region usually tends to assume full control of all of its own business activities, while the home country is very often treated as just another market.

Companies using this model have the following characteristics in common: broad geographical spread, mature standardized products, fairly low product and process technology and a strategic focus on downstream activities. In the past, this structure has been favored by firms in the automotive, beverage, container, cosmetics, food and petroleum industries. On the downside, this option has drawbacks similar to the worldwide product structure.

• **National subsidiary.** Under this structure, each overseas entity reports directly to the CEO, with no intervening layers of management. Sometimes subsidiary management may report to a local or regional board of directors on which the parent company is represented. This structure suits companies that are highly decentralized. Headquarters does not have direct responsibility for a subsidiary's line or staff operations. The corporatewide system is tied together through various functions, such as planning, technology transfer and finance. Given its decentralized focus, this option has all the advantages and disadvantages of an international holding company.

• **Functional.** Here a company organizes around its major business functions. For example, reporting directly to the CEO might be executives responsible for worldwide marketing, manufacturing, administration and finance. The approach is frequently used in some extracting industries, such as mining and steel, in companies with a highly integrated product line and in small companies. Offsetting the benefits of integrating important functions are the costs of poor geographic coordination and difficulties in integrating the company into a unified operation.

• **International division.** In its purest form, this mode gives a separate geographically based unit of the company exclusive authority and responsibility for operations outside the home country. The unit head usually reports to the CEO. The design is for companies whose basic business thrust is domestic and who regard international markets as separate entities. It is not suited to firms with a global focus. Inter-divisional cooperation can be difficult.

● **Pure matrix**. This approach seeks equal emphasis for product, geography and function. It has two key characteristics: (1) Organizationally, there is a dual or multiple chain of command, and (2) behaviorally, there is lateral (dual) decisionmaking and a culture that can foster conflict management. Although there is no single matrix model, the most common approach is dual reporting along product and geographic lines. A more flexible model is the matrix overlay, which allows companies to organize along a traditional framework-emphasizing product, geography or function – but with built-in structural accountability for the other two functions.

Pure matrix has almost become a dirty word within corporate corridors. It is very difficult to manage and requires a lot of management time to install. The matrix overlay attempts to address these problems. It can offer the benefits of building accountability for all functions into the organization without the onerous management stresses presented by a pure matrix structure. Matrix overlay is growing in popularity.

● **Mixed structure**. This alternative seems to embody two or more organizational formats within the same company – typically, some self-contained global businesses, along with one or more regional divisions. Another common setup is the use of an international division to handle selected parts of the international operations, a couple of global businesses and several domestic divisions. This option is ideally suited for large MNCs. It emphasizes the unique needs of different businesses, e.g. patterns of worldwide competition, demand and supply. The format can create a synergy through which management can effectively allocate and coordinate product, geographical and functional resources. The structure does, however, demand a high degree of flexibility and creative approaches to management and administration.

2. Building a Competitive Organization in the 1990s

Building an organizational structure that not only withstands competitive challenges but also provides the springboard for corporate growth is one of the critical problems facing today's chief executive. In BI's survey of CEOs from 400 companies worldwide, the two organizational goals that CEOs cited most frequently were enhancing customer responsiveness and creating a company that values entrepreneurship and a profit orientation.

Making the Customer King

In developing a corporate structure that enhances customer responsiveness, Square D's chairman and CEO, Jerre Stead, "destroyed every manual I could find. We do not have organizational charts, either. I do not believe in them. The organizational charts keep somebody busy changing something. To me, the organization serves one purpose only: meeting your long-term goals through serving customer needs."

Novo Nordisk CEO Mads Ovlisen believes "it is important for us to not only talk about being close to the market but to have everybody in the organization actually feeling it and being motivated by it." Ovlisen considers the removal of the extensive approval process at corporate level, formerly a hindrance to strategic business unit (SBU) initiative, the most important aspect of the company's current organization. "We've allowed the people who really know the business to take care of it."

Dow Chemical's management concurs that a spirit of risk-taking and entrepreneurship is essential to sustain innovation and respond to change. They have taken this one step further in supporting managers' potentially risky endeavors. "You shouldn't fire risk-takers," says CEO Frank P. Popoff. "You should reward them and try to discourage them from making the same mistakes over again."

New Modes of Organization

The CEOs who responded to the survey believe that the organization must foster entrepreneurship, but they often differ with regard to what type of organization this mandates. However, although many dislike the term "matrix," an increasing number are of the view that a large, far-flung company necessitates a form of matrix organization.

"If you really think about it, any organization today is a matrix organization," says Square D's Stead. "The degrees may differ...but there is no way you can meet your customer needs in today's markets outside of a matrix, unless you happen to produce one single product that meets everybody's expectations around the world. This is an exception that may apply to a small number of companies. So most firms are going to end up with the matrix. The key issue is accepting it and making it work in the best possible way."

The question then is how best to achieve the balance between global coordination and geographic focus. Although no clearly dominant type of organization can be identified from the survey findings, two basic concepts did emerge:

(1) The international division structure (i.e. grouping all international operations in a separate corporate group reporting to the CEO) has been largely abandoned.

(2) The functional organizational structure is confined to a small minority of companies, typically those with simple product-line mix.

• **Square D**.   In the late 1980s, Square D abandoned a product- and function-driven organization and adopted a market-oriented structure that can be described as a customer-focused matrix. Stead points out that matrix structures can work effectively only if the right kinds of people are placed in charge and decision points are clearly established to avoid time-consuming effort to reach a consensus.

• **Dow Chemical**.   A pioneer of matrix organization, this firm created a single management system with objectives ranging from specific financial criteria, such as return on investment or market share, to broader business goals—developing a new product or penetrating a new market. Depending on the priorities of each business, one of the three matrix components—function, product line or geography—is designated as primary in that business's decisionmaking process. Dow concentrates on opportunities in individual countries rather than regions, except where there is an explicit manufacturing, logistical or marketing interaction among a combination of countries that produces some advantage. Popoff views each country as an entity with its own special characteristics and believes that efforts to group countries by region often lead to over generalization and bad decisions.

How Decentralized Is Today's MNC?

In creating a structure that is most responsive to customer needs, a key question is how far to go with decentralization. The majority of MNCs surveyed have introduced a strong element of decentralization into their decisionmaking process and organization. About three fourths of the survey respondents believe that decentralization improves the functioning of the company even though it imposes a special management challenge in terms of ensuring uniform strategic vision and cooperation among different SBUs.

One of the key steps toward decentralization is limiting the role of the corporate headquarters vis-a-vis SBUs and eliminating unnecessary layers of management.

- **General Electric (GE)**.   At GE, the entire second and third echelon of management was removed in the mid-1980s. As few as four management levels now exist between the factory floor and the executive office (the CEO, two vice chairmen and executive vice president), while before there typically were nine levels. Staff functions were redefined dramatically from monitoring, control and approval to facilitating the job of line managers through partnership.

The final decision on whether to undertake a given initiative always rests with the business group. Under GE's existing management system, "the head of a business cannot come back two years later and say, 'That was a very bad direction you gave me, Jack [Jack Welch, CEO],'" says Paul Van Orden, executive vice president. The head of each business is expected to tell the CEO that while his idea may be very interesting, it will not be pursued, because of excessive risks, opportunity costs or poor fit with GE's established operations.

- **Hanson PLC**.   Hanson has developed a corporate culture that stresses decentralization and flexibility. Corporate headquarters focuses on motivating operating managers toward profitable change and reinvestment of cash flows, leaving the running of day-to-day operations and the generation of cash to the managers of the business units. These managers operate in a highly autonomous fashion and are responsible for expanding their businesses, increasing productivity, enhancing customer service and managing brands through appropriate marketing strategies.

Career paths and promotions reflect the emphasis on actual operations rather than administration. For example, people are traditionally promoted from headquarters to the subsidiaries.

- **Square D**.   Here, the decisionmaking process was decentralized several years ago. "When I came on board," says Stead, "nobody could approve a capital outlay of more than $100,000. Today, a business unit president can authorize up to $500,000." This decentralization accelerated decisions and increased the entrepreneurial energy among managers. "In the past, I had managers cutting back on capital outlays when they were under budget. Some would not submit projects with a 40% discounted cash-flow rate of return. If we can get a 10% or 12% return, give it to me. Our people now understand the need for incremental investment even if their sales performance at a given point may be weak," he adds.

Building Cooperation Among SBUs

The need for cooperation among different company units is increasing as decentralization of the decisionmaking process becomes more widespread. There are various approaches to encourage cooperation. Not surprisingly, the dominant ones include stepping up communications across regions, product divisions and functions and team-building through meetings and social functions. The supplementary steps include setting codes and policies (broad corporate guidelines rather than restrictive "what-to-dos and how-to-dos") and corporatewide training. By and large, companies agree on the necessary steps to build cooperation regardless of the MNCs' region of domicile, size or industry.

● **Motorola**. The corporatewide commitment to quality at Motorola has become part of the corporate culture, helping to ensure communication and cooperation within the company. The process has transcended Motorola's home-country orientation and made it easier for a common commitment on the part of Motorola's employees worldwide.

Top management makes it very clear in its internal and external communications that the success of the US-based company is not an American success but of "Motorolans" wherever they happen to be, and this contributes to company pride and esprit de corps.

3. Shell: A Global Management Model

Although thought of as primarily an oil and gas trader, for more than 60 years Shell has been a major chemical producer. Shell companies are also active in the production and sale of coal and metals. The basic ownership structure of this diversified group is built around three holding companies. The two original holding companies (in London and Amsterdam) own the shares, directly or indirectly, of all the operating companies and service companies in more than 100 countries. A third holding company, Shell Petroleum Inc, holds the shares of the group interests in the US.

Managing in 'Three Dimensions'

The key to Shell's management model lies within this structure. Shell seeks to avoid consolidation of a diversified business by creating a constellation of independent businesses within a "three-dimensional matrix" that allows the independent operating companies to draw upon global resources in terms of regional, sectoral and functional management.

These resources are available through nine service companies. They provide the means to coordinate, monitor and control the global policies and objectives of Shell; and they provide specialized advice and services to the operating and associated companies. The key personnel in the service companies are experienced managers and specialists who have extensive working knowledge in particular disciplines – for example, in exploration techniques, financial management or running a petrochemical plant. The majority of senior managers in the service companies have had firsthand experience in running operating companies in various parts of the world (although Shell Oil Co, the group operating company in the US, is run independently and does not participate in the system of advice and services provided by the service companies).

Also located in the service companies are three central trading units dealing, respectively, in oil, chemicals and coal. Here again the philosophy of independent operation within the group is applied. Transactions between group companies take place in accordance with commercial market mechanisms; and although a group trader may be the preferred supplier and purchaser for group companies, it also engages in considerable third-party business in its own right.

The Operations-Services Relationship

The Shell organization contains several hundred operating companies situated throughout the world. Most of these are 100% owned by Shell, but some are joint ventures. The operating companies are run autonomously, with no interference in their day-to-day management. They draw up their own business plans and manage their companies in accordance with local market conditions, while conforming to certain standards that are upheld throughout the group, including accounting practices, safety standards and protection of the environment. But all operating companies draw on the same "three dimensions" of group management expertise:

● **Regions**.   Since the setting up of Shell Petroleum Inc as a separate holding company, the regional structure has been reorganized into five regions. Five regional coordinators act as shareholders' representatives.

The regional coordinator is responsible for monitoring, operating companies' profits and approving dividends and investments.

- **Sectors**. Shell's operations are divided into six business sectors: (1) upstream oil and gas; (2) downstream oil, which comprises manufacturing, marine, supply and marketing; (3) natural gas; (4) chemicals; (5) coal; and (6) metals. The Committee of Managing Directors appoints a number of sector panels, each of which includes some managing directors and senior company executives. The sectoral organizations are concerned with strategy and plans for the country, regional and worldwide businesses.

- **Functions**. There are nine departments specialized by function. They provide advice and assistance in the following areas: finance; legal affairs; materials; planning; public affairs; research; health, safety and environment; information and computing; and human resources and organization. It should be noted that these are not skeletal but fully staffed activities. The operating companies rely on functional experts to help them develop their business plans and to give advice on systems and management techniques. The business plans will later be reviewed by the regional coordinator, who calls upon sectors and functions for assistance as necessary.

Inherent in the matrix structure of Royal Dutch/Shell are various checks and balances. The chief executive of each operating company is responsible for preparing an annual country business plan. In preparing this, he may ask for the assistance and advice of one or more of the nine functional departments in the service companies. He may also call for technical and marketing advice from the relevant sector organization.

Shell considers that the key reason for the success of the Shell matrix is that almost all the senior management in the service companies have had long-term experience in operating some companies. Unlike other major oil companies, few of Shell's senior executives have made their careers in central office management without extensive hands-on experience.

There are disadvantages, too: The receipt at headquarters of collective, simultaneous responses from operating companies, and the nonstandardization of computer hardware and software and of certain management practices can give rise to inefficiencies. But Shell believes that allowing operating companies the freedom and initiative to make their own decisions—moving quickly to adapt to changing market conditions—outweigh some of the productivity gains that can be made by large-scale consolidation.

4. A Checklist for Headquarters Evaluation

What is the role of corporate headquarters? The effect of mergers and acquisitions (M&As), collaborative ventures and restructuring activities on corporate organizations is pressuring management to find new and fresh solutions to this question. Yet there is no simple menu of options for redefining the mission of the corporate center. Frequently the solution lies in a close analysis of internal and external variables.

The following is a checklist of issues and questions for executives to contemplate in their search for a flexible corporate nucleus that can add value and coordinate complex global operations.

• What are the company's strategic needs regarding its corporate headquarters?

• Is headquarters currently trying to do too many things? Are there ways to create a more focused approach?

• How well does the existing headquarters' structure accomplish its most important tasks? Where can improvements be made?

• How would you grade—on a scale of one to 10—how well the corporate center handles its major responsibilities? Management guru Peter F. Drucker outlines seven main tasks for headquarters:

> (1) Define the mission of the business, develop strategies and plans, set objectives and make decisions that relate to these matters;
> (2) Set the standards, the values and the example of how things are to be done;
> (3) Develop the firm's human resources and identify the next generation of leaders;
> (4) Create and implement the best corporatewide organization that will meet its business strategies and needs;
> (5) Establish and maintain those external relationships that are of central importance to the company's performance;
> (6) Partake in and lead key ceremonial activities;
> (7) In concert with the board of directors, act as the most effective organ for dealing with any major crisis.

• What "world-class" skills are present in the various headquarters units? What might the company reasonably expect to have in the next three years? (The strong skills currently on board will help define appropriate headquarters roles.)

• Which two or three of all the possible activities that headquarters can perform are of critical importance to the company's success? (These should receive the lion's share of total headquarters resources.)

• What is the role of headquarters among key competitors and other companies of comparable size, technology, age and product/geographic diversity? Does a benchmarking analysis yield important differences with regard to one's own company?

• What are two of the most attractive alternative scenarios to the current role, organization and size of corporate headquarters? Does a rigorous examination of the strengths/weaknesses of these scenarios suggest the need for a change?

• What results does a review of environmental and industry conditions yield in terms of the role and size of MNC headquarters? Have you factored environmental issues—economic, legal, political, sociocultural, regulatory and technological—into the headquarters' equation? What changes to headquarters does an analysis of the market, competition and customers suggest?

• Does the headquarters structure facilitate and enhance the company's various characteristics, such as size, technology, stage in life cycle, extent of product and geographic diversity, level of vertical integration, degree of subunit interdependency, location of major capital resources and use of acquisitions and collaborative ventures?

• Have you examined the influence of corporate management and culture on the role and size of headquarters? For instance, how does the leadership style of the CEO, quality and experience of senior management, traditional modus operandi, culture and history, distribution of power and morale affect the center's structure, its strengths and weaknesses?

• What influence does the overall structure of the company have on the role and size of headquarters? What does an analysis of the following variables reveal: strategic plans, organizational structure, financial systems, legal framework and systems for control, coordination, communication and decisionmaking?

5. 'Planned Parenthood': Why Headquarters Must Fine-Tune Its Role

Pressures to globalize, restructure for a single EC market and keep one step ahead of Pacific Rim competitors are forcing many multinational corporations to rethink the role of their corporate headquarters. McKinsey & Co, together with the UK-based Ashridge Strategic Management Center, offers a fresh perspective on maximizing the value of parent headquarters. The following examines the McKinsey-Ashridge "focused corporate parenting" theory and the five headquarters roles it has identified.

Five Parenting Models

According to Michael Goold, director of the Ashridge Strategic Management Center and coauthor of *Strategies and Styles* and Nathaniel Foote, senior engagement manager at McKinsey & Co, parent headquarters can no longer afford to operate as a jack-of-all-trades, playing different roles for its various businesses. The only way it can provide superior value is to specialize in a single parenting role. The selection of this role is based on an analysis of headquarters' strengths and weaknesses as well as the specific needs of each business unit.

To assist headquarters in its search for a focused parenting role, McKinsey-Ashridge outlines three permanent roles (controller, coach and orchestrator) and two temporary ones (surgeon and architect). The permanent roles are used to manage the ongoing, day-to-day relationships between the business units and the parent. The temporary roles are employed during major transformations, such as restructuring operations after an acquisition.

Following is a summary of the main characteristics of the five roles:

• **Controller.** The controller manages with a decentralized, hands-off style and uses very stringent profit and budget targets. Each business unit is treated as a separate stand-alone entity to maximize accountability. According to Goold, the focus is more on meeting quarterly and budget goals than on the long-term horizon. Managers are typically given considerable autonomy to manage their operations, but are frequently replaced if they fail to meet financial targets. There is little parent involvement in strategy, minimal headquarters staff and low over-head.

Controllers frequently rely on acquisitions rather than organic growth to expand significantly. The controller style matches the parenting needs of diversified conglomerates as well as mature or commodity-type industries in which competition is predictable, techno-logical or product innovation is slight and there is little need for costly, long-term and risky investment decisions. Foote cites the UK-based con-glomerate BTR as a controller.

• **Coach.**   The coach occupies the middle ground, operating business units as autonomous stand-alone entities in order to nurture indepen-dence and initiative. At the same time, however, the coach encourages a transfer of skills and ideas from business to business, and from head-quarters to the various operations. The real challenge behind the coach role is striking the right balance between autonomy and coordination. Difficulties may arise in trying to garner sufficient information at head-quarters without imposing undue bureaucratic burdens on the operat-ing units. Managers are motivated and evaluated on both financial and strategic criteria. Individual business units develop their own strategies, with final approval from parent headquarters.

The coach encourages a transfer of skills and ideas by rotating man-agers among various businesses. Parent headquarters also maintains a small coordination unit. This group serves as a liaison and channel for communications among operations. Industries suitable for the coach role include consumer goods, marketing services and newspapers. Ac-cording to Goold, the coach works for firms in which the marketplace and source of competitive advantage are similar from business to busi-ness. For instance, in a consumer-goods company, each unit may seek a competitive edge by relying on a strong brand image or similar product positioning strategies. Foote says Nestle and Unilever are coaches.

• **Orchestrator.**   An orchestrator uses a hands-on style to coordinate the various business units in order to realize synergies and economies of scale. Many functions of the business system are centrally managed by parent headquarters, such as manufacturing, R&D and finance. This style is appropriate where investment decisions are large and long-term, markets are dynamic and corporatewide concerns are as important as local business issues.

The added value comes from the close involvement of headquarters in strategy and decisionmaking. But there is a down side. This parenting role has high overhead costs, and headquarters involvement can lead to interference. Problems may also surface in motivating managers and creating clear accountability. The orchestrator usually operates in highly integrated industries, such as oil, steel, consumer electronics, mining and financial services.

• **Surgeon.** The surgeon is typically an acquirer that specializes in buying undervalued companies with poor track records and breaking them apart, retaining a few operations and selling off others to recoup acquisition costs. The key challenges to the surgeon are how to make the right decisions on what businesses and managers to keep and how to maintain morale. A skillful surgeon acts swiftly once the decision to acquire or restructure an entity is made. After the restructuring, surgeons operate as controllers. Hanson is a good example of a surgeon.

• **Architect.** Architects focus on creating synergies when restructuring or acquiring businesses. They operate as either coaches or orchestrators once they have integrated their operations. The key challenge for the architect is correctly identifying possible areas of synergy. Goold cites ICI's acquisition of US-based Stauffer Chemicals as an architectural role.

Benefits of a Single Parenting Role

Goold and Foote cite important advantages of focusing on one specific management role for parent headquarters:

• A firm can sharpen both its strategy and portfolio of businesses. Decisions to remain, enter or divest a business depend on whether the parent possesses the appropriate skills both to manage and to add value to the operation. Whether a company seeks to expand via acquisitions, greenfield investments or joint ventures, the right parenting style allows management to concentrate on businesses to which it can add more value than other competing parenting companies.

• MNCs are forced to focus on the skills in which management excels. Too often, the value of the parent headquarters is diluted or lost when headquarters tries to be all things to all businesses. The single parenting approach also reduces a company's vulnerability to corporate raiders and leveraged buyout teams that claim they provide a better management alternative.

• Adopting a single parenting role sends a clear message to all operations of what headquarters is and what it expects.

• The approach offers a wide range of parenting strategies. At one end is a parenting role for the diversified conglomerate. At the other end is a style for MNCs with closely related businesses.

6. Choosing and Crafting a Parenting Role for Headquarters

Foote and Goold also suggest that management analyze a firm's business portfolio to identify the headquarters style that will add value, reduce risks of a hostile takeover or leveraged buyout and send a uniform signal of what it wants and expects. This analysis should focus on three criteria:

• **The degree of synergy between businesses.** MNCs with little or no synergy between operations are best managed with the decentralized, hands-off style of a financial controller. However, if a firm's profitability depends on a high degree of synergy and integration, headquarters must rely on the hands-on coordinated approach of an orchestrator. In the middle is the coach style, which suits MNCs that realize synergies by exploiting similarities in strategy and sharing ideas and skills between businesses.

• **The magnitude of risk in investment decisions.** The higher the risk in an investment—in terms of amount and length of the payback period—the greater the need for an active parenting style, such as an orchestrator. For instance, an orchestrator's deep involvement in decisionmaking is needed when a few large but critical investments can place an entire company at stake. The controller fits firms in which investments are low in risk and cost and the payback period is no more than two to four years. The coach is appropriate for investments with intermediate payback periods (e.g. a consumer product launch that may not realize payback for four to six years).

• **The nature of the competitive environment.** Goold identifies three types of market battles—open, fierce and stable—to help MNCs classify business units. Controllers can add value to businesses facing "stable" battles in which the business situation is predictable, competitors' positions are stable, key factors for success are clear and new entrants have little impact. The coach is best at managing businesses operating in "open" battles, characterized by a moderate level of market uncertainty, fighting that is not head-on, some key criteria that are unclear, market openings for new competitors and no clear winners. MNCs should opt for the orchestrator role if their businesses are engaged in "fierce" competition. Here competitive uncertainty is high; competitors meet head-on; and dramatic changes in a company's fortunes are possible.

Crafting a Single Parenting Style

The above analysis often uncovers tough choices, say Foote and Goold – either a radical restructuring of the company's business portfolio or a dramatic change in how parent headquarters must operate, or both. Some companies may be able to capitalize on major new developments, such as the appointment of a new CEO, to launch a major overhaul of headquarters and the business portfolio. Most, however, must work within existing managerial, organizational and financial constraints. Moreover, since the CEO's style and personality determine a particular management style, making a change in midstream is a formidable challenge for any CEO. Nonetheless, Goold and Foote say, MNCs can take incremental steps to revamp headquarters and the business portfolio and pave the way for a single parenting style.

According to Foote, a headquarters center has four basic "levers" it can pull to better manage and add value to operations: i.e. redefine the business units; develop or improve strategy; motivate management to perform; and upgrade organizational capabilities and resources. How headquarters operates these levers depends on the single parenting style it has selected. Foote and Goold offer some techniques on how MNCs can apply these levers differently to specialize in a single parenting style:

• **Redefine the business units.** MNCs focusing on a controller style will want to reorganize operations into separate stand-alone entities. Companies opting for an orchestrator approach will want to combine and centralize key operations like manufacturing, sourcing or strategic planning to maximize synergies and economies of scale. Coaches specialize in organizing operations into separate stand-alone entities linked by central mechanisms such as worldwide product managers. Care must be taken to organize these central mechanisms so that they add value by channeling strategic and operational information between businesses. Otherwise they become just an extra bureaucratic layer.

• **Develop or improve strategy.** Controllers reorient the strategic thinking of the center and business units to focus on short-term financial goals and specialize in developing new cost-cutting and margin-improvement techniques. Orchestrators groom "visionary" strategic planners at headquarters who can skillfully factor all operations and issues—such as competitors' responses and future scenarios for market and technology developments—into a long-term strategic equation. Coaches pull together at the center a small team of seasoned strategic planners who have gained wide exposure through various assignments in the field. This group specializes in operating as "devil's advocate" and grills individual business-unit managers to help them fine-tune their strategies.

• **Motivate management to perform.** MNCs can make significant headway in developing a single parenting style by changing how headquarters designs, controls and monitors such key management systems as the budget, strategic planning and performance evaluation. At one end are controllers who install tight budget and financial systems to motivate and evaluate managers. At the other end, orchestrators judge managers on qualitative strategic measures, rather than hold them accountable to rigorous financial and budgetary targets.

• **Upgrade organizational capabilities and resources.** Coaches strengthen managers by installing procedures to regularly rotate executives between different product lines and geographic regions. Orchestrators expose managers to all stages of the business—technology development, sourcing, manufacturing, marketing and distribution, and customer service. Controllers, however, emphasize building up a managers' expertise within a specific business. No resources or time are spent in encouraging executives to learn about the operations of other business units.

7. Sony: A Centralized Management Approach

One of the best examples of centralized management is Japan's electronics giant Sony Corp. Although external factors have been exerting influence on Japanese firms to move toward decentralization, Sony continues to use headquarters management as part of its approach to globalization. Under centralized management, most major business functions are controlled at corporate headquarters and all major management decisions are taken in the home office.

Global Strategy

Worldwide, Sony has five strategic goals:

(1) To build more nonconsumer businesses while solidifying its leadership in consumer electronics;

(2) To pursue global development of the software side of its consumer electronics business, using CBS Records as a springboard;

(3) To augment its overseas production capacity by expanding existing facilities and setting up new ones;

(4) To develop in-house individual human resource capabilities; and

(5) To strengthen Sony's financial soundness even further, primarily through tightened inventory controls, a critical approach to capital investment decisions and promotion of greater cost-efficiency in research and development activities.

Role of Headquarters

To ensure that its goals are being met by all of its subsidiaries worldwide, Sony has developed two management techniques for its global network: zone management and global localization.

● **Zone management**.   Sony recently initiated this management approach for all worldwide operations. Each zone headquarters located in Europe, the US, Japan and Southeast Asia is responsible for optimizing and supervising all its common business functions: financing, production location, research and development, marketing strategy and human resources.

The introduction of zone management has brought about significant changes in corporate headquarters during the past 10 years, as has the company's continuing growth in both corporate and country headquarters. New responsibilities have been added, which include the overseeing of operations as well as effective communications with country headquarters.

Sales, manufacturing and product planning are generally decentralized and within the purview of the country headquarters, but all final approvals come from corporate headquarters. In addition, long-range financing and long-range business planning worldwide are still centralized at corporate headquarters.

● **Global localization**.   Instituted by Akio Morita, chairman and CEO, this policy states that the company must be a good corporate citizen in each local community, even while its operation is globally oriented. Furthermore, the company should manufacture its products in the markets in which it sells. Local markets should be utilized, and the company should be involved in community affairs.

The Senior Corporate Board at headquarters, led by Akio Morita, is responsible for domestic and international business operations. These include companywide long-term planning, long-term coordination of production, regional strategy and other aspects of long-term worldwide operations.

US Operations: A Management Microcosm

A vital part of Sony's globalization efforts, Sony Corp of America has two major roles: as a trend-setter in marketing and as a major corporate manufacturing base. In order to accelerate the firm's expansion in the US, Sony Deputy President Masaaki Morita relocated to the US in the fall of 1987 and assumed new responsibilities as chairman of Sony Corp of America. In this position, he is poised to make strategic business decisions affecting the US market.

● **Local goals.** In addition to internationalizing Sony's manufacturing operations and management systems, top management plans to procure more parts from local suppliers and to expand research and development activities abroad. The acquisition of CBS Records was a critical first step in the global expansion of Sony's software business. Future goals for Sony Corp of America include expansion in both consumer and nonconsumer products, e.g. new technologies, semiconductor technologies and high technology.

● **Melding with headquarters.** Sony Corp of America follows the headquarters policies of *zone management and global localization*. The chairman of the corporation Board of Sony Corporation of America is also a member of the Senior Corporate Board in Tokyo. He works with the Senior Corporate Board to develop and initiate future corporate strategies (business development investments, long-range product planning and technological innovations), and he is also responsible for operations and plans for all the US product groups and country headquarters.

8.   Reynolds Picks Lausanne as European Nerve Center

Reynolds Metals, like many non-EC companies that are intent on securing a strong competitive position in Europe, has reevaluated its Euro-

pean organization and is creating a strong central European base in order to coordinate its operations across the Continent.

While many companies are looking at the value of a regional headquarters as a response to economic integration in Europe, Reynolds believes that Europe's irrepressible economic, political and cultural diversity makes a European-based central management team essential.
Indeed, Reynolds Chairman and CEO Bill Bourke says the company's
decision to create a headquarters office in Europe would have been
made "with or without 1992."

A Europe Divided

Under the old organizational structure, managing directors of each of
seven European subsidiaries reported to the president of Reynolds International at the home office in Richmond. In addition to being responsible for Europe, the head of international juggled 25 direct reports worldwide. The result in Europe was chaos. "You had salesmen
from four or five different Reynolds companies calling on the same accounts—and selling the same product lines—which was a very un-
healthy situation," says Bourke. On the manufacturing side, Reynolds
had duplicate operations in many countries for aluminum, aluminum
sheet and extruded products with no "total plan for Europe to go for
the cheapest source and best quality," he goes on.

A fragmented organization in Europe, managed from the US, also
worked against Reynolds vis-a-vis competitors. European players in the
aluminum business, like Pechiney in France, VAW in Germany and
Alusuisse in Switzerland, are big and government-owned. "If we were
going to be successful in competing against them," says Bourke, "we
needed the scale of being pan-European."

Creating a Eurobase

A headquarters operation seemed the best way to start to bring unity to
the organization. In 1987, a small office (Reynolds Europe) was established in Lausanne to oversee manufacturing, distribution and marketing throughout Europe. Managing directors of country subs now report
to a president of Reynolds Europe, who in turn reports to the head of
Reynolds International in Richmond. Other managers based in
Lausanne include a CFO, an executive vice president in charge of manufacturing operations and several vice presidents who assist in functional areas such as marketing.

Reynolds Europe now provides a "single voice" in Western Europe to
represent Reynolds Metals and a coordinating organization to help

Reynolds subs complement, not compete, with each other. Bourke cites some of the benefits:

• **A rational sourcing plan.** Under the direction of the president of Reynolds Europe, a sourcing plan has been developed for Reynolds packaging operations that goes after (1) low-cost manufacturing sites and (2) tailors the output of each factory to specific product lines. Aluminum foil production has shifted from Belgium to plants in Italy and Spain that will serve all of Europe. Capacity at Reynolds's Spanish sub Industrial Navara del Aluminio (Inasa) is being expanded by about one third to 75,000-80,000 tons a year to keep pace with anticipated growth.

• **Speeding up the decision process.** With the old structure, major decisions had to be made in Richmond by the head of international. Most of that authority has now been delegated, with the exception of budgets, which are approved in the US.

• **Pan-European marketing.** A consumer-product strategy is developed in Lausanne for each product line. Aluminum foil, which Reynolds previously sold only in Spain, Belgium, Luxembourg, the Netherlands and France, is the first target for expansion to other European markets. Advertising strategy is also being fine-tuned to account for "spillover" between countries. "To advertise on television and radio in France you may have to spend a lot of money," notes Bourke, "but it doesn't mean it won't be seen by Germans and Swiss or vice versa."

• **Power in size.** "Reynolds Europe can represent all of our employees and customers to speak with one mouth. I think we have more clout today—not only with the EC, but also with individual governments—than we had when we were fragmented," reflects Bourke. In particular, Reynolds's voice in the influential European Aluminum Association has been greatly strengthened by designating the president of Reynolds Europe as its single representative.

A Neutral Site

One of the initial problems with the new organization has been the loss of authority among the top country managers. "There's bound to be ruffled feathers," says Bourke. "Once you experience the luxury of little or no supervision you tend to resent having a boss who visits you regularly and knows what's going on."

This resentment can also have nationalist overtones. Bourke recalls that when Ford Europe was formed, the firm lost nearly half its management in Germany because it chose to locate the headquarters in London. "In the minds of the Germans, that was selling out to their English brother," says Bourke. He adds, "There's a lot of talk about a United Europe, but, believe me, European nations are every bit as economically nationalistic as they were 200 years ago."

Faced with the same decision at Reynolds, Bourke chose Lausanne because the city is neither in southern or northern Europe. Although Reynolds sacrificed on the expense side in order to locate in Switzerland, Bourke says he "didn't want the Italians or Spanish to think we were abandoning them by going to Hamburg, Germany."

9.   To Have or Not to Have: The RHQ Question

When considering establishing a regional headquarters (RHQ), companies need to answer the following questions:

• Do we need a regional office at all? Can we handle the business as effectively from our headquarters?

• What role could a regional office play? How important is this in view of the company's strategic plan and its competitive environment?

• If there is to be a regional organization, do we need one or several offices? How will these be structured? What reporting relationships should we establish among these offices and with the parent company?

• Where should we locate this office or offices?

The RHQ Decision

Several factors typically affect a company's decision to set up an RHQ:

• **Size.**   This is perhaps the single most important factor: Small companies, even if the business potential were to justify it, generally face resource constraints too severe to warrant the logistics and expense of having an office thousands of miles from home. Conversely, a large company may establish such an office as a long-term investment, even if it's not immediately cost effective.

• **Perception of the region.**   Another key element is the company's perception of the target region and how it fits into the overall corporate strategy. Obviously, a firm that expects its major growth over the next decade to come from this region has more reason to commit resources to it than some other area.

• **Degree of corporate decentralization.** Relatively decentralized companies are more likely to want a local regional presence than highly centralized ones (except for those that are so decentralized that each individual country operation runs quite independently and thus needs to report only to corporate headquarters).

• **Corporate culture.** Are international markets considered a residual business, to be picked up only when home markets are slack? Does the company see a need to manage a certain region differently than other markets? Is senior management truly interested in the region — no matter what may be said in the formal strategic plan?

• **Nature and volume of the business.** Is the business large enough to justify such an office? Do the products require specialized support — sales or service — from the vendor? Do the products require new market development? Or are they fighting for market share against strong competitors in a slow-growth environment? Are there a number of product lines that would help spread the cost of such an office?

• **Competition.** A company may need the competitive edge that comes from having rapid access to information, customers and decisions, and from a better understanding of local conditions.

Advantages of an RHQ

• **Rapid identification of opportunities**. The most important argument for having a regional office is to enable the company to discover opportunities much faster and more effectively than either corporate headquarters, which is too far away, or country managers, who may lack a sufficiently broad global perspective. The RHQ is best positioned to identify both general opportunities — for instance, trends in governmental policy that may indicate an opening or closing of markets — and specific ones: "We can sell a million widgets a year to Taiwan if we find the right local partner." This may be particularly true in countries where the firm does not have a substantial presence and there is no local management to sound an early alert.

• **Information gathering**. Most companies recognize in the abstract that knowledge and experience are valuable corporate assets, but these qualities reside in individuals who may leave or be reassigned. A regional office is a central point for data collection; it is close to the ground and a structure that can ensure continuity even when individuals move on. It also can act as a clearinghouse for information between countries and headquarters, screening input for accuracy and providing it in usable corporate-specific forms.

● **Fast reactions in the field**.   By delegating decisionmaking power to the regions, companies can ensure that their customers get quicker answers and assistance. In this era of rapid communications, that might not be critical (although telecommunications in some countries are not that good); what is critical is that a regional office is likely to be in closer touch with the situation than corporate HQ and thus able to make better decisions.

● **Local attention where needed**.   For similar reasons, RHQs may provide more effective oversight of country businesses; regional managers are well placed to deal with local conditions and concerns while not losing the overall corporate perspective. This can be particularly important in the early stages of development. One executive whose company eliminated its RHQ conceded that the strongest operations did all right; however, two "developmental" country markets quickly lost ground and were cut, weaker country businesses declined over a period of about three years and had to be sold or closed, and the company's licenses were left almost unattended.

● **Functional support**.   An RHQ is able to provide important functional support while spreading the cost over a larger base than would be possible for individual country operations. At the same time, the company's functional experts are close enough to tap into information sources at the country level and thus can provide specific assistance.

Disadvantages of an RHQ

Some problems are inherent in RHQs, and are a necessary risk, but others occur frequently enough to be considered when a company is deciding whether or not to have an RHQ in a particular region.

● **Complicated communications**.   For companies accustomed to easy two-way communications between corporate HQ and country management, adding an RHQ may hinder, rather than facilitate, interchange. Such an intermediary can easily degenerate into an expensive post office that no one takes seriously. Even in the best of situations, companies have to guard against the kind of overgrowth that leads to a regional bottleneck in communications and decisionmaking, not to mention duplication of effort.

- **Additional expenses.** Although an RHQ requires little apparent investment, being merely rented space with relatively inexpensive equipment, the costs do mount up. Expatriate executives are expensive: most companies provide perquisites that double or triple the usual cost of an executive in the home country. Yet using only local nationals is likely to hamper the communication and interchange that is the most fundamental rationale of an RHQ. It also adds a new administrative burden — especially for companies that have no other offshore offices in the country.

- **Distance from senior corporate management.** Occasionally, overseas-based executives will find the disadvantages of being far from the corporate center outweigh the advantages of being close to the countries for which they are responsible. Companies with RHQs and corporate HQs in totally different time zones tend to be the worst affected, particularly those that are rather centralized. They may find that other units located in or near corporate HQ have an edge in competing for resources.

- **Difficult to attract high flyers.** US executives often note that the career path to top management seldom involves substantial overseas experience; this may deter them from accepting foreign assignments. Companies thus have to enhance the compensation package considerably to attract suitable talent — and even then, they may fail. European companies usually have less trouble in this respect.

- **Pressure at home.** Spending a lot of time traveling is a fact of life for most executives assigned to regional offices, especially those in large territories. Frequently the spouse will not be able to work in his or her chosen career, or maybe not at all. These factors, combined with immersion in an unfamiliar culture and language, can put a lot of pressure on families. Other worries are the children's education and the difference in lifestyles. Executives may be concerned about children who grow up without sufficient exposure to their mother tongue. Problems at home resulting from this may have repercussions on morale at the office.

10. Choosing an RHQ Site

While every company must set its own priorities for a regional headquarters (RHQ), it is easier to decide if all the relevant factors have been
considered. A host of details need consideration before renting premises and moving in families. The list of questions — covering from mo-
mentous to trivial — is considerable, as it is important to avoid overlook-
ing problems that can resurface months later. The following list of
questions should be exhaustive enough for most companies.

General Business Climate

(1) How stable is the country, socially and politically?

(2) What is the government's attitude toward regional headquarters
and foreign investment?

(3) How much red tape is involved in obtaining government approval
for a headquarters operation?

(4) What are the economic strengths and weaknesses of the country?
What are GDP projections for the next five years?

(5) How strong is the currency?

(6) How much corruption is involved in doing business in the country?

Transportation

(1) Is the city located near those markets and facilities that must be visited on a regular basis?

(2) Is it well located in relation to corporate headquarters, the RHQ site
and other cities with operations under its control? How long does it take
to reach the airport from the office?

(3) Is the airport efficient? Is it necessary to meet visitors or can they
make their own way to hotels and the RHQ office?

(4) Is suitable hotel accommodation available at short notice?

(5) Is local transport adequate? If staff need their own cars, what will it
cost them or the company? Can cars be rented for visiting executives?

Communications

(1) How reliable are phone links between corporate HQ and the proposed regional RHQ, and between the latter and existing/planned facilities in the region?

(2) How long does it take to have a telephone, switchboard and telex installed? How much do international telephone calls cost?

(3) How reliable is the local telephone service?

(4) Are cable, telex and facsimile facilities available and reliable? How much do they cost?

(5) How reliable and speedy is the postal service between the office and corporate HQ? How efficient is the local postal service? Are private messengers available, and at what cost?

(6) Can air freight services be used in lieu of the mail to move small parcels? Does red tape hinder customs clearance?

(7) Are post office boxes readily available? Can the local postal service handle mail addressed in foreign languages without difficulty?

Services

(1) Are local banking facilities adequate? Can the banks provide financial and alternative information on other countries managed by the RHQ?

(2) Are accounting, advertising, auditing, insurance, legal and other services adequate and readily available?

(3) How accessible and adequate are libraries and other sources of data and information needed by the RHQ?

(4) Are data-processing facilities available?

(5) Can office equipment be purchased/leased?

Taxation

(1) What legal structures (e.g. branch, subsidiary) are available for the RHQ, and what does it cost to suitably establish the RHQ?

(2) Will the tax authorities demand that the RHQ show income, and if so, what is the tax burden?

(3) Will the RHQ's offshore income be taxed? How are commissions from offshore sales, foreign dividends and interest received from abroad taxed? If licenses are issued, what is the tax on royalties, technical fees and management fees?

(4) Are tax concessions granted for export promotion activities?

(5) Will exchange controls create problems?

(6) What is the personal tax burden on expatriate executives? Are exemptions granted for time spent outside the country?

Office Space

(1) Is suitable office space available and what does it cost? Are deposits required? Are large rental prepayments necessary?

(2) Is cleaning, air conditioning, etc. included in the rent?

(3) Are local taxes levied on office rents?

(4) How reliable are electricity and water supplies?

(5) Can additional storage space be obtained?

(6) Is air conditioning available outside normal office hours, such as for the operation of data-processing equipment?

Staffing

(1) How readily available and qualified are local personnel in different categories? What are normal salaries for secretaries, bookkeepers, typists? What are the expected (legal or customary) fringe benefits?

(2) Can reliable agencies recruit or recommend office personnel?

(3) Can temporary office staff be obtained at short notice?

(4) Are high-quality junior executive personnel available? What are the salaries and fringe benefits?

(5) Can they be recruited through agencies?

(6) What fringe benefits are usually granted to expatriates of other foreign companies in this location (e.g. club memberships, chauffeurs and cars, household help, home leave, cost-of-living allowances)?

(7) What is the attitude of the local people toward being employed by foreign companies?

Housing

(1) Can expatriates rent suitable housing easily and at reasonable cost? Are deposits or advance rental payments required?

(2) Does rent include fittings and household appliances? Are taxes, building maintenance or other service charges extra?

(3) Should the company consider buying or even building apartments or houses for expatriates?

(4) Are Western-type household furnishings readily available in the area and at reasonable prices?

(5) Is household help available, at what cost? Is language a problem?

Education

(1) How accessible are suitable primary and secondary schools?

(2) Do conveniently located suitable schools have places available, or do they have waiting lists or bond-purchase requirements?

(3) What is their total cost?

(4) Do they provide transportation? What does it cost?

(5) Are kindergarten and nursery school facilities available, and at what cost?

(6) Do expatriates in this location expect their employers to pay for travel costs of children being educated elsewhere, and how often?

Personal Income Tax

(1) What is the personal tax burden on expatriate executives?

(2) Are exemptions granted for time spent outside the country?

(3) Are expatriates taxed on fringe benefits, such as the value of home-leave transport paid by the employer?

(4) Are expatriates taxed on housing allowances or for free housing, and what is the rate they are charged?

(5) Are expatriates taxed on income from foreign sources?

Personal Transport

(1) Are personal cars necessary, and for which level of executive do companies usually provide them?

(2) What are the import rules and requirements for new and used cars?

(3) Are local cars available? At what price?

(4) Is local public or private transport available and convenient?

(5) Can spouses rely on the availability of public transport, or do they require a second car?

(6) Is self-driving advisable, or are chauffeurs recommended?

Cost of Living

(1) How does the cost of living compare with expatriates' home base?

(2) How fast is the cost of living rising?

(3) Will expatriates require separate cost-of-living allowances?

Entertainment and Cultural Activities

(1) What good private clubs are accessible to expatriates? At what cost?

(2) What facilities do clubs have? Do they have waiting lists? Can they be bypassed by buying bonds or corporate memberships, and at what cost?

(3) What sports facilities are available (golf links, swimming pools, beaches, tennis and squash courts, marinas, etc.)?

(4) What cultural activities (concerts, stage plays, etc.) go on in the city? Are arts festivals being staged regularly? What is the quality of movie houses, TV, libraries, local newspapers, etc.?

(5) What is the quality of local night clubs and restaurants?

(6) Do universities offer extramural courses?

Medical and Health Facilities

(1) What are the standards of available medical facilities?

(2) Do expatriates usually leave the city for medical care, the treatment of certain illnesses or for other health reasons such as pregnancy?

(3) What is the cost involved to go elsewhere for medical reasons?

(4) How good are dental services? What do they cost?

(5) Does the climate favor particular afflictions?

Cultural Adjustment

(1) Are major cultural adjustments necessary for the expatriate family, and are these adjustments difficult?

(2) Will expatriates, spouses, and families find the environment agreeable?

(3) Can expatriates and the local population communicate in a common language?

(4) Are spouses allowed to work, and is employment available?

(5) Do spouses and children have opportunities to keep occupied?

Personal Security

(1) Is personal security a major problem for expatriates?

(2) What is the crime rate, and is violent crime above average?

(3) Would a political change entail personal danger for expatriates?

11.　How Loctite Prospers With Three-Man Headquarters, Country Managers

For US-based Loctite Corp, a fast-growing manufacturer of adhesives and sealants that in 1987 derived 50% of its $337 million in sales from international operations, setting up an international division in which authority and responsibility rest primarily with strong country managers has proven to be the most efficient and flexible organizational approach. It is a system that complements the company's decentralized management style, integrated product lines and its emphasis on marketing and service.

Less Is More at Headquarters

According to Ted Patlovich, senior corporate vice president and international group president, the company's international operations are organized to optimize its competitive response worldwide in the areas most critical to its business: adaptation to local demand, guaranteed quality and strong technical support. "Our philosophy is not to have a huge headquarters staff—but to provide all the support and expertise we can on the local scene," he says. Patlovich sees headquarters' major role as one that provides strong strategic direction for international operations. At corporate headquarters in Newington, Connecticut, Patlovich—supported by a staff of just two people—oversees all international operations. These include 28 wholly owned subsidiaries, four joint ventures and distributors in 50 countries.

Loctite has divided the world outside the US into three regions—Europe, Latin America and the Pacific—where the bulk of its activities are focused. Each is managed by a regional vice president, who reports to Patlovich. Managers responsible for country operations report to the regional head.

The three-person international division headquarters is bolstered by two corporate staff functions specifically created to promote a global flow of product information. Loctite's corporate R&D is handled by a worldwide New Business Development group (NBD) responsible for all research and new product development. On the manufacturing side, there are corporate vice president of manufacturing and technologies at plants in each region. In addition, NBD coordinates the flow of new product ideas from overseas through its own country representatives who report to NBD at headquarters. These representatives conduct market research and report their findings to NBD every month.

How the Country Subs Fit In

Loctite manufactures in just three countries outside the US—Ireland, Brazil and China. Its other overseas operations are essentially marketing and service subsidiaries, responsible for sales and marketing, technical services and applications R&D in their respective countries. The primary responsibilities of each country operation are: satisfy local custom needs; manage the growth of country specific businesses; help cross-fertilize ideas and execute global strategies.

Loctite's emphasis on country managers to fulfill these objectives features the following:

• **Operating independence.** Once their annual business plans are approved by headquarters, country managers have bottom-line responsibility for "running a total business," says Patlovich. This includes determining what products to sell, developing marketing plans, setting prices and monitoring day-to-day business operations.

For example, giving country managers final say on what the product mix should be in their markets—particularly when new products are launched—allows for a more targeted approach. Patlovich says when some country managers were asked to sell adhesive for bonding denim (primarily for unhemmed blue jeans), they advised headquarters that in their markets, jeans are sold with hems sewn, affording Loctite few sales opportunities.

• **Coordinated regional marketing.** When possible, Loctite tries to introduce new products with consistent packaging and advertising throughout the region. But when adaptation is necessary, the country manager is consulted about appropriate changes.

• **Local managers with headquarters training.** In general, the company hires local nationals as country managers but tries to ensure that they know how things are run at home. For instance, a Chinese executive selected to run Loctite's new operation in China is spending two years in Newington before taking over in Beijing.

• **Language skills.** In addition to employing local nationals as country managers, Patlovich notes that most overseas managers speak several languages. He adds that versatile language skills are a requirement of the job. This has proved to be particularly helpful in coordinating regional strategies.

• **Frequent travel.** Patlovich meets with regional managers about every three months to facilitate strong communication links throughout the international division. In Europe, country managers meet as a group at least 10 times per year.

• **Video communications.** Video is increasingly used to share application innovations among operations in other countries. For example, the Japanese operation, which has pioneered several applications in the electronics industry, has videotaped presentations on its techniques. Managers of other Loctite subs have been able to use the application to improve service for their own customers that are foreign subsidiaries of Japanese electronic firms.

12. How Sandvik AB Decentralized to a More Responsive Structure

The Sandvik Group is one of Sweden's largest exporting enterprises, active all over the world through more than 100 companies in over 40 countries. Some 90% of the group's sales are generated outside Sweden. The company maintains local production, warehousing, distribution, technical service and delivery systems in order to service its customers internationally. In 1986, the group employed about 24,000 and invoiced sales of Skr127 million. Below, BI examines how Sandvik restructured to meet their strategic, operational and financial needs.

Sandvik's Setup Before Restructuring

By the mid-1970s, the group's organization had solidified under the following structure:

• The group had four business divisions, plus subsidiaries in major markets. Each division had profit responsibility, and the subsidiaries had separate sales forces for each product line or business. All subsidiaries and most divisions reported directly to the president. The subsidiaries also reported to the division heads on a functional (dotted line) basis.

• There was a large, strong group staff and a powerful corporate management team.

• Formally, all positions had explicit responsibilities. This was reinforced by the fact that all Sandvik managers had lived with the system for many years. An extensive system of regulations, termed Sandvik Guidelines, governed the general modus operandi.

• Informally, Sandvik was (and remains) a relatively small company. The managers got to know each other and learned to work closely with one another.

One of the most glaring weaknesses of this format was the operating difficulties of the subsidiary president, who was burdened by multiple demands and reporting relationships. The president of the group also had enormous responsibilities and a large span of control. Finally, the heads of the four business divisions did not have full control of their product lines internationally.

The deep and prolonged recession of 1981-83 led to a substantial decline in volume within most business sectors. In 1981, the group took corrective measures, including a reduction in personnel strength by about 7,000. During the latter part of 1983, the group stepped up the pace at which it was shedding money-losing operations. This was not enough, however, and the company decided to take further steps.

On Jan. 1, 1984, the Sandvik Group was organized as a number of discrete companies—an arrangement intended to permit increased decentralization, efficiency and profitability. At the same time, the staff units of the parent company were greatly reduced. A month later, a new president and CEO were appointed.

How the Restructuring Worked

• Six separate business areas now make up the basis of the organization. Each business area is handled by a product company that is responsible for the development, production and sale of the group's products. In each major market, the product company maintains a subsidiary of its own or has a division of a conjoint Sandvik company. The board of each business area is composed of the Sandvik president (who serves as chairman), an individual from the group legal function (who serves as secretary), the business area managing director and a couple of his senior executives. Outside the main markets, Sandvik's products are marketed by four regional companies:

AB Sandvik International, headquartered in Sandviken, is responsible for marketing in the former USSR, Eastern Europe, the PRC, the Middle East, Africa (apart from South Africa) and other territories.

Sandvik Latin America Inc, located in Miami, is responsible for marketing in Latin America, other than Argentina, Brazil and Mexico. Operations within this region are conducted to a large extent through local subsidiary companies.

Sandvik South East Asia Pte Ltd, which has its head office in Singapore, sees to the marketing of the group's products in Southeast Asia, through local subs and agents.

Sandvik Asia Ltd in Poona, India, develops, produces and markets cemented-carbide products in India, Sri Lanka, Bhutan and Nepal through its own sales offices and agents.

• The six product companies are self-contained units. They have their own staff and line operations and are responsible for the success or failure of their own business. These firms hire, fire and lay off; conclude union agreements; and plan and manage operations.

• At the group level, Sandvik now operates almost as a holding company that limits the authority of the product companies only in certain areas. They are, for example, forbidden to sell their own stock and are required to follow corporate policies on personnel, finance, technology, etc. As Sandvik's president has noted: "An important task for Sandvik was to bring in a new organization in which initiative and responsibility would be decentralized so that every business unit would be able to choose the optimum strategy and tactics by which to conduct its activities."

• Two special companies, AB Sandvik Central Service and AB Sandvik Information Systems, provide the group with conjoint support services. Each is responsible for its own profits. Their biggest customers are the Sandvik units within Sweden; but they also sell their services to subsidiary companies outside Sweden and to external customers. AB Sandvik Central Service is active mainly in the areas of logistics, personnel accounting, real estate management, and information and advertising. AB Sandvik Information Systems provides services in the areas of systems development, computer technology, data processing, telecommunications and data communications and training.

The reorganization reassigned most of the 500 former group staff specialists to the six business areas and the two service companies, although a few did lose their jobs. The reassignments left a group staff of about 50. The current staff functions—auditing, economy, finance, legal affairs, market and technology, market communication, personnel, public affairs, R&D and taxes—support the operating units and perform specialized tasks for the group as a whole.

• Planning has also been decentralized. Under the old organization, a large staff prepared two- and five-year plans on an annual basis. Today, plans are developed and approved by each business area; the head of each business area reviews the plan with the group president, but he neither approves nor disapproves it. All plans are consolidated at the group level.

Making the Changes Work

After the new structure was put in place, the company took several important steps to ensure that it worked in practice. These included:

• **Leadership.** The appointment of a new president helped galvanize a spirit of change and direction throughout the organization. His knowledge of the company (gained through almost 20 years of service), business acumen, self-confidence and personal energy made a strong impression on the employees. Further, his in-depth knowledge of business issues, such as finance and technology, has kept line and staff executives on their toes.

• **Training.** Everybody from group managers to supervisors attended a three-week training program that focused on: financial controls, management training and leadership psychology. The program reinforced the fact that Sandvik was changing and provided guidelines for adjusting to the new environment. Top managers from the business areas served as instructors for most parts of the course.

Prior to the training, employees received questionnaires requesting their input on a variety of issues. The same survey was repeated about five months later; it indicated improved boss-subordinate relationships, work climate, etc. This approach made it possible to agree on group and business area goals and to make them widely known.

• **New logo.** Another means of getting people's attention inside and outside of Sandvik was to redesign the company logotype. This was done in connection with the partitioning of the group into separate companies. An information campaign in the local and international media presented the new logo while publicizing the group's reorganization.

The changes had lowered costs, improved profitability, reduced internal bureaucracy and resulted in a more pronounced customer orientation. Productivity also rose, despite the fact that the average number of employees was reduced by about 8,000, or 25%, from 1980 to 1986. One of the ongoing goals of management is to continue to raise productivity levels.

While the restructuring has been largely successful, it is not without drawbacks. The two biggest glitches are:

• **Staff too small.** Some group staff units feel that the product companies and subsidiaries in many cases are too small to be able to build up sufficient professional knowledge and experience within specialized fields. Training, experience sharing and general advice is the approach so far.

• **Conflicting objectives.** The head of the holding company in a large country may be pressured by the managers of two or three product companies to take certain actions that may conflict with the needs of the group in the country. The paradoxes crop up at many levels, but they are recognized for what they are: the challenges that have to be mastered to keep the benefits of decentralization.

13. How Unisys Turned a Hostile Takeover Into a Successful Merger

When Burroughs Corp and Sperry Corp merged to form the world's second largest computer company, Unisys Corp, management faced a prodigious challenge. A highly competitive industry left little room for error as the firm sought to dispel the aftermath of a hostile takeover while reorganizing over 100,000 employees in 120 countries. In any merger, the uncertainty of change as well as the inevitable downsizing of the corporate organization threaten staff morale and customer confidence. With Unisys, these risks were compounded by the unprecedented size of the merger and the menacing mood engendered by Burroughs's hostile takeover of Sperry. In Europe, there was the additional factor that the new operation spread across many countries and cultures.

However, the Unisys merger strategy appears to have met the organizational challenge with a strong bottom line to prove it.

What Made the Merger Work

At the outset, EAD president Graham Murphy says, "We saw that our main priorities were people issues—both customers and personnel." Accordingly, the implementation of changes in the corporate structure was geared towards minimizing uncertainty while creating commitment to a new, stronger organization. Following the guidelines established by Unisys Chairman Michael Blumenthal, the management of Unisys EAD adopted a merger strategy for the Burroughs-Sperry union in Europe:

• **Move with speed.**   Two weeks after the announcement of the parents' merger, the key managers for Unisys EAD were selected; three days later the first staff meeting was held. Within three months, a new European headquarters in Uxbridge, England, was built, country managers were chosen, a financial plan was agreed upon and responsibilities from the top to the bottom of the organizational chart were defined. At the half-year point, a series of seminars was scheduled to explain internal structural changes to customers, reassuring them of the Unisys commitment to sustained product quality and service. While Murphy says the compressed timetable was "extremely demanding," it was the best way to remove any doubts that might have led to diminished personnel and customer support.

• **Emphasize merit.**   Although the creation of Unisys was the result of a heated takeover battle between two competitors, Blumenthal stipulated that the style of implementation would be a merger—with merit serving as the principal criteria guiding staffing decisions. In the selection of managers for the new company in Europe, Murphy points out that they aimed for "a conscious distillation of all that was the best from the former companies." As a result, appointments of both the managers at the EAD headquarters and the country managers represent a balanced mix of ex-Sperry and ex-Burroughs personnel. (See Unisys EAD Headquarters chart, p. 39.)

• **Structure around a new culture.**   It is not often that a corporation has a free hand to establish the organizational structure at the same time that it is trying to build a new culture. According to Murphy, "We paid as much attention to the culture of the new enterprise as to the structure." The objective: create an intensely market-driven firm.

First, a shallow organizational profile in Europe was designed to ensure management's direct involvement in the market. Second, the foundation of the reorganization of the European division was the restructuring of the Burroughs and Sperry marketing forces into "line-of-business" units (LOBs). At the regional and country levels, LOBs for key market segments—financial services, public sector and transportation, and industrial and commercial are now the fundamental building blocks of the organization. (See Unisys UK Subsidiary chart, p. 39.)

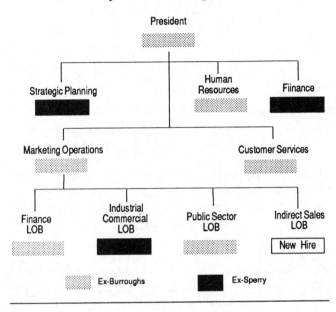

Unisys EAD Headquarters

President

Strategic Planning

Human Resources

Fiinance

Marketing Operations

Customer Services

Finance LOB

Industrial Commercial LOB

Public Sector LOB

Indirect Sales LOB

New Hire

Ex-Burroughs   Ex-Sperry

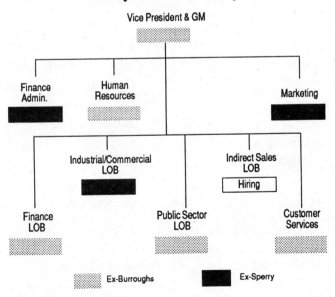

Unisys UK Subsidiary

Vice President & GM

Finance Admin.

Human Resources

Marketing

Industrial/Commercial LOB

Indirect Sales LOB

Hiring

Finance LOB

Public Sector LOB

Customer Services

Ex-Burroughs   Ex-Sperry

Assignments in the new organization have been clearly defined by LOBs. Thus, from the beginning, Unisys employees have had a strong awareness of the new company's mandate and of their specific role in achieving corporate objectives. Consistent standards for management performance have been emphasized, based on such criteria as employee and team development, the Unisys image in the marketplace, customer satisfaction and conventional financial objectives.

• **Make the structure consistent.**   To facilitate effective communication and planning among the national companies and the European headquarters, the new management structure is consistent across the region. In addition, groupings of countries (i.e. the Scandinavian group and the Iberia group) link common cultures and languages to encourage sharing of marketing and financial resources. The managers of each product segment report directly to their country vice president/ general manager, but also have dotted-line accountability to the European headquarters marketing manager.

• **Establish a new headquarters.**   Prior to the merger, Sperry ran its European operations from the US, while Burroughs maintained a small marketing and support operation in Europe. In keeping with the effort to create an organizational structure that reflects a strong market orientation, the decision was made to base the European headquarters in Europe. This decision, Murphy says, "has created a much stronger European identity for the company" to meet the specific requirements of the marketplace. The European operation has also been given a stronger voice in developing international strategy at the top of the corporation. Murphy was appointed to the parents' management board, which oversees the operations of Unisys worldwide.

14. Watching the International Angles When Reorganizing

Corporate restructuring, when undertaken as part of a rationalization program, raises special management concerns. These rise markedly when the organization being restructured has domestic as well as international operations. The story below draws on the lessons from the experience of a large US-based firm with worldwide operations.

Company B was one of the world's leading and most diversified manufacturers of packaging products. Total sales of the US-based parent exceeded $3.5 billion, about 15% of which were generated overseas. In the early 1980s, the firm's senior management undertook a major restructuring, after having determined that an excessive cost structure was undermining returns and adequate shareholder value. Fear that the company might be targeted for a hostile takeover generated a further impetus for change.

Recognition of the need for reorganization was widespread. In the words of one foreign executive, "The restructuring and downsizing were long overdue. The company had coasted along comfortably for years, without pushing its various businesses harder to produce. Over time, growing layers of bureaucracy turned decisionmaking into a complex exercise. An intrinsically simple business had become complex; it was high time someone came along to pull it up by its bootstraps."

Steps for Improving Returns

• First, a corporatewide program for reducing costs was applied over a three-year period, trimming operating expenses (as a percentage of sales) from about 10% to 8%, and yielding annual savings well in excess of $60 million.

• Second, certain existing assets were liquidated, realizing almost $400 million. Businesses that could not contribute to the fulfillment of corporate objectives were sold or closed down. The criteria for these decisions were clear: to become the high-quality, low-cost producer in every area of business in which the corporation competes and to continually improve that position.

From this exercise, Company B learned the importance of casting a hard eye on its marginally performing businesses, especially the international ones. Close scrutiny focused attention on the inordinately high real costs of the management time and on the corporate resources involved in efforts to boost performance in these operations.

• Third, building upon the foundation of its traditional basic businesses, management sought to invest the proceeds of these sales in acquisitions. The object was to identify areas that offered possibilities for higher, profitable growth. Through a strategic planning process, several major industries were analyzed for their potential to meet these criteria, as well as for entry opportunities. Three were selected and investments were made.

Downsizing the International Operations

Early in the restructuring process it was decided that corporate head-quarters would refrain from dictating how overseas affiliates (largely self-contained units) should reduce their expenses. Instead, hq studied the return on equity of each affiliate and set tough profit targets. Each affiliate general manager was responsible for the methods by which the targets were achieved.

The downsizing inspired a major change in the structure of the organization. The international division staff and its role were severely reduced; the corporation reorganized away from an international division to a worldwide product structure. Regional headquarters were eliminated and the international hq operation was cut over a four-year period. Divisional staffs, including some with international responsibilities, were also reduced.

As to the elimination of regional headquarters, a senior executive said, "At the time, I thought it was wrong, but in retrospect I see it was not a mistake. For one thing, it yielded immediate and very real cost savings. A more long-lasting effect was that it allowed country managers to take greater responsibility for running their own operations."

Lessons From Downsizing

In the course of its cost reductions and restructuring, Company B learned several lessons the hard way. (Not the least among them was that even with a successful reorganization focused on profitability, the company was unable to avoid being taken over.) The most important tips that other firms may find useful include:

• **Understand the change in demands on management.**   When you reorganize to a worldwide product structure, realize that the division executive typically will have little or no international experience. It may take him a while to understand some of the finer points of operating in key foreign markets, thus slowing decisionmaking. He may also be reluctant to take what he perceives as risks in an unfamiliar environment.

Even for an experienced international hand, the transition can be demanding. Particularly when domestic operations account for a large part of the product business, it will take some time to get used to the different concerns of international and domestic operations and the changes in management style that may be needed as a result.

• **Be willing to let go.**   Do not be afraid to decentralize the locus of control in your international business to the local level. Decentralization does not mean that senior management is ignoring the affiliates. What is required is that management be clear on goals, approve the affiliates' business plans and set up appropriate monitors to track results. Company B found it was able to do very well without a bevy of specialists in international planning, finance, marketing, human resources, etc.

• **Understand the pitfalls of cutting muscle.**   In your eagerness to downsize, be very careful to provide for the future of the corporation. Planning as a staff function may be eliminated or drastically reduced. But appropriate resources must still be made available to ensure quality thinking about the long-term direction of the business. The concern about future competitiveness is even more important in the R&D area.

• **Bite the bullet on your head count.**   Plan and execute the scope of a corporate early retirement program and then stick to it. Morale suffers badly when new "early retirement" drives are announced every two or three years.

15. How US Firms Organize Their European Treasuries

When it comes to treasury organization, there are no set solutions that apply to all companies. Each firm must decide what type of geographic organization it needs based on the specific nature of its business operations and the treasury functions it wants to perform. However, a survey of 14 well-known MNCs conducted by one Fortune 50 firm did have two specific findings that all US firms with European operations should consider.

(1) Most US companies that have significant operations in Europe site their regional treasuries on the European side of the Atlantic. Regional treasuries satisfy the need for daily contact with operating management, financial institutions and the general economic and political environments of markets and production sites. They also eliminate the inefficiencies that are caused by the time difference between the US and Europe, as well as high T&E expenses and extensive travel time.

(2) Most European treasury units report directly to corporate headquarters and not to European divisional headquarters. Of the 14 companies surveyed, 10 have units that report to corporate headquarters and four have units that report to European headquarters. There are several reasons for this:

• In most cases, the European treasury services various product groups within the company. If that treasury reported to any one

Survey of 14 Regional Treasuries

Department function	Perform function
European netting system	14
Centralized exposure management	13
Cash management studies	12
Capital-structure recommendations	12
Exchange/interest rate forecasts	12
Leasing	11
Determining FX strategy	11
Dividend analysis/determination	11
Managing insurance programs	9
Issuing guarantees	9
A/R collection responsibility	8
Approving fixed-asset investments	5
Budget participation	5
Approving fixed-asset investments	3
Countertrade	2
Factoring company	2

product group, it would be difficult to maintain services to the other groups.

• Many of the functions of the European treasurer, such as determining dividends, capital structure and cash levels, are of a corporate or fiduciary nature. The person determining these issues should not report to the management of the companies involved.

• European treasurers carry out many functions that are not operational line functions, such as maintaining shareholder relations and supporting the US treasury in carrying out projects in Europe.

• In many cases, the managers of product groups in the US prefer to have the European treasury group report into corporate treasury. This provides increased financial control of European operations and an independent viewpoint on major financial policy issues.

• Closer ties between the European and corporate treasuries boost the overall technical know-how and effectiveness of the treasury staff. They also ensure greater consistency in policy and objectives.

• A reporting relationship with HQ gives the European treasurer more clout when dealing with financial institutions, because he is perceived as a corporate representative and not just a divisional treasurer.

General Motors: The Complete Menu

Of the 14 firms surveyed, General Motors (GM) operates one of the most active European treasuries. Its regional treasury office offers extensive operational and day-to-day support to its European units, whose consolidated sales are about $12 billion. The office was set up in Brussels in 1986 to support the operating units with an enhanced treasury capability in their local time zones. Established with a staff of nine, it was added to GM's existing Belgian coordination center to facilitate the financing of the automaker's eight European manufacturing sites and 22 sales units, while taking advantage of the tax holiday offered to BCCs.

The regional treasury office, or RT, interacts mostly with GM's subsidiaries in Germany, the Netherlands and the UK because of those countries' liberal exchange controls and banking rules. Since in-house banking services are simply not allowed for operations in Italy, Spain and Portugal (manufacturers can deal only with authorized banks), the RT acts mostly in an advisory capacity for these units, dealing with questions on foreign exchange, funding and other treasury matters. Specifically, the European RT offers regional units the following services:

• **Foreign exchange risk management.**   Each subsidiary makes transactions only in its local currency. Where permitted by local regulations, subsidiaries buy spot and forward contracts through the RT. The RT establishes forex-position limits for itself as well as for each subsidiary. It reports its own positions daily to GM's main treasury office in New York. It reports subsidiary positions to New York twice a week.

• **In-house banking services.**   The RT takes deposits from cash-rich subs and offers loans to operations that need financing. However, subsidiaries are allowed to go elsewhere if they can get a better deal from a local bank. "We can usually provide competitive arm's-length interest because our fixed costs and overhead are low," says European Treasurer Scott Bihl. For example, GM tries to reduce costs by keeping its multicurrency accounts in London rather than in Brussels, where banking costs are higher. There is no precise reporting schedule, but contact is maintained with the treasurers in the field so that the RT knows whether they need funds or have excess cash.

The RT can also advise operating units about long-term financing structures or implement those structures on its own books to minimize aftertax funding costs. The RT is now actively developing this function, and the long-term side of the business is expected to grow in the future.

• **Training designed to increase the level of treasury expertise in European operations and to promote treasury efficiency.** To do this, GM offers subsidiary treasurers six-month stints at the regional office giving them a chance to broaden their horizons. "We find that European treasury people are highly qualified and used to dealing with different currencies and markets," says another GM staffer. "However, the six months here helps them to see problems at a wider level than they do in their local jobs."

PPG's Scaled-Down Approach

At the other end of the scale, PPG Industries operated one of the leaner European treasuries. Through July 1988, PPG's Paris-based regional treasury supported the financial activities of 12 European subsidiaries. The RT was led by European Treasury Manager Bob Howard, who, as a member of the international treasury section of the US parent's treasury department, reported functionally to the US-based treasurer.

Although PPG's 1987 European sales were $1.2 billion and its regional assets $1.5 billion, its RT was extremely lean, staffed only by Howard and a secretary. Says Howard, "We didn't want a centralized European treasury organization unless it fully replaced the existing activities in our 12 companies in Europe. We find that many companies have created another level without eliminating the costs the unit was supposed to save."

PPG could maintain stripped-down RT because its day-to-day treasury needs are modes. Country finance managers are encouraged to maintain financial control over their operations and to show initiative in carrying out daily activities. In the key countries of France, Italy, Germany and the UK, a local manager handles the national cash-pooling program that was set up with Howard's help. The various companies in these four countries send weekly reports to the country's lead financial manager, advising him of cash flows for the next six weeks.

Since PPG sells glass and paint to industrial purchasers and large distributors, its subs are not burdened with heavy daily cash flows from numerous retail outlets, and this makes cash management easier. Furthermore, because transport costs are heavy, most of its European business is confined to domestic markets, limiting cross-border business transactions and forex risks. The small amount of cross-border business that does exist was netted monthly on a bilateral basis between RT and each subsidiary.

Every year, meetings are held in each country to coordinate the financial plan for the coming year. The plan forecasts the dividend capacity of each subsidiary in light of expansion or development plans. It also lays out the expected supply and demand of the region's internal funds, the funding that will be needed from external sources and the banks that will be used for funding. The local financial managers must operate within this framework.

The annual meeting also reviews cross-border forex flows to see if it is worthwhile to centralize certain transactions. To date, the opportunities have been limited and the costs of changing the present decentralized system not equal to the potential savings. However, the European operations are growing every year, and it may be necessary to manage forex flows more centrally in the future. Says Howard, "The annual review helps us reexamine the situation so that we can change our strategy if we need to."

16. Financial Organization at Ciba-Geigy

With its small home base in Basel, Switzerland, Ciba-Geigy has built its success on product divisions with worldwide responsibilities. It has decentralized operational responsibilities to adapt better to conditions abroad, while at the same time relying on centralized support divisions to focus expertise and maintain control. As a key support function, finance has organized itself along centralized lines but has also retained a significant decentralized component. Finance Director Walter Zeller was interviewed about Ciba-Geigy's finance department and how it has organized to reap the advantages of functional centralization while keeping the benefits of a decentralized geographic orientation.

A Companywide Matrix

The company is organized in the following way:

• The general managers of Ciba-Geigy's nine major product divisions each report to the executive committee, which in turn reports to the CEO (see diagram, p. 48).

• The support functions, including finance, control, legal services, R&D and production, also report to the committee as separate entities. How-

Ciba-Geigy's Business Organization

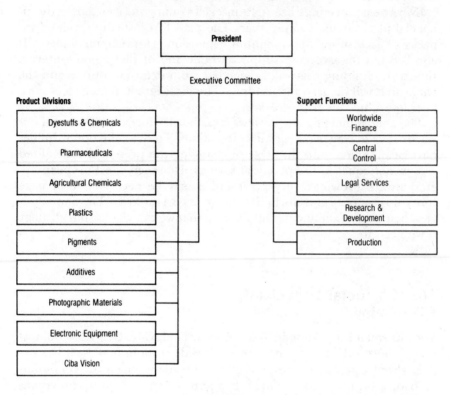

President

Executive Committee

Product Divisions

- Dyestuffs & Chemicals
- Pharmaceuticals
- Agricultural Chemicals
- Plastics
- Pigments
- Additives
- Photographic Materials
- Electronic Equipment
- Ciba Vision

Support Functions

- Worldwide Finance
- Central Control
- Legal Services
- Research & Development
- Production

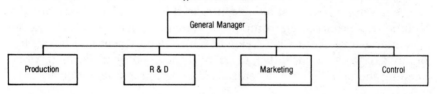

Typical Product Division

General Manager

| Production | R & D | Marketing | Control |

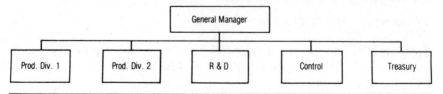

Typical Major Affiliated Company

General Manager

| Prod. Div. 1 | Prod. Div. 2 | R & D | Control | Treasury |

ever, each product division also has its own R&D, marketing, production and control staffs, which report directly to the general manager of the division.

• In addition, the divisional control staff reports on a dotted-line basis to the central control group. (The company's other divisional functions, such as R&D and production, do not report to the central functions.)

• At the country level, some of the major subsidiaries sell and, in some cases, produce goods for one or more product divisions. (Some affiliates also have R&D facilities.)

• Each affiliate also has a control staff and a treasury staff that report directly to the subsidiary general manager. The control staff reports on a dotted-line basis to the control staffs in the product divisions, while the treasury staff bypasses the product divisions (which have no treasury staff) and communicates directly with the central finance group.

This matrix organization calls for a good deal of discussion and compromise among various managers, but the company is kept on a straight course by clearly stated corporate policies and guidelines geared toward improving long-term earnings growth. All Ciba-Geigy managers must try to do the following:

• **Create productivity gains.**   The executive committee relies both on ratios (e.g. sales per employee) and financial data (e.g. contribution to consolidated profits) when it reviews productivity levels in the field. Says Zeller, "In addition to looking at key figures such as sales per employee, we also set goals agreed upon at the unit level; each unit discusses how it can improve its own productivity." Like the product divisions, the support functions are measured for productivity gains.

• **Build market share.**   Increased productivity helps Ciba-Geigy offer customers better goods at lower prices. The firm also seeks to boost its share in its existing markets through enormous outlays for R&D and through expansion into related new product markets. Says Zeller, "We have two alternatives for obtaining new technology: We can develop it in-house or we can make an acquisition."

• **Guard against forex volatility.**   While 46% of Ciba-Geigy's sales are generated in European currencies that are parallel with the franc (because of EMS stability and the Swiss franc's informal link to the Deutschemark), another 28% of sales come from North America, 13% from

Asia, 8% from Latin America and the remaining 5% from elsewhere. As the US dollar fell in the 1980s, both Swiss franc sales and aftertax profits fell dramatically. Clearly, protecting the company against foreign exchange fluctuations must be a top corporate priority, and every manager must be aware of it.

Geographic and Functional Coverage

To enable finance to play its essential role in supporting this strategic focus, Ciba-Geigy has adopted an intriguing organizational approach. "The finance function is organizationally equivalent to a product division," explains Zeller (see diagram, below). Like the product divisions, the two central financial groups—central control and worldwide finance—report to a member of the executive committee. Central control is responsible for the MIS system; it provides consolidated financial information to the executive committee and to all management levels of Ciba-Geigy. The worldwide finance group includes parent company treasury (PCT), finance group companies (FGC), countertrade, intercompany invisible management and capital markets transactions.

To take full advantage of the benefits of centralized finance while ensuring the primacy of operational decentralization, the activities of worldwide finance have been organized along both functional and geographical lines:

• **Finance group companies organized geographically.** Its 20 staff members include area treasurers for Europe; the Middle East and Af-

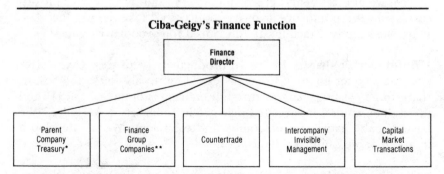

Ciba-Geigy's Finance Function

Finance Director

| Parent Company Treasury* | Finance Group Companies** | Countertrade | Intercompany Invisible Management | Capital Market Transactions |

*Includes forex trading and hedging, cash management, cash investment, accounts payable/receivable, credit management, and export credit and insurance.
**Includes treasurers for Europe; Middle East and Africa; US, UK and Far East; and Canada and Latin America.

rica; the US, UK and Far East; and Canada and Latin America. Based in Basel, FGC discusses all major financial decisions with the overseas subsidiaries and consults with them for planning, policy and supervisory purposes. While PCT handles all treasury concerns for the parent and product divisions, FGC serves as a strategic and communications link between the foreign subs and the treasury, administration and capital markets groups at headquarters. Subsidiaries can take responsibility for many of their short-term financial needs, such as borrowing in local currency and cash and credit management, but there are four operations they cannot perform independently: borrowing forex, borrowing for one year or longer, giving company guarantees for loans and taking out mortgages.

- **Parent company treasury is organized functionally.** Its 70 staffers are divided into teams with worldwide responsibility for FX trading and hedging, cash management, cash investment, accounts payable/receivable, credit management and export credit and insurance.

As stated above, FX management is the top priority. Given the firm's emphasis on long-term growth, the FX strategy incorporates not only short-term transaction hedging but long-term operational adjustments as well. Says Zeller, "We do not change direction from week to week or month to month; our strategy is for the long term. We cannot shift our supply or production points every year as the relationships between currencies change. When we look at new investments, we have to take into account the current relationship between hard and soft currencies, but we keep in mind the long-term effect, too."

- **Three worldwide finance departments, five people each, are also organized functionally.** There is one department for intercompany invisible management and another for capital market transactions. The latter provides for the long-term funding and investment needs of PCT and FGC and is responsible for a number of Ciba-Geigy finance companies.

A third unit looks after countertrade. This group is located in the finance function rather than in marketing (as it is at other firms) to allow the countertraders to take an impartial view of opportunities and to concentrate expertise in one place. It works closely with the export-credit unit of PCT, since countertrade is regarded as one of several ways of generating business opportunities in countries short of foreign exchange. Says Zeller, "We want the countertrade group to look at situations objectively. When they see a problem in a country that can be solved by countertrade, they go to the product division and say, 'This will cost you a 2% premium.' Then the product division can agree or disagree." Countertrade operates as a cost center, charging only the premium for handling products obtained in the barter operation.

Financial Democracy

FGC and PCT work closely together to fund worldwide operations. They generally prefer to lend intercompany, thus utilizing Ciba-Geigy liquidity. The major exceptions are loans to risky countries or situations in which a local currency loan would serve as a hedge. Subsidiaries generally borrow Swiss francs or easily traded major currencies such as US dollars, Deutschemarks or UK pounds. They are charged at the same rate the parent would receive for an investment in that currency, and they thus pay slightly less than they would have had they borrowed the funds from a bank.

FGC and PCT not only cooperate with each other but share financial responsibility with the operations managers as well. For example, if the dyestuffs division wants to make a sale to a risky country, it must consult PCT to find out whether additional risk can be absorbed within the aggregate limits set for the company as a whole. If not, the finance director will ask the executive committee to increase the ceiling or require the product division to sell for cash. PCT must also approve customer credits with maturities exceeding one year.

The process of discussion and coordination leads to control in a "subtle democratic way," according to FGC Manager Francois Bochud. "We try to maintain a consensus on how the financial situation is developing. In addition to frequent contact by telephone and telex, group treasurers come to Basel once a year, and we get out there from time to time."

17. Organizing for Global Marketing: The Elusive 'Best' Structure

Since multinational corporations (MNCs) ventured abroad decades ago, they have been searching for the optimum organization structure to integrate their foreign and domestic marketing activities. The challenge they have faced—and continue to face—is how to maximize the international potential of their products and services without diluting their domestic marketing efforts. Despite extensive experimentation and the allocation of vast amounts of money and executive time to the issue of corporate organization, no single structure has emerged as the ideal, even for companies in the same industry.

In the end, every company chooses an organization structure based on a number of highly individualized factors:

• The nature of its business;

• The diversity of its products;

• The extent and distribution of its international sales and manufacturing;

• The company's competitive position;

• Corporate culture.

• The degree of centralization of marketing decisionmaking desired by senior management. This is often determined by the availability and depth of management at the overseas subsidiaries, since it cannot work without highly capable people in place in the field.

Types of Structures

The International Division. International divisions are a natural outgrowth of traditional export departments. The main benefits of an international division are:

• **International specialization.** It provides a central corporate management group focused exclusively on doing business outside the home country and on coordinating international activities. It provides the easiest way to concentrate scarce managerial resources on international operations, and since international divisions tend to have relatively small staffs, they often have lower costs as well.

An international division brings together executives and salespeople with an interest in international business and, usually, with international expertise, ability to speak foreign languages and other cross-cultural skills. Many of these people already have experience marketing one or more of the company's products as well, experience typically gained when they were on the domestic side of the business. Therefore, their internationalism serves as an additional, rather than a sole, competence. In many (but by no means all) MNCs, a transfer from a product division

to the international division is considered a promotion or at least a plum
assignment.

• **Increased coordination.** An international division reduces the potential for duplication of effort, because all business activities associated
with a given country are placed under one "roof" — usually a country
subsidiary (XYZ Company France, XYZ Company Brazil, etc.) that reports back to the head of the international division, sometimes directly,
but usually through a regional headquarters.

• **Unified image.** At the country level, the international division has
the advantage of simplicity for those who must deal with the company.
There is one president of XYZ Company France, and it is easy to
present a consistent corporate image. Having a single subsidiary in a
given country fosters close relationships with national and local governments.

• **Attention to international markets.** Most important, the existence
of an international division helps ensure that the overseas market and
individual country markets get proper attention. A product might have
huge potential abroad, but if domestic sales are increasing, too, a product division might not want to allocate the necessary funds to develop
the overseas market. It is the responsibility of the head of the international division — who is not accountable to the heads of the product divisions — to see that the product is marketed in other countries. Indeed,
he may elect to spend a large share of his division's budget building foreign sales for the product if he thinks it is especially promising. (However, he may have to battle with the product division head to obtain adequate supplies of the product if it is a hot seller at home — a situation
that illustrates one of the most serious shortcomings of an international
division structure.)

International divisions also have their shortcomings:

• **Conflict with product groups.** Part of the reason for the decline in
popularity of the international division was that it created deep structural conflicts within companies that were increasingly organizing their
domestic operations by product group. As the product groups were
usually larger and had much richer budgets, they prevailed in many disputes and began to usurp the international division's authority in marketing (and other functions as well).

• **Lack of product specialization.** International divisions, by definition, create product generalists rather than specialists, because their personnel must market many products at once. It is not uncommon for a handful of salespeople in a country to be responsible for marketing a company's entire product line. In the case of industrial manufacturers, this can mean hundreds or thousands of items. Complicated products, not surprisingly, are often neglected, while simpler, easier-to-use products get the most attention. For this reason, consumer products are easier to market through an international division than high-tech industrial items. The unequal marketing effort and the complaints generated back home in the product divisions making complex products have been major contributors to the abandonment of the international division by many companies.

Worldwide Product Groups. Today many globally oriented companies, particularly highly diversified ones, make their product divisions or groups responsible for their own international marketing. According to James Bolt, founder and president of Executive Development Associates, a Connecticut-based international business management consulting firm, "The greater diversity of product lines, the more likely it becomes for a company to manage foreign business through a worldwide product division." For many firms, organizing along product lines has proven to be a successful formula: Corporations using the world product group structure have grown about 50% faster than those using regional or international divisions, explained Bolt in a recent paper entitled *Global Competitors: Some Criteria for Success.*

The world product group addresses many of the problems associated with the international division:

• **Product specialization.** International marketing personnel are product specialists and, as such, are usually more attuned to customers' needs. It is somewhat easier to foster a team atmosphere, since everyone—from transportation to distribution to sales to service—is familiar with the products and has a vested interest in maximizing sales on the global market. This cooperative attitude contrasts sharply with the "we-they" syndrome that is often associated with the international division approach.

• **Incentive to sell to foreign markets.** Inherent in the world product group organizational form is the notion that product groups, given full credit for their foreign sales, will not drag their feet on international marketing but will seek overseas orders to increase their profitability.

Indeed, many corporate executives believe that world product divisions provide the widest scope and latitude for individual decisionmaking and risk-taking.

The main drawbacks to this type of organization:

• **Lack of coordination in international marketing efforts.** Duplication of effort often arises when more than one product is marketed by separate groups with separate strategies in the same country; the more products, the greater the risk of the right hand not knowing what the left is doing. The classic horror story is the one about two product general managers from the same company meeting outside a mutual customer's office — or a government official's office — each with no prior knowledge of the other's visit. Such incidents can be not only embarrassing but costly as well.

• **Lack of country specialization.** The fact that there is no headquarters international staff may result in a watering down of international and country-specific expertise.

The Regional Organizational Pattern. While similar to the international division configuration in theory, regional systems vary in a number of respects. In a regional organization, each region's top executive (who may be called a general manager, managing director, vice president or president, depending on the company's hierarchy of titles) reports directly to a senior corporate executive, typically the president of the company or an executive vice president. It is this direct reporting relationship that distinguishes a true regional organization from an international division with regional subdivisions, in which the heads of the regions report on a line basis to the head of the international division. (However, to complicate matters, some regional organizations do have a *staff* executive at corporate headquarters responsible for coordinating international matters.)

From a marketing perspective, a key difference between the two forms of organization is that an international division normally has one executive who is ultimately responsible for worldwide marketing. With a regional pattern, the head of marketing for each region has the final responsibility for marketing to all the countries within that region. The marketing managers for each of the various countries or subsidiaries report to this individual. Two important advantages of such an approach are:

• The likelihood of duplication of effort in a given region is reduced.

• Coordination is enhanced.

However, many of the drawbacks associated with international divisions are also associated with regional organizations:

• **Lack of specialization**. Like international divisions, regions foster the creation of product generalists and dilute the attention paid to complex products.

Hybrid Patterns. A hybrid refers to a single structure that incorporates a combination of organizational approaches throughout the company. Pure organizational forms are increasingly rare among global corporations. In some cases, what were once pure organizational patterns have become blurred over the years, in some cases because of mergers and acquisitions with companies organized in different ways. In other cases, pure organizational patterns were altered due to changes that occurred in product mix, markets or management.

Some companies have deliberately tried to fuse various forms of organization together to create more workable systems for their particular needs and circumstances. Hybrid forms use two or more organizational patterns concurrently throughout a company. Some firms call such approaches "matrixes," although that term appears to be falling into disuse, perhaps because it connotes a certain formality and rigidity at a time when companies are trying to stress organizational flexibility.

Mixture Solutions. MNCs that have adopted organizational mixtures use one approach for certain products or divisions and another for other products or divisions. Some of a company's product groups might have responsibility for marketing their own lines overseas, while others might turn over their international marketing to a central international division. The kinds of companies that use mixtures are typically those with highly diverse product lines.

Mixtures may occur when the overseas business of one or more product groups grows so large that top management decides the product groups can no longer handle their overseas operations simply as an extension of their domestic business. An international division may then be set up to assume responsibility for marketing those products abroad. In other cases, acquisitions or mergers between companies with different organization structures results in a mixture pattern. When a company with a worldwide product group format acquires a company with an international or regional pattern, management may decide to let the two systems coexist for a period of time, or indefinitely, or until they prove to be incompatible.

● **Best of both worlds**. Both hybrids and mixtures allow a company to take advantage of the best attributes of an organizational pattern while at the same time minimizing its inherent weaknesses.

The Network Approach. As global corporations are becoming ever larger through foreign acquisitions, joint ventures or direct investments overseas, a number have decided that none of the conventional organizational forms work for them. At the same time, these companies are trying to stay flexible, maintain the ability to respond quickly to fast-changing technology and become product innovators. Companies like this have decided that the only way to accommodate their needs is through a new concept of organization called the "corporate network."

A networked company is one in which all employees in all parts of the world create, produce and sell the company's products through a carefully cultivated system of interrelationships. Middle-level managers from R&D, marketing, distribution, etc. discuss common problems and try to accommodate one another. Information need not travel along inflexible routes or organizational lines. This system provides several benefits:

● **Enhanced communication.** The network system works in contrast to traditional corporate organizations, discussed earlier, which divide companies according to either products, functions or geography — or some combination of these. In those systems, information travels according to a set chain of command.

The network approach involves no formal chain of communication. Marketing people in France are encouraged to speak to manufacturing people in Singapore. Lateral relationships spur innovation, new product development and better quality control. Supporters of the network approach perceive it as the only true way a company can be innovative in today's bureaucratic world.

● **Reduced bureaucracy.** Networking puts greater decisionmaking responsibility in the hands of middle managers, who are not required to clear every detail and event with higher-ups. Fred Guterl stated in *Business Month* in January 1989, "The corporate network is not so much a new organizational structure as a departure from the whole idea of structure. Management control is replaced by coordination."

2
Planning and Investment

18. Corporate Planning in the 1990s: 10 Key Functions

A generation ago, planning departments enjoyed high status within the corporate organization. Conceived by business school professors and put into practice by the US's emerging multinational giants, corporate planning was the leading-edge management "science." Planning mechanisms were characterized by highly structured formats and a strong degree of central administrative control. Planning units had large staffs and supervised elaborate planning procedures. the job of planners was, in a very real sense, to plan the future course of the company.

Today, most corporate planners downplay their formal planning roles and instead emphasize their functions as "facilitators," "communicators" or "consultants." Experience with such largely unforeseen upheavals as the two oil crises of the 1970s and the stock market crash of 1987, coupled with the increasing need for flexibility and rapid local response, has revealed the shortcomings of the centralized approach: It was overly bureaucratic, and it took power and accountability out of the hands of the line managers and division heads who should be wielding them.

A typical planning system in the 1990s aims to ensure the smooth running of the global corporation. The planning department has become an information "switchbox," receiving information on a vast array of issues and strategies from field units and filtering this data to make it accessible to top management. In the opposite direction, it sends essential macroeconomic assumptions and directives on mission and strategy from top management to operating units and provides them with support and consulting services.

What Today's Planners Do

BI conducted in-depth interviews with 17 of the world's leading international companies on three continents for insights into their approaches to global planning. The planning departments examined ranged in size from two staff members to 60. Clearly, the scope and nature of their functions vary substantially. Nonetheless, planners in global organizations face similar challenges and have developed broadly analogous working methods. The following are the 10 most frequently mentioned functions of corporate planners:

• **Compilation of information for top management.** In a large MNC, it is usually impossible for senior managers to absorb all the varied data being sent from the operating and staff units. Strategic planning departments play a key role in screening the raw information and packaging what top executives need most in a manageable format. Typically, planners compile summary data on achievement of strategic or budgeted goals, current financial targets of divisions, divisional strategic plans, competitor intelligence, regional and global economic reports and special research studies.

• **Competitor research.** Although most competitive information is likely to be collected at the divisional level, corporate planning departments frequently research global competition. This function becomes critical, as diversified global companies find themselves competing against similarly globalized firms across industries and regions. For example, Eastman Kodak competes with Canon in both copiers and photographic equipment. A divisional analysis that focuses on only one of these industries would provide an incomplete picture of the competition.

• **Forecasting.** The majority of corporate planning departments develop (or acquire from outside consultants) certain overall assumptions or forecasts to guide divisional planners. In some cases, these are limited to very basic macroeconomic figures. However, when the company is heavily dependent on essential commodities, assumptions may also include commodity price ranges.

The main purpose of these forecasts is to provide a consistent framework for divisional plans. But corporate planners at several firms insist that these assumptions are only guidelines. Adherence to them is not mandatory for planners and managers at the divisions who usually make their own regional or industry-specific projections — sometimes based on assumptions from headquarters — which may in turn be used by the corporate planning group for its own forecasting process.

● **Consulting services.** Several corporate planners emphasize that they see their roles less as representatives of corporate authority than as consultants charged with assisting the divisions in developing their own plans and strategies. And extreme example is Pirelli, where the divisions actually pay "consulting fees" for the services of the company's planners, who compete, to some extent, with outside consulting firms. Moreover, to prove their value as objective experts, Pirelli planners also offer their services as consultants on a fee basis to other companies.

Services provided by the typical corporate planning department to operating divisions include planning methods, formats and step-by-step processes; planning critiques; competitive analysis; industry analysis; and special projects, especially those that require time or expertise unavailable within the division.

● **Creating a common language.** Many planners in global organizations see part of their role as introducing harmony into a variegated system by creating common languages and terms of reference. For example, they may devise standardized reporting formats, so that figures that portray return on investment, market share and so on are understood throughout the organization, as well as by top management.

● **Communicating corporate "culture."** Together with top management and the personnel and corporate communications departments, corporate planning helps project the corporation's culture throughout the organization and even outside. The planning department typically fosters the culture by emphasizing the strategic orientation adopted by the company (e.g. and aggressive move to high technology). While top management uses personal visits, speeches, internal communications and high-profile actions to spread its message, planners can serve a valuable function by integrating cultural factors into the corporate planning process.

● **Establishing and communicating corporate objectives.** The extent to which centrally mandated goals must be incorporated into divisional strategies varies from company to company. But all the MNCs interviewed required a minimal level of conformity with top management's goals. Planning departments inculcate corporate goals in a variety of ways — including them in the planning formats sent out at the start of the planning cycle, arranging conferences at which top managers articulate their goals for the corporation, distributing papers or memos prepared by top management outlining the firm's overall objectives or by simply communicating informally with division heads.

● **Group facilitation and team leadership**.   Planners organize and coordinate meetings and conferences, which are attended by various mixtures of top executives, division heads and product or industry specialists. In connection with these meetings, planners often put together preparatory material, analyze key issues, set the schedule, introduce themes and issues, lead discussions or decision-making groups, compile conclusions and communicate strategies or goals arising from the meetings. In some instances, regular meetings or conferences organized by the corporate planning department are integrated into the planning cycle; in others, meetings are called on an ad hoc basis.

● **Developing planning methods**.   Most planning departments have devised and refined a variety of specific techniques and procedures for strategic planning. Some are based on internal expertise, some on the ideas and methods used by outside consultants and some on the views of top management. At present, few planners interviewed are developing new or different planning methods. Thus, although development of a planning discipline is an essential function of corporate planning, it is not necessarily an ongoing activity.

19.   What Goes Into a Plan?

BI's interviews with MNCs revealed that the content of global strategic plans varies widely. This is due partly to different corporate philosophies and partly to varying degrees of delegation to the divisional level. Nevertheless, virtually all plans prepared by operating divisions must include these basic elements:

● **Sales and income goals.**   These objectives are perhaps the single ingredient of corporate plans that is universal to all the companies interviewed. In some instances, top management sets the goals at corporate headquarters, whereas more bottom-up-oriented firms may allow the divisions to determine their own sales and income targets.

● **Mission statement.**   The formal expression of the company's raison d'etre, these statements often come from top management in a process separate from the regular planning cycle. Corporate missions range from general aspirations (e.g. to be useful to society) to very specific goals (e.g. to become the global leader in a particular industry over a certain time period).

• **Economic analysis.** In most cases (as indicated earlier), corporate planners provide the divisions with a set of economic assumptions. However, these tend to be very broad – mainly limited to macro-economic indicators such as GNP, inflation and unemployment. Divisional planners are expected to use these assumptions as a starting point, conducting a more detailed economic analysis specific to their region or industry.

• **Competitor analysis.** Most plans typically pay some attention to evaluating competitive threats. Several of the firms BI interviewed furnish the divisions with a detailed summary of the types of competitor analysis to be carried out by the divisions and suggest how such information might be used. In some cases, however, competitor analysis is left entirely to the divisions. Notably lacking from the majority of cases was any appreciable focus on such current corporate concerns as customer needs or market characteristics. Although these "qualitative" issues may be addressed at the divisional level, virtually none of the companies deal with them in a standardized planning format.

Cutting Paperwork at Whirlpool

One firm that has minimized the written material divisional planners need to submit is Whirlpool Corp, the US-based appliance manufacturer. Whirlpool's planning process makes the operating units responsible for developing their own business strategies. Indeed, the corporate planning department has a staff of only five. "Our function is to run the planning process globally," says Harry Burritt, director of corporate planning and development, "not dictate strategy."

Whirlpool's plans for operating units use standardized formats to facilitate consistent measurement. But these procedures are kept to a bare minimum. "Last year, we went to three forms," says Burritt. "One of these is an executive summary, which is a blank sheet of paper. What we have learned over time is that if you can simplify your strategy on a couple of pieces of paper, then you probably have a pretty good one. This does not mean the strategy is simple, but you've thought about it enough so you can really bring out the key points that are the core of the strategy." He adds: "I don't mean to imply that the requested output of the process is limited. In fact, the operating units are expected to provide a detailed path to achieve our corporate vision. That's a pretty tall order, because the vision is very aggressive. We're expecting our divisions to become world leaders. The answer to how they are going to do that is obviously not simple."

20. The CEO's View of the 1990s: Globalization and Quality

There is little doubt that the political and economic changes of the 1980s have left a legacy of increasing global competitiveness. In surveying more than 400 CEOs worldwide, BI focused on discovering those factors that executives feel will most strongly affect their business during the coming decade. In addition, BI wanted to learn which strategies and management styles companies considered crucial to maintain profitability during a turbulent decade.

Defining the Global Marketplace

Executives point to key factors they believe will shape the global marketplace of the 1990s: greater globalization of markets, more customer insistence on quality, increasing competition, regional trading blocs and the rapid pace of technological development.

● **Globalization of markets**. CEOs see further erosion of geographic barriers as the major factor affecting businesses worldwide. Although this perception is particularly acute among North American executives, European multinational companies rank globalization ahead of the creation of the single market as a key force changing the marketplace of the 1990s.

● **Customer demand for quality**. Among European executives, this issue ranks number one, while North Americans and Asians rank it number two. In absolute terms, though, North American firms are more concerned about quality than are Asian firms. This indicates that European firms for the most part lag behind Asian and North American firms in quality-improvement processes, while US firms lag behind Asian companies.

● **Increasing competition and technology**. These two factors were ranked within the top five influences on business conditions in the 1990s. The market will increasingly penalize MNCs that fail to become more responsive to customer needs, or to bring products to market quickly or to generally strengthen their competitive position.

● **Regional trading blocs**. A majority of companies consider the European Community's single market initiative to be the most important regional trend affecting their competitive position. The ranking reflects the widespread perception among corporate executives that the economic importance of Europe will increase in both absolute and relative terms as a result of the consolidation of the EC member states' markets.

The order in which the effects of other regional trends on MNCs' businesses – the political and economic restructuring of the Soviet Union and Eastern Europe, the opening of Japan's domestic market and the unification of the US and Canadian markets – are ranked show a close correlation to the geographic proximity of the respondent's home region. Thus, the second most important trend for North American respondents is the unification of the US and Canadian markets; for Asian respondents, it is the liberalization of Japan's domestic market; and for European respondents, it is the transformation of Eastern Europe.

Corporate Strategies

Developing a "clear strategic focus" for responding to the fiercely competitive marketplace is the challenge for today's CEO. It is critical to balance the firm's need to maintain efficiency and low production costs, while remaining adaptable to specific markets and delivering a high quality, well-serviced product. This is essential, since the top strategic goal of MNCs today is achieving and maintaining customer satisfaction.

● **Expansion techniques**. When developing strategies for expansion, "strategic alliances," such as joint ventures and licensing agreements, were favored overall by companies over "acquisitions." Larger corporations, however, ranked acquisitions about equal to strategic alliances, reflecting both their ability to obtain cheaper capital and their desire for control. The lowest-ranked expansion strategy, is "de novo/start-ups." As Paul Van Orden, executive vice president of General Electric put it, "If you want to be in a developed-country market and don't already have a customer base there, the cost of getting in is often prohibitive."

● **Streamlining operations**. In evaluating overall operations, almost three fourths of the survey respondents chose "automate/apply advanced technology" as the best way to lower costs and increase the pace of product differentiation. Furthermore, many executives acknowledged that as competition gets keener, they must continually reexamine all aspects of their business in light of new technology and new applications of existing technology. Some noted that where real competitive gains appear feasible, they are ready to commit substantial staff and financial resources early to promote the development of a new technology or application.

● **Ensuring quality**.   By a wide margin, respondents selected a quality-driven culture as the most important approach to ensuring product and service quality. In its broadest application, a corporate culture driven by quality was defined by executives as a companywide effort, involving every employee from the top managers down to assembly-line workers, and every product operation and staff function.

● **Strategic planning**.   To be able to respond to rapid technological change, new and differentiated products and transformations in the marketplace, most respondents favored "decentralized planning conducted by business units."

The Role of the CEO

CEOs think that flexible decisionmaking based on shared strategic vision will be the determining characteristic of successful companies in the 1990s. This concept means delegating decisionmaking powers to line managers, eliminating management layers and instilling entrepreneurial drive within business units.

The CEO and top management have, therefore, become motivators, advisers and facilitators, rather than the order-giving moguls of the past. They and the headquarters staff work closely with operating units. Today's CEO is instrumental in setting a strategic direction, but does it as a member of a corporate team.

This transition is illustrated by one US *Fortune* 100 company that strives to shape its decisionmaking process via an inverted organizational chart. The customer is on top of the chart, followed by product-service managers interacting directly with customers. The CEO is at the bottom of the chart, helping the entire organization meet its ultimate goal of satisfying customer needs.

● **CEO priorities**.   Setting strategic direction is the CEO's number one priority. Without a clear-cut strategic focus, a company finds it increasingly difficult to respond effectively to the changing demands of the marketplace. The CEO's other top priorities—organizing/managing, encouraging innovation/new technology and building relations with customers and investors—all flow from the strategic direction.

● **Managing trade-offs**.   One of the most difficult aspects of the CEO's job is to establish a trade-off between short-term and long-term corporate objectives. Many CEOs report that only by keeping the strategic vision can they even begin to correctly prioritize options.

Objectives of Organization

Enhancing responsiveness to customers and instilling entrepreneurship/profit-orientation are the two most important goals influencing organization, regardless of geographic base, size or industry. The three other important factors are attaining quality objectives, encouraging innovation and new technology and promoting flexibility/ease of adapting to change.

Interestingly, central coordination of business decisions has a very limited influence on the shape of corporate organizations and is expected to decline further in coming years. This is consistent with CEO desires to develop a responsive entrepreneurial corporate organism.

● **Matrix management.** An increasing number of CEOs believe that a large, far-flung company must have a form of matrix organization. The key question is how the product dimension of the organization should be related to the geographic dimension, and vice versa.

● **Decentralization.** The majority of companies surveyed have introduced a strong element of decentralization into their decisionmaking process and organization. More than half of the respondents currently describe their companies as either highly or somewhat decentralized. This proportion is expected to increase to two thirds over the next three years.

At present, North American companies tend to be more decentralized than European or Asian firms, but in the next three years the phenomenon of decentralization is expected to be equal among geographic groups. That is, Asian and European companies are planning to adopt major decentralization initiatives in coming years. Most respondents believe that decentralization improves the functioning of the company even though it imposes a special management challenge in terms of ensuring uniform strategic vision and cooperation between different strategic business units.

21.   US Industry's Drive to Be Competitive for the 1990s

How US industry will compete with innovators in their respective fields, not only from Asia and Europe, but also from within the US is critical to the survival and growth of American industry. The strategies companies adopt and the factors they base their business on may very well determine the future industrial growth of the US. In an informal survey of industry leaders, BI found that while the companies queried uniformly agreed that exchange rate movements had little influence on how they planned for the future, almost all conceded that they were in the process of reexamining their operations to improve competitiveness and cost reduction needs.

Many US companies have met this problem head on. As James Conner, executive vice president of Motor & Equipment Manufacturers Association, commented, "You must be careful when you make broad statements such as, 'US firms still have a long way to go before they will be competitive.' Companies like TRW and Eaton are world-class competitors by any measure, and they have been for years." Nevertheless, US industry across the board will have to make the push to be number one. As one US export manager noted, "If we don't put ourselves on top, even our neighborhood delis may be run by foreign MNCs."

One thread common to the manufacturing companies is the strategy to push away from the assembly line and into manufacturing cells, mimicking the Japanese approach to manufacturing. Two companies interviewed by BI have taken an aggressive approach to managing foreign competition. Both have developed a unique approach to strengthening their company, albeit the common tactic is the drive to reduce costs and redesign manufacturing.

Federal Mogul's Strategy

About one third of Federal Mogul's business is international, with approximately 10% of that coming from exports. FM has 25-30 plant locations overseas. It also has a network of 20 regionalized worldwide warehouses to maintain strong ties with customers. The company manufactures a variety of bearings and its major competitors are the European SKF and FAG.

FM is confident that it is progressively directing its manufacturing and marketing to make it a formidable worldwide competitor, edging out Japan, Korea, Canada and Mexico. The company has increased its market share and has a booming business as suppliers to the auto, aircraft and truck industries.

• **Effect of the dollar.** FM has benefited from the dollar's drop, particularly where it competes with the Japanese. FM has attempted to capitalize on dollar-related price benefits by also stressing other factors such as availability, quality, packaging and cataloging. Its original equipment and replacement parts business is up 15-20%. While part of that is attributable to a new marketing push, many of FM's customers' sales were boosted by the dollar's decline. That, in turn, led to more sales for FM. This also bodes well for future sales, because replacement parts will eventually be needed to service the original equipment installations.

● **High tech or not?.**   FM is spending its R&D money not on expansion into high-tech products but in concentrating on two issues: materials research, i.e. the use of new materials such as plastics in making bearings, and the employment of manufacturing techniques to improve quality and decrease costs. FM is investing in new automation and systems like laser measuring devices to improve accuracy. It is also using statistical process controls.

The company has no intention of switching to high-tech products because their bearings are necessary in many manufactured products. Barry Murphy, head of FM's investor relations, recalls that during World War II, the Allies tried to bomb all of the bearing plants in Germany to prevent the production of tanks. Citing this history, FM believes that the US government will always support an indigenous bearings industry.

● **Dealing with foreign competition.**   The Japanese have been hit by import duties and they are planning to build plants in the US in order to compete. However, FM has developed a good customer relationship and has strategically positioned its factories to meet customer demand, particularly important since many of them are operating under JIT (just-in-time technology). To compete in the original equipment market, and particularly in the aftermarket, a company has to be located where its customers are. That is one of the reasons the Europeans have become a real competitive factor in the US.

● **Corporate survival.**   There is a strong revival now of the "rust bowl." Murphy believes that a lot of companies—not only FM, but also Dana, Eaton and others—are emerging in a stronger position after a few tough years. The companies that couldn't compete either merged or went out of business, and the survivors are now reaping the profits from these corporate departures.

FM is placing a major emphasis on improving competitiveness through manufacturing. It has built a plant in Pennsylvania (at a location where there is a strong work ethic) that incorporates new technology and involves "manufacturing cells," units responsible for complete products, rather than assembly-line production. On the management side, the company is using team leaders rather than foremen. Through labor-saving techniques, it expects this new plant to make it the lowest-cost manufacturer of ball bearings.

Plant With a Future: Caterpillar Inc

Caterpillar (CAT) has developed a long-range corporate strategy to minimize its vulnerability to cyclical downturns. The impetus behind the broad-based cost reduction program is twofold: (1) demand for its products is not expected to return to historic levels; and (2) in the future, CAT will be moving away from manufacturing component parts to purchasing more parts from lower-cost suppliers.

As part of a cost-reduction effort, Caterpillar has been developing a new manufacturing method called Plant with a Future (PWAF). As described by Pierre Guerindon, vice president in charge of manufacturing general offices, computer-integrated manufacturing technology and European plants, PWAF has evolved in two phases.

The first plateau was aimed at reducing overall costs by 22% from the 1981 base. This involved the following cost-cutting: new corporatewide cost accounting and reduction measures; corporate downsizing; plant closures to reduce excess capacity; outsourcing of component parts where the alternative suppliers were more cost effective.

The second plateau includes a goal of reducing costs permanently by at least another 15% over the first plateau, and then holding that gain. Says Guerindon, "The tactics we pursued in the 'first plateau' won't continue to yield enough gain to accomplish this additional reduction. But PWAF will get us there."

How PWAF Works

The strategic focus of PWAF is to modernize CAT's worldwide manufacturing base to become the lowest-cost supplier of high-quality products. The plan is to make plants "the least-cost source for core elements of production." Twenty percent of vital components will be produced in-house. The other 80% will be purchased from outside suppliers. Previously, 60% or more of parts and components were manufactured by CAT.

CAT plans to: consolidate plant facilities, selectively automate (replacing equipment only when it is most cost effective to do so) and simplify and integrate manufacturing. New concepts involve moving from assembly-line production to cell manufacturing. By the end of the decade, manufacturing space will be reduced 25%. Correspondingly, manufacturing capacity, the number of units that can be built, will be adjusted to meet worldwide demand.

22. What Is a Global Company?

Though seemingly similar—indeed, some would say interchangeable—the concepts of the multinational corporation (MNC) and the global corporation are not the same. A traditional MNC sells to several countries, adjusting product offerings, manufacturing practices and marketing strategies as needed, usually at considerable cost. A global corporation, on the other hand, strives to sell the same products or services everywhere and run its operations on one standard, at a relatively lower cost. It treats the entire world—or at least major portions of it—as a single market.

"Many companies that think of themselves as global are really multinational," says Martyn Roetter, a director of Arthur D. Little's North America Management Consulting Directorate. "Most of these firms began as local companies that became national, then expanded by selling in an overseas market and creating an international vice president." Although these companies were enterprising in realizing their international potential, they are not truly global in perspective, according to Roetter, because "they are essentially a collection of national businesses."

In truly global companies, very little decisionmaking occurs that does not support the goal of treating the world as a single market. Manufacturing, distribution and product development are normally planned and executed on a worldwide basis.

Sony Corp is one of the best-known global firms. Neil Vander Dussen, vice chairman of Sony of America, says: "We are entering an age of borderless competition. In the 1990s, we believe our company must possess four characteristics: We must be more global, more localized, more integrated and more decentralized. These four characteristics may seem contradictory; but they are, in fact, mutually supportive."

Key Differences

A global company, then, is defined by the following factors:

• More products sold outside the home country than in it;

- Localized, rather than centralized, decisionmaking;

- R&D implemented wherever necessary—often in foreign labs;

- Company stock usually listed on several foreign exchanges;

- Shareholders spread around the world;

- Nonnational executives on the fast track to top management;

- Significant number of nonnational directors on board;

- Trade barriers not a threat to business;

- Multiple identities and loyalties successfully managed, in part through a fluid chain of command; and

- Global image bolstered, rather than confined by, strong home-country identity (if the company has one).

For traditional MNCs, the defining attributes are the following:

- Home territory still the major market;

- Foreign subsidiaries operate as appendages of headquarters, which makes the major decisions;

- Research conducted and products designed at headquarters;

- Company stock listed on home-country stock exchange only;

- Shareholders mainly in home country;

- Overseas management staffed and directed primarily from headquarters, with few nonnationals on fast track;

- Very few or no nonnationals on the board;

- Decisionmaking strongly affected by national boundaries and trade barriers;

- Clear, unambiguous chain of command; and

• Narrow—and limiting—home-country identity.

23. Philips: 'Thinking Global, Acting Local'

Flexibility is paramount for the Dutch electronics giant Philips as it pioneers the transition from a European-based multinational to a global company. Executives stress that products, marketing and distribution must remain responsive to local markets within the company's new transnational framework.

In a development regarded as a corporate model for the 1990s, Philips is shifting management responsibility from its national organizations to product divisions that span national frontiers. At the same time, the company is focusing on its core activities of electronics and lighting, and divesting from nonrelated businesses.

The move toward a more streamlined company with global manufacturing and marketing strategies is a response to the changing competitive environment.

Shifting Responsibility to Product Divisions

Traditionally, Philips' "national organizations" have enjoyed a high degree of autonomy—a formula that worked well during an era of high tariff barriers. Now the company is reshaping itself on a global pattern through changes that include:

• **Transferring responsibility from the functional and geographic organizations** to the product divisions, with consumer electronics, electronic components, and information technology and communication as the three interlinked core divisions.

• **Reducing the autonomy of the national organizations** to ensure a clear worldwide manufacturing and marketing strategy for each product division.

• **Spinning off peripheral activities** into joint ventures, selling them outright or increasing their independence by selling shares to the public.

• **Rationalizing production on a global scale** with each product division formulating its own manufacturing strategy and some divisions centralizing production in "mother factories" to lower costs.

• **Streamlining management** by bringing the interlinked product division directors onto the board.

Balancing Global Strategies With Local Tactics

Top executives stress, however, that the new outlook does not mean Philips headquarters at Eindhoven will be imposing rigid global policies on the national organizations. President Cornelis van der Klugt emphasizes that the philosophy behind the changes is one of "controlled decentralization," a flexible structure aimed at maximizing the benefits of international strategies and local knowledge to achieve both scale economies and targeted marketing.

Dr. M.D. van Hamersveld, marketing support manager for Philips' consumer electronics division, comments: "We have to be highly effective in product creation. This means thinking internationally in a more centralized way and making the product divisions the entrepreneurial drive behind the company. We can't stay in business by inventing different products in every country. But that doesn't imply a few people in a building in Eindhoven know what is going on everywhere. They desperately need the input of the key markets. Our goal is to integrate the strengths of transnational product divisions with the local sensitivities of our national organizations."

An important step is placing competence centers in the crucial markets where the competition is most intense and technological innovations originate. The domestic appliances joint venture with Whirlpool, for example, is based in Italy and car electronics in Germany. Product ideas from these and other centers will be spread through the corporation.

Second, the company is bringing together multidisciplinary teams to work on product development, pooling the know-how of specialists in development, design, manufacturing and marketing to speed the process of bringing products to the market and ensure their all-round effectiveness from technical, commercial and marketing viewpoints.

Philips executives believe this goal of achieving an optimum balance between the technological and marketing requirements of products and launching them at the right time to meet market demand is a prime reason for harmonizing global strategies with local input. "The international product axis underlies corporate policy," says van Hamersveld, "but the contribution of national organizations is vital in pointing the direction for local marketing and distribution, in dealing with national regulations and handling relationships with governments."

Adjusting to Product Life Cycles

According to van Hamersveld, the interplay between transnational and local elements varies during differing stages of the product life cycle.

● **Early adoption phase—global approach**.   Philips' consumer product innovations are launched internationally in Europe, the US and Japan, targeting homogeneous consumer groups, drawing on the full weight of the corporation to add impact to the launch, and benefiting from the cost savings of centralized manufacturing and standardization. This stage lasts two or three years.

● **Maturity phase—local influence**.   As the product enters the main stage of its life cycle, the company draws more on its national resources, using local marketing muscle, relations with distributors and sensitivity to the area to give the product a local edge in national markets as competition intensifies. This take the form of adding local modifications to the global concept in terms of both product specification and marketing. This stage lasts 5-10 years, depending on the kind of product.

● **Decline phase—global economies**.   The final stage in the cycle, when profit margins drop, does not justify the resources required for adding a local touch to products , and Philips reverts to the cost savings derived from a global merchandizing approach. This phase usually lasts another four to five years on average.

Philips' "global television chassis" is an example of the company's approach to standardization. The basis of the set will use common technology and components as far as the world's differing broadcasting and electrical power systems allow. This makes for cheaper, more efficient and flexible production. At the same time, technical specifications, cabinet styling, colors and brand images can be altered to suit the requirements of specific markets.

"Our aim is to exploit the value and strengths of national organizations more than we have in the past," adds van Hamersveld.

Standardization in consumer electronics is of necessity more complex than for global products such as Parker pens or McDonald's hamburgers. Often, differentiation is not a matter of choice. On a technical level, plug fittings, power cycles and broadcasting systems vary from country to country. From the cultural point of view, differing requirements for items such as shavers, varying attitudes regarding cooking, etc. affect products from region to region.

On the other hand, the fact that many consumer electronics products are composed of hardware systems with software inputs makes them more easily adaptable to globalization. "Software in the form of records, tapes, compact disks, videos and computer programs is easily varied from region to region to suit local tastes," comments M.M. Polak, general affairs manager at Eindhoven.

Distribution: A Crucial Local Asset

Distribution channel policy is the area of Philips' global strategy most attuned to local requirements. "Looking at the traditional marketing elements of product, price, promotion and place, the latter probably has to be adapted most to local conditions," says van Hamersveld. This is because of the complex variation of sales channels from country to country, despite a trend for dealers to merge into larger enterprises.

The powerful distribution and dealer networks built up by Philips' national organizations all over the world are considered a crucial competitive asset that the company will continue to nurture from within its new global framework. Van Hamersveld comments: "Our Japanese competitors who began with selective distribution in many countries are now facing decisions on how to enlarge their distribution networks and change their agent structures. The volume of certain businesses means that you need good local structures, and that is one of Philips' strongest points. No other company has the type of power balance among dealers that we enjoy. The Japanese are still wondering how we did it. The answer is that we have been in some countries for many years and are thus very well integrated into the local distribution structures."

24. Co-Steel's Winning Growth Strategy in a Contracting Market

Engineering a rebound in a depressed marketplace is no easy feat. But for Co-Steel Inc, a Canada-based MNC, a good niche strategy and a lean approach to organization has turned the threat of a declining market into an opportunity for growth. Despite rising tariff barriers, strong foreign competition and a real decline in the price of its manufactured product, Co-Steel has nevertheless averaged 15-20% growth annually.

In the face of a protracted industry downturn, mini-mill producers have developed some natural advantages over the large steel producer, including lower cost processing and smaller, more flexible plant facilities. However, Co-Steel has taken those advantages several steps further. The key to its success was the implementation of a strategy embracing several crucial features:

• **Leading-edge technology.** According to CEO Ronald Fournier, investing in leading-edge technology has been "the life blood" of the firm since the 1960s. At that time, Co-Steel pioneered a steelmaking technique that eliminated eight stages in the production process, resulting in considerable reductions in plant, labor and raw material costs. From 1977 to 1987, the rate at which Co-Steel was able to melt scrap metal increased from 20 to 120 tons per hour. At the same time, unit consumption inputs were cut as much as 50%.

To maintain this edge, Co-Steel invests more than twice its annual depreciation expense into plant maintenance and is always on the lookout for ways to improve. Co-Steel has traded technology with major operators in North America, Europe and Japan through licensing agreements, and its efforts to sustain product quality and diversification have paid off. For example, in the US plant, which opened in 1980, production has expanded from a base of one product—rod for steel applications—to include 95 out of the 97 principal markets for that steel product.

• **International diversification.** Hedging against the risk of rising tariff barriers, Co-Steel built plants abroad to ensure access to its key foreign markets. In addition to its Canadian facility in Ontario, the firm has plants in New Jersey (to serve the US market) and in Sheerness, England (from which it serves the European market).

• **Just-in-time manufacturing.** Co-Steel's plants are located near major cities, giving it ready access to steady supply of raw materials—namely waste metal. This also reduces the transportation and distribution costs of the finished product. By locating plants close to the customer, Co-Steel can offer just-in-time deliveries, and that is something Fournier notes, "the importers cannot do."

• **Keeping overall costs low.** Co-Steel has kept a close watch on inexpensive subsidized steel coming in from LDCs. "We are concerned about competing with the Brazilians and the Koreans who have labor costs of US$3 per hour," says Fournier. Co-Steel's objective, he claims, is to keep our employment costs below the cost of oceangoing freight for these offshore producers. "If we do this, they can have zero cost of labor and we can still compete."

Clearly, this cannot be done on a straight salary differential basis. Co-Steel pares away at overhead by keeping a very lean organization. Subsidiaries have complete operating autonomy. Headquarters management consists of a staff of only three senior executives.

To maximize efficiency in this decentralized operation, management encourages open lines of communication from the shop floor to the CEO, and employees at all levels are encouraged to participate in the decisionmaking process. "Our objective is to push decisionmaking down to the lowest component level in the organization," Fournier says. Much time is spent providing on-the-job multiple-skill training. Additional employee incentives include a profit-sharing plan that pays out on average 12.5% of pretax profits.

25. Acquisition/Partnerships, Supplier Relations Help MCI Build a Global IT Company

Eight years after it tested the waters of international telecommunications, US-based MCI Communications charged into the new decade as a major global player. Using a combination of strategic alliances, strong supplier relations and innovative acquisitions, MCI has become a highly profitable provider of information technology (IT).

Acquisitions/Partnerships the Key

MCI started way behind AT&T in international service. In fact, MCI didn't offer international direct-dialing to most of the world until 1988. During the past few years, though, the company has made dramatic inroads into international service. It now services 72 countries directly and provides access to 101 others. It owns a piece of the latest, privately laid fiber-optic cable under the Atlantic, part of another serving Hawaii, as well as regional systems between Australia and New Zealand and a Caribbean fiber cable that links Florida to Colombia.

One of the reasons for the company's rapid expansion is skillful use of both acquisitions and alliances.

• **Springing off the telex market.** In 1988, MCI bought RCA Global Communications from General Electric for $160 million. That made MCI the world telex leader. While the takeover provided network redundancy, the acquisition gave MCI new corporate customers for its advanced services like fax transmission, electronic mail, private networks and packet switching.

Going Global

In 1990, MCI bought a 25% stake in Infonet Services, a worldwide data network and computer services consortium whose other shareholders are the national phone administrations of such nations as Germany, Japan, Australia and Singapore. That $27.5 million investment makes MCI the largest of Infonet's shareholders.

MCI has also entered into network partnerships with two major carriers, British Telecom and Japan's Kokusai Denshin Denwa (KDD). Through these alliances, MCI is able to offer a full menu of worldwide communications and computer services.

Expanding in the US

MCI is also using acquisitions to become a bigger player in the US. The company recently bought urban rights-of-way from Western Union. That network will be integrated with the rest of the MCI backbone to increase offerings to large businesses and government agencies. Ultimately, this acquisition means MCI may be able to effectively provide all-purpose service to US customers that now obtain local service from one provider and long-distance and other services from another.

Becoming Price/Cost Competitive

Other factors lie behind MCI's rapid expansion as well.

● **Upgrading technology.** The most important decision was the move to enhance and expand its technological infrastructure. During the last five years, MCI has spent over $7 billion, including $1.2 billion this year.

● **Slashing prices.** A crucial factor for this investment was MCI's need to enhance price competitiveness. Every MNC has this as a goal, but for companies in IT, it is even more important — particularly for those operating in the US, which is MCI's major market. (MCI controls about 15% of the market. This should rise to 17% when it completes its $1.25-billion takeover of rival Telecom.) In the US, long-distance carriers must constantly decrease rates as the result of the 1984 divestiture of AT&T. Last year, MCI cut prices about 6% for US services.

● **Building on supplier relations**.   Another way MCI stays competitive is through its global sourcing policy. Unlike AT&T, MCI does not make any of its equipment. Instead, it buys its large digital switches from Northern Telecom (Canada), its smaller switches from DSC Communications (US) and its large international switches from L.M. Ericsson (Sweden). Fiberoptic cable and electronics come from Fujitsu (Japan) and the satellite relay equipment from divisions of Rockwell (US).

Most of the mainframe computer equipment running MCI's network comes from IBM. The IBM alliance has vastly upgraded the quality of MCI's service; it has also brought in flocks of new corporate and government customers, IBM included.

One by-product of its emphasis on developing good supplier relations is that MCI is able to cost-effectively stay in the forefront of technological developments. For example, Fujitsu developed a new single-mode optical fiber, which it offered to MCI for installation. With its suppliers providing MCI with products they developed through their own internal research, MCI avoids the massive R&D costs of its competitors, which last year alone were over $2.8 billion.

26.   Weaving a Safety Net for Strategic Alliances

The advantages of cooperative ventures – the ability to leverage scarce corporate resources, share the high costs and risks of product development, preempt competitive threats on the home front and enter overseas markets rapidly – can evaporate if management does not maintain a balance between cooperating with competitors and protecting the firms's contribution to the venture, be it technology, capital or marketing expertise. Below is a review of practical protective steps taken by successful alliance-makers, along with legal pointers offered by Joel Marcus, managing partner at Los Angeles-based Pettit & Martin.

Many executives characterize strategic alliances as marriages, implying a close relationship that nevertheless has the potential for conflict. The following checklist is structured around that metaphor.

The Courtship

● **Conduct preliminary risk assessments**.   Before signing a letter of intent, experienced firms conduct a thorough analysis of the risks of co-

A Prenegotiation Checklist

- Is the partner a direct competitor, and in what markets?

- How critical is the venture to the partner's long-term business strategy, i.e. how much does it need the venture to meet strategic and tactical objectives?

- What are your bargaining chips to inhibit a partner from extracting valuable contributions from the venture?

- What is the partner's track record on cooperation?

- What measures have you taken to protect your contribution — whether it is technology, capital or a marketing expertise?

- How much protection is provided for the technology under patents?

- What other mechanisms are in place besides broad-scope patents, which are not an effective deterrent under many countries' intellectual-property laws?

- Have you considered filing a patent but then regularly supplementing the application with additional information so that it never actually gets published and reaches the public domain?

- What measures are available to protect know-how, which is perhaps the most valuable yet most difficult contribution to safeguard?

operation. Executives frequently rely on a prenegotiation questionnaire to identify trouble spots, assess whether the benefits of cooperation outweigh costs and map out strategies to minimize risks (see box above).

- **Detect early-warning signals.** Marcus points out that certain actions during the early stages of negotiation can serve as "red flag indicators" of high-risk relationships. He advises clients to seriously reconsider the cooperative approach if a potential partner employs some of the following tactics: (1) up-front demands for proprietary data, (2) a guarded posture, (3) eagerness to outline spending plans and commitments without adequate due diligence, (4) little evidence of "good faith" or (5) undue pressure to close the deal quickly.

Another useful way to expose high-risk deals is to hold forthright discussions at the outset about each partner's strategic objectives, plus why and how the venture will help each company achieve its long-term goals. Marcus says these discussions usually help uncover hidden agendas and enable the company to sever negotiations promptly before losing valuable technology and corporate assets to an ill-conceived alliance.

The Marriage Contract

• **Have a tightly focused objective.** A well-defined agreement that zeroes in on the areas and methods for cooperation can add a strong dose of protection because it minimizes the chance that trade secrets and technology will migrate to an ally-competitor. The contract should also include periodic checks and reviews to ensure that the venture is meeting its stated objectives on schedule.

• **Create a separate stand-alone entity.** Marcus says that the use of a separate company for cooperative ventures—particularly joint-technology development endeavors—can minimize a host of protection problems. First, this ensures that the aggregate technology and know-how contributions of each partner are legally and jointly owned by all participants. If properly structured, any future spinoffs or second-generation products from the cooperative endeavor will also be jointly owned and controlled.

Suppose Company A and Company B are competitors in a broad range of products, but enter a joint-technology development agreement to improve the manufacturing process for product Z. Both partners contribute technology and know-how, but the research is conducted in Company A's R&D center. Company A identifies innovative ways to use Company B's technology for new applications and enhancements for many of its other products. However, unaware of this valuable discovery, not only does Company B fail to receive the appropriate licensing and financial rewards, but it inadvertently helps Company A become an even more formidable competitor. Says Marcus, "This risk can be alleviated by having all rights to the technology and its applications owned jointly through a separate company with proper back licensing."

• **Establish benchmarks.** Although most of the discussion on protection centers on technology or marketing expertise, partners contributing capital must also hedge against the risks. Defining milestones for the alliance is an effective strategy for safeguarding financial partners. For instance, Marcus represented Japan's Kirin Brewery in a joint venture with US-based Amgen. Amgen's contribution centered on its technology plus $4 million in cash, while Kirin provided $12 million of the $24 million aggregate value. Kirin minimized the risks to its investment by providing the capital in increments, each of which was contingent on Amgen's achieving certain technological milestones by certain dates. The strategy also satisfied Amgen's protection needs. Under such a tight schedule, Amgen would not have time to furnish all the technological details and valuable know-how behind its research to Kirin, thereby preserving Amgen's technological edge.

Staying Married—For Better, Not Worse

● **Foster mutual dependence.** For ventures involving technology, many companies ensure that know-how and technology exchanges travel on a two-way street. Other MNCs point out that the greater the number of links between partners, and the greater the reciprocal needs for each other's markets, capital and technology, the less likely one partner is to stab the other in the back.

Many alliance builders also maintain mutual dependence by ensuring that they always reserve to themselves a critical piece of know-how or value-added. Marcus cites the example of an alliance between two US MNCs (Company C and Company D). Company C was responsible for developing and manufacturing the product that Company D would distribute and sell in the US. The latter, however, requested a second source of supply in case its partner encountered any business or financial difficulties. In response, Company C—which was obviously interested in preserving its technological lead—provided a second US company with partial know-how. This way, the second supplier—which was subsequently acquired by Company D—still needed to rely on Company C for some essential bits of technology.

● **Establish an alliance coordination unit.** Having a central liaison group to monitor and control who works with the partner and what information is shared can add an extra measure of safety. Many executives warn that trade secrets and know-how can slip into the hands of a partner-competitor through casual conversations and contacts.

27. Farmer or Hunter: Why Firms Acquire Companies

With corporate acquisitions all the rage, and companies worried over who will be the next target, BI has discovered that the process of acquiring companies can be classified roughly into six categories. If companies that are the focus of takeover attempts can determine into which category their purchaser falls, trepidations over management control, employment and career pathing may either be alleviated or, in the worst case, reinforced.

Target companies are endlessly concerned over what the future of the company will be after acquisition and, more to the point, what their future will be with the firm. Acquisitions often result in many changes, not all of them pleasant to the target company. Through interviews with MNCs, BI has found that acquirers that are most experienced (by virtue of having done many acquisitions in the past) are those most likely to effect a smooth and successful transition. To them, post-acquisition management is a normal, everyday affair. Acquirers with less experience in acquisitions are often the most conscience ridden and concerned about errors of commission and omission.

Acquisitions over the past few years have not been uniform either in concept or implementation. There have, however, been enough similarities for BI to define the following six different acquirer groupings based on both the motives and frequency of acquisition.

● **Carnivores**. These are the companies that consider acquisition as part of their daily business activity. Carnivores are unfazed by organizational and restructuring problems and their human implications. Their management policies are well established to deal with all possible problems and their managers are equipped to handle integrating the acquisition into the parent, often severing part or all of the takeover company's existing management.

Carnivorous takeover companies include Unilever (Anglo/Dutch), which has taken over about 50 companies in the last five years while divesting itself of a similar number; Esselte (Swedish), which uses acquisitions to grow the parent, purchasing about 10 firms a year and integrating them into its system; and Electrolux (Swedish), which expects takeovers to bring strong bottom-line performance and is willing to mold the target in order to bring in results.

● **Dairy farmers**. These acquirers increase the shareholder value of their company by multiplying and increasing the value of the herd and then "milking" it. As with any well-run farm, they do whatever is necessary to nurture the herd. From time to time, they sell off nonproducing animals and replace them with healthier beasts. Usually, dairy farmers do not interfere with the operation of the herd, except for insisting on financial performance.

Hanson Trust is an excellent example, having built a $2.5 billion company from practically nothing. This company is a cattle dealer and feels that hands-on management would distract them from their basic activity of buying and selling. For this reason, senior management is usually kept in place. In both their recent acquisition of Kidde and a previous acquisition of SCM, Hanson Trust's chief executives remained on board.

● **Vegetarians**. One of the least threatening acquirers, these companies often have unclear objectives. Acquisitions tend to be opportunistic, although they may be used to reposition the parent. Vegetarians used to be commonplace on the M&A list, but a general refocusing on core business rather than diversification has made them much less common. Several executives in this group said that they keep their acquisitions as "corporate pets." As long as everything goes well, the pet is left to its own devices. When failures arise, though, truth squads are often sent in to solve the problem.

● **White hunters**. These are the corporate raiders. The new twist to this group is that they often go after game much larger than themselves, to whit, the takeover of JWT by an unknown UK supermarket-trolley maker headed by Martin Sorrell. Although their acquisitions often appear to lack industrial or commercial logic, hunters believe that they are performing a needed function in forcing lazy managements to make better use of undervalued or underused assets. The white hunters have no set policy for post-acquisition management of their purchases, often leaving the target in limbo awaiting eventual dismemberment or disposal.

● **Gentlemen shooters**. These companies are the most common among European acquirers, tending to make one acquisition at a time and then only rarely. Their purchases are usually strategically motivated and their targets are integrated in the company. Companies that are sought for acquisition are usually courted for some time and are rarely the focus of a hostile takeover.

Because gentlemen shooters are so infrequently involved in takeovers, problems may arise afterward. Often it takes a year or two of relatively depressed performance before things are operating smoothly. Among the gentlemen shooters were Burroughs, with its bid for Sperry Corp. L.M. Ericsson, which purchased Data-Saab, and General Motors, which purchased EDS. Each of these had important strategic implications for the bidder, and while Sperry complained at the onset, structuring of the company under a new corporate identity (Unisys) helped smooth the way.

• **Cross-breeders**.   A new set of hybrids is beginning to emerge in Europe. It involves the mating of companies from different nationalities that have united to form a new European multinational, many times destroying their national identity in the process. While trans-European alliances were often attempted in the past, national rivalry often sank the union. This time Europeans appear to have focused on the need for unity in creating a power that can successfully compete on a global scale. While it is too soon to tell the tale, the groundwork is certainly in place.

Leading examples of this new breed are crosses between Asea of Sweden and Brown Boveri of Switzerland in heavy electrical equipment; between the state-owned SGS (Italy) and Thomson (France) in semiconductors; and between CGE (France) and ITT (US) in telecommunications.

28. Acquisition Strategies:
Six Frequent Traps and How
to Avoid Them

Acquisitions are a double-edged sword. While they can provide fast, cost-effective growth, studies show that over 50% fail to meet the buyer's original objectives — and some have proved disastrous for the acquirer. Senior executive interviewed by BI stress that acquisition failures can usually be traced to conspicuous, fundamental mistakes made by the acquiring firm in conceiving or executing its strategy. The acquisition traps mentioned most frequently by seasoned managers are summarized.

Trap #1: Overestimated Revenues

Scores of executives concur that the single most dangerous error made by acquisition-minded firms is placing too much credence in sales/ earnings projections. Overestimated future revenues can convince the acquirer that the target is worth a premium price and can sometimes lure management into heavy debt to finance the deal. If the growth rate falls below expectation, operating profits may barely cover interest charges. Typically, the parent then cuts costs and reduces capital investment and R&D, potentially eroding its competitiveness.

A glaring example is Fluor's 1981 takeover of St. Joe Minerals Corp. Based on projections that St. Joe's earnings would surge from $120 million in 1980 to more than $300 million by 1985, the US construction firm took a flying leap into debt to buy its target for $2.2 billion. The commodity gluts of the 1980s wrecked even these estimates: By 1986, St. Joe was barely at break even, while its parent struggled under a mountain of debt. By early 1986, Fluor's market value had tumbled to $1.3 billion—nearly $1 billion less than it had paid for its acquisition. While the Fluor case is extreme, a number of executives admit their own firms have fallen for unproductive acquisitions based on over optimistic growth projections.

• **Avoiding the trap**. Managers say the best way to sidestep this potential pitfall is simple, but hard to do: Never take extrapolated growth figures too seriously. In fact, it is a good idea to take the figures and then discount them by 20% or 30%, or in some cases even 50%. Does the target still look like a good deal?

Trap #2: Underestimated Needs

A second trap is underestimating the target's future cash requirements. While acquirers expect that a troubled firm will need heavy post-acquisition investment, the cash-trap firm shows deceptively healthy growth and profits. Only after the acquisition does the buyer suddenly find it has to invest more and more to keep its prize viable. Europe abounds with such firms, often family-owned companies that have achieved a respectable size but have drifted into a poor strategic position.

• **Avoiding the trap**. How can you tell if a company will turn out to be a cash trap? If an acquisition target exhibits any of the following characteristics, look again: low market share in a low-growth industry segment; declining profit margins; a disproportionate share of revenues generated by old products; R&D spending below industry norms; or a pattern of losing major accounts. While there may be a strategic reason for acquiring such companies, buyers should have no illusions that future growth can be funded through the acquisition's own cash flows. Instead, acquirers should map out a financial strategy that recognizes the need for major cash injections and allows for quite a long payback period.

Trap #3: Too-Loose Controls

Failure to counterbalance decentralized decisionmaking with watertight financial reporting can lead to insurmountable problems. Companies with successful acquisition track records—among them Electrolux,

Hanson Trust, BTR—combine both elements. But many acquirers, European firms in particular, hesitate to impose strict reporting rules on new units, particularly when the unit has good management and a successful track record.

This was the case of one midsized European conglomerate that went on an acquisition binge during the 1970s: It allowed managers wide latitude to make both operating and strategic decisions and failed to install tight financial controls. After several years of growth, the group suffered heavy losses in the early 1980s. In 1984, a new management team discovered that the conglomerate's engineering activities had been losing money and piling up liabilities for several years. Lax accounting procedures camouflaged the fact that it had unforeseen exposure totaling $20 million. Already heavily in debt, the firm's profitable activities could not come close to covering liabilities of this magnitude. Despite a stringent program of asset disposal, cost reduction and increased short-term borrowing, the company was saved from bankruptcy only when its bankers agreed to take the responsibility of a major liability in return for a sizable parcel of preferred shares.

● **Avoiding the trap.**   Says a consultant from McKinsey & Co., "A lot of companies tolerate sloppy reporting in the name of decentralization. When a downwave arrives—as it always does—these companies are the first to hit bottom." Clear requirements for frequent reporting of key financial, production and competitive data are a must. In the beginning, it is better to ask for too much information than to ask for too little.

Trap #4: Overconfident Diversification

Many acquisitions are made for the sake of diversification into new but related products/markets. In the case of these "concentric acquisitions," the danger for international managers is that they will buy a business that has only superficial links with the acquirer's core activities. In such cases, the acquiring firm erroneously feels it knows enough about the business to manage it successfully. Says an acquisitions analyst with a leading management consulting firm: "The problem is that very often your knowledge isn't deep enough. It's enough to get you into trouble, but not enough to get you out of it."

A medium-size MNC providing pest-control services fell into this trap when it acquired an industrial cleaning firm. As both firms sold contract services to institutional customers, the buyer felt they were compatible. But the businesses had crucial dissimilarities: Cleaning services are characterized by many players and intense price cutting; there are fewer pest-control firms, and margins are much higher. The buyer immediately increased the cleaning services' prices—losing customers. Moreover, the acquisition's rapid personnel turnover became a drain on management time. After years of losses, the acquirer divested.

● **Avoiding the trap**.   The key to a sound move on this score is to check the terrain, i.e. make sure that the competitive circumstances in the targeted sector are favorable—and investigate the depth of supposed similarities. Not only should the buyer be able to help the acquired firm in areas such as marketing, product development and manufacturing, etc., but it must also ascertain whether the injection of such strengths into the target will give it a fundamental competitive advantage.

Trap #5: Underestimated Competition

Another danger is that the potential synergies of an acquisition may tempt the acquirer into trying too much too soon and underestimating the competition. L.M. Ericsson's diversification into the highly competitive office information systems market has plunged the firm into a sea of red ink. In principle, the purchase of two small Scandinavian suppliers, Facit and Data-Saab, made a natural fit with the Swedish firm's core business—state of the art telephone networks.

Instead of competing in just a few segments, Ericsson aimed at offering fully integrated offices systems all across Europe and the US, coming to bat against the likes of IBM, Xerox and Olivetti. The costs and problems of this grand strategy have been a drain on the company's resources. In 1986, the company posted a Skr805 million loss; in 1986 and 1987, Ericsson's US operations were scaled down, production was cut back and some 5,000 employees were let go.

Says the planner at a rival firm, "Data-Saab and Facit were just a couple of small competitors, and both had serious problems to begin with. Even when combined, they couldn't generate the revenues needed to cover product development across a broad line…and Ericsson's own telecommunications profits were not nearly sufficient to fund R&D in both areas."

● **Avoiding the trap**.   Says one French electronics industry executive, "If you're diversifying into an area where the competition is very powerful, then you're asking for trouble. We've made that mistake time after time." Similarly, companies should be very wary of using acquisitions to diversify into fields where rising development and marketing costs will create funding problems for the parent. Other options, such as entering into a competitive alliance, with an established player, may well give the firm a greater chance of success at a more affordable price.

Trap #6: Failure to Divest

Some growth-oriented companies find themselves acquiring more and more businesses while hanging on to others that are poor performers or that no longer mesh with the firm's future plans. This failure to balance acquisitions with divestitures can be dangerous to the parent for two reasons: (1) making sick businesses well and acquiring new ones are both full-time occupations, and few companies have the resources to tackle both tasks simultaneously; and (2) clinging to some units — even healthy ones — that no longer fit a firm's strategy ties up capital that could be used better elsewhere.

A firm believer in divesting nonstrategic units is the Anglo-Dutch giant Unilever. In recent years, it has acquired a number of firms to sharpen its focus on food and personal care and household products. At the same time, the firm has disposed of an equal number of businesses in areas such as building products and transportation.

A company that found itself overwhelmed by its inventory of businesses was the Beecham Group. Through the 1970s and early 1980s, Beecham was a UK industrial success story, using acquisitions both to expand its core prescription drug business and to diversify into sectors such as cosmetics, food and beverages, adhesives, do-it-yourself, etc. The firm had a knack for ferreting out good takeover targets, but it never sold anything off. By the mid-1980s, with sales growing at 15% per year, growth lagged at only 7% annually, and earnings per share had stagnated. The implications for a publicly traded company were clear: Beecham had to improve performance — or risk attracting bids from raiders bent on wringing better figures from the company. In June 1986, Beecham suddenly announced plans to dispose of virtually all noncore activities and to dedicate itself again to health- or personal-care products. While top management claims Beecham only undertook a long-overdue tidying up, some insiders believe that the company's concentration on miscellaneous activities has eroded its long-term competitiveness vis-a-vis such rivals as Glaxo, Upjohn and Schering-Plough.

● **Avoiding the trap.** Divestment decisions are rarely easy, especially if the superfluous unit is a big-volume producer. Nevertheless, most managers stress that if an acquisition-oriented company cannot discipline itself to initiate systematic disposal of nonessential assets, the cumulative financial and managerial stress of piling new businesses on old ones may dangerously weaken it.

29. Advance Work on Logistics Smooths Launch of Alliance

As MNCs increasingly join forces to compete in today's tough global environment, one of the biggest challenges facing management is designing and negotiating a workable competitive alliance (CA). Executives interviewed for a BI study advise firms to iron out as many operational and management kinks to collaboration as possible before the parties meet at the negotiating table. For example, the successful launching of the 50:50 joint venture between EniChem SPA of Italy and UK-based Imperial Chemical Industries PLC (ICI) was achieved through intense work by executives of the two chemical giants to resolve delicate issues in the prenegotiation phase.

Careful preplanning offers potential alliance partners several advantages. The process provides an opportunity to fine-tune negotiating strategies, to clarify each company's needs and wants and to test the chemistry of the proposed alliance, in terms of corporate structures and personalities. Since the exercise should reveal whether cooperation is feasible, it can help firms avoid forging ahead with an ill-conceived venture. As the EniChem-ICI case shows, having executives from each partner join together in removing obstacles to cooperation can also ease the task of combining corporate staffs, management styles and cultures.

The ICI and Enichem Match

Deteriorating competitive conditions in the maturing polyvinyl chloride (PVC) market prompted ICI and Italy's state-owned EniChem SPA to form the European Vinyls Corp (EVC), a 50:50 JV, established in 1986. As a front-runner to the negotiations, each partner organized teams — which included marketing, finance, legal, research, manufacturing and technical experts — to analyze the logistics of creating the competitive alliance. Beginning in mid-1985, the groups worked together for about a year to sort through a number of complex issues.

According to Harry Richter, president of ICI Italia, "The work of these teams enabled us to iron out problems at the onset. It laid the groundwork for smooth, timely negotiations." The partners were able to reach final agreement relatively quickly and launch the JV in October 1986 because the teams resolved the following key issues in the pre-negotiation phase:

• **Asset transfers to the venture.**   In structuring EVC, the two teams decided against merging their manufacturing assets or transferring ownership of these facilities to the venture for several reasons: First, the live and depreciation schedules of the different facilities and equipment made it difficult to accurately assess their value and devise a systematic accounting system. Second, the production of PVC at both firms was tightly integrated with other manufacturing operations. It would have been neither profitable nor operationally feasible for the companies to withdraw and then combine their PVC production.

Third, given the depressed conditions in the petrochemicals market, there was no guarantee that the venture would actually reverse the dismal profit outlook for the two companies. If the project failed, the partners believed that it would be easier to disband a JV that had not merged manufacturing assets. Consequently, the manufacturing assets and all related personnel remained with the parent companies.

• **Additional rationalization measures to eliminate surplus capacity from the older, more costly plants.**   Both MNCs agreed to reduce capacity. However, the issue had to be treated very delicately, given the political and employment ramifications. On paper, the partners' rationalization plan seemed imbalanced because ICI had already undertaken significant steps to revamp its operations. ICI thus had to convince EniChem to follow a similar strategy. In order to persuade EniChem management that the rationalization plan was equitable, ICI prepared a very detailed presentation on its previous effort. Besides discussing the results in terms of reductions in production capacity, ICI staffers also reviewed the effects on their company and on the market, and offered forecasts on how additional consolidation moves would affect the industry and the JV.

• **Combining corporate and management structures.**   According to Richter, by having the two teams work together, "We were able to make significant progress on the problem of meshing two very different corporate cultures—a publicly owned Anglo-Saxon MNC with an Italian state-owned company." The two sides agreed that the JV would adopt a management style similar to ICI's, a structure that embodied the concept of teamwork. However, EniChem, an outgrowth of the reorganization of the Italian petrochemicals industry, had been created only in

1983. The Italian firm had not had the time to foster team management and was not used to the older company's approach. The joint feasibility study gave both sides an excellent training ground for working together and for smoothing implementation of the team concept in the JV.

- **Setting up the headquarters on a neutral site.** ICI and EniChem elected to site the JV in a third country because they "wanted a location that was in neutral territory to reduce the risk that one partner would try to dominate the venture." But the logistics had an interesting twist: EVC's legal headquarters is in the Netherlands, allowing it to benefit from the Dutch tax treaty network; however, the venture's management is actually located in Brussels.

According to EniChem Vice President Tomasso Giardino, the Brussels base is strategically positioned so that the companies can centralize operations and achieve greater efficiency in marketing and overall coordination. Brussels's key responsibilities include strategic planning, marketing and manufacturing outposts. EVC maintains local operating companies for manufacturing and marketing in Germany, Italy, Switzerland and the UK. In other major markets, such as the Benelux countries and France, the JV has only sales and marketing organizations.

The raw materials for PVC production is purchased by EVC, and the Brussels management group undertakes distribution and allocation of these among the manufacturing sites in Italy, Switzerland and the UK. Combining all raw material purchases enables EVC to secure more favorable prices and conditions from suppliers.

The Brussels center has also developed a central processing and accounting system for all orders: Customer requests and invoices are transmitted from local operations to the hub for processing; Brussels designates an appropriate manufacturing plant to handle the order; the latter then ships products directly to the customer.

30. The International Side of Mergers and Acquisitions

In the heat of US merger-acquisition mania, many players seem to be ignoring the implications for international operations—and it may come back to haunt them. Most investment bankers and executives interviewed by BI are downplaying international issues, citing the need to first integrate domestic operations. Yet a few are warning that too little

attention is being paid to the effect of mergers on foreign operations—
and this will negatively affect the bottom line.

Experts say that the magnitude of the work load involved in consum-
mating the deal domestically—targeting the price, arranging the financing, analyzing the tax effects, coping with antitrust considerations and
blending domestic operations—means integration of international activities can be treated only as an afterthought. Attempts to integrate too
much too soon may damage the deal.

Still, whether management takes action at the initial phase of an acquisition or in the post-merger phase, attention to the international
ramifications is critical. According to BI's 1984 Profitability Survey,
many firms involved in the merger blitz—General Electric and RCA,
Philip Morris and General Foods, R.J. Reynolds and Nabisco, Baxter
Travenol and American Hospital Supply, Monsanto and G.D. Searle—
generate sizable earnings from foreign operations. For some of them,
foreign sales count for 25-37% of the total, foreign assets take up to
46% of the whole. These numbers cannot be taken lightly.

Below, a few key questions to consider when integrating international
operations.

**What organizational structure: yours, mine—or a whole new
design?**   In any merger, management must combine not only different
corporate cultures, but also different organizational structures. Where
two MNCs are involved, the process takes on added complexity. The
key question is how responsibility for international operations is allocated among some or all of these elements: corporate headquarters, line
or staff international divisions, worldwide product groups, regional
structures (of the parent or a division) and country units.

For example, when one firm has placed international operations in
worldwide product groups without a corporate international coordinating group and the other has a line international division, major steps
probably must be taken to achieve a coherent approach. An imbalance
can result when each has multiple businesses in a key country, and one
unifies under a single-company umbrella while the other has units reporting to product divisions at HQ.

When the partners have similar structures (General Electric and RCA
are both generally organized along worldwide product group lines),
overall integration may be relatively simple. When two MNCs with different structures marry, management may well have to design a new organization pattern compatible to both.

Human resources: How do you reassure overseas managers?   All
mergers and acquisitions take their toll on the employees involved. At
the first hint, visions of redundancies and power struggles begin to

dance in managers' minds. Those in the acquired firm assume they will be the losers. The problem is multiplied when the firms are multinational. Given a concentration on US matters, managers in the field are likely to feel even more vulnerable than US counterparts. While top management is trying to figure out its international strategies and organizational changes, it can expect loss of productivity, key people and market share to more stable competitors.

Both domestically and internationally, the acquiring company must help employees and management adapt to operating as one combined unit. The best way to achieve this difficult feat is to put a single senior manager in charge of the process. Some of the particularly international aspects of the process include:

• Allocating responsibility for reorganizing overseas operations. Should US headquarters design the organization chart and have local management implement the strategy? Or should HQ give the responsibility to overseas management in order to bring local employees into the merger process?

• Resolving conflicts when one firm uses US nationals to run overseas subs and the other relies on local personnel.

• Sorting out potential conflicts between two sets of regional headquarters; evaluating country managers and sorting out their responsibilities — particularly if the new firm winds up with two in the same market.

Distribution networks: How do you combine them? A massive, loyal distribution system is a major weapon against the competition. Outside distributors will experience the same insecurities as international managers. The trick is to combine the strengths of two networks, avoid duplication and ensure distributor loyalty before your competitors pick them off.

Regulatory complications: Where do other governments come in? Some governments may be hostile to a newly created US giant and the competitive threat it poses to national corporate champions. A few governments can invoke antitrust legislation, which allows them to review the proposed US merger to analyze the domestic effects of the acquisition. Canadian regulations forced the sale of some Gulf operations during the Gulf-Chevron merger. A fair number of governments will make it extremely difficult and expensive to carry out any consolidations.

31. Making Synergy a Post-Merger Reality

The allure of synergies frequently brings corporate suitors together — with ambitious expectations of how they will strengthen the bottom line. All too often, however, post-merger management fails to exploit synergies to their fullest potential. In incorporating Glidden into ICI Paints, management developed an innovative approach that has allowed them to realize both profit and strategic objectives. The highlights of ICI's plan yield valuable pointers for other firms:

• **Understand what you want up front.** According to Richard Stillwell, vice president of acquisition and planning, the paints group established very specific qualitative and quantitative synergy targets while the acquisition was negotiated. ICI was clear that one of its primary objectives was to merge the companies so as to maximize R&D potential and develop a technological edge. (This is a critical part of managing synergy successfully — too often, efforts to cut costs through rationalization result in delay or neglect of the equally important process of building technological strengths.)

• **Tie synergy to the bottom line.** While many firms are clear on their qualitative goals in managing synergies, the actual financial impact is easily ignored or misunderstood. ICI put a firm price tag on synergy when it negotiated the Glidden acquisition (management declines to reveal the exact amount, but it was in the 3-15% range of the $580 million purchase price). That was just a first step; ICI is now keeping score in dollars, to ensure that the expected value of synergy is being realized.

• **Keep your approach simple and direct.** Stillwell says he has tried to avoid "endless committees bogging the whole thing down in bureaucracy." He describes himself as "a one man committee," whose charge it is to monitor and facilitate the merging of synergies. His approach consists of "a combination of high profile and informality to help the process flow most effectively." On a daily basis, Stillwell interacts with the functional and product managers, often acting as an intermediary to bring different parts of the organization together. On one occasion, for example, Stillwell served as a facilitator for an agreement whereby Glidden will now source raw materials from ICI at considerable savings over sourcing from outside suppliers.

In addition, Stillwell pays close attention to the integration of Glidden into the strategic planning process at ICI. He is secretary of both the IBT and the advisory council and will be meeting with the council to present a progress report on synergy. Participation in discussions at the most senior level of the organization allows Stillwell to keep managers abreast of merger developments at the top of the organization as well as at the operational level.

- **Link synergism to manager's performance.** According to Stillwell, part of his role is to ensure that individual managers regard synergy as part of their key performance objectives. "Half the battle is discipline — making sure that people continuously think about the benefits and maintain those benefits high on their daily agendas. If they know they are being monitored personally, they are more likely to make things happen."

- **Continue to explore synergy potential.** While preacquisition targets can provide important guidelines for identifying synergies, they are seldom completely accurate. As the companies get to know each other, the process of understanding and matching capabilities is ongoing. While some synergies may not work as well in practice as they did in theory, unexpected complements can yield considerable cash benefits. Currently, there are close to 80 synergy projects under way in such areas as R&D, purchasing and manufacturing operations — adding up to several million dollars in reduced costs that will hit the bottom line in the first year of the merger.

32. Partnerships for Growth

While most start-ups rely on venture capital, SDA Systems, a young California-based firm, utilized sponsorship from four global semiconductor and telecommunications majors to smooth its start-up and early product development in integrated circuit computer-aided design (IC CAD). Reevaluation of this experience and refinement of the concept led to the "technology partnerships" subsequently launched with Japan's Toshiba Corp and Italy's Innovative Silicon Technology (IST).

SDA's start-up strategy aimed to fill two voids in the CAD market that existed when the firm was founded in 1983. First was the lack of a satisfactory basic framework for IC design. Most IC makers have either developed CAD operating systems in house or pieced them together from systems offered by various CAD vendors. Second was the arm's-length relationships between commercial systems that lag behind the rapidly changing needs of IC designers.

The technical side of SDA's effort was realized in the SDA Design Framework, which provides IC designers with a foundation that allows them to develop their own specific applications on various hardware systems. This gave SDA sole possession of a key niche in the IC design chain.

A Win-Win Approach

SDA's strategy of turning to semiconductor makers as "industrial sponsors" instead of the usual start-up approach of using solely venture capital made it possible to achieve these objectives. The company's founder and chairman, James Solomon, convinced four firms—the semiconductor divisions of US-based Harris Corp, General Electric and National Semiconductor plus Sweden's L.M. Ericsson—to support his concept. Together, they contributed a total of $6 million of the initial $10 million capital (they now supply about half of the total $19.3 million capitalization), with the remainder coming from venture capital sources brought in to provide independent business guidance. The arrangement was advantageous for all parties involved:

• SDA received **more consistent support from investors** with vested interests in CAD solutions, instead of just aiming for a return on capital. According to SDA President Joseph Costello, "We targeted firms that were considering building such systems internally at high cost and risk; we offered an opportunity to share the risk, reduce costs and obtain better ongoing support from a commercial CAD company responsive to their needs."

• The sponsors were able to offer **direct input into definition and development of SDA's design framework and CAD tools** through "resident engineers" at SDA's lab. Says Thomas Sanders, vice president of Harris Semiconductors: "This link allowed us to access a potentially world-class CAD system at an early stage of its development and customize it for our own purposes."

• **Product development was kept on track** by getting actual industry users involved early so that SDA's engineers were in constant touch with industry requirements.

• **An initial market base was virtually ensured** to SDA for its early products—even though there was no formal obligation on the sponsors' part—as the more active sponsors were involved in their design.

• **SDA gained a competitive edge** resulting from continuous guidance from major CAD users via the resident engineer interaction with SDA

R&D staffers. The overt support of the four majors also enhanced confidence in SDA's products in the wider industry market.

Flies in the Ointment

While the approach was quite successful from both founder's and sponsors' viewpoint, it was not perfect. Several weaknesses prevented the full realization of the sponsorships' potential synergies—especially those deriving from the resident engineer program. SDA's hindsight may help other firms avoid similar pitfalls:

• **Lack of structure.** The main problem may have been SDA's lack of clarity on the nature and benefits of cooperation beyond the sponsors' capital input and involvement in early product development—and a corresponding lack of a management structure. Says Costello: "There wasn't any formal reporting or monitoring structure to guarantee full utilization of rights and fulfillment of obligations and thus ensure mutual benefit for all parties."

• **Unbalanced commitment.** Partly as a result of the structural weakness and largely owing to internal corporate politics (e.g. "not-invented here" beliefs) and priorities, there was a wide variation in the sponsors' degree of commitment. Companies that put more effort into product development work through the resident engineers or that bought more SDA products—such as Harris and Ericsson—enjoyed greater influence. By itself, the equity stake was insufficient to ensure active ongoing participation from all the sponsors.

• **Less than ideal coordination.** Management of the SDA relationship was often divided among several groups in the sponsoring companies. On SDA's part, Costello (then operations vice president) was responsible for managing SDA's ties with the sponsors as well as carrying out his other tasks. Coupled with the loose structure, the coordination problem mushroomed.

Trying Nonequity Partners

SDA subsequently addressed these problems (and the fact that it is now a viable company and not a start-up operation) with another variation on the sponsorship theme: nonequity "technical partnership" agreements with Toshiba and IST. According to Costello, the primary goal of the technical partners was "a tight relationship with a CAD supplier so they could influence the development of CAD tools and develop software based on our design framework." For SDA, the links helped keep its offerings in step with its main industry users. This goal was attained through a formal structure with the following objectives:

- **Building a deeper level of interaction.** The partnerships built on what was considered a "secondary benefit" in the start-up period—the synergy arising from the resident engineer program. SDA received the right to place its engineers at its partners' laboratories. And the partners were also able to initiate joint development projects and enjoy as much access to SDA design framework as SDA's own R&D staffers. Such access was also offered to the industrial sponsors.

- **Establishing a formal management structure that ensures all sides fulfill their commitments.** Each partner named a dedicated program manager, to be matched by an SDA counterpart. Formal quarterly reviews were implemented for both program managers and resident engineers. Semiannual management meetings keep SDA and the partners abreast of each other's business and technology-development plans.

- **Writing into the cooperation agreement incentives for ongoing cooperation.** The partners have continuing financial commitments: Besides a substantial up-front technology-transfer payment, Toshiba and IST (and future technical partners) have to pay quarterly "technology maintenance" fees and meet guaranteed annual purchase targets for SDA products.

33. The Down Side of Competitive Alliances and How to Cut Your Risk

With more MNCs embracing the competitive alliance (CA) as a way to stretch resources in the global marketplace, management must walk a fine line between cooperating and preventing today's ally from milking the arrangement in order to become a more formidable competitor. The Japanese, in particular, are often fingered as culprits who use collaboration to rob partners of comparative advantage, be it technology or markets.

Robert B. Reich and Eric D. Mankin charge that "joint ventures with Japan give away our future." The scholars caution that JVs "seem dangerously shortsighted. In exchange for few lower-skilled, lower-paying jobs and access to our competitors' high-quality products, we are apparently prepared to sacrifice our competitiveness in a host of industries." Technology and market access are the most vulnerable assets in an alliance. Many MNCs fear their Japanese partners will simply learn the selling channels or copy the technology and then drop their partner to go it alone. But many skilled corporate practitioners of CAs protect themselves by relying on certain techniques.

● **Have a tightly focused objective.** Clearly outline the areas of cooperation and the methods to avoid the risk that trade secrets and technology will migrate. Twenty-four years ago, Varian Associates (US) established a JV with NEC to manufacture and market Varian's semiconductor-making products in Japan; a mismatch of objectives doomed the venture. According to Larry Hansen, executive VP at Varian, problems and the firm's loss of technology were a result of Japanese regulations restricting foreign firms to minority ownership. NEC, with 51%, took responsibility for staffing and managing. Once operations started, it became clear the staff's goal was not to sell Varian products; they were interested in acquiring the know-how and technology behind them. This forced Varian to withdraw.

In the 1981 ICL-Fujitsu link to develop a new generation of mainframes, the contract clearly delineated the functions of each partner and restricted cooperation to the single product. Says David Dace, director of collaborations at ICL, "We were not going to mortgage the entire company." Japan's Nippon Glass and the US-based LOF Glass teamed up to supply the rapidly growing market for auto glass in Korea created by the influx of US and Japanese investment. LOF contributed special technology plus its entree with US automakers, Nippon its production prowess and insider status with the Japanese automotive firms.

● **Protect your competitive advantage.** UK-based ICL's distribution network offered Fujitsu a gateway to Europe. ICL protects its network—and its market—from its partner by ensuring that it adds value to all products introduced through the CA (e.g. it does all design work for the mainframes). The contract for a Mitsubishi-Westinghouse JV specifies that its products are sold through the US parent's network. Westinghouse thus secured a measure of market protection by keeping its powerful sales channels at arm's length to the JV and to its partner.

● **Clearly designate liaison points within the parent organization.** Many executives warn that trade secrets and know-how can slip into the hands of the partner/competitor through casual conversations, etc. By designating a central liaison, MNCs can maintain control over who works with the partner and what information is shared.

34. GM-Fanuc Robotics Venture Armed for Global Competition

A 50:50 JV between General Motors Corp (US) and Fanuc Ltd (Japan) has helped both companies realize their goal of becoming a world-class volume robotics manufacturer. The venture allowed the partners to capitalize on their individual technological strengths and realize strategic objectives that neither could achieve alone.

In 1981, GM set out to become a major player in robotics and to bring the benefits to its car-making operations by the end of the 1980s. But GM faced two dilemmas: (1) it had a narrow product line in robotics, centered on the numerically controlled spray-painting system (N/C painter) and (2) bringing robots to the factory floor required installing 14,000 units. "This did not give GM much time," says GMF President and CEO Eric Mittelstadt. Consequently, GM decided to seek an alliance. Of 10 candidates, Fanuc was selected for the following reasons:

• **Similar objectives**. GM and Fanuc both wanted to become volume producers offering a multiplicity of models. Most other firms wanted to concentrate on top-of-the-line models or systems for the factory of the future. GM wanted to start with a product designed to meet current needs and then build up to the factory of the future.

• **Complementary technological and market strengths**. GM contributed the sophisticated N/C painter, its expertise in software and knowledge of application and engineering requirements of the North Atlantic markets. GM also had skills in systems integration for its customers—a plus for Fanuc, whose Asian clients adapt the robots to their own production needs. Fanuc furnished the venture with its own global leadership in numerically controlled systems, plus its reputation for low-cost, highly reliable products and expertise in electronic and mechanical hardware.

Another benefit stemmed from Fanuc's lack of substantial ties with the Japanese auto firms. In general, opposition may surface within GM to alliances with the Japanese, particularly cooperation in manufacturing technology. Employees fear that knowledge may leak to Japanese competitors and bite GM in the auto market.

Setting Up Shop

In June 1982, GMF was established as a separate legal entity headquartered near Detroit. Each partner contributed $5 million for initial capitalization. The JV has a six-member board, with three from each partner; decisions require a two-thirds majority. GM nominates the president and CEO, Fanuc selects the chairman.

The partners agreed to cooperate in the development, manufacturing and marketing of robots for 10 years. GMF does its own R&D and has a cooperative agreement with GM under which it gains access to the parent's development work. Fanuc provides production and manufacturing expertise, but the venture is free to source components and products from outside suppliers.

Building a Management Style

While the agreement highlights the synergies between the two partners, "strategies and elegant contracts will get you nowhere if a venture is not effectively managed," says Mittelstadt. GMF's operating management principles, outlined below, laid the groundwork for current gains:

• **Strong commitment, rapid response.** Fanuc has consistently demonstrated a strong commitment to the venture. Early on, for example, GMF's managers realized they needed a spot-welding robot to meet market demand. GMF engineers went to Japan with design and technical specs; 14 weeks later, the robot was on display at the Osaka trade show. A few months later, the JV bid on a large order, but the customer wanted GMF to lower costs by 30%. "We sent Fanuc an eight-page facsimile outlining the reasons we needed to meet the reduction. The very next day, Fanuc told us the cost reduction would be met."

Relaying GM's commitment to the venture proved more difficult, given the arm's-length relationship between GMF and the US parent. However, GM has purchased a substantial portion of Fanuc's robotics production through GMF.

• **Foster trust.** For instance, when GMF began operations, a competitor asked Mittelstadt how GM was going to protect itself. The competitor suggested his way of operating with the Japanese was to license everything to cover and protect his company. In Mittelstadt's opinion, this was one competitor GMF did not have to worry about. "The Japanese can sense if a partner is covering himself. They will do likewise and do a much better job."

- **Build human resources.** Says Mittelstadt, "We needed to build our staff quickly. Whoever was qualified got the job — regardless of seniority or background." As a result, the average age of GMF employees is under 30. Of 700 employees, less than 100 are from GM and only four from Fanuc. Thus, the JV has largely avoided the need to reorient worker loyalties. GMF trains employees to adhere to the philosophy, "It's my job." From the janitor to the senior executive, "it is everyone's duty to understand GMF's business. A customer may call on any phone, and we want employees to be able to assist them."

- **Create a corporate culture.** Asserts Mittelstadt, "A crucial factor in my decision to take GMF's helm was a guarantee from the parents that I would really be a CEO with full independence in the JV's management." As a start-up venture, GMF could not adopt the management and more bureaucratic decisionmaking styles of either partner. Thus, GMF operates with a very participative management approach that allocates responsibility to all levels. This requires that top management be very communicative about profit and sales projections and strategies. GMF holds monthly meetings with staff. At a one-day employee seminar to discuss operations and management, three employees spoke about their levels.

- **Build cooperation at lower levels.** In the agreement, GMF assumed responsibility for software and Fanuc for hardware. As each had engineers with expertise in both fields, senior management had to convince them that successful cooperation required each side to sacrifice their personal interests to meet new business objectives.

- **Avoid the "big brother" syndrome.** GMF rejects arguments that success in the robotics industry requires only a "big brother," or captive customer. Such a relationship, Mittelstadt argues, can often produce more damage than reward. "When top management demands that all plants use the products of a venture, it provides the factory managers with a very good scapegoat on which to blame all problems." Therefore, GMF structured its relationship to GM on two different levels. In R&D, GM and GMF operate as partners; but for sales and marketing, GMF is an arm's-length supplier. This enables GMF to circumvent the "malicious obedience" phenomenon.

35. Getting Started in Mexico: Amway Finds Adaptation Leads to Rapid Growth

More liberal official attitudes toward incoming foreign investment have let US-based Amway International, a direct-sales consumer products company, begin a major distribution operation in Mexico in 1990. The firm, whose 1990 sales were $2.2 billion, has found the country to be an excellent market: First-year sales are expected to reach $15-20 million, more than double original projections. Amway Mexico has grown rapidly and is moving ahead with expansion plans that include manufacturing.

The company's unique organizational structure and extensive sales network helped it get off to a fast start in Mexico. In the first months of operations, some 15,000 Amway salespeople ("distributors") from the US and other countries came to Mexico to recruit local distributors. Unexpected interest allowed the company to register about 65,000 distributors there.

Amway chose the northern industrial city of Monterrey for its headquarters. "We wanted to be a bigger fish in a smaller pond," says Managing Director Russ Hall. "We were a little afraid we'd get lost in Mexico City." It set up distribution centers in several other cities and contracted for legal and public relations services in Mexico City. Besides buying products from its home office in Ada, Michigan, the Mexican subsidiary receives extensive help from its parent's international division. Advisers are sent to Mexico to assist with marketing, lab testing or products under local conditions and so on. Moreover, headquarters has an "open door" policy that gives overseas affiliates direct access to all levels of management to solve problems in areas such as supply and manufacturing.

Surmounting Obstacles

To be successful in Mexico, the Amway system had to be modified to conform with local laws and cope with a general lack of service infrastructure in several key areas. The roadblocks Amway faced included the following:

• **Adjusting organizational structure to meet legal requirements.** By meeting the basic investment, financing and long-term foreign currency balance requirements of Mexico's new foreign investment regulations, Amway has been able to keep contact with the government to a minimum.

One difficult legal task, however, was to change the organizational system so that there was "absolutely no labor connection between Amway and its individual distributors," according to Warren Kaufman of Goodrich, Riquelme & Associates, a Mexican law firm that deals mostly with MNCs. The aim was to avoid responsibility for social security payments and income tax withholdings. Under the new approach, each Mexican Amway distributor must register as an individual business. Amway assists new distributors in meeting these requirements.

• **Finding an adequate payment system for distributors.** This has been the firm's major stumbling block. In the US, Amway receives advance payment from distributors through a computerized direct-debit banking system. In Mexico, such a system exists only in Mexico City and is available only to certain companies. However, the government's decision last May to privatize the banking system has fostered a more innovative attitude among Mexico's bankers. The company is now working with a bank to establish a direct debit payment system soon.

• **Underdeveloped national shipping and delivery systems.** In the US and Europe, Amway uses home delivery to get products to its distributors, but no shippers in Mexico offer adequate service. Therefore, the company has set up eight distribution centers in six cities—where distributors collect product shipments directly—and plans to move into at least four more cities over the next six months. It has also worked closely with Estafeta, the Mexican express delivery company, and can now deliver products in two to six days to those areas not served by its own depots.

• **Inadequate communications systems.** The firm uses the rapidly expanding toll-free 800 telephone system offered by Telmex, Mexico's newly privatized phone company, to receive orders from its distributors. Although the service is notoriously inefficient and costly, the company has had few problems. It has experienced delays, though, in acquiring a dedicated line for computer communication between the Monterrey office and outlying distribution centers.

• **Official red tape.** Amway has also been delayed by the trademark registration and health authorization process for imported products. The firm has found the average wait in Mexico to be three months, compared with only one month in Europe.

• **Too much, too soon.** Paradoxically, Amway has also run into problems because of its rapid growth. "To be honest, we weren't prepared for so much demand," admits Marketing Director David Casanova. "The company had to double its initial staff and accelerate the development of its product distribution system through Estafeta."

36. How Tambrands Tackled Daunting Soviet Market

"If you experience any pain, dizziness or shortness of breath, discontinue this exercise immediately." When Senior Vice President Paul Konney of Tambrands Inc, the Lake Success, New York-based manufacturer of feminine hygiene and health products, reads this warning on an exercise machine at his company's fitness center, he is reminded of his involvement with Tambrands' Soviet joint venture (JV). Yet despite hardships, the firm believes the benefits of expanding its global business to include the area formerly known as the USSR, building a presence in the huge Soviet market and taking advantage of perestroika have outweighed any operating obstacles Tambrands faced in its Ukrainian venture.

Laying the Groundwork

Tambrands first began to explore the possibilities of a Soviet JV in 1985. From the start, management faced the challenge that the Soviet government in the mid-1980s was primarily interested in foreign investment in capital goods and high technology, not consumer products like tampons and sanitary napkins. Still, Tambrands' management adeptly moved from a 1987 letter of intent to a formal JV agreement in 1988, and to full operations in 1989.

Konney attributes Tambrands' relatively smooth progress to several factors: management's enthusiasm and commitment to establish a brand franchise in the Soviet Union, its recognition of the need for a unique strategy to surmount official resistance to a consumer-goods venture and its implementation of a clear plan of action. The Tambrands' strategy had four key elements:

• **Development of a raison d'etre: The cotton concept.**   To win over the then Soviet government, Tambrands focused on the substantial savings of cotton the Soviet economy would realize if the venture went through. The company provided in-depth analyses that showed how existing feminine hygiene products in the Soviet market required four times as much cotton as Tambrands' items. Management used world cotton prices to prove that the annual savings translated into about $700 million.

• **A high-profile champion of the cause.**   Tambrands needed to gain access to the top echelons of the Soviet government. The question, of course, was how? Management decided to try to enlist a world leader, preferably a woman, who could open the doors to the Kremlin. Tambrands found the perfect champion in the UK's then-prime minister Margaret Thatcher. She was a close friend of President Mikhail Gorbachev and was in regular contact with him; she was interested in women's health and welfare; and she was eager to develop UK-USSR trade. It was a stroke of luck for Tambrands that the Soviet JV was the brainchild of its UK subsidiary. Thatcher introduced Tambrands' proposal to the Soviets in 1986, and "whenever negotiations reached a stalemate, she frequently nudged the venture along," says Konney.

• **A thorough search for a committed partner.**   When Tambrands began looking for a partner in 1987, it focused on Moscow, where the central government firmly controlled all resources and economic decisions. Unable to find a suitable partner, however, Tambrands redirected its efforts to the republics. (Given the recent erosion of the Kremlin's power, Konney says companies may now want to begin their search for partners in the republics, rather than in Moscow.)

Eventually, Tambrands selected the pharmaceutical ministry in the Ukraine for several reasons. The Ukraine was the breadbasket of the former Soviet Union, accounting for one half of total agricultural output, as well as roughly one fifth of total industrial output. Market possibilities are thus considerably greater in the Ukraine than in other regions. The republic is also strategically well situated for transport. In addition, the region's pharmaceutical ministry has the most efficient distribution system and actively promotes better feminine hygiene.

• **Creativity and flexibility in structuring deals.**   Even though Tambrands initially set out to establish one Soviet JV, the result to date has been three separate operations, representing a total investment of approximately $10 million: a JV to manufacture Tampax tampons, another to produce sanitary napkins (both in the Ukraine) and a cotton processing plant in St. Petersburg (Russia). With the cotton plant, which was purchased in 1989, Tambrands can vertically integrate production of tampons and sanitary napkins. This acquisition is also a vehicle by which management could comply with 1989 export regulation amendments and repatriate capital via export sales. Konney notes that the purchase of the cotton plant highlights a Western firm's need for flexibility. It must be prepared to make unplanned changes to its Soviet operations because of new regulatory and political developments.

Launching Operations

For positive publicity reasons, Konney recommends that a Soviet venture set its official start-up for a symbolic holiday or date. In Tambrands' case, the date selected was Soviet Women's Day, March 8 (1989).

From the JV's inception, Soviet-made Tambrands tampons and sanitary napkins have been well received. In fact, they are the only available disposable items on the market. Two of the venture's greatest challenges are keeping up with demand and ensuring that middlemen do not buy up pharmacies' entire inventory of the products and resell them for higher prices on the street.

The venture has had to contend with other operational problems, for which Konney offers the following insights:

- **Cultivate a solid management team and work force.** MNCs should try to replace expatriate managers with local people as soon as possible. Having a Soviet general manager to navigate the bureaucracy, interpret new regulations and hire and manage workers can make a big difference.

Tambrands' Soviet general manager has played a pivotal role in building a dedicated work force. Konney explains that it can be difficult to motivate workers who are accustomed to getting paid whether they work or not. A key motivating factor for Tambrands' work force was the Soviet manager's suggestion to build a cafeteria and offer free meals. Because of food shortages in the USSR, many workers were eager to work for Tambrands to obtain steady meals. In fact, the firm regularly ships a variety of foods from the US and Europe to the workers' cafeteria.

The venture's local managers also helped resolve the company's shortage of accommodations for visiting executives or expatriates on temporary assignment. The Soviet managers were important players in finding an appropriate house to acquire, negotiating the transaction and overseeing renovations to convert the building into several apartments.

- **Establish an effective on-site training program for budding Soviet marketers.** Perhaps one of the greatest obstacles an MNC faces is transforming employees who are accustomed to a state-managed economy into Western-style entrepreneurial managers. Visa restrictions — the scarcity of long-term or multiple-entry Soviet visas for Westerners and US limits on the number of visits from Soviet nationals — preclude relying on expatriate marketing executives or sending Soviet personnel to the US for extensive training.

- **Negotiate pricing.** Substantial differences between the official and market rates of the ruble can cause difficulties for firms in terms of pricing. Soviet bureaucrats, of course, are reluctant to discuss anything but the official rate. However, if a JV bases its prices on that rate, its goods will be priced out of the market. At the time of Tambrands' JV agreement, the official ruble/dollar rate was $1:R0.625, whereas the market rate was R10:$1. With a mixture of practicality, diplomacy and subtle persuasion, Tambrands' management was able to negotiate a more realistic rate with the government. The partners finally settled on a ruble/dollar rate of R2.5:$1.

- **Develop a mechanism for repatriating profits—and be aware of countertrade's shortcomings.** Because exchange controls make it almost impossible to convert rubles to dollars, most companies rely on countertrade to repatriate profits. Tambrands, for example, was paid with bleached cotton — its main raw material — instead of rubles. Management then used some of the cotton at its Ukrainian facilities and exported the rest for hard currency.

However, the firm had to solve two problems before it could export Soviet cotton successfully. First, management needed to substantially upgrade the cotton's quality to meet the world market's standards. Second, it had to comply with a 1989 decree that prohibited all exports of anything but final products. As noted previously, Tambrands acquired a cotton processing facility in St. Petersburg so that it would be in compliance with this regulation and could also sell the cotton for hard currency. Profits from the export sales are then channeled to Tambrands' UK subsidiary.

37. Schlumberger Copes With Hungarian Privatization

The deal by Schlumberger Industries (France) in late 1989 to acquire the Ganz Electric Meters/GEM enterprise underscores the complexities confronting Western firms investing in existing Hungarian enterprises. Capitalizing on the "privatization" mood prevalent in official circles, the French company—after considerable effort—was able to resolve most problems. Despite the difficulties, the arrangement foreshadows a different investment approach for the 1990s by Western companies in Hungary, one that favors partial or complete acquisitions, particularly when sizeble deals are involved.

On the surface, the Schlumberger agreement was relatively straightforward. In reality, however, it was anything but. One of Hungary's oldest and best-known enterprises, GEM—which manufactures switches as well as gas and electric meters—was technically approaching bankruptcy. Taking advantage of the situation, Schlumberger—assisted by the French consulting company ROI—purchased a 75% stake in GEM for $8.6 million.

As part of the deal, the French company agreed to invest an additional $4.5 million worth of production licenses, know-how and equipment within 18 months. Schlumberger—which will take over the management of the enterprise—also plans to install an automated energy-saving production control system. The company intends to introduce new products as well.

To arrange the contract, however, the French firm had to face and settle a number of essential issues:

• The ambiguity of ownership posed by the workers' council running the Ganz enterprise had to be overcome. As this council legally was not allowed to sell parts of the enterprise, GEM was first placed officially under the control of the Ministry of Industry.

• Subsequently it was reorganized as a one-man limited liability company.

• In compliance with the Hungarian Business Association Act, Schlumberger first formed a joint venture with the Budapest Holding enterprise (the state), registering the JV as a limited liability company with a low foundation capital of Ffr4 million ($65,000) to get the deal started quickly.

• To enable the purchase of GEM's machinery, the "Ganz" brand name and other properties by the joint venture, the capital was substantially increased for operating purposes.

• The joint venture then concluded the purchase of GEM's assets. Additional land and buildings were also leased from Budapest Holding.

• In order to start new operations free of debt, Ganz Electric Meters, now reorganized as a one-man limited company, paid off all its outstanding obligations using the $8.6 million from Schlumberger. Then the one-man company initiated its own liquidation.

• At that point, all of GEM's holdings and brand name were the property of the expanded JV in which Schlumberger had a 75% stake.

Ironically, the end result is that the state has managed to sell 25% of its holdings to itself. But the government also succeeded in bailing out a bankrupt enterprise and securing substantial amounts of operating and development capital from Schlumberger.

As one Hungarian manager noted, "Schlumberger got a good deal. Why would the French have acted so fast otherwise?" But the convoluted process exemplifies the experimental and hasty nature of privatization in Hungary. The practice has also led to underpricing some of the country's valuable assets.

38. Vienna Gets Competition as East-West Trade Center

With growing attention being given to East West (E-W) trade potential, more Western companies are considering setting up a special office to coordinate their dealings with EE. For many, the question remains: where? Vienna, heretofore the uncrowned capital of E-W trade, now faces challenges from Brussels, Paris, Frankfurt, London and the latest — Berlin.

Not Really a Choice

Where a firm should locate depends much on the EE markets in which it plans to be active. Companies with established EE operations located in Brussels, Paris, London or Dusseldorf are likely to stay put, but the growing interest in Vienna as an EE center is obvious.

In deciding in favor of Vienna, companies report their preferences are based on straightforward reasoning:

- **Proximity.** Prague and Budapest are an easy drive from Vienna; day trips are simple to arrange. EE personnel also can usually get to Vienna with few problems. Vienna offers at least two flights daily to all EE capitals and many lesser cities as well.

- **Visa support.** For those businessmen who still need a visa, all EE countries—even Albania—are represented in Vienna.

- **Financing.** The Austrians understand EE currencies, countertrade needs, EE leasing and other aspects of supporting a sale. Sufficient trading houses are on hand to deal with nearly any CT requirement.

- **Languages, staffing.** With borders now open, in parts of Vienna Hungarian or Czech is more readily heard than German. From sales managers to secretaries, personnel with knowledge of EE languages can be found.

- **Favorable tax status.** Depending on the organizational formula chosen, the Austrians will give an EE operations or sales office special tax consideration.

- **Local infrastructure.** The city is livable, transportation good, schooling available in most Western languages (including American and Japanese) and costs are manageable. Prices for some items are high, but inflation is negligible.

Taken together, these reasons apparently place Vienna above its other West European challengers. For fullest market penetration, more companies will be opening offices in the individual EE countries themselves, but as that occurs, firms find even greater need for a coordination center not too distant that can understand and deal with the problems that arise in the EE field offices.

39. The Tokyo Option: PPG Shifts Asian HQ to Push Expansion

US-based PPG Industries Inc has marked a clear breach with conventional cost considerations by moving its Asian HQ from Hong Kong to Tokyo—the world's most expensive city. A leading producer of coatings, resins, chemicals and glass, PPG is making the switch to emphasize Japan's pivotal role in its regional strategy, both as a market site and as a potential source of new technical expertise. The decision does not presage any erosion in the dominance of Hong Kong and Singapore as regional HQ sites, but it does underline the importance that US MNCs are according Japan.

Historically, North America has been the main focus of PPG's business. In 1985, over 85% of its net corporate sales were derived from operations in the US and Canada. PPG established its first Asian joint venture in 1967—Asahi-Penn Chemical Co, a 50:50 arrangement with Japan's Asahi Glass Ltd—but it did not expand its regional activity much beyond that JV until the late 1970s.

According to William Harris, PPG's senior vice president international, the renewed interest in Asia was partly a response to sluggishness in PPG's core chemical and glass lines in the US. "We believe our profit situation can be improved by operating in the Far East with its higher growth rates. There is strong potential there for expansion in our core industries," he says.

In the past several years, PPG has built a presence in four critical markets. In Taiwan, it established a 55% venture with local investors to make silica (for reinforcing rubber) and announced a chlorine-caustic soda joint venture with state-owned China Petrochemical Development Corp. PPG's 50:50 Korean JV—Dongju Industrial Co Ltd—produces automobile coatings. In China, the firm is building a joint-venture float glass plant in Shekou and is providing technology and equipment to the country's first commercial silica plant in Nanchang. In Japan, apart from a variety of licensing agreements in the glass and coatings sectors, PPG is studying how it can develop specialty chemicals for industrial application with Nippon Oil & Fats Co Ltd (NOF).

A Long Way From Pittsburgh

Until recently, all of PPG's international operations outside Canada were coordinated from parent HQ in Pittsburgh. Operations are primarily handled by four globally managed product groups: glass, coatings and resins, chemicals, and the newly formed instruments and systems. PPG's international division functions as a coordination unit, conducts market research and provides assistance in negotiations.

Asian operations were first handled exclusively by three product groups from Pittsburgh. After deciding to intensify the Asian effort in 1984, management recognized the need for dedicated, on-site management. "We had to have a headquarters staffed with a high-powered individual from each product group to study market opportunities for core products as well as to provide insights on the use of new technology in the region," says Harris.

Hong Kong was chosen as the location because of its strong financing sector and convenient transportation to other regional markets. The regional HQ began operations on Jan. 21, 1986, under new PPG Far East President Rod Watters, who previously served as Alcoa of Australia (Asia) Ltd's managing director in Hong Kong.

A few months later, the company decided to make the move to Tokyo after meetings of top corporate management identified Japan as the company's key country in the region. Harris acknowledges that the decision to move could prove expensive: Costs in Tokyo are "significantly higher," he says. Nevertheless, management concluded that establishing capacity for market study and monitoring functions in Japan, along with the opportunity to build ties with customers in key industries overrode Hong Kong's cost, tax and geographic advantages.

Three Key Attractions

The swing factor was the global importance of Japan's economy, as well as the prominence of many Japanese companies in industry segments vital to PPG. Besides the fact that Japan accounts for about 75% of Asia's GDP, three particular features of the Japanese economy attracted PPG's attention:

• **Automotives.** "Japan is becoming the center of the world auto industry," notes Harris, and Japanese companies are closely linked to developing opportunities in this sector in Korea and Taiwan. The auto industry is the main end-user for PPG's core product groups. Building up ties with leading automakers in Tokyo may also open up opportunities to supply the growing number of Japanese firms investing in the US.

• **Access to advanced technology.** Says Harris, "There's a lot of R&D work in Japan in areas that are of interest to us. We want not only to stay aware of but also participate in this work." Until 1984, PPG had a joint R&D project on membrane cell technology with Asahi Glass. A focus of its future interest will be Japan's highly advanced specialty chemicals industry.

- **Potential for strategic alliances.** According to Watters, "This location will allow us to establish direct relationships with many leading Japanese customers in our key industry segments that are headquartered in Tokyo." Adds Harris: "We are looking for business partners with which we may have complementary technology." One example is PPG's relationship with NOF, a leading chemical maker noted for its high technical standards and aggressive international stance.

Setting up strong ties with Japanese producers may also boost PPG's regional opportunities. The rising yen has prompted a revival of Japanese offshore investment interest in Asia — the auto and ancillary industries in Korea and Taiwan are major beneficiaries.

Ambitious Targets

The Tokyo office opened officially on Jan. 1, 1987, staffed by Watters and one representative each from PPG's four product groups who report directly to their group vice presidents in Pittsburgh. In line with PPG's existing matrix organization, the Tokyo headquarters performs a coordinating function. It tracks regional business conditions and looks out for opportunities that could benefit the product groups.

PPG aims to build a strong position in all four product groups based on strategies derived from market studies conducted in Tokyo. A key focus will be on building relationships with the major Japanese auto companies with a view to supplying them in Japan and, possibly, in the US as well. Harris hopes that the location in Tokyo will help boost PPG to $1 billion in gross sales from the Far East by 1994, up from less than $100 million in 1985.

40. Wholly Owned
Investments in China Are
on the Rise

Put off by the credit squeeze that is trapping many joint ventures (JVs) in China, an increasing number of companies are turning to 100% foreign-owned investments. In addition, Chinese officials are taking a more accommodating stance toward wholly owned foreign ventures

(WVs) as they recognize the benefits of bringing in new technology and know-how without putting up cash.

Pros of Sole Ownership

Interviews with MNCs currently operating or looking to invest in WVs highlight some of the pros and cons of going solo in China:

• **Flexibility.** All companies cite the freedom to make day-to-day operating decisions without consulting a Chinese partner who may have a very different idea of how things should be run. "There are no limits on the reaction time," says John Marsh, director of international business development at 3M. "When you are ready to make a move in a very difficult environment, you just do it."

As the enterprise grows, there is also much more flexibility to diversify. "If you want to expand or reinvest, it may be very difficult to move beyond your original charter if you have a partner," says Marsh.

• **Protecting technology.** Companies also cite fewer difficulties with technology transfer. In the case of proprietary formulas, this may be particularly important. However, Tim Gelatt, a specialist in Chinese law and partner with Paul, Weiss, Rifkind, Wharton & Garrison, cautions: "Companies may think they can avoid losing their grip on technology, but the fact that they will employ some Chinese staff inevitably means a transfer of knowledge must take place."

• **New industry niches.** According to William Kinch, chairman and president of Grace China Ltd, wholly-owned ventures are ideally suited for companies that come in with a "niche deal." In 1987 when Grace opened its first plant to produce can sealing compound, "we basically started a new industry," Kinch says. "Before, each little canning plant would mix the stuff up itself." In contrast, Grace is currently looking at another investment in rare earths where the Chinese already have a lot of technology. In this case Grace will go for a JV to enhance what the Chinese have already developed.

And the Obstacles...

Companies considering wholly owned projects should also be aware of the many difficulties associated with these ventures.

• **Stiff foreign exchange (forex) requirements.** Balancing forex requirements against revenues is more restrictive with a WV, especially if selling into the domestic market is the objective. One US MNC that already has several JVs in China recently backed away from a WV proposal because the firm was told by the Chinese it would have to export 70% of its output (by volume). A senior legal counsel involved in the deal commented: "If you're looking at China as a low-cost manufacturing source for products that you are going to distribute in other markets, there's no problem. But if your objective is to sell domestically, a high export requirement won't fit."

• **Labor hassles.** Hiring and firing workers, dealing with labor bureaus and the party organization are often problems that a foreign firm would pass on to its Chinese partner in a JV. When 3M opened its operation in Shanghai, it was obliged to hire inexperienced workers selected by the foreign service bureau. The company soon took on the Shanghai Investment & Trust Co as a consultant to help bypass middlemen when hiring people.

Grace was able to hire directly using advertisements in local papers, but the company still had some difficulty releasing the new employees from their original work units. Kinch notes that Grace's Chinese-born general manager (also a US citizen) has been very effective in helping with labor problems.

• **Legal ambiguity.** Although a law governing WVs was passed in 1986, it is not developed as well as the legislation governing joint ventures. Critical gray areas include expropriation and corporate liability.

• **How much autonomy?** Although WVs can enjoy significant management autonomy—including substantive provisions in the WV law to prevent interference by local officials—they live with fundamental constraints. WVs are approved based on their potential to earn hard currency, while most firms are more intent on access to the local market. In addition, government agencies have strict "watchdog" powers in the initial approval process and in such areas as finance and mergers or in implementing other changes to local organization.

41. How MNCs Assess the Risks as Hong Kong Nears 1997

The deadline for China's recovery of Hong Kong, slated for midnight June 30, 1997, is now edging onto the planning horizons of MNCs with operations in the British colony. While the critical question of how China will administer the territory is still up for speculation, it is not too soon for companies to begin seriously evaluating the risks and opportunities involved. The following section, based on interviews with over 15 MNCs with operations in Hong Kong, discusses some of their perspectives and plans.

Most executives interviewed — particularly those who are not Hong Kong-born Chinese — express cautious optimism over the PRC's ability to cope with the transition without eroding Hong Kong's advantages as a regional sourcing, financial and headquarters site. The rationale for this optimism is the fact that Hong Kong provides as much as a quarter of China's forex revenues. In any case, the bulk of MNC investment is in people: "We're not worried; our branch office can just pick up and go," notes a US banker.

Moreover, many MNCs believe that the process of its absorption in to the PRC will open up more opportunities than it will create risks and are thus boosting their positions often in stark contrast to local investors. Company A, a US equipment MNC, has set up a fully owned sales and service operation to serve the colony and China's neighboring Guangdong province. A US-based consumer goods company is considering building a sizable Hong Kong operation "as a point of political entry into the PRC," according to the firm's Asia/Pacific manager. According to a Japanese banker, most of the rising Japanese investment in Hong Kong aims to secure entry into the southern China market through a base in post-1997 Hong Kong. The influx of new or expanded MNC offices also provides major market opportunities.

Nevertheless, firms are aware of the risks. Among the most often cited are the following:

• **Possible crossover of PRC restrictive rules on business activity.** Says an executive for a major US office equipment maker: "We maintain a regional headquarters operation in Hong Kong. If there are changes in the liberal procedures for free exit-and-entry, communications or capital movements, we may move it to Singapore." The Asia/Pacific manager for a US chemical firm concurs: "We will monitor how our ability to repatriate profits and maintain management control might be affected."

• **Negative side effects of the PRC's growing interest in Hong Kong's economy.** While the aggressive expansion of PRC-linked banks, trading companies and manufacturers is providing a fillip to the local economy, the Hong Kong-born Asia manager for a US chemical firm is concerned that "Hong Kong's business environment is being subtly transformed. We deal with PRC people more and more commercially and must cope with their different priorities. We've already lost one supply contract because of their fixation on price, even at the cost of quality."

• **Deteriorating economic conditions in Hong Kong as 1997 approaches.** Although its export-led economy has been robust, protectionist action abroad is bound to slow trade and economic expansion. Anxiety over the territory's political future may also depress long-term investments, undermining export competitiveness: Such worries contributed to the virtual standstill of fixed capital formation from 1982-85. Moreover, the much-praised infrastructure may deteriorate by the early 1990s if the government delays major construction projects such as a new airport.

• **Ebbing confidence among local professionals and the middle class.** Skepticism over Beijing's promises not to alter the territory's capitalist system for 50 years has spurred a substantial exodus of professional and managerial talent. Echoing the concerns of several executives, the vice president of one US MNC admits, "Staffing is our number one problem now in Hong Kong. We seem able to retain only Hong Kong Chinese who already have foreign passports and thus we have to employ more expatriates than we would like." One indicator of the leaving trend is the rapid rise of applications for "good citizen certificates," attesting to a clean police record, and used almost exclusively for visa applications: After topping 23,000 in 1985, applications soared to 38,200 in 1986.

Some analysts believe that 1991-92 is likely to be one of the most touchy periods. With only five years to go, individuals and companies will have to decide whether to stay or leave. Economic difficulties or social unrest could accelerate the exodus.

Preventative Medicine

Executives who were interviewed offered some prescriptions to cope with both short-run problems and longer-term risks:

• **Exercise care in staffing.** To cope with the serious attrition experienced in its Hong Kong office ("the highest rate in our company worldwide"), a leading US equipment maker now tries to recruit mostly Hong Kong-born Chinese who already have "safe havens." Adopting a similar policy, one US electronics firm also arranges overseas work assignments for its key Hong Kong staffers to secure passports, then sends them back to the territory.

Such practices can alleviate the "1997 jitters" among valuable staffers. However, one executive admits, "this solution can breed tensions between higher-paid returnees and employees who may have no intentions of departing."

• **Stay light on your feet.** Company A's Asia/Pacific vp says: "We are making a small-scale investment without any manufacturing facilities. Despite our confidence in Beijing, we believe larger assets may not be prudent given the undeniable long-term uncertainties."

• **Keep close watch on China's fluid political situation and policies.** Since hopes for a favorable transition rest mostly upon the shoulders of a group led by Deng Ziaoping and Premier Zhao Ziyan, companies should track the outcome of current political infighting. Statements by Deng and other Chinese leaders decrying proposals to expand popular representation and maintain the separate powers system in post-1997 Hong Kong continue to undermine local confidence in China's aims.

42. JVs in Korea: Points to Consider

While most foreign companies prefer to run wholly owned subsidiaries abroad, a joint venture is often the most effective and practical organization for operating in Korea. Indeed, it may be the only viable option in light of Korean government rules and guidelines emphasizing local ownership.

BI interviewed a broad range of experienced managers of JVs in Korea. Overall, they believe the advantages of JVs outweigh the disadvantages. Here are the specifics that were most frequently mentioned:

The Pros...

• **Access to the local market**. JVs benefit heavily from a well-positioned local partner's marketing and distribution channels. The duplication of the highly personal system of marketing in Korea would require a substantial investment of time and money.

• **Protection of product and marketing.** Many firms view an investment (which in Korea usually means a JV) as the best way of controlling the marketing and sales of their products and protecting their technology and know-how.

- **Incentives**. Korean incentives are generally equal to or better than those of other developing nations. Inducements such as five-year tax holidays and 50% reductions in major taxes for three years attract foreign investors.

- **Financial benefits**. In a JV, the local partner's financial contribution reduces the risks and costs. In some cases, the Korean company directly or indirectly handles financial dealings (including "facilitative" payments) that the non-Korean firm wishes to avoid.

- **Government support**. Companies with maximum local participation often have an edge in supplying and operating important manufacturing projects. Korean firms have sometimes approached foreign MNCs with JV proposals specifically encouraged by the government.

- **Liberalized investment rules**. During the 1980s, many of the primary barriers to foreign investment in Korea were dismantled. These reforms, along with the prospect of further liberalization, point to more favorable terms for foreign partners.

- **Skilled labor**. An efficient, educated and skilled work force is available. Foreign firms frequently find their Korean partners the best source for white- and blue-collar workers.

- **Moderate wage levels**. Wages have risen substantially since the late 1970s, eroding Korea's labor-cost edge. For now, however, labor costs are still lower than in industrialized countries and are balanced by high productivity.

...And the Cons

- **Limited control**. The operating problems resulting from the sharing of authority in a JV may be formidable. MNCs commonly complain of problems in cooperation on the part of the Korean government and the local companies.

- **Cultural and language differences**. JVs often founder on differences in cultural background and business philosophy. For example, Koreans share a very strong degree of homogeneity and national pride, a direct manner of speaking and an adherence to Confucian principles of conflict avoidance and hierarchical arrangements.

• **Red tape**. Decisions made at high governmental levels do not always reach working-level officials quickly. To many foreigners, the mass of red tape and the need for follow-up can be draining.

• **Restrictions on areas of business**. Specific government approval must be obtained when a JV wants to expand into a line of business other than the one initially authorized.

43. Coping with Officialdom When Investing in Korea

Although government leaders in Korea generally look favorably on foreign investment, Seoul's bureaucracy is often a major cause of administrative delays and managerial headaches for multinational companies operating in that country. To help companies cut through the red tape, this Business International study offers some tips on how to manage relationships with Korean officialdom.

• Recognize and respect the high status of government officials in Korea. They are public directors, not civil servants. Avoid any actions or statements that may be construed as attacks on the pride, or "face," of an official or the government.

• Be aware of the varying attitudes toward MNCs in key government ministries. The Economic Planning Board (EPB) is often more liberal in its thinking, favoring policies that MNCs support; some bureaus in the Ministry of Finance agree with the EPB, but others do not. The Ministry of Trade and Industry has traditionally been more conservative in its actions toward MNCs, but recently has adopted a more favorable stance. Among the most conservative offices are the ministries for communications, agriculture and fisheries, and health and social affairs.

• Understand the differences between higher- and lower-level officials and their impact on policy implementation. Upper-echelon officials are likely to be much more knowledgeable about and friendly toward MNCs, but lower-level bureaucrats wield broad discretionary powers. Thus, agreement at higher levels does not necessarily ensure compliance further down the ladder.

• Before submitting an investment application, find out which ministry will make the decision and which others may be involved. (But don't ask local bureaucrats who has this power—instead, consult your country's diplomatic representatives in Korea or private sector organizations.) Try to sound out these officials' views; your aim is to obtain their informal encouragement prior to applying.

• Don't expect laws to be implemented exactly as they're written. Interpretation is a key part of Korea's legal system, and internal policy guidelines often have a larger bearing on implementation than do the laws themselves.

• Don't surprise officials with new positions or demands during formal meetings. Discussions between executives and senior officials generally occur for two reasons: (1) to present the foreign position and learn the government's attitude prior to the submission of paperwork, and (2) to sign the documents once the deal has been made. It might help to brief the people reporting to those you're scheduled to meet, so they may inform their bosses before your meeting and cushion any shocks.

• Don't assume that your potential joint-venture partner will fully support your position in private discussions with government officials. While many Korean firms have excellent contacts with relevant ministries, some have privately asked officials to strike certain "disagreeable" clauses of their proposed JV contracts.

• Don't expect bureaucrats to treat the information you give them as confidential. Recognize the danger of a leak, stress the importance of secrecy to officials and keep the time period between the submission of information and final approval (or withdrawal) of the application to a minimum.

• Don't submit an application or document and then sit back and wait for results. Follow up with an inquiry in case additional information is required.

• Don't try to be "too Korean." Foreigners are expected to be more straightforward, and excessive politeness may be interpreted as a lack of sincere interest.

44. Steps for Setting Up Shop in Vietnam

Despite Hanoi's eagerness to attract foreign investment, winning project approvals remains a lengthy, bureaucratic process that takes several months at best. US attorney Sesto Vecchi of New York-based law firm Kaplan Russin Vecchi & Kirkwood visited Vietnam as a consultant for the UN Center on Transnational Corporations. Upon his return, Vecchi, who practiced in Saigon from 1966-74, outlined the steps it currently takes to win approvals for foreign-invested operations.

• MNCs seeking to set up shop in Vietnam first must complete the government's foreign investment application in both English and Vietnamese and submit seven copies to the State Committee for Cooperation and Investment (SCCI) if the project will be located in Hanoi. Proposals for areas outside the capital first must be vetted by the appropriate People's Committee (the Ho Chi Minh People's Committee, for example) before they're submitted to the SCCI for okays.

• Although the SCCI hands down the final decisions on projects, applications are passed through six other agencies for assessment, including the Ministry of Finance, the central bank, the Ministry of External Economic Relations, the State Planning Commission, the Scientific and Technology Commission and the Council of Ministers. "It's said each organization has only 10 days to comment, but that seems far too optimistic," asserts Vecchi.

• Vecchi strongly urges newcomers to the reform-bound country to consult one of about 10 local investment service companies (ISCs) attached to all the major ministries and agencies before submitting applications. "Although not compulsory, it appears to be important to work with the appropriate ISC," he stresses. The ISC also can assist in the search for a local partner.

• Although Vietnam's private sector is allowed under the Foreign Investment Law to participate in foreign-invested JVs, Vecchi says most partners "almost certainly will be state enterprises" at this stage in its economic development. While the SCCI likes to play a "neutral role" in negotiations between JV partners, "it's probably a good idea to keep the SCCI informed of discussions and progress," he advises.

- The project review period can last two to three months — and longer if the application first must be approved by a People's Committee. If it's a large project, the SCCI may need to go back to the Council of Ministers to resolve conflicts. The bottom line? Don't expect one-stop investment services yet.

45. Pepsi Clears Last Hurdle to Launch Punjab Venture

By 1988, PepsiCo Inc's efforts to set up a joint venture in India had come to be viewed as the litmus test for the government's much-publicized economic liberalization program. After more than three years of battling with the Indian approval process, the company's application to set up a food processing-cum-soft drink venture with Vollas, a member of the Tata group, and Punjab Agro Industries Corp (PAIC), an enterprise owned by the Punjab state government, cleared the Project Approval Board and the union cabinet of ministers, India's highest decisionmaking body.

In part, Pepsi owes its success to steady and skillful piloting through a tortuous approval process, involving rigorous scrutiny by governmental committees, plus heated debates in Parliament and the national press and a final seal of approval from India's highest governmental body. But of equal importance is the flexible approach Pepsi took in order to satisfy tough government demands. In the end, Pepsi agreed to entry requirements in India that it has rejected in the 150 other countries in which it operates.

Perseverance Is Key to Success

The proposed venture, which promised to metamorphose Punjab's fruit- and vegetable-processing industry, passed the various committees with flying colors and garnered widespread support among the state's farmers and politicians. Why then was the go-ahead so long in coming? M.Z.A. Baig, principal executive officer of Tata Services Ltd, who steered the proposal through the bureaucratic labyrinth, ascribes the drawn-out approval process to a determined soft-drink lobby bent on torpedoing the project. Although the Pepsi case was more politicized than most, local business's testy attitude toward foreign investors is by no means limited to soft drinks and food. Baig advises companies to fight their battles in the marketplace, not the political arena. He offers these suggestions for MNCs that want to crack the Indian market.

● **Be sensitive to the government's position**. The strongly entrenched soft-drink lobby packed more clout than most other industry groups. Three producers, representing more than 85% of the market, managed to mobilize support in both the ruling party and the opposition. Yet, the government's bold political decision to let Pepsi in clearly demonstrates that New Delhi can withstand formidable pressure from domestic lobbies. Nevertheless, the government still had to protect itself from accusations of caving in to MNCs and, therefore, imposed some tough conditions on the venture.

● **Be ready to dig in for the long haul**. Foreign companies serious about making entry into India need to have the ability to persevere against overwhelming odds. In this case, PepsiCo's critics exploited the country's anti-Western bias by claiming that the firm should be barred from India because it represented an alien culture.

● **Accentuate the positive**. Be aware that MNCs have a poor track record in India. Although Pepsi's case rested largely on the promise of export commitments, the company had to convince many skeptics. Examples of failed pledges abound. A venture between General Foods of the US and Kothari to make freeze-dried coffee and protein foods has sought more time to fulfill its five-year Rs990 million export obligation. Meanwhile, Bata India Ltd successfully lobbied to reduce its export obligation from 75% to 33% in its collaboration with Adidas of West Germany.

● **Present a united front with your partners**. The three PepsiCo partners countered the government's suggestion that the soft-drink concentrate unit be split from the food-processing venture by arguing that the project's components were interdependent and inseparable. And Tata realized PepsiCo would not be totally committed to a truncated project if the soft-drink unit were eliminated. In the end, local producers' arguments that foreign investment was inappropriate for the low-technology beverage industry did not wash because they ignored the contribution PepsiCo would make to food-processing and packaging technology.

● **Be flexible**. PepsiCo's proposal was not chiseled in stone. The firm offered several revisions and finally agreed to unprecedented concessions.

Terms of the Deal

After three years of haggling, Pepsi agreed to the following government-imposed conditions:

• An export commitment equal to 50% of total ex-factory production costs. Only 80% of foreign sales can be products the venture makes. The other 20% must be agricultural and processed food products from a government-approved list, which the JV buys from small-scale producers. In addition, the export obligation will run for 10 years instead of the customary five.

• No dividends or capital can be repatriated until the export obligation is fulfilled.

• The foreign exchange inflow:outflow ratio is set at 5:1. Over the 10-year period, forex outflow—for imported capital equipment and raw materials, engineering fees and dividends—is projected at Rs370 million, while export earnings of at least Rs1.94 billion are expected.

• Soft-drink concentrate sales should not exceed 25% of total revenues.

• The venture cannot use foreign brand names on products for the domestic market. Although this is standard policy, it is likely to be more rigorously applied in the PepsiCo case. Ramesh Vangal, PepsiCo's director for business development, said the firm plans to come up with brand names that combine foreign and Indian ones.

• Raw material imports must adhere to the import policy in force and are subject to full customs duties.

3
Marketing

46. Most Frequent Mistakes in Market Analysis/Business Planning

Military strategists discovered long ago that a frontal assault on an entrenched enemy was the most likely road to disaster, even with overwhelmingly superior forces. Companies have found the same to be true of market entry without revolutionary product improvement. Below are some of some of the most common errors that can foil your company's marketing success.

(1) Not understanding the competition in terms of:

- Their ability and motivation to respond to your entry;

- Their past actions vs what is currently in some stage of preparation;

- How deeply entrenched their customer base is;

- Overestimating internal strengths and underrating weaknesses.

(2) Not understanding the customer and relying on secondary research rather than firsthand exposure to the market via focus groups can lead to these failures:

- Underrating customer loyalty to competition;

- Not understanding customer needs;

• Overestimating customer willingness to take risks, spend money, make changes—i.e. underestimating the inertia factor;

• Underestimating trade channels as a factor that affects your success.

(3) Analyzing past history instead of projecting a changing future for your markets—i.e. using inaccurate assumptions about the external environment can result in:

• Failure to translate the effect of megatrends on your market;

• Failure to maintain a global marketing information network to spot trends surfacing in other countries in your industry that affect your customers, but are not yet a factor here.

(4) Underestimating cost and time required can arise from:

• An advertising budget that is too small. Advertising "share of voice" usually must be two points higher for a one-point share of market increase, and this does not include the cost of obtaining initial trial and awareness (i.e. after launch);

• Launch blindness. The inability to see and plan beyond the first risk to the need for second and third waves. No long-term battle plan;

• Tendency to skimp on cost of doing a thorough up-front analysis cost (a tiny fraction of total market entry cost);

• Underestimation of the time required for a thorough market test, and of the time required for distribution, trial and awareness.

47. 18 Questions to Ask Before Launching a New Product

Opportunities exist all over the world for international companies that want to create stronger markets for goods now sold effectively only in their domestic markets. Such markets can be broken down into two categories: those where the product is not heavily consumed and local competition is not very strong (Type A), and those where the product is not consumed at all and where no local competition exists (Type B).

In Market Type A, consumption of the product is not usually linked to purchasing power. In Type B, low standards of living, low purchasing power and low industrialization, are often the reasons for nonuse of the product. In the latter market, it is usually necessary to overcome an affluence/consumption lag—that period of time that generally elapses between changes in income and changes in expenditure patterns. Often, it may be no more than a matter of making consumers aware of products that are now within their means.

Selling to both types of markets requires an intense investigation of the psychological buying habits of consumers and putting into action a creative sales policy to foster the market. Before an attempt is made to sell an established product outside its national market, a company will have to answer the following questions:

• Does the product fill the same need or serve the same purpose in the new market that it does in the domestic market?

• Can it be serve a different function than that for which it was originally created?

• Is the market so segmented that it will fill both categories?

• Do the product-use conditions differ from those of the domestic market?

• What alternatives can be made to adjust to the absence of these other products?

• What will the influence of the product be on the market? Are there other products already on the market that could influence the use or nonuse of the product?

• Is competition likely in the local market from local firms? From other firms in countries where the product is common? How long until there is nonlocal competition?

• Can the product be sold to a similar class of trade as that in the national market?

• Can distribution of the product fit into existing channels, or will new ones be required?

• What changes in pricing policy will be necessary until the product catches on and sales volume rises to a profitable level?

• Will educational efforts be necessary to teach consumers the use of the product? Will distributors and retail outlets selling the product need training?

• Can these costs be absorbed, or will growth of the market be too limited? What alternatives are there?

• Are there any government or local regulations affecting the contents, packaging or labeling of the product? Could these arise in the future?

• What is the likelihood of the product becoming obsolete before the market develops to its fullest extent and biggest volume?

• Will the product need to be upgraded along the way or changed to avoid obsolescence? Will the highest expected volume absorb additional costs?

• Is there any chance that the market will change in the future in ways that would make the product lose its usefulness or function? Is it possible to determine the product life span based on experience in the domestic market?

48. Developing Expertise on Foreign Markets

The battle to expand world sales is swinging from the production area to the marketing front. To keep pace, a firm must develop expertise on foreign marketing conditions for a more intense penetration of the existing overseas market and of the larger one on its heels.

On pages 133–135 is a checklist for use as a guide in developing information on foreign markets. It outlines the minimum information every firm seriously interested in expanding worldwide sales should have at hand. It can also serve as a tool for the traveling executive, a reminder of the major points to cover in reports on the markets visited.

Each entry is stated as briefly as possible. Each should stimulate one or more questions. For example, under point 8 of Legal, a firm should know how easy or difficult it is to obtain patents and register trademarks; the cost of obtaining and maintaining them; the rights a firm owning a trademark has (and doesn't have); if a firm with a strong patent or trademark position can exclude certain competitive products from the country, or be excluded by a competitor with such a position.

Import Regulations

(1) Import licenses, quotas, exchange allocations.

(2) Methods of valuing imports for customs (invoice value, domestic market value, whether from related company, etc.).

(3) Preferential tariffs through membership in trade blocks, individual rulings.

(4) Trade agreements, preferences for certain countries.

(5) Other import taxes and turnover taxes on imports.

(6) Other nontariff barriers (health, size laws, etc.).

(7) Antidumping law and practice.

Port and Transport Facilities

(1) Major ports.

(2) Warehousing facilities.

(3) Cost of warehousing.

(4) Warehouse repackaging regulations.

(5) Free ports or free trade zones.

(6) Manufacturing in free trade zones.

(7) Port taxes and fees.

(8) Unloading delays.

(9) Status of internal road and rail transport systems.

(10) Cost and advantages of various forms of transport.

Distribution Patterns

(1) Nature of importers (private, state, etc.).

(2) Common types of importers (manufacturers' reps, foreign sales subsidiaries, etc.).

(3) Import practices (inventory, consignment, etc.).

(4) Marketing channels (how goods move from importer or manufacturer to final buyer).

(5) Regional distribution centers.

(6) Compensation mechanisms for entities handling goods.

(7) Nature of retail outlets.

(8) Number of different types of retail outlets (chain stores, department stores, mail-order houses, supermarkets, etc.).

(9) Nature of competition among wholesalers, retailers.

(10) Local or foreign-origin bias of government, consumers.

(11) Packaging practices.

(12) Characteristics of salesmen and compensation methods.

(13) Profitability of wholesalers and retailers.

Credit

(1) Credit terms normally extended to importers.

(2) Credit terms normally extended by local manufacturers.

(3) Credit terms normally extended to retailers.

(4) Retail credit buyers (charge accounts, etc.).

(5) Credit-rating agencies.

(6) Extent of credit competition among suppliers.

(7) Level and nature of installment buying.

Advertising

(1) Level of technique.

(2) Responsiveness of buyers.

(3) Local manufacturer, wholesaler, retailer attitudes.

(4) Percentage of sales spent on advertising.

(5) Largest agencies, their billing and clients.

(6) Services offered.

(7) Direct creation and placement of advertising by sellers.

(8) Major media (plus statistics on consumer exposure).

(9) Cost of major media.

(10) Ad agency compensation techniques.

(11) Sales premiums, special offers, trading stamps, etc.

(12) Tie-in promotion.

Legal

(1) Rules of competition on:
  (a) collusion,
  (b) discrimination against certain buyers,
  (c) promotional methods,
  (d) variable pricing,
  (e) exclusive-territory agreements.
(2) Retail price maintenance law.
(3) Cancellation of distributor or wholesaler agreements.
(4) Quality of product laws and controls.
(5) Packaging laws.
(6) Warranty and after-sales exposure.
(7) Price controls, limitations on mark-ups or mark-downs.
(8) Patent, trademark and copyright laws and practices.

Statistics—Collect Figures On:

(1) Population by language, religion, ethnic groups.

(2) Population by age, income, major occupations.

(3) Population by regions and centers—with growth rates.

(4) Numbers of households and rate of creation.

(5) Percentage of households with car, radio, refrigerator, TV, washing machine, running water, electricity.

(6) Per capita personal disposable income, broken down by region.

(7) Personal and household consumption pattern; changes over 10 years.

(8) Government purchases of goods and service, by product groupings and agency.

(9) Type, number and purchasing of state enterprises.

(10) Imports and exports, by product and by origin or destination.

(11) Statistics on market for your products (internal production plus imports less exports).

49. A Practical Guide to Exploring US Market Entry

Before entering the US market, a foreign investor can take several steps to ensure a better understanding of potential problems.

Secondary Research

The first thing a company should do is have a report on the industry prepared that:

(1) Digests everything pertinent written in the trade press over at least the past three years, including legislative matters, technical trends, whatever the trade association is working on (not just marketing) and anything else in the news;

(2) Documents and analyzes brand share, total market figures and total market sales, in dollars and in physical volume by major regional market by month for a least three years;

(3) Records advertising expenditures by brand for three years by quarter and compiles examples of advertisements for each significant competitor;

(4) Contains as much competitive intelligence as possible on each competitor — financial statements and stockbroker opinions, both on the company and on the overall market for those that are publicly traded, complete data on key executives, etc.

Primary Research

(1) Use qualitative research to get the feel of the market, including:

• Focus panels of consumers discussing (and perhaps trying) your product.

• Personal visits. It is very important for one or more senior-level executives to spend time in the market. This will give a background against which to weigh the reports and recommendations to come.

• Visit key trade contacts — e.g. wholesalers and buyers — people who interact directly with your end users and who will be involved in your distribution.

• Interview service company senior contacts: ad agencies, market research, legal, accounting, investment banking firms, etc.

(2) Use quantitative research to undertake:

• Competitive consumer-product testing, including extended use tests.

• Testing markets under a variety of assumptions.

• Evaluation of other concrete options, like copy testing of alternate themes, alternate packaging or merchandising display concepts.

50. The Critical Role of Marketing in the New Europe

When it comes to the single European market, marketing garners the most concern and attention of senior executives responsible for Europe. Companies are revising or refreshing marketing approaches to Europe through a variety of techniques, some that are quite innovative:

• **Retail focus.** Because Colgate's management believes that retailing is moving into a decade of consolidation, it places priority on strengthening its relationships with retailers. To accomplish this, Colgate Europe now avoids the somewhat artificial distinction between the disciplines of sales and marketing. Instead, it uses the word "commercial" as an umbrella term to cover both these functions, as well as service, and to promote the idea that all three are intertwined. It offers "commercial" as opposed to "sales" or "marketing" careers.

• **Industry marketing.** In 1988, Data General introduced the concept of "industry marketing" into its European business through a system of "competency centers," organized according to the vertical markets on which the company is focusing in Europe. Although the centers are located in different countries, each has Europewide responsibility for a particular function — e.g. service and distribution.

• **Global account managers.** Allen-Bradley uses global account managers to sell and service major European MNCs, such as Nestle, Michelin and ICI.

• **Pan-European market information systems.** Both NCR and Colgate are establishing such systems. Like many other firms, they are convinced that high-tech computer and communication systems, which will keep their many operations in constant touch as well as connect them with suppliers and customers, are crucial to long-term success in the New Europe.

• **Subsidiary specialization.** Mitsui, whose country subsidiaries have heretofore carried out their own distribution of a range of products, is moving to pan-European sectoral or product specializations for each country operation. For example, one country will handle fertilizers and another dairy products.

• **Centralized physical distribution.** In general, US and Japanese companies appear more intent than their EC and EFTA counterparts on centralizing physical distribution and using computer networks to track sales patterns. A major part of Foxboro's European strategy, for example, has been the creation of a centralized warehouse in the Netherlands from which it can serve all its European manufacturing operations. Data General has set up a similar facility in Frankfurt to use for assembly and as a central order processing and shipping point.

• **Pan-European product and advertising strategies.** NCR has been following this tack. Before it initiated its pan-European marketing strategy in 1986, its product messages were not consistent from country to country. In fact, even the NCR logo was not standardized in all cases. Now the advertising, graphics and thematic messages have been standardized, and early results indicate a much greater degree of target audience awareness than previously existed. For consumer product manufacturers, the obvious limitations on cross-border marketing are language, ethnicity, and national or cultural preferences. Nonetheless, in Colgate Europe's view, strong forces, not the least of which is the EC move toward integration, are pressuring companies to undertake Europewide advertising. The ability to develop essentially universal messages will enable Colgate and many other consumer goods firms to maximize the money they spend on marketing and achieve a consistent image throughout Europe.

51. Merloni's Strategy to Go On and On and On...

Building strong brands is one of the keys to successful marketing in Europe. The following shows how Italy's home appliance maker Merloni Elettrodomestici is promoting its Ariston brand, and examines the corporate strategy behind the campaign. It is based on an interview with Vittorio Merloni, president and major shareholder of Merloni.

All-Important Image Building

Since 1985, Merloni has been hard at work enhancing the image of its flagship trademark Ariston. This has involved substantial costs, but Merloni executives say the expense been paid off.

The company's UK advertising jingle highlights the reliability of the brand: "Ariston, and on and on and on and on." The jingle is supported by the company's success. From 1985-1989, it more than doubled its share in the Italian white goods market and now claims a number three ranking worldwide, after Electrolux (Sweden) and Whirlpool (US).

The key elements of Merloni's brand strategy include:

• **Choosing the right image.** The most delicate stage in the image strategy is deciding the kind of message you want to get across to your market, explain Merloni managers. At Merloni, the choice has been based on two markets, retailers and the general public. "Retailers are interested in the product itself, while the individual buyer identifies more with the kind of feeling a trademark is linked to."

Accordingly, Merloni's advertising and image-building efforts reflect two messages. One underscores the "winner" element of the company, symbolized by its sponsorship of one of Italy's leading football teams, Juventus. "It's a way to be a 'hero'; a top performer," says one Merloni manager.

The other image it wanted to convey was that of a "good friend you can trust." Merloni says the best example of its soft pitch approach to the individual market is the campaign built around its Margherita washing machine. A series of highly polished advertising spots tell the story of "Margherita, the washing machine with a woman's name." Each spot features a woman in a range of different roles and circumstances. The actual washing machine is not seen until the end.

• **Bombarding your market.** Executives at Merloni proudly say, "You can't get by a day without running into Ariston somewhere." Ariston advertising is planned according to a global calendar that the company uses to coordinate and maximize each of its products. Advertising efforts include a mix of television, print (newspapers, magazines and industry publications) and sponsorships (Ariston sponsors one of Italy's most popular midday game shows, *Bis*).

• **Sending the right kind of financial message.** Merloni feels its financial policies, including listings on both the Milan and Rome stock markets, are part and parcel of the image it is trying to project. Merloni's Portuguese subsidiary (Portugal's leading manufacturer of household appliances) is also listed on the Lisbon market. Other listings in foreign markets are under consideration.

Laying Out the Survival Strategy

However, image is insufficient on its own. Merloni, who headed the Italian employers' federation (Confindustria) in 1980-84, is convinced that the unifying European market will translate into the survival of the fittest — and the biggest. According to Merloni, the number of players in the world white-goods industry will shrink to "no more than five" by 1992.

Merloni's overall strategy for success is based around other important elements as well:

Vittorio Merloni's golden rule of thumb to guarantee a competitive position in any market is based on achieving "at least a third of your largest competitor's market share." All of the group's efforts are ultimately geared at keeping within this "one-to-three" ratio. Given the rapid pace of corporate marriages in the white-goods industry worldwide, Merloni feels it also has to move quickly.

Merloni's first major step toward its critical mass target involved the acquisition in 1987 of Turin-based Indesit with a line of 350 models of products running from stoves to designer washing machines. Indesit, a long-time popular trademark in the European market, had run into financial difficulties, but still retained recognizable trademark and production facilities that made it interesting as a takeover target. Other acquisitions are likely to be in the cards for Merloni.

Merloni operates subsidiaries in France, the UK, Germany, Holland, Portugal and Spain, with agents tapping businesses outside these countries. Merloni's overseas sales organization coordinates a network spanning from Latin America to the Far East.

In addition, through its Merloni Progetti subsidiary, the group sells its know-how abroad. Merloni Progetti designs and builds plants, including turnkey facilities in Eastern Europe and in developing countries. Despite its own considerable international muscle, Merloni still feels that it is impossible "to go it alone" to create the kind of economies of scale that will survive into the future.

• **Knowing the market.** One of the first things Merloni came to grips with was the fundamental change in its traditional customer base (the Merloni product line includes washing machines, cooking ranges, refrigerators and microwave ovens). "People shopping for appliances are not just mothers anymore," explains one company official, "and if they are, they're probably holding down an outside job, too." The company has also begun to focus on the singles market (male and female), limitations in home appliance space, and eating habits that vary from one country to another.

The other important reference point guiding Merloni's marketing team is the need to come up with products that make one's old washing machine at home appear obsolete. Explains one of the company's Milan-based executives, "Italy produces over 14 million units. It is the number one European maker of household appliances, second in the world only to the US. Japan is third. Refrigerators, washing machines, etc are already widespread here and most everywhere else, so the real business is replacement."

● **Keeping an eye on the future.** Because "a lot of people hang on to their washing machines until they fall apart," Merloni says the R&D team devises ways to motivate people to buy new machines. The group's mandate is to come up with increasingly advanced and modern appliances (this, the company believes, is what will eventually separate the winners from the losers in the industry). One major step in this direction for Merloni was the introduction of microwave ovens and refrigerators into the product group, the latter equipped with four separate areas featuring different cooling levels.

Things like reduced size, speed in operation, and reduced energy and water consumption are other points Merloni considers when developing or improving a product. The company is also moving toward the production of appliances that can are programmed to detect and correct breakdowns, and to help run the household. Merloni's dream refrigerator will tell its owner when it has run out of eggs and order fresh supplies from the corner market.

● **Learning how to keep customers happy.** After-sales service heads Merloni's priority list. The company sees it as "one of our main lines of communication with our customers." In fact, Merloni executives say that customers ultimately judge the reliability of the company's trademark as much on follow-up service as on product quality. To drive the point home, the company ran a fairly successful advertising campaign featuring a reassuring female Merloni employee telling the public, "Behind Ariston there's Ariston."

Merloni executives claim their slogan is for real. Computerized production and distribution keeps delivery time down. The company has also launched a marketing system dubbed "Serra Project," which essentially allows a customer to pick out a household appliance via an interactive video terminal installed in selected sales outlets. The central computer in Fabriano memorizes the request, processes the production program and issues a shipping order for direct transport from the factory to the customer's home.

To respond quickly to distress calls from customers with broken washing machines, Merloni keeps a fleet of 800 service vans throughout Europe. The vans keep in constant radio contact with the service centers to receive customer calls. The company's service department is also backed up by a data processing office, which manages a vast amount of technical and design details that can help provide a speedy answer to a problem. The data network also feeds into its general data base all of the data it gathers from its service people in Italy and abroad. This ensures continuous checking of a model's after-sales performance.

● **Bringing automation to the factory.**   Once the decision had been made to bring Merloni into the big league, the next phase involved a major outlay on "technological innovations." Computer screens flicker from just about every desk throughout the Merloni organization. The firm's extensive network allows for valuable cost-cutting coordination from the factory floor and the warehouse down to the sales office. Computer-aided-design (CAD) terminals have helped shave a full two years off Merloni's idea-to-production four-year cycle.

Computer-controlled robots at Merloni's quality-control center at Comunanza run 100 different tests every four minutes on the company's washing machines. The computers that run the test cycles memorize all the pertinent information. This is later used to provide an identification trail for each unit. The company believes this feature is fundamental in providing optimum after-sales service as it allows a repair technician to check the data base for problems that may already have been recorded during the quality-control testing.

At the company's factory at Albacina, the collection and sorting of parts, and the movement of finished machines from warehouse to production line, are done automatically via a system of magnetically guided carts. The whole system is managed by a central computer that also regulates loading and unloading, as well as optional routes. Merloni hopes to increase the level of automation over the next couple of years. A pilot project under way at Melano Marischio is already testing a procedure for assembling and sealing refrigerator cabinets with a group of multiuse robots.

Aside from increasing overall efficiency, Merloni's efforts to automate and computerize its production systems should also drastically reduce the company's failure costs stemming from things like mechanical mistakes and cabinet flaws.

• **The human element**. Last, but highly important, in the Merloni game plan for the future comes the group's 6,000-strong work force. The company invests heavily in an in-house training program and in external training.

Managers are on a strict management-by-objective scheme that stresses performance and overall quality. Vittorio Merloni likes to remind people that the Ariston trademark was developed from Aristide, the name of his father (and founder of the original Industrie Merloni in 1930). Aristide comes from the Greek word "Aristo," which means "the best." Merloni people are expected to toe the family line.

52. Using Niching to Squeeze New Sales From Maturing Markets

Niche marketing—tapping narrowly defined parts of larger business segments—is a key element in multinational response to the twin problems of maturing product cycles and rapid technological change. Using strategies first implemented by the world's leading automakers, more consumer and industrial marketers are relying on niches to exploit opportunities that brand-name leaders may have missed or have purposely ignored. In the following checklist, some of the characteristics of a successful niching strategy and a few pitfalls that firms should avoid when putting this marketing technique to use are detailed.

• A niche must be clearly identifiable, in the marketplace and in the mind of the marketer. A niche brand should be positioned precisely, or it will fall prey to mass market competitors possessing superior promotional resources and strong customer loyalty. Marketers are advised to strive (1) to define as narrowly as possible a particular customer need; (2) to identify a potential market for it; and (3) to create the product necessary to satisfy it.

Differentiation is critical: In order to survive, a niche must serve a need for which there is no adequate substitute. This is particularly true in relation to other products in the company's own line. If consumers conclude the product is not truly separate, it could be "cannibalized" by a fellow brand. At Du Pont, for example, niche products are backed by a written marketing action plan that clearly defines the distinct customer needs driving its introduction to the marketplace.

• Niches should complement other elements of company strategy. MNCs must carefully tie the niche product to its overall pricing, distribution and market communications strategies. A "stand-alone" niche rarely can be developed into a profitable segment, which is the next step in a product's evolution to lucrative mass market status.

• Focus on high-growth markets where the firm is already well positioned. This will help the niche marketer defend its position. Sources of strength that should ideally be present are low-cost production capacity; the ability to apply proprietary technology; high brand-switching costs for customers; and special advantages in marketing or distribution.

Without such strengths, even favorably placed firms may be vulnerable to competition from a flood of "me too" marketers, who copy the product and ship it from a low-cost base in the LDCs. Although companies may cope with this challenge by stressing a high degree of after-sales service, most executives agree that ultimate success in a niche will be determined by who holds status as the lowest-cost producer. A company should be prepared to exit a niche once it forfeits this position.

• Take advantage of technology. Many promising niches are uncovered through ongoing technological improvements in pricing, packaging and new feature additions. Conversely, the pace of change often exposes an existing niche product to new competition. Thus, survival in a niche requires companies to continuously keep pace with adjustments in product references.

• Prior research is vital. A General Foods executive cites three key disciplines needed to tag a market niche. "The first is observation, the second is learned intuition, otherwise known as insight, and the third is intestinal fortitude—that is, the ability to withstand internal opposition from established brand managers who fear the idea intrudes on their turf." The best sources of observation and insight are the consumers themselves, as well as members of the corporate sales team.

Marketers also utilize quantitative data on consumer trends and industry structure and rely heavily on competitive intelligence. This latter knowledge is most useful in identifying weaknesses in a competitor's strategy that can create the opening for a niche product. Marketers should amass detailed information about a competitor's marketing and distribution systems, targeted markets, technological strengths and weaknesses, and financial capabilities.

• Keep your own plans under wraps. Competitors in the larger market should be either ignorant or uninterested in the niche – at least at the time of entry. One managing director of an oil products niche marketer comments that his own firm's competitive approach is "low investment, low overhead, low profile."

• Timing is critical. Once a niche product is identified and tested in preliminary consumer surveys, it should be put into the marketplace quickly. The objectives are to build demand quickly and create a defensible base, thus raising the market entry cost for competitors.

53. Adapting a US Sales Approach for the UK Market

Marketing strategies developed in one country may have to undergo significant adaptation when extended abroad – even to markets with the same language or similar cultures. The US-based Dell Computer Corp found that it had to substantially alter its successful direct-response manufacturing and marketing system when it branched out into the UK. Below is a look at how the company assessed the differences in the markets and how it altered its basic business approach for the UK.

Dell Computer Corp (until June 1987, PC's Ltd) was founded by Chairman and CEO Michael Dell in 1984. Almost 70% of the firm's computers, which are manufactured and configured at its Austin, Texas, headquarters complex, are sold into the corporate market. According to an industry analyst, one of the reasons that Dell has been so successful in selling into corporate offices is its strong direct response marketing program, which has allowed for low overhead and prices.

The Word in the UK Is 'Proactive'

When Dell decided to expand operations internationally in late 1986, its first target was the UK, principally because of the common language of the two nations. However, the company soon realized that it was looking at a very different market, one that would demand a significantly changed strategy. According to Andrew Harris, managing director of Dell Computer Corp Ltd (DCCL – the UK subsidiary), the key barrier faced in the UK market was that UK corporate and individual buyers were not familiar or comfortable with the US practice of using the telephone to purchase expensive machinery. Says Harris, "Buyers in the UK are reluctant to spend their money unless they can physically feel and see the quality of a product, whereas telephone buying is already a respected way of buying in the US."

Moreover, the UK market is much smaller than that of the US, where even a passive sales approach generates sales simply because of the sheer volume of prospects. However, there is a silver lining: With the UK's high degree of concentration, a new entrant might find it easier to have a much greater relative impact (assuming a proper marketing strategy) than would be possible in the more dispersed US market. The implications of these combined factors for DCCL's marketing strategy convinced management that it would have to work more proactively in pursuing sales. The major changes eventually focused on the following areas:

• **Building customer comfort.** The psychological barriers to direct-response marketing impelled DCCL to adopt a two-pronged promotion campaign using direct press contact and advertising to build brand name recognition and comfort with the direct-response system. The relatively homogeneous nature of the UK press allowed a concentrated campaign to reach almost all the UK specialist press simultaneously. Harris relates that a press blitz, organized for DCCL by Sterling Public Relations Co, resulted in about 60 published articles on Dell's products and distribution method (especially on the advantages to the customer) within two weeks. There were more than 100 articles published within a month. This campaign was followed by reviews of Dell's products in the specialist press and an intense advertising campaign.

• **Tailoring the advertising.** DCCL's advertising approach was also distinct from its US parent. While the US advertisements herald the quality and low price of Dell's computers, the UK advertisements — developed by White, Collins, Robinsford & Scott — focus on the benefits for buyers of "dealing direct." The DCCL advertisements assure UK consumers that US users "have found that ordering a computer over the phone doesn't mean you are left on your own. In fact, you get something no dealer can give: a direct relationship with the designer and manufacturer of your machine."

The UK advertisements incorporate a feature not seen in the US versions: a coupon for written information. According to Harris, "This feature allows prospective buyers to make initial contact with us through written material, which also provides us with some basic data on their needs. We then follow up with telephone calls—precisely the reverse of the method used in the US."

Dell's promotion campaign in the UK has concentrated on its high performance models. According to Harris, the lower end of the UK market (e.g. for first-time users) was already dominated by IBM and makers of IBM-compatibles, such as Amstrad PLC. DCCL has emphasized its association with a quality manufacturer (i.e. PC's Ltd) and worked to promote its high performance models through its advertising and with aggressive pricing.

• **Working the field.** Harris also formed a field task force that has been actively contracting major corporations in the UK either through traditional direct methods of phone calling or through DCCL's advertisements. The concentration of UK corporate offices near London enables DCCL to keep down the costs of this more proactive marketing approach. The office for the UK operation is located in Berkshire, about 60 kilometers west of London, putting 60% of the market within 100 miles.

Setting Up Shop

A major decision Dell had to make early on was to determine what kind of operation to run in the UK: Would the UK branch merely be a sales office, or would Dell invest in an integrated complex, similar to the Austin headquarters, which combines sales, design, production and administration. Management decided on the latter course for operational reasons.

Months of analysis and discussions with vendors showed that DCCL could best ensure product quality by setting up a full-scale operation in the UK and could actually cut costs by doing so. "A number of our vendors make components for our system in Europe or in the Far East. If the part is made in the UK or EC, we don't have to pay duty or the cost of transporting those parts from Europe to the US and back. Importing directly from the Far East also saves on shipping, as well as the administrative costs of moving parts through our Austin factory and purchasing teams," says Harris. DCCL will also gain better control of inventory.

Harris claims that DCCL has gained a foothold in the UK. "Within two months of launch, we had 2% of the personal computer market." This has prompted DCCL to begin its backward integration. The firm has moved into a far larger facility with a 25-year lease. Initially, only final configurations were made in London on machinery basically sourced from Austin, but with a new production line, the firm will be able to work back on the production process until the Berkshire office fully replicates the functions in the Austin complex.

54. Selling to Rural Areas

International companies marketing consumer products in developing countries (LDCs) face the problem of whether to confine sales activities to urban areas, invariably the countries' economic centers, or try to reach the rural population as well, which in certain LDCs may not yet have reached the cash-economy stage. Many companies consider the rural markets too difficult and/or costly to reach, but others are attempting to cover this part of the developing country market. Following is a checklist (based on actual corporate experiences) of marketing techniques aimed at penetrating outlying LDC markets.

Distribution

• Generally, do not let your marketing strategy be stymied by traditional concepts and do not hesitate to utilize or create sales channels.

• In large LDC countries, consider carving up the market into many small sales areas and subareas, and installing several layers of multiple-function intermediaries — e.g. dealers/wholesalers who also perform retail functions. Union Carbide successfully used this strategy in Indonesia.

• If your company uses distributors, make it clear that applications are always welcome, even if a distributorship is not actually available in a given area. This way you can build up a reference file of potential distributors to choose from when an opening does occur.

• In evaluating prospective distributors, check such indicators as volume of sales, size and location of storage facilities, and types and geographical scope of retailers served. It may also be useful to find out retailers' opinions of the distributors you are considering. Evaluations are best performed in person.

• Transportation is crucial in serving a rural market, so gauge accurately whether prospective distributors can handle shipment of your goods.

• Familiarize your distributors with your complete line of products and their main selling points.

• Similarly, make sure that you are well acquainted with markets they serve. Distributors may be able to give you tips: for example, if the product has to go through many hands before reaching the point of sale, you will know that sturdy packaging is required.

• In many African countries, where foreign-controlled trading companies such as Unilever's United Africa, the French CFAO and SCOA, or Denmark's East Asiatic have historically dominated the import-export and local markets, let the trading companies do your distribution work for you. Their long familiarity with the pitfalls of African bureaucracy and their contacts with government officials will save you many headaches.

• Remember that in many LDC countries, import-export functions have been taken over by the state and you will have to distribute through a state trading corporation.

• In Africa, consider using the well-established network of market "mothers" as retail outlets. African women manage the small-change sales in almost every country and control a good deal of local capital as well. Your African banker should be able to recommend the leading market "mother."

• Consider hiring a special sales force for rural areas made up of local part timers, students, and others available at a rate lower than that paid your regular salesmen. Also, consider setting up a network of mobile vendors on bicycles; mobile vendors may be particularly suited to introducing unfamiliar products to unsophisticated rural consumers.

Research

• Recognize that conventional market research may be of limited use, but need not be ruled out totally.

• A good indicator of whether a product will do well in a rural market is the degree of success it has enjoyed in the poorer sections of the urban market.

• However limited your formal research, include some face-to-face interviewing, which may sometimes entail small payments to individuals polled. For example, you might construct a street or market display, and then poll curious passersby as to whether they would buy the product(s), what price they would pay, and so on.

• Do not overlook the importance of cultural idiosyncracies that can make or break a product. For example, some colors carry unfavorable connotations in certain countries (e.g. in some African countries the use of red in product promotions may be considered blasphemous).

• Similarly, learn the important symbols and totems in these areas. Among certain Africans, for example, lions, elephants, rhinoceroses, and tigers can represent strength and vigor.

Advertising and Promotion

• Since illiteracy rates are high in rural districts, strive to develop product identification through nonverbal means. Use a package logo that clearly identifies the product pictorially. Emphasize color, package shape and design.

• Among other wordless promotion techniques, experiment with repetition of identical posters, possibly as many as 50 in a row showing just a picture of your product and its name.

• Use filmed advertisements for showing before and during intermissions at movies. Cartoons and cartoon characters have a wide appeal.

• Use billboards to advertise your products along a network of roadways where they will reach a large portion of the country's (money-carrying) travelers. But check whether picture billboards are acceptable.

• Use local radio stations to bring your commercial to a semiliterate audience through the growing network of transistor radios in the Third World (in Africa, several countries bar commercial advertising from the air).

• Do not underestimate unusual advertising media — e.g. camels carrying your company's name on a banner in certain parts of Africa.

• Consider putting promotional teams in booths close to retail stores or at market places, to draw people into stores who might otherwise overlook your product.

• A brightly painted sound truck stationed at the market or moving through a village can be an effective sales medium. Normally the vehicle will offer only free samples, but it may also have full sizes available for purchase and may even do double duty if it is also selling in bulk to local retailers.

• Make your product the sponsor of a movie or of a sporting event. Distribute samples and give sales talks during intermission.

• Seek the endorsement of an athlete or entertainer who is as well known in rural areas as in the cities. This technique was successfully used by a Brazilian company, Cacique de Alimentos, when it named its Cafe Pele after the soccer star.

• Consider a consumer-collector promotion, such as enclosing one of a series of pictures of sports stars (or entertainment stars or simple collectible items such as recipes) in each package.

55. How Northern Telecom Is Winning Share in Japan

In 1986, the Canadian multinational Northern Telecom, working through its US and Japanese subsidiaries, became the first foreign supplier to clinch a major deal with Japan's goliath Nippon Telegraph and Telephone Corp (NTT). Now, Northern Telecom is branching out as a supplier to private common carriers and has hooked up with a Japanese partner to support distribution and service. How Northern got into Japan and is sustaining momentum provides some valuable lessons in the ways of the Japanese market.

Patience Pays

Six years after Chairman Edmund Fitzgerald's initial dialogue with NTT (including 18 months of negotiations and another two years to build and pass muster with a made-to-order test system), Northern Telecom won out over AT&T for a $250 million contract to supply NTT with its DMS-10 small-capacity telecommunications switches. Northern's DMS-10s are manufactured in the US in Raleigh, North Carolina. A wholly owned subsidiary in Japan covers marketing and sales, customer service and technical support.

Although the first contract is still "formally" valued at $250 million, the potential value is probably double that. As Northern Telecom proves itself in the implementation and service phase of the DMS-10 contract, NTT will recognize the economies of scale to be enjoyed by procuring related features inherent in the DMS-10, says Howard Garvey, president of Northern Telecom Japan.

Winning in Japan

Several factors were key to Northern's entry and continued success in Japan. Among them were the following:

- **Reputation for quality.** "Japan is not a market you can dabble in," says Allan Toomer, vice president for rural switching and network products in Raleigh. "If your product's performance isn't proven, don't try to go to Japan." He says that the US was just the right proving ground. According to Toomer, selling US-manufactured telecom products in Japan has a distinct advantage that boils down to the well-known Japanese concern for quality. In fact, Toomer speculates that some Europeans may have been competing early on for the original NTT bid, but the race narrowed to Northern and AT&T because of "respect for the Bell system, which is the world's best."

- **Japanese focus.** A US telecommunications procurement pact with NTT was certainly a plus when Northern decided to export DMS-10s from the US. However, Garvey stresses that the more important focus was building on a global strategy of which Japan is a critical piece. That approach has certainly paid off for the company. According to Toomer, 40% of the output from the DMS-10 factory in Raleigh goes to Japan and that the total business has doubled.

- **Commitment from the top.** Both Garvey and Toomer concur that this element has made a big difference for Northern Telecom in Japan. Fitzgerald helped them get in the door, but more important, he has traveled back and forth over the past several years to reinforce the relationship. "That has impressed the Japanese," says Toomer. Fitzgerald's determination also unified the company internally, he adds. Given the time, effort and money that were needed to succeed, management in the US had to feel that the venture was serious. Support also came on the ground in Japan, where Northern established its marketing subsidiary in 1984.

- **Negotiating savvy.** Northern learned several lessons on how to conduct negotiations with the Japanese. For one, "You don't sit down across the table and hammer things out. You put items on the table and then go away and discuss them separately," says Garvey. In negotiations and as an operating principle, Garvey summarizes the best tack to take: "Opportunities in Japan relate directly to the amount of effort put forward in working the Japanese way."

• **Continual improvement efforts.** Northern has been responsive to the needs of its tough customer to make the product even better. Garvey says that the contract has had a visible quality-boosting effect on Northern Telecom. It "cuts across product lines" and goes beyond hardware to software and service, where the firm is "enhancing performance to the 'nth' degree" and exploring global applications for products.

In Japan, Garvey says, the company is "honing the way we engineer and the way we deliver" to meet Japanese standards. One way is through a tie-up between Oki Electronic, a top global telecommunications supplier, and Northern Telecom Japan. According to Garvey, the partnership, which assists in logistics and commissioning, will serve as a "comfort factor" as Northern Japan moves into volume supply. He mentions two other principles that have served Northern well: "Success is a matter of being patient and understanding the customer's needs"; and "turning our views into their views is the best way to address the customer."

• **US-Japan coordination.** Northern's US and Japanese subsidiaries work closely together to serve the customer in Japan. Toomer says his division "takes the language barrier seriously" and has an arrangement with North Carolina State University to provide language instruction to technical personnel and others who need it. There is also a strong emphasis on human resource exchanges between Tokyo and the US. "We like the Japanese to experience the product here," says Toomer. Training Japanese personnel involves a minimum of six weeks on-the-job training in Raleigh.

True to the Canadian parent's credo that the only way to do business in Japan is to be a Japanese company, Garvey says his sub plans to have better than a 90% local population by 1992 — including his handpicked Japanese successor when he departs. He adds, however, that some expatriates will always be on site (mostly engineers and other system support people) because "technical depth will continue to be in North America."

56. How CompuServe Moved Into Japan's Information Services Market

CompuServe, the computer communications subsidiary of US-based H&R Block Inc, took its first step into the international field in April of 1987 with a foray into Japan's information services market. Its arrangements with Network Information Forum Corp (NIF), a 50:50 joint venture between Fujitsu Ltd and Nissho Iwai Corp, show how a medium-sized service company is able to utilize licensing in order to exploit a promising international opportunity without large capital outlays or major management commitments.

The deal with NIF offers access to CompuServe's on-line services and NIF's own vernacular services to Japanese users based on an exclusive license from the US firm. NIF has been licensed to use in Japan know-how developed for the US CompuServe Information Service (CIS) and has gained an exclusive distributorship for CIS in Japan.

The Turning Points

CompuServe's management was initially surprised by and lukewarm to its Japanese suitors (who had formed their alliance in response to the planned liberalization of Japan's telecommunications sector). The company's lean human resources were fully devoted to building up its domestic services. CIS, for example, has grown by 20-25% p.a. since its start-up in 1980 to over 350,000 subscribers and currently accounts for almost half of CompuServe's $85 million turnover, according to Maury Cox, executive vice president for CompuServe.

The US firm's enthusiasm soon warmed, and, after months of talks, CompuServe chose to cooperate with NIF. Licensing offered "a way to formulate this venture so that it would not detract from our ability to further build our US market and indeed would allow us to enhance our service with international connections," Cox adds. "To do a joint venture, we'd have to assign several people more than we had available for this effort."

Structuring for Economy and Protection

The pact was designed to secure proper value and protection for CompuServe's know-how and to ensure strong support for NIF to make the venture a success — without having to resort to large-scale inputs of

CompuServe's management resources. Key features include the following:

- **Scope of the license.** CompuServe granted NIF access to a substantial part of the CIS application software plus marketing and administrative savvy, which NIF will use to develop and offer its services in Japan. NIF will also be linked to CIS through CompuServe's computers in the US and will redistribute access to CIS to Japanese users under a long-term distributorship; the technology license does not have a set term. NIF's Japan services, the CIS gateway and a two-way electronic mail link has already opened. A gateway to Japan will be established so that CompuServe's US subscribers can access NIF under a cross-licensing pact.

- **Training and ongoing consulting costs are covered in the license's lump-sum payment.** Besides conducting training classes for NIF staffers in the US, CompuServe assigned one full-time staffer to stay in Tokyo for about a year to assist day-to-day implementation. After the service comes on line, ongoing consulting will take place primarily during semiannual review sessions to be held alternately in Tokyo and Columbus, Ohio. In these three-day seminars, CompuServe will update NIF on new services and will provide training for additional capabilities as requested. NIF will be charged separately if it uses up the yearly allocation of consulting time.

- **Royalties.** CompuServe will receive a lump-sum license fee in millions of US dollars, ongoing royalties on the know-how used by NIF and revenues derived from NIF's resale of CIS in Japan—all dollar-denominated. The ongoing royalties will be calculated as a percentage of the gross revenue earned from NIF's Japan service. CompuServe will provide NIF with the billings for CIS (based on the time used and the category of service accessed) for rebilling to the Japanese user; the reverse will hold when the gateway to NIF is opened.

In setting the lump-sum fee, says Cox, "we determined the minimum amount of money that we needed for our bottom line in order to allow us to train and support NIF properly in lieu of other strategic opportunities. We also considered the number of man-hours that were put into developing the software as well as the value of our expertise that will allow NIF to avoid stumbling blocks in this business. We structured an ongoing royalty as an incentive for ourselves to get involved in helping them develop both the interface and new offerings."

Because of the weakening dollar, Cox acknowledges, denominating the royalties in dollars "has worked incredibly well for the Japanese";

however, he denies having any sense of lost opportunity. "We saw the value of the technology in US dollars. As a medium-size US company with little international business outside of this, we really do not have much of an incentive to worry about the foreign exchange issue."

• **Intellectual property and market protection.** CompuServe clearly delineated the license to include only a portion of the CIS application software and not CompuServe's industry-related services or proprietary operational system and network software. The standard nondisclosure and confidentiality clauses extend beyond NIF, largely at the insistence of NIF's parents. "The two Japanese firms didn't want information transferred from NIF to their other units because of potential conflicts within Fujitsu and Nissho Iwai," says Cox.

CompuServe's domestic market and future overseas ventures are guarded from potential competition from NIF by the stipulation that NIF has rights to use CIS technology only in Japan. However, NIF does enjoy first-refusal rights to market the combined services in specified Asian countries, such as Taiwan and Korea.

• **Clear definition of the technology-transfer process.** Scarcely less important than defining what was being transferred was how: "We put a great deal of pain into predefinition of how software would be documented; what the content and duration of training classes would be; and the level of people that would provide the training," explains Cox.

Such strict definition also helps hold down the impact of this operation on CompuServe's ongoing operations. "We've been able to draw part time on different functions to train and support NIF, and we haven't had to put a significant number of people to work on a full-time basis. Moreover, we didn't want to be committed to certain projects internally and then have to make a second decision on resource allocation because NIF needed something more," Cox adds.

57. SmithKline Cracks China Market With Two-Tier Distribution

When SmithKline Beckman, now a subsidiary of SmithKline Beecham, established a joint venture (JV) in Tianjin, China in the early 1980s, penetrating the domestic market was its greatest challenge. The venture produces and sells both brand-name drugs (such as Tagamet) and over-the-counter medicines (such as Contac cold tablets and Zentel deworming agent). When SmithKline first entered the arrangement, management was in the dark about the country's drug-distribution system. And because the firm's Chinese partners were almost entirely production-oriented, they weren't able to shed much light on the subject.

Today, Tianjin SmithKline (TSK), has a two-tier marketing and distribution network, and with a promotion program that it regards as highly successful. Since the October 1987 start-up, the JV's sales have climbed to 100% of production—and it's working off an order backlog.

Taking on the formidable marketing task was Chien Wu, vice president for business development in China, who acquired in-depth knowledge of the local pharmaceutical distribution system during his two-year tenure as TSK acting general manager. He instituted a multifaceted marketing and promotion program, and hired and helped train the local marketing team (he continues to supervise the team from the US with frequent visits to China). Personnel from SmithKline's Philadelphia headquarters also helped with training and provided information about promotion strategies used by the US parent in other foreign markets.

Knowledge of the local market and its distribution system was accumulated over several years. Before launching products in China, Wu and his associates visited several distributors, hospitals and pharmacies, and held a large number of seminars and sales meetings.

The Marketing Force

● **Recruitment**. Wu assembled his marketing team by recruiting local Chinese—mostly recent college graduates (some with a pharmaceutical background) who had no prior working experience.

● **Training**. Visiting SmithKline marketing specialists provided formal product and marketing training; some received supplementary training at the US headquarters. Wu says the performance of the 25-member marketing contingent, composed of "product planners" and sales people, has been outstanding.

● **Compensation**. In addition to salary and regular performance-based bonuses, the sales force receives a small commission. TSK is tempering its use of such incentive pay, however: In egalitarian-minded China, much larger compensation for some staff could be resented by other employees.

Two-Tier System

Unlike many other foreign JVs in China, TSK distributes its low-priced, over-the-counter drugs through China's traditional system, and supplements this with a Western-style sales network to market its brand-name prescription medicines.

● **The traditional network**. China's system consists of large local wholesalers that are on three levels. First-level wholesalers supply drugs to major cities such as Beijing, Tianjin and Shanghai. Second-level units service medium-sized cities with an average population of 300,000; third-level concerns handle counties and cities with 100,000 people or less.

When TSK sells through first-level wholesalers, some of the product trickles down to the second and even third level. As a result, it broadly penetrates the market. It also sells direct to second-level distributors who attend company seminars and sales meetings, but it doesn't seek out third-level ones. Sales volumes simply don't justify the effort.

● **The Western approach**. The firm also uses the door-to-door approach, sending a sales force directly to hospitals, pharmacies and clinics. Tagamet, TSK's brand-name ulcer drug, is the only product now sold this way. The company's trained sales force, while comprising personnel with good academic backgrounds and product knowledge, is small compared with the market's size. Because customers tend to order the drug in much smaller quantities than over-the-counter items such as Contac or Zentel, this sales-intensive approach is more suitable for higher-priced drugs.

Promotion Program

● **Advertising**. The JV has developed ad campaigns for China's three major advertising media: TV, newspapers and magazines. The message differs according to the target audience, which can be the consumer, a physician or another intermediary.

TSK's most successful TV commercial, for its Zentel dewormer, first ran in October 1989. The company pitched the drug as capable of killing most intestinal parasites (such as roundworm and pigworm) with only two tablets (although some hearty parasites might take three to seven days to destroy). Through these advertisements, the message has reached every part of China, Wu said. TSK followed up with a new TV commercial that underlined how the drug, especially if taken by children, can improve food nutrition that might otherwise be taken by these parasites.

TSK hired a local advertising agency that presented the commercials Chinese-style, focusing primarily on product information and content. Its other TV ad campaign, a more Western-style one for Contac cold capsules, was created by a Hong Kong-based agency and also was successful. TSK executives believe an effective message is more important than the presentation. It runs the commercials in conjunction with local programming, buying specific time spots directly from China Central Television (CCTV). It believes this is as productive as the more expensive, and less flexible, national advertising campaigns run in conjunction with Western programming.

Magazine advertisements are directed mainly at physicians and pharmacists, and to a lesser degree to sales people in the pharmaceutical industry. Newspaper advertisements are directed toward the consumer.

One indication that the advertisements are paying off is consumer willingness to pay more for TSK's brand-name drugs, even though comparable generics (e.g. deworming agents, cold tablets and ulcer drugs) have been available in the country for years. The quality of its pharmaceuticals appears to make the additional expense palatable to the Chinese consumer. (In regard to pricing, SmithKline said authorities have been cooperative in agreeing to JV management's price suggestions, and flexible about allowing changes.)

● **Seminars.** Equally important in the marketing effort has been a series of seminars and sales meetings. Held periodically, they are tailored to meet the needs of physicians, pharmacists and first- and second-level wholesalers.

● **Direct mail.** The JV also has launched an ongoing direct-mail campaign, based on a carefully culled computer data base list of hospitals, physicians a drug stores. Selective promotional materials are sent to this target audience.

Success Factors

TSK believes its marketing efforts have been successful for several reasons:

(1) Its strategy of working within the traditional Chinese distribution system to achieve widespread market penetration. This is viewed as the most important factor.

(2) Direct personal contact with Chinese wholesalers. Wu says the relationships he's been building for years are paying off.

(3) Attention to detail in product presentation. For example, the packaging looks as good as what is found on the shelves of drugstores in the West. Wu believes foreign investors make a mistake in downgrading packaging or altering presentation for Third World customers.

Wu says TSK thinking has changed from the belief that production should drive the company to an emphasis on marketing and sales. "The reason we're successful is that we have the best marketing and sales capability among all the pharmaceutical JVs," he claims.

58. Making the Most of Brand-Name Sales in the Indian Market

These days, Indian shops are prominently displaying well-known consumer labels such as Van Heusen and Benetton (clothing), Chesterfield and Rothmans (cigarettes), Raymond Weill and Titan (watches), North Star and Adidas (footwear), Oil of Olay (cosmetics) and Barbie (toys). This trend—also seen among high-tech and industrial items—reflects a relaxation in New Delhi's regulations that made it tough in the past for MNCs to market under foreign brand names in India.

The Official Name Game

Although few clear-cut rules cover the use of foreign product names in India, the approval process is generally similar to that for overseas collaboration. For example, products that match official export priorities, promise to generate foreign exchange, include significant local or high-tech content, or are internationally noted for quality, have the best chance of winning official approval. Local partners are not permitted to pay for use of the name, but MNCs often sidestep this with offshore accounts or third-party payments.

• **Industrial products**. Most drugs, precision electronics equipment, or computers—such as Gould oscilloscopes or Digital Equipment's VAX series—can be marketed under original labels. (Permits hinge on the fact that local partners don't pay for the name. However, MNCs often turn to offshore accounts or third parties to get around this law.) New Delhi also accepts foreign names and model-number suffixes for mass-produced precision engineering products (from ball bearings to valves) that require complex production technology. Most of these items, however, have high local-content levels and involve substantial transfer of technology.

- **Consumer goods**. Export criteria are weighed more heavily for consumer-goods products. But officials take a fairly liberal attitude toward the use of a foreign name by licensees for brand names like Van Heusen and Wrangler that export a high percentage of output.

Maintaining Your Brand Name

The following are important tips for playing India's name game:

- **Pursue public-sector partners.** Pierre Cardin (PC) has sought a link with the Indian Tourism Development Corp (ITDC) to market its clothing and accessory lines under its international brand name. PC officials believe that associating with the state concern may cut official friction and facilitate the opening of retail outlets at most ITDC hotels.

- **Explore export-processing zones (EPZs).** Foreign companies setting up shop in EPZs agree to export at least 75% of output (and hit 30% value-added levels). In exchange they are permitted to sell the remaining 25% locally—often under the foreign brand name. Although Coca-Cola's attempts to use EPZs as a route to local brand-name sales failed, firms marketing less controversial products may be more successful.

- **Franchise.** Licensed retail outlets are rapidly gaining MNC favor. The law is silent on using brand and trade names on outlets, so chains like Benetton and Mothercare can open local shops under original names. In a clever variation, Playboy franchises (licensed by Fashion Sport) operate under the name Rabbit Show—allowing for a close association with the original brand. Products sold in outlets may be marketed under the name brand or a locally coined one.

- **Coin a compound label.** If you can't market under your original brand name, add a locally derived word or suffix. Multinational companies already pursuing this route include Maruti Suzuki (cars), Carrier Aircon (air conditioners), L&T Honeywell (dot-matrix printers) and Wilkinson's Wiltech. Ties between the foreign firm and its local compound name can be reinforced through well-placed advertisements.

• **Adopt an Indian label.** Take an Indian name, then gear promotional campaigns toward educating local buyers about its foreign-brand roots. Japanese firms have mastered this technique, particularly in electronics: Now most Indians know Orson is really Sony and Videocon is National.

Advertisements highlight the names of collaborators or make the point more subtly. Sony, for instance, tells Indian customers: "In case of a problem, please take your Orson TV set to the nearest Sony service center." This approach is ideal when your products basically are assembled kits, and foreign brand names on service centers often are as reassuring as they are on products.

• **Big name brands can fail.** A big name doesn't necessarily translate into sales. The list of failed foreign-branded products is long and distinguished. Marketers of Tang, Close Up and Double Cola all found that a well-known foreign name is no substitute for product quality, proper positioning, reasonable pricing and effective distribution. Expensive locally produced foreign name brands—especially consumer products—often fail in the face of smuggled and imported counterparts.

• **Shop around.** Most of India's major cities now have surprisingly well-stocked "customs notified" shops that legally sell foreign goods. Given only marginal price differences, most buyers prefer foreign goods. MNCs setting up local operations should consider this when forming local tie-ups.

59. Coca-Cola's Use of Corporate Sponsorship in Spain

In most of the EC, corporate sponsorship may now be an overworked part of the total communications package. In Spain, however, the concept is still novel and is one way for companies to generate goodwill among opinion leaders, the media and consumers. In Spain's complex and fiercely competitive soft drink market, Coca-Cola Espana is known for its corporate sponsorship of the arts. Sponsorship also awards the company brand-name identification with its youthful consumers. Below are some of the key elements of the company's approach:

• **Long-term commitment with very little tangible return.** Like other companies that make corporate sponsorship part of communications strategy, Coca-Cola Espana does not count on an immediate and measurable return. In fact, the return is hard to measure at all. The strategic concept corresponds to the contribution that Europe's younger generation thinks companies should be making to society, particularly if they sell products that could come to be considered "superfluous."

• **Focus on youth.**   In 1988, the company became the sole sponsor of the Spanish National Youth Orchestra, known by its acronym, the Jonde. Significantly, no one in the orchestra is over 26. Also, Coca-Cola's partner in this sponsorship is the Socialist government's Ministry of Culture. The company's contribution is P20 million, which covers around 25% of the Jonde's total annual budget, while the state-supported Institute of Stage Arts & Music and a few private contributors foot the rest of the bill. Coca-Cola's initial commitment to the Jonde is for one year.

"These young people work extremely hard to develop their futures as musicians," said Rocio Ruiz do Velasco, a member of the team that implements corporate sponsorship at Coca-Cola Espana. "We decided to sponsor the Jonde because we believe in what we are doing."

• **Gifts beyond grants.**   Cash grants are only the tip of the iceberg. Coca-Cola Espana devotes additional company time and resources to "work" the sponsoring. Traditional tools will be used to provide the Jonde with a larger audience and at the same time multiply the impact of Coca-Cola's message. Coca-Cola Espana will produce a documentary film on the orchestra, a record and a benefit concert. For a company that uses the theme "Youth is the future" in its product advertising, the sponsorship is a perfect fit.

• **A range of sponsorship activities.**   While support of the Jonde is the centerpiece of Coca-Cola Espana's cultural sponsorship program, the company also reaches out to other target groups: the scientific community, with a sponsored research competition on food and nutrition in relation to health and sports achievement; and schoolchildren, with nationwide essay contests.

Coca-Cola also sponsors a variety of youth championships in tennis, skiing, sailing and basketball. For these grassroots sporting events, Coca-Cola Espana provides everything from trophies to transport to refreshments, as well as financial support.

In 1992, and throughout the run-up to the Barcelona Olympics, Coca-Cola will benefit as a sponsor of the Spanish track team.

• **Publicity gauged to fit the project.**   For arts programs, the company intentionally keeps a low profile: Coca-Cola's trademark does not appear on Jonde printed material. Credit goes to Coca-Cola Espana SA but, says Ruiz do Velasco, "the credit line deliberately is not printed in large type."

The tack is different, however, for sporting events, where the red and white Coca-Cola trademark is highly visible.

60. Taking Advantage of Trade Fairs for Maximum Sales Impact

For competitive reasons alone, participation in trade fairs—often an underrated marketing tool—is becoming an essential component of any global marketing strategy. But the trade fair also makes excellent financial sense. Experienced firms find it is one of the most cost-effective ways for an MNC to serve existing markets and expand into new areas.

In Europe, trade fairs have long been major marketing events. Today, however, trade shows are an increasingly important marketing venue in other regions, especially the traditionally tough markets in Asia and Latin America. US Commerce Department officials say that with a few exceptions, liberalized import restrictions in developing countries have expanded the horizon of trade fairs beyond local producers, attracting companies from all over the world. Taiwan's Taipei World Trade Center, opened in 1986, operates exclusively for trade exhibits. Commerce officials say the quality of shows in Latin America varies according to local political and economic conditions, but the major national multi-industry shows are generally well attended.

Advantages of Trade Show Marketing

Corporate exhibitors and international show consultants cite numerous benefits trade show participation offers:

• **Targeted audience.** According to William Mee, president of the US Trade Show Bureau, more than 86% of all attendees represent "buying influences" (managers with direct responsibility for purchasing products and services). Of equal significance is the fact that trade show visitors are there because they have a specific interest in the exhibits. And Trade Show Bureau research has shown that most participants interested in a particular product have not received a sales call for as long as a year prior to the show.

• **Cost effectiveness.** Marketing through trade shows offers major cost savings over direct selling. Surveys conducted by the McGraw-Hill

Laboratory of Advertising Performance and the Trade Show Bureau show the average cost of a direct sales call to be $230, while similar contact made at a trade show costs only $107. The same surveys also report that up to five direct sales calls are required on average to close a sale—bringing the total cost to $1,265, vs a total of $290 for a sale developed through a trade show. For marketing in foreign countries, the savings from trade show participation can be even greater.

- **Enhanced corporate image.** Trade fairs afford a rare opportunity to promote the corporate name to a highly select audience—and savvy companies make a concerted effort to use trade fair participation as an intrinsic part of their image strategies. Whether a firm is seeking to sustain a leadership image or raise its profile in a new market, trade shows provide more direct visibility to potential customers than any other form of advertising.

Image considerations also work in the negative. "A company's absence from important industry trade shows is likely to raise questions concerning its commitment to the market and to providing customer support," says Jerry van Dijk, vice president of Cahners Exposition Group, a leading international trade fair consulting firm. "If IBM pulls out of the banking show, the perception could be that IBM has given up on that market."

- **New product testing.** Although not all companies contacted make frequent use of trade shows to introduce new products, those that do say that it has proven to be a faster way to reach key customers than use of other traditional marketing strategies. Many say the opportunity to display and demonstrate the actual product has a much greater impact than verbal or print promotion alone.

Trade shows also present an ideal forum to conduct market research on new products before a production commitment is made. Using an exhibit to demonstrate prototypes of new products "can save millions of dollars if the interest turns out not to be as strong as anticipated," says van Dijk.

- **Competitive intelligence.** Visiting competitor exhibits at a trade fair provides one of the best ways to identify those product areas where a competitor may be emphasizing promotional efforts. It is also a good way to identify distinguishing features of a competitor's product—particularly when it is new to the market.

- **New market intelligence.** Participation in foreign fairs can offer excellent opportunities for gathering market intelligence on new or particularly difficult markets. For example, Benjamin Martin, a vice president in the international division of Anchor Hocking Corp, notes that in "using trade fairs, you really find out valuable cultural information that may prompt significant changes in features such as packaging and labeling or even discovery of markets for products that are no longer selling domestically." Martin, along with marketing executives from several other companies, suggests that trade fairs are an effective way to establish or strengthen a distribution network abroad.

How to Make an Exhibit Pay

Recognizing the benefits of trade show participatioñ is only the first step in making the most of what can be an expensive undertaking. Who represents the company and how they do it are the real keys to success. Unfortunately, the tendency in many companies is to view fairs as either a nuisance assignment or a junket; the quality of representation gets short shrift. Experienced executives suggest the following pointers to help ensure that a firm gets the best possible return on its trade show investment:

• **Support from top management is essential.**   Corporate respondents unanimously agree that successful exhibitions depend on the support of senior management, right up to the CEO level. In some cases, senior executives can play an influential role at the show itself. This is particularly true in Europe, where it is established practice for top managers to appear on the trade show floor. One of the companies that follows this practice is Olivetti. Says Joachim Schafer, "Olivetti is likely to have the heads of its own foreign subsidiaries in the US, Asia and Latin America on hand to speak directly to potential buyers from those parts of the world."

• **Preshow promotion helps.**   Before a company attends a show, management should have a good idea of who is going to be there, i.e. high-level executives, technical people, distributors. The selection of booth personnel, display techniques and promotional approaches should be tailored to audience demographics.

• **Set written objectives.**   Regardless of whether the primary purpose of the exhibit is to capture sales at the show or after, corporate respondents say it is critical that expectations be well established prior to the show and that these be clearly communicated to company representatives. Companies note that in Europe there tends to be a greater emphasis on booking orders on the spot. In the US, on the other hand, broader marketing goals such as image promotion tend to take precedence over floor sales.

• **Train booth personnel.** Although many companies say they often do not have the time or budget to provide extensive preshow training, most say it can make a big difference in how well the show goes. At Minnesota Mining & Manufacturing Co (3M), Corporate Manager of Meetings and Trade Shows Hugh Morrisey says that "the majority of the divisions do have a preshow meeting where they talk to booth personnel both about show objectives and trade show selling techniques."

• **Follow up systematically.** Develop a system to evaluate postshow performance and to track qualified leads. Some companies use extensive quantitative tallying through computer transmission. For example, at 3M, trade show leads are transmitted directly from the trade show floor back to the home office.

61. Selling to the UN: Profits From an Overlooked Market

Multinational companies go to great lengths to develop export markets, often ignoring one of the world's largest and most varied international markets, the United Nations. The UN's worldwide network of agencies, programs, commissions and offices all purchase goods and services from outside suppliers. But companies are often deterred from cracking this market by the legendary UN bureaucracy, the inherent complexity of the organization, and—most important—a lack of information about how to get started. However, for the company that invests even a modest amount of time and effort, the rewards can be substantial.

The UN buys more than $750 million of goods and services each year. (The total amount of purchases generated by UN-related programs, including expenditures made by governments receiving loans from international lending institutions, approaches a staggering $20 billion annually.) The range of items used by the UN defies easy description because it includes virtually anything and everything.

All UN affiliates represent markets for office supplies and equipment, furniture and motor vehicles. Beyond that, the sky's the limit. One UN affiliate, the International Civil Aviation Organization (ICAO), buys training aircraft, flight and air traffic control simulators, airborne and ground communications and navigation systems and other high-tech equipment. It also retains consultants to do studies, design systems, supervise systems installation and manage projects.

The ICAO is just one of more than two dozen UN agencies, some of which are equally specialized. The World Meteorological Organization, the World Health Organization, the International Telecommunications Union, the International Fund for Agricultural Development and others are major buyers within their respective fields. But the biggest UN buyer is the UN Development Program (UNDP), the world's largest channel for multilateral technical assistance. UNDP works with 152 governments and 35 international and regional agencies to promote higher living standards and economic growth in the developing world. At any given time, UNDP provides financial and technical support to about 5,000 projects that include agriculture, industry, education, energy, transportation, communications, public administration, health, housing and trade.

Approaching the UN

• **IAPSU.** To make it easier for potential suppliers to deal with the UN, the Inter-Agency Procurement Services Unit (IAPSU) was set up within UNDP. In effect, IAPSU is an information clearinghouse that helps match up suppliers and UN customers. It is the contact point for potential suppliers to all UN agencies, handling the initial screening and then sending information about the supplier to those agencies most likely to need its products or services.

The best, and easiest, way to get on UN supplier lists, particularly for regular or routine procurement, is to get in touch with IAPSU. (Its address is Palais des Nations, CH-1211 Geneva 10, Switzerland.) Even companies that already sell to UN agencies should contact IAPSU, because it may open doors to other UN operations that could lead to more customers.

• **Contacting agencies directly.** There are also other ways to plug into the procurement system. Companies can directly contact those agencies that can use their products or services. They can check the public announcements of requests for bids on large, multi-million dollar projects financed by IAPSU. For more information, contact IAPSU.

• **Business Contact Days.** Another entry is IAPSU's Business Contact Days. These are held in connection with IAPSU's annual meeting of procurement managers from the various UN agencies. Company representatives get an opportunity to meet face-to-face with UN purchasing executives, display or discuss their products and services and learn more about supplying the UN. In recent years, Business Contact Days have been held in Denmark, the Netherlands, Sweden, Norway and Canada.

How UN Procurement Works

In order for companies to approach the UN market realistically, it's important that they understand how UN purchasing operates. For most suppliers, the UN represents an excellent market for incremental sales, but not for regular business. UN agencies buy when they have specific needs, whether for a particular aid program in a developing nation or for their own use, and stop buying when the need is filled. Thus, a company that wins a contract to supply a UN program with bicycles, earthmovers, fertilizer, industrial training programs or anything else one year, may not get another order for several years.

● **Small orders.**   Every UN unit sets its own criteria for what comprises a small order, based on the type and volume of its purchases. A small order at some agencies may be less than $5,000, while other agencies regard a small order as under $50,000. Each UN agency requires a minimum of three price quotes for each small order, but these can be requested from previous suppliers or prescreened potential suppliers.

● **Large orders.**   For large orders, UN agencies operate a system of international competitive bidding. Low price is the main criterion, but quality and the ability to meet technical specifications and delivery requirements are also highly important.

Preferential Suppliers

Companies from industrialized economies should be aware that the UN, as a matter of policy, is trying to increase procurement from three categories of countries: developing countries, those where accumulated nonconvertible currencies can be used, and those considered to be underutilized major donors. The latter—notably the Scandinavian nations and Canada—are nations whose governments make substantial voluntary contributions to UNDP, but whose suppliers receive a disproportionately small share of UN orders. It is no accident that the IAPSU meetings and Business Contact Days mentioned earlier have been held in those countries: the objective was to encourage companies in those countries to become UN suppliers.

The practical effect of the UN's policy is that it seeks quotes from suppliers in the preferred categories whenever possible. But it frequently cannot find a qualified supplier in these categories, and it then requests bids from other companies on its roster. As a result, the industrialized nations still provide most of what the UN buys. For example, the Pan American Health Organization (part of the World Health Organization) recently awarded nine contracts ranging in value from $50,000 to $189,000. Three went to US firms, two to British, two to Swiss, one to Panamanian and one to a Brazilian company.

4
Trade and Supplier Relations

62. Why MNCs See Countertrade as a Potent Marketing Tool

The traditional US corporate dislike of countertrade (CT) — often viewed as deals in which a capital goods exporter gets paid in bananas — is rapidly giving way to the view of CT as a pivotal marketing and financial strategy. Many firms that abjured any involvement with this "primitive" practice have watched their sales ebb while other, more flexible companies sign deals and snap up available business. And as more countries jump on the countertrade bandwagon, MNCs are looking for more effective ways to use this device.

A BI survey of 130 US companies engaged in CT shows that a growing number of firms acknowledge that CT is not a temporary phenomenon and are organizing to meet the challenge. Highlights of the survey's findings follow:

Paying for Products

• There are numerous examples of companies that not only use CT to facilitate and support their own exports, but have also set up trading subsidiaries that contribute significantly to the corporate bottom line, handling both the parent's commitments and those of third parties.

More and more executives — including top management, international marketing directors and financial officers — realize that successful overall performance is increasingly synonymous with the ability to generate the means to pay for exports. Without imaginative financing, LDC demands and sales opportunities may go unfulfilled because of severe constraints on payment capacity. Moreover, banks with shaky loans in LDCs and manufacturers with huge sums of blocked local currency in various parts of the world are beginning to look at the trading function, i.e. CT, as a possible tool to solve financial—rather than marketing—problems.

• It is noteworthy that while almost half of the 130 companies surveyed have a marketing person to head CT responsibilities, in 27% of the cases this function is filled by an executive with direct treasury or financial responsibility. This illustrates the growing importance of using CT as a financial mechanism not only to promote exports, but in many cases to hedge financial risks or even to repatriate blocked funds. (Executives with a purchasing background or responsibility, or with specific product expertise, accounted for 10% each in the category of key executives responsible for CT. The remainder were spread among such backgrounds as strategic planning, international business development, market research and special projects.)

CT as Finance: Some Techniques

• Some of the more aggressive and experienced MNCs will initiate a CT proposal when a partner country tightens exchange controls. Specifically, they negotiate an advance purchase of CT goods, setting up an escrow account in another country to settle the transaction. The assets side of the account shows the hard-currency value of CT products the MNC bought, which are used to offset the liabilities for the goods it sold. This lets the MNC keep up the flow of deliveries that would otherwise have been suspended for nonpayment.

• Another novel way that CT helps expand available credit is by enabling a trader to bypass a bank's limits on and credit-risk evaluation of a country. One trading house said it concluded a deal in which a commercial bank issued 80% of the transaction's value as a loan to the commodity trading house. The remaining 20% was taken by the trading house itself. The risk was on the trading house, not on the country and the end-buyer of the CT deal.

This trading house strongly recommends that MNCs offer CT as a backup if the LDC cannot obtain normal export financing or cannot absorb the cost.

• "Such prenegotiated CT alternatives should clearly have the LDC importer pick up the cost of the subsidy and the trading house fee," the trader noted. "Presenting such alternatives not only shows the MNC's goodwill, but also makes the LDC aware of the cost involved in doing business the CT way."

• Perhaps the most talked about (and least practiced) aspect of using CT as a financial technique is as a way to repatriate blocked funds or to remit frozen dividends—particularly in Latin American and Southeast Asian markets. Only a limited number of such transactions have been completed successfully; most falter over the question of official vs parallel exchange rates and the risk of devaluation.

One consumer-goods executive who used CT to unblock funds from his company's Brazilian manufacturing subsidiary said, "The only way you are going to get your dividend out is to earn the cash to do so in hard currency—and now is the time to do it." He set up a Brazilian trading operation, which gained access to the subsidiary's blocked cruzeiros and used them to purchase local goods. It then exported these products and remitted part of the hard-currency proceeds to the US parent company.

63. Countertrade Watch: Benefits and Pitfalls of Evidence Accounts

The use of evidence accounts, a relatively underused documentation tool that allows monitoring performance of countertrade (CT) transactions, has spread from Eastern Europe, where it originated, to a number of developing countries including the PRC, India, Brazil, Venezuela, Bangladesh and most Middle Eastern nations. While especially useful for firms that have several subs or product divisions engaged in extensive CT in a given country, evidence accounts make excellent sense for any MNC with ongoing long-term CT commitments.

In most cases, evidence accounts are split into two subaccounts. One records contracts signed by a company for purchases from, or sales to, a country. The other itemizes payments in settlement of the contracts. Evidence accounts can be official or unofficial. If a company countertrades with only one partner in a country (a foreign trade organization—FTO—a state-trading organization or a private sector importer), a bilateral record is kept by both parties. Should the firm deal with several partners in the same country, unofficial accounts may be carried by each of the involved entities.

Since neither officials in the foreign trade authority nor central banks can keep track of a company's total purchases in their country, new CT demands may be imposed. To safeguard against such a possibility, the company should aim to get an official evidence account — or one kept by the import license-issuing authority.

The Advantages...

• It is possible for a company to bypass lengthy case-by-case CT negotiations. The exporter does not have to get involved in counterpurchase negotiations for each sale to a country that routinely demands CT. This is because evidence accounts solve the often tricky problem of linkage — or securing official approval for applying purchases to fulfillment of CT obligations.

• Payment for nonfulfillment of CT obligations can be avoided or delayed. This is possible since evidence accounts usually span three to five years. The balance (incoming goods vs outgoing counterpurchases) need not run neck and neck. Should a signatory to an evidence account agreement not fulfill its purchase commitment, the balance would be tacked on to its purchase obligation for the following year.

...And the Drawbacks

• It is not always easy to dispose of goods. Calling in a trading house to help is usually frowned upon by the FTO; the idea is that a third party not take advantage of a bilateral agreement.

• Making advance purchases may be risky. An evidence account cannot guarantee that the other party will fulfill its side of the bargain.

Like any CT deal, a fundamental consideration with evidence accounts is that an MNC must offer what the government really needs. For instance, one automotive MNC has been able to set up evidence accounts with the PRC and Zaire to get paid for sales of autos and trucks — items that both governments deem necessary. But a large US manufacturer of plastics reports no luck in establishing evidence accounts in Eastern Europe. The reason: FTO officials say they see no long-term need for the material, although they are interested in talking one-shot deals.

McDonnell Douglas has had good results with evidence accounts: For over 20 years, the aircraft company has kept an ongoing account open with the Yugoslav FTO for sale of its DC-10 planes. It has used the account to fulfill a total takeback commitment of $90 million and still has an excess credit of $10 million. The firm also negotiated similar arrangements for sales to the PRC and Korea.

64. How to Evaluate Foreign
Distributors

Firms using overseas distributors and agents know how critical the selection of good representatives can be. One high-tech marketing manager said, "An ineffective foreign distributor can set you back years. It is almost better to have no distributor than a bad one in a major market." The division president of a major multinational comments, "The agent-selection process is precisely analogous to the recruiting and hiring process, and we give it equal care." The checklist below presents key factors companies should consider when evaluating promising candidates.

For most companies, distributor evaluation breaks down into two broad categories: what to look for and where to go for the information. All agree that the best sources of information are in the target market.

Questions such as, "How effective is the company?"; "Can it really cover the market?"; or "Does it have political clout?" are almost impossible to answer adequately long distance. Therefore, most companies interviewed in Business International's survey send executives to the scene to not only interview distributor candidates and to verify their facilities, but also to talk with potential customers.

Smaller firms, which cannot afford on-site inspection, use a combination of networking among industry peers and selective telephoning to recommended contacts in the target market. Another favorite technique is to ask the prospective distributor for a local market plan and competitive analysis to use as a basis for evaluation.

"Lengthy questionnaires are generally not answered, and they are in any case a poor reflection of reality," says one export manager. "If we cannot visit the market, we get our financial information from the standard sources. We telephone as much as necessary to get third-party opinions that we know we can trust. We also ask the potential distributor to demonstrate his capability by describing to us in some detail how he is going to market our products."

And what if the information is unsatisfactory? "Proceed very carefully," cautions the president of a small industrial equipment firm. "It is always possible to make a trial agreement with minimum purchase requirements, but you must be sure that local laws will let you get out of it if things go wrong."

Before signing with a distributor, exporters should satisfy themselves on the following points:

• What is the distributor's financial standing? Do not overlook any of the available methods of checking credit abroad, but be aware that published figures are not always complete or accurate. Verify them through first-hand visits or reliable third-party opinion.

- Check the distributor's reputation with customers. Experienced companies take time to ascertain the agent's standing with customers, suppliers, the local business community and others in the industry (even competitors). "We look for factors that will help us forecast the effectiveness of the representative," reports the head of a West Coast export management company. "How aggressive is the company? How ethical? How does it treat customers? Does it handle good products?" The question of political clout can be decisive, the executive notes: "We lost part of our business in Indonesia when one of our distributors was unable to persuade the government to lift some discriminatory import regulations."

- Determine the nature of the distributor's existing business. "The best new distributors are those who already know your business because they already sell products to the same market segments," advises the head of an electronic equipment exporter. "Unfortunately, they sometimes handle competing products. In that case, we look for a firm handling related equipment, or a firm with the same level of technical expertise."

  Through careful questioning, the company tries to determine how much the distributor makes from each existing product line, "so we can get an idea of how important our products will be and how much effort we can expect from the distributor." It also looks at the company's historical sales record to determine where it may be headed. In addition, the exporter asks what other foreign manufacturers the distributor represents, "so that we can check with those companies about the distributor's performance."

- Find out the extent of the distributor's market coverage. "Nearly all potential distributors claim to cover their entire national territory," a major exporter says, "but if this is not true, you run the risk of setting up a distributor—or worse, an exclusive distributor—who cannot reach all your available customers." Benchmarks that the exporter looks for include the appearance of the company's physical facilities ("We always check in person"), the size and the level of training of the distributor's sales force, and the number of the firm's sales outlets. "You should attempt to find out what market segments the distributor serves and what is his market share in each," the exporter counsels. "This may be your basis for awarding several exclusive distributorships in one country—each for a specific market segment."

- Determine the distributor's own business strategy. "Look carefully into the representative's own corporate and personal goals to judge to what extent they coincide with yours," suggests a market manager doing business in Asia. "Will he ultimately want to manufacture under license or joint venture?" The manager tries to make a prior estimate of what kind of help the distributor will require in terms of price, credit, delivery, sales training, communication, personal visits, product modification, warranty, advertising, warehousing, technical support and after-sales service. "Knowing this in advance will help avoid unpleasant surprises," says the manager.

• Test the distributor's commitment to your business. "In effect," says one international sales manager, "our first agreement with a distributor is a test of his commitment." The company tries to set reasonable conditions, such as an initial stock order, a certain level of effort in advertising and promotional campaigns, minimum sales targets, some degree of investment in sales and technical training and a willingness to give adequate market feedback. If the distributor agrees to all of these conditions, then "we know that he is interested."

65. How Companies Get Around Forex Problems in the PRC

A key operational dilemma for MNCs in China is finding uses for earnings obtained in the local currency. Because simple conversion of the renminbi for payment of expenses incurred in foreign exchange or for homeward remittances is blocked, investors and their local partners must devise ways to get around it. Below are some tips on how MNCs can deal with the problem.

• **Export the venture's output.** Some MNCs have placed a portion or all of the products generated by a PRC joint venture (JV) for sale on the world market. This approach is strongly favored by Chinese authorities. Company A, a manufacturer of industrial controls, now depends on its PRC JV for components formerly purchased from outside suppliers, thereby providing the JV with a ready export market. The parent insists that the JV's prices and quality be competitive.

However, exporting may not be the preferred solution for some companies. As one US executive puts it, "Everybody goes to China with visions of the domestic market. MNCs are already satisfying demand for the products they make outside of China, and there are better places to set up plants if it's low-cost manufacturing for export that you're after. So, unless you absolutely have to, why export the product?"

• **Export an alternative product—if you can find it and no strings are attached.** Finding an exportable commodity is complicated. The Chinese already export most of what they can (through state foreign trade corporations that guard their prerogatives jealously), and the low quality of other products often makes them unsalable on the world market. Still, some firms have succeeded in using renminbi profits to purchase finished Chinese goods for export. International Hydron, which has a 50:50 JV (Shanghai-Hydron Contact Lens Co), uses its renminbi earnings to buy cotton medical products for sale to US customers in the medical supplies field.

A second option is investing in another operation that makes goods for export. Typical candidates are firms that produce an established line of export goods and that need capital for expansion and modernization. International Hydron has also adopted this strategy. "Under a contract with the factory and the government," says Ed Hopkins, vice president for international business development, "you become eligible to take your profit out of that factory in goods it is already producing for export."

As a rule of thumb, International Hydron plays it small in these deals, since bigger deals require negotiations with the central bureaucracy. "We've tried very specifically to stay under $10 million, so we have to deal only with the local governments," Hopkins notes. "The smaller you are, the better it is."

• **Look further afield.**   Sometimes contracts with local officials do not suffice. By widening contacts beyond provincial officials and specific government ministries, companies can gain access to higher authorities, which may make solving the forex problem easier over time. For example, a company may want to trade the product of its JV for the exportable good of another enterprise. While ministerial lines remain hard to cross, some executives feel they can enhance a deal's prospects by taking the lead as go-betweens with the ministries involved.

• **Buy dollars from companies that need renminbi.**   Even before the Provisions to Encourage Foreign Investment offered limited forex trading through the Bank of China, a few JVs had begun using this method. "We've had the most success with hotels," says the finance manager of Company A. "They are net forex generators because all their foreign guests pay them in dollars." To facilitate such exchanges, monitor them and earn a handling fee in the process, the PRC has established forex adjustment centers in major cities around the country.

• **Press the authorities for solutions.**   PRC officials realize companies are facing problems, but their position is that economic goals must come first. Nevertheless, the government will sometimes listen to company complaints as part of an effort to head off any additional dampening of foreign interest in investing in China. Says one manager who needs forex to make import payments: "We are constantly talking to the government, asking them to remedy the situation. We press them to recognize that some import-substitution ventures have a need for foreign exchange, and can't entirely be the burden of the venture. In some cases, they did give us relief."

Some ventures whose products substitute for imports are allowed to charge the customer part-forex/part-renminbi for domestic sales. Permission to do this was authorized for several automotive JVs, including American Motors Corp's Beijing Jeep plant.

• **Source locally.** By cutting back on imports that are needed to produce for the Chinese market, firms can slash forex needs. While this seems to be an obvious solution, companies must look far and wide for factories that can deliver components of the proper quality and on a reliable schedule. Usually they don't find them. The executive of one company manufacturing in China laments, "An awful lot of the things we need are simply not available yet in China or, if they are, they are not of sufficient quality. We've done pretty well with some of the routine parts, but things like electrical components and special connectors are hard to come by."

66. Trends in Global Sourcing: Exporting From Latin America

Many MNCs with subsidiaries in Latin America are trying to maintain earnings momentum by boosting exports inside and outside the region. Other than responding to their own needs to employ underutilized local plant capacity and to generate foreign exchange, MNCs are also often urged to hike exports by governments anxious to service onerous hard-currency debt burdens.

According to a BI study of more than 50 US and European MNCs, two basic conditions in Latin American economies now favor export operations:

• **Production costs have been pushed extremely low** by devaluations and recession. Mexico, Brazil and Central American nations now rank among the lowest-cost sourcing points for worldwide exports, especially in labor-intensive lines. By contrast, unit labor costs in most Southeast Asian economies have risen steadily in the last decade. The downside risk is that the attraction of cheap labor sites for export-oriented operations may be eroded by automation. Companies also point out that amassing higher profits in devalued local currencies is needed to return comparable results to the parent entity.

• **Export incentives are widely available.** The debt crisis and accompanying balance-of-payments shortfalls have made export capability a key factor in investment approvals and eligibility for incentive payments.

Techniques for Building Exports

Besides participating in proliferating countertrade arrangements, MNCs are adopting various alternative strategies to make their Latin American operations more export-oriented:

• **Regional assembly and finishing of materials.** Parts and components are sent duty-free on consignment basis by MNCs to regional subs for shipment to the foreign parent or other affiliates. This type of set-up has flourished in Mexico under the *maquiladora* system; it has also shown good results in some Central American states, e.g. Costa Rica, El Salvador and Guatemala.

One small but aggressive MNC believes Latin America offers ideal sourcing points for traditional products: "We are using Brazil as a prime part of our international supply network, as we have used India," says a spokesman.

• **Diversion of existing export markets** in favor of Latin American production facilities at the expense of parent or other non-Latin American plants. Although this tactic runs the risk of inciting strong opposition from labor unions back home, one consumer and intermediate goods manufacturer claims to be thriving in Brazil and Mexico, largely because of the exports from its plants there to Third World markets. According to a senior parent company executive, "The Brazilians are as productive as the Koreans. As a result our costs in Brazil are very competitive with our plants in the Far East."

• **Establishment of world-scale manufacturing facilities** within the context of a long-term regional strategic plan. One diversified high-tech company that manufactures its products globally has made Brazil the major export base for some of its automotive components and parts. These products are shipped to original equipment manufacturers in other parts of the world as well as to the parent. A giant intermediate products maker has responded to Brazilian government pressure to export by drafting a long-term plan: "We are looking at various types of world-scale facilities that we can put into Brazil and that will be complemented by the local supply of raw materials."

• **Technology transfers** to independent or minority-owned Latin American companies to produce exports. Although licensing is primarily used in Latin America to secure positions in local markets, a number of MNCs have begun licensing local firms to manufacture finished products and components for export to the foreign licensor or to third parties overseas.

Success in exporting depends on Latin American products' being globally competitive in both quality and cost. But views are mixed: while there are some questions about the quality of consumer goods, executives surveyed are convinced that the quality of finished goods or components they source from Latin America can be equal to goods made at home.

67. Preshipment Inspections: How to Reduce Costly Delays

Since the early 1980s, MNCs operating in less developed countries (LDCs) have faced the headache of preshipment inspections of imports and exports. The purpose of the inspections is to check price, quantity and quality of shipments. Each government determines how these checks will take place, but many are hiring independent auditing firms to carry out the inspections on their behalf. Probably the best-known outfit is Swiss-based Societe Generale de Surveillance (SGS). Below is a look at what happens when SGS is called in.

What Happens During the Inspection

SGS first studies the proforma invoice to ensure that the prices quoted are within the accepted price range prevailing in the country of origin or in the relevant international market. SGS is not interested in verifying the exporter's cost or in inspecting the exporter's books. They do, however, match the proforma invoice price with the company's price list. If the prices quoted on the proforma invoice and on the company's price list are higher than the "prevailing market price," SGS may ask the exporter to explain the difference. Price differences within reasonable limits are never a problem, according to Henry Holzer, SGS director of special projects in New York. Once the proforma invoice prices have been accepted, an inspector will be sent to check the shipment.

The physical inspection, which according to some companies lasts about 30 minutes, takes place in the manufacturer's or seller's warehouse before the shipment is sent to its port of embarkation. The inspector randomly selects a few items to determine whether the quantity and quality of the goods meet the specifications detailed in the invoice. Occasionally a sample is taken for laboratory tests.

Once the inspector verifies the correct quantity and quality of the goods, the containers are closed and sealed. Under special circumstances, SGS may reinspect the goods at any point, including at the time of loading. Upon finishing the inspection, SGS issues a Clean Report of Findings, which is required both for customs clearance and to obtain payment through a commercial bank.

10 Ways to Save Time and Money on Inspections

Firms are generally not happy when SGS or one of its competitors gets into the act, contending that the procedures are costly and time-consuming. But there are several ways that knowledgeable firms can use to expedite the process.

● **Appoint a coordinator**.   Assign the task of learning everything possible about inspections to one individual in your organization. This coordinator should read and file all information coming from governments and from the inspecting firm. The coordinator should also attend the inspections to observe how they are conducted, answer any questions that arise and learn what could speed up the process.

● **Establish regular contacts**.   Get in touch with the local office of SGS to schedule an appointment and obtain an advance supply of printed instructions and forms. Meet the people you will be frequently dealing with on the phone. Until a solid working relationship is established, don't stint on trips to the local branch of your inspecting firm.

● **Learn the paperwork ropes**.   To avoid unnecessary delays, learn how to complete the one-page Request for Information/Inspection (RFI) form and have it double-checked before it goes out. It will be returned to you if it is not properly filled out. Be sure someone on the other end of the deal is following up on the government paperwork; otherwise, you will not have all the necessary documentation.

• **Have full background documentation.** Don't forget to attach your company's price list, typed or printed on the company's letterhead, to the RFI form. If your prices are higher than the prevailing market prices, be prepared to explain the peculiarities of your product (i.e. your widgets use silver screws instead of copper ones).

• **Identify your shipment.** Use SGS's reference number (this is usually the import license number) on all correspondence to ensure proper identification of the transaction.

• **Watch the licenses.** Since the import license (or equivalent document) is the governing document in the country of importation, all information related to the inspection must agree with this license. Don't combine several licenses into one final invoice unless it clearly shows breakdown per license.

• **Book in advance.** As soon as you know the date your shipment will be ready for inspection, alert the inspecting company. SGS does not require that all documentation be completed before you request inspection. However, it is not authorized to issue final reports until it is in possession of the import license (or equivalent document).

• **Combine shipments.** If you are planning to make several shipments to different countries around the same date, you may be able to arrange one inspection. Check first to find out how your local inspecting office handles simultaneous transactions.

• **Warn ahead.** If you have any questions or anticipate any problems, procedural difficulties, etc., discuss them with SGS in advance so they can be resolved by the time the shipment is ready to move. SGS is allowed to discuss inspection matters at any time, but it can address pricing matters only when it has received an import license or equivalent document.

• **Spoilage prevention.** If you export perishable goods, inquire about the applicable rule; SGS says it will try to give priority to perishable goods.

68. How India's Modi Xerox Meets Protectionist Laws, at a Solid Profit

Modi Xerox is a joint venture (JV) of Modi Group, one of India's largest family-owned companies, and the UK-based Rank Xerox Corp, that produces Xerox 1045 and 1025 copiers. The JV evolved in two stages. The first was a 100% export-oriented unit, Indian Xerographic Systems, 51% owned by Rank Xerox. Once Rank Xerox determined that it could produce state-of-the-art xerographic equipment in India, it moved into the second stage and set up a manufacturing plant to serve the local market.

Modi Xerox, formed in 1984, serves this purpose, with ownership split three ways: Rank Xerox and Modi each own 40%, and the remaining 20% is held by outside shareholders.

While reforms in India helped cut government red tape in recent years, foreign firms still face strong protectionist regulations. As a foreign venture, Modi Xerox is subject to a minimum 30% export obligation based on the f.o.b. value of exports as a percentage of the ex-factory value of production. It is applicable for five years with a possible extension for another five. And, the JV must achieve 85% local content by its fifth year. Complying with the rules, though, often runs at cross purposes with profitability given the following circumstances:

• **Local growth discouraged.** Because export levels are pegged to total production, the export obligation discourages domestic expansion.

• **Bureaucratic delays.** Getting an advance export license for overseas orders normally takes four months. Filling orders therefore takes at least eight months, often too long to be acceptable in the highly competitive export market.

• **Rigid export licensing procedures.** Once issued, the advance license is inflexible—it allows no changes. That means a new license—marking the start of a new four month delay—is required whenever a customer decides to switch models or an exporter wants to divert the consignment to another buyer.

• **Costly import substitution.** Key raw materials, such as copper wire and sheet metal, must be sourced in India at several times the price of foreign supplies. Excise taxes and other duties can add as much as 200% to input costs. Last year, about 40% of gross sales went to taxes and duties.

Despite these handicaps, the f.o.b. value of Modi Xerox exports has been well above the stipulated 30% and export revenues have soared. As for indigenization, the JV has achieved 60% local content value on one line of copiers and 25-30% overall.

According to B.S. Kalara, director of exports for Modi Xerox, there are a number of steps that enabled the firm to prosper despite regulatory burdens:

• **Take the export commitment seriously.** First and foremost, says Kalara, be willing to meet the commitment. Kalara himself closely monitors export figures on a monthly basis. Too often, companies do not seriously intend to fulfill their export obligations. They are prepared to face the music (penalties may take the form of fines or denial of further import licenses or concessional funds), or they anticipate a waiver of either the requirements or penalties.

• **High product quality.** Installed at a cost of Rs375 million, the Modi Xerox plant is the largest investment made to date in India's copier industry and incorporates the latest xerographic manufacturing techniques. It is one of only two plants in the world where all copier-related technologies are under one roof, according to Kalara. With this investment in facilities to produce a line of copiers of comparable quality as that manufactured in Europe, Modi Xerox can sell subassemblies to Xerox plants in the Netherlands and in the UK, while maintaining a substantial technological lead over its competitors in India.

• **Enlist HQ support from the MNC partner.** Rank Xerox's worldwide marketing network has been a big help for the JV, serving as its export agent and providing full customer support. Overseas sales have helped the company achieve higher capacity utilization—critical to profitability. Modi Xerox concedes that no new entrant could match a substantial export sales record this quickly on its own.

• **Explore new export avenues.** Modi Xerox has tapped new markets, participated in major international trade fairs, and experimented with countertrade to increase exports. For example, it exported a consignment of 40 copiers to Zimbabwe under a collaborative arrangement with the Minerals and Metals Trading Corp, one of India's largest public trading houses.

69. Export Pricing

The following three factors are most frequently cited by international companies as impacting their export pricing strategies, according to S.

Tamer Cavusgil, director of an international business development program at Michigan State University, East Lansing, Michigan:

(1) Nature of product or industry.   A specialized product, or one with a technological edge, gives the firm price flexibility. In many markets there is no local production of the product, government imposed import barriers are minimal and importing firms all face similar price escalation factors. Under such circumstances, firms are able to remain competitive with little adjustment in price strategy.

A relatively low level of price competition usually leads to administered prices and a static role for pricing in the export marketing mix. In such instances, a skimming pricing is often utilized. Over the years, however, as price competition evolves and technological advantages shrink, specialized and highly technical firms must make more market-based exceptions to uniform export pricing strategies.

Fluctuations in raw material availability and price as well as predator pricing strategies by competitors (most notably the Asian NICs) are factors that demand greater flexibility in export pricing at some companies. Other companies negotiate fixed-price agreements with suppliers prior to making a contract bid.

(2) Location of production facility.   Many companies produce exported products in their home country. In some cases, exports are not large enough to justify foreign sourcing and manufacturing. In other cases, export trading zones make it financially feasible to keep manufacturing at home. The problem with this type of strategy is that the company is tied to conditions prevailing in the home market and thus reduces the company's local pricing flexibility. Economic, political and natural calamities have been known to take their toll and forced export prices up. The same can be said of trade embargoes that keep out needed raw materials and thus affect export prices.

Those companies that manufacture abroad, closer to export markets, often have greater pricing flexibility in overseas markets. Similarly, when production facilities are in great enough numbers, companies may choose to cease production until conditions improve. These companies find it easier to respond to foreign exchange fluctuations.

(3) Distribution system.   The channels of export distribution may dictate pricing strategies. Subsidiary relationships will offer greater control than distributor relationships. With independent distributorship, control usually extends only to the landed price received by the exporter.

Discount prices for intermediaries have to be established. Also, the costs associated with exporting (promotion, freight service, etc.) must be assigned to either the intermediaries or the manufacturer/exporter.

Manufacturing exporters obviously have much to gain from reducing the number of intermediaries between the manufacturer and the customer.

Alternative Approaches to Pricing

The three most common export pricing methods are: rigid cost-plus; flexible cost-plus; and dynamic incremental pricing strategies.

● **Rigid cost-plus.** The complexity of export pricing has caused many managers to cling to a rigid cost-plus pricing strategy in an effort to secure profitability. This strategy establishes the foreign list price by adding international customer costs and a gross margin to domestic manufacturing costs. The final cost to the consumer includes administrative and R&D overhead costs, transportation, insurance, packaging, marketing, documentation and customs charges, as well as the profit margins for both the distributor and the manufacturer. Although this type of pricing ensures margins, the final price may be so high that it keeps the firm from being competitive in major markets.

● **Flexible cost-plus.** This strategy is identical to the rigid strategy in establishing list prices. Flexible strategies, however, allow for price variations in "special" circumstances. For example, discounts may be granted, depending on the customer, the size of the order, or the intensity of local competition. The primary objective in this approach is profit. Thus, pricing is still a static element of the marketing mix.

● **Dynamic incremental.** This strategy is based on the assumption that fixed and variable domestic costs are incurred regardless of export sales success. Therefore, the only variable is the international customer costs that need to be recovered in export prices. This makes it possible to maintain profit margins while selling exported products at below domestic prices. (Note: this practice amounts to predator pricing and is illegal in some countries including the US.)

Strategies for Adjusting to Currency Fluctuations

● **Weak domestic currency**

● Stress price benefits;

● Shift sourcing and production to domestic market;

- Expand product line and add more costly features;

- Minimize local borrowing.

- **Strong domestic currency**

- Shift sourcing and production overseas;

- Trim profit margins and use marginal-cost pricing;

- Borrow locally;

- Give priority to exports to strong currency countries.

70. Using Supplier Relations to Boost Quality

Beginning in 1985 as an effort to improve product quality, US-based Baxter Healthcare Corp, an $8 billion manufacturer and marketer of health-care products and services, totally redefined and revamped its supplier relationships. The company has achieved major cost savings and quality improvements through a far-reaching program centered on an innovative concept known as "Valued Managed Relationships" (VMRs).

The original purpose of the VMR was to transform the traditional adversarial relationship between a company and its suppliers into a true partnership through unusually broad, profound and close cooperation. So successful have VMRs with suppliers been—Baxter now has many of them around the globe—that the company has begun transferring the concept to its relationships with customers (mainly hospitals) and is using these relationships in other corporate functions, notably product development and logistics.

Baxter seeks to manage the entire supply line using VMRs—from the supplier's supplier to the customer's customer. Baxter has begun on the supplier side, but even here the customer is king: All efforts at improvement are focused on the ultimate users' requirements. As Vernon R. Loucks, Jr., chairman and CEO, puts it, "We are no longer just in the business of selling products. We are in the business of helping our customers meet their profit objectives."

Suppliers that fulfill a formidable list of standards and requirements are given "certified" status. This means a supplier has a proven quality system that guarantees products meeting Baxter's requirements 100%

of the time. With certification, incoming inspection and testing at the company are virtually eliminated. Certified supplies are delivered on an as-needed basis directly from the supplier to Baxter's production lines.

Setting Up a VMR

Baxter has formulated a set of criteria and developed a structured process for selecting companies with which it will establish a VMR:

Strategic Fit. Baxter considers it essential that a VMR mesh with the overall business objectives and approach of both partners.

Mutual Benefits. The relationship must be a true win-win situation for both partners.

Long-term Commitment. Baxter views a VMR as a long-term commitment rather than a series of one-time deals. At first, Baxter agreed to one- or two-year commitments, but now requires at least five years because it believes real benefits come only after an extended period of cooperation. "To tell the truth, we are looking for partners that will work with us forever," says Loucks.

Flexibility. These relationships require changes in both companies' existing business practices and organization and demand a different mind-set from traditional attitudes. Such changes do not happen quickly.

For example, employees must consider the goals and needs of the VMR before those of their own department. And managers have to shed the pervasive attitudes that exist in the standard supplier-customer relationships: "Disclose as little as possible," and "your win is my loss."

The entire organizations of both companies are brought into the process. Working relationships are established and expanded at all levels, functional and staff, including top management. "Key people have to be involved early," says Jerry Arthur, vice president of distribution staff operations. "This is really important because people's jobs change as a result of these relationships."

Managing an Unfamiliar Relationship

At the outset, senior managers from both firms develop common goals, clarify and rationalize their respective requirements and define precisely what they expect from the VMR. These items are formalized in a "contract," which also forecasts the precise savings each side anticipates. (It is essential that, over time, the cost savings be reflected in lower prices.)

Partners must agree to share vast amounts of information, resources and systems, including detailed process control statistics. In some cases, the data exchanged are so integral to Baxter's or to its suppliers' operations that they enter into confidentiality agreements. Each VMR develops and introduces joint measurement systems to measure both quantitative and qualitative results, on the premise that an unmeasured activity cannot be properly managed.

Every Baxter department has a direct link with its counterpart at each partner. In addition, at the beginning, each VMR is assigned an account executive who coordinates the overall effort and advocates the VMR's interests in the face of employee resistance, which is almost inevitable. But if VMRs create difficulties for some, they have resulted in surprising and positive changes in employee attitudes.

5
Finance

71. How Finance Helps Allied-Signal Compete in Today's Global Market

Through acquisitions and divestments, Allied-Signal Corp, the $11 billion aerospace, specialty chemicals and automotive MNC, has forged a structure that it hopes will help it achieve the lowest costs of any producer in its global markets.

The New Role of Finance

Allied's efforts to remain competitive through dramatic restructuring had an enormous impact on the role of the CFO. The corporate raider phenomenon brought into sharp focus the importance of company valuation by proving that a going concern can be worth less than its assets. For corporate CFO Donald R. Kayser, the legacy of the takeover wave is the need for managers to ask themselves how they can run their businesses in a manner that creates as much value as a corporate raider could.

The finance function must determine why such a valuation gap might occur and recommend steps to narrow it. To enable the firm to pursue its long-term goals without sacrificing short-term performance, finance officers work jointly with operating officers to articulate corporate strategies and to evaluate their impact. Explains Kayser, "The finance function works with business units to prioritize strategies in line with overall financial objectives and to recast the strategies as circumstances change."

The higher profile of finance in the planning process makes strategy more dynamic and flexible, permitting the company to adjust quickly to changing circumstances, to capture new opportunities and to better quantify its objectives. The time horizon of the strategic plan has been effectively shortened from five years to three, with a very strong focus on the annual plan. The longer time frame of 10-15 years is considered a "strategic vision."

Financial Strategies

In addition to its role in strategic planning, the corporate finance function supports Allied's strategic goals by performing the following functions:

• **Reducing the cost of capital.** To raise cash for restructuring and to remain a low-cost producer, Allied urgently needed inexpensive money. To this end, Allied established a global fund-raising program that is managed centrally from its Morristown, New Jersey headquarters. "We try to capture windows of opportunity anywhere in the world and to arbitrage credit differentials between various markets," explains Roger Matthews, assistant treasurer corporate finance.

Vital to Allied's ability to tap global markets for low-cost funds is its single-A credit rating. To maintain this rating, Allied strives to keep its debt/capital ratio at 35%. Finance has compared the benefits of increased leverage with the drawbacks of a reduced credit rating and decided against adding more debt. This relationship and the pros and cons of debt are frequently revisited, however.

One reason Allied finds a steady A rating so important is that the company's radical transformations over the past few years have raised the risk of making its identity less clear to the markets. Explains Kayser, "While the CEO, the director of investor relations, senior operations executives and myself have worked very hard to convey to our US and foreign investors the company's strategic vision, the rapid pace of our acquisitions and divestitures have inevitably confused them." Allied's constant credit rating acts as an anchor amid rapid change.

• **Managing bank relations.** In addition to courting investors, Allied's finance department has had to manage relations with another valuable source of funding: the firm's banks. Allied has moved from transaction- to relationship-oriented banking in order achieve maximum benefits from its financing strategy. Purely negotiated deals are relatively infrequent, however. Allied typically opts for competition, using a restricted bidding process, one in which four or five institutions are invited to submit their bids. The invitations are meant not only to compensate banks for their quality of service, but also to reward those that have developed innovative financial ideas for the company. On the commercial banking side, Allied values access to significant, reasonably priced credit lines meant to provide credit capacity for extraordinary situations (e.g. a pending acquisition) even when market conditions are not favorable. This thinking reflects the company's strategic opportunism more than it does any large, day-to-day demand for bank credit. "We have a $2.4 billion revolving credit to back up our commercial paper program, but we rarely use more than $500 million at any one time," says Kayser.

- **Determining the best sourcing pattern.**   Global sourcing is critical to Allied's competitive position. For example, the firm has a profitable operation in Brazil that manufactures high-quality automotive components for operations in Europe and the US. The low-cost facility "is an important element in our ability to be competitive in all our geographic markets around the world," says Kayser. Allied also has large manufacturing units in Taiwan and Singapore for its electronics businesses. Sourcing decisions are business- (operations-) driven, but the CFO is intimately involved. "If you have manufacturing units in 20 countries around the world, the finance department must structure such operations financially, taking into account tax-effectiveness, cash flow and currency fluctuations," says Kayser.

- **Evaluating the performance of subsidiaries and their managers.**   The CFOs of each sector work closely with their general managers to evaluate the performance of operations. Top management sees market share, low costs and new-product development as the keys to good financial results. Given the dynamism of Allied's business strategies, however, specific performance measures are always changing. "We change performance yardsticks as our objectives evolve in response to the external environment," says Kayser.

Financial targets are set individually for each business unit and are constantly reevaluated. "We do not operate on the basis of a standard hurdle rate," says Kayser. "We feel our strategic and financial planners are sophisticated enough to deal effectively with each individual situation, taking into account both the specific circumstances of a unit and overall corporate objectives."

A significant judgmental input is also required to temper the inadequacy of the classic yardsticks, which include discounted cash flows, return on investment, internal rate of return, net income and return on assets. "How can you measure a business unit on the basis of unadjusted ROA," asks Kayser, "if you deal with an acquisition unit? What do you do with purchase accounting, the step-up and goodwill?" If one business unit has grown internally and the other has expanded through acquisitions, measuring both by the ROA standard is inconsistent. Similarly, the performance of a mature business run to generate cash flows must be measured differently from that of an embryonic business run for growth.

72. Critical Factors in Performance Evaluation for the 1990s

In surveying major corporations, BI found that the systems used for evaluating performance—that is, judging the success of both business units and their managers—often need to be brought up to date. However, firms should move cautiously before making any radical changes, because the findings show that even a seemingly minor modification in structure, strategy or reporting (made in response to the factors listed below) often has a domino effect on virtually every aspect of a company's evaluation system, from its profit centers to its performance indicators, standards of success and incentive plans.

When reevaluating their performance measurement systems, companies should take into account the effects of the following events or trends:

• **Rampant corporate restructuring.** Whether undertaken to foil takeover attempts or simply to improve a corporation's competitive position, restructurings typically involve some combination of acquisitions, divestitures, name changes, a thorough revamping of financial operations, downsizing and the elimination of layers of middle management.

• **Unprecedented wave of mergers and acquisitions.** At one extreme of the 1980s "merger mania" were the hostile takeovers of underperforming companies, usually accomplished through leveraged buyouts (LBOs), that left many of the LBO targets mired in high-cost debt. At the other extreme were the better financed, cross-border strategic acquisitions by global competitors to round out their international operations or gain a new technology or a strong brand name. Whatever the reason, restructuring has put many firms in a defensive posture and forced them to apply the same techniques to evaluating the performance of their business units that raiders use to value a target company's stock.

• **Weak US dollar.** Adding further impetus to the wave of hostile takeovers among US-bed MNCs was the weak-dollar environment that prevailed through the mid-1980s. The cheap dollar encouraged foreign investors to buy US corporations because it made the US a relatively low-cost manufacturing site. The result was a record number of foreign takeovers of US companies. Even firms not directly affected by the upsurge in M&A activity have found that a weak dollar dramatically complicates the process of evaluating business units. This is equally true for US subsidiaries of foreign-based parents and foreign subsidiaries of US parents.

• **EC single market initiative.** The competitive pressure spawned by the EC's 1992 integration plan has also contributed to merger fever. As the EC strives to eliminate economic boundaries and turn itself into a single market, companies based outside of the EC fear being "locked out." As a result, many are reassessing the strength of their European operations and the potential of European markets. However, the assessment process is further complicated by Europe's pending installation of its own multilateral financial system and by US businesses' increasing conversion to local currency, or European Currency Units (ECUs), as their functional currency under Financial Accounting Standards Board (FASB) Rule 52.

• **Globalization of the world's capital markets.** The stock market crash on Oct. 19, 1987 awakened both government and business to just how globalized and interdependent the world's capital markets have become. Because of this globalization, MNCs have new opportunities to raise funds in offshore capital markets; but differences in accounting and disclosure rules can make listings on overseas exchanges costly and challenging. For today's internationally oriented companies, gauging the response of investors — and not just those in the home country — has become a critical aspect of evaluating foreign operations.

• **Differences in accounting for acquired brands.** The heightened cross-border takeover activity of recent years has had yet another effect on MNCs, particularly consumer products manufacturers. Companies that have developed brands internally complain that the stock market does not adequately recognize the value of such brands. The reason is that a major asset — brand loyalty or customer goodwill — is omitted from the balance sheet unless a takeover occurs. The differences in treatment between acquired and internally developed brands distort the competitive and unit-to-unit comparisons needed for performance evaluation.

• **Latin American instability.** While the rest of the world coasted through a decade of disinflation, Latin America remained hyperinflationary. Maxidevaluations, double- and even triple-digit inflation, exchange controls and political instability combined to make doing business in the region especially difficult. "If you leave your cash in Latin America for too long," says Howard Goldstein, CFO of Xerox Corp's Latin American Group, "your money may not be worth much." Hence, many firms are taking special measures to incorporate cash flows into their performance evaluation systems for Latin America.

• **Global tax reform.**   Tax reform in many countries has changed the economics of manufacturing abroad for US firms. Thanks to the Tax Reform Act of 1986 (TRA86), the US has become something of a tax haven relative to other countries. Moreover, a growing number of US corporations find themselves saddled with excess foreign tax credits. As their incremental tax dollars now flow to foreign rather than to domestic tax authorities, these companies are determined to reassess both foreign operations and intercompany transfers much more closely, with an eye toward managing their taxes better at the local level.

• **Changes in US rules for accounting for taxes.**   After TRA86, new US accounting rules for taxes were introduced as part of FAS Rule 96. These rules require firms to switch from the deferral method of accounting for income taxes to the liability method. According to Tom Dodson, manager of Exxon's accounting policy division, "The net effect is a new element of increased volatility in corporate earnings, especially for multinational companies that use the US dollar as the functional currency." Reassessing foreign operations' performance in light of these new rules has become critical to identify tax-effective profit improvement ideas, such as possibly hedging forex translation gains and losses and shifting inventory around to help recover deferred tax assets.

73.   Revising Systems to Evaluate Performance

The dramatically changed nature of global competition that began in the 1980s led many MNCs to develop different strategies for each of their product lines. Often these strategies involve reorganizing profit centers and introducing new performance criteria. Interviews with senior executives point to critical issues firms must consider when devising new operating unit evaluation systems.

• **Adapting systems to strategy.**   For many corporations, the most difficult aspect of adapting their systems to strategy is determining how to balance multiple objectives, such as short-term shareholder profitability, against the long-term growth the company needs to remain competitive. Management's choices determine how the company defines its profit centers and key performance criteria. The changing business environment has resulted in a reevaluation of the standard for performance evaluation. Of the firms surveyed by Business International, 54% now use strategic business units (SBUs) as the basis for evaluating profitability, while 31% focus on subsidiaries. (Only a decade ago, 42% focused on subsidiaries for evaluation purposes, while 31% zeroed in on SBUs.)

In addition, companies that seek to maximize product quality often set specific quality standards as their prime performance criterion, while firms aiming to expand internationally are more concerned with volume or market share. The survey found that leading-edge firms increasingly view quality and cash flow as equally important.

• **Developing key performance indicators.** For most companies, defining performance measures is a continuing task. The result is considerable diversity in the way even the most common yardsticks (like ROS and ROA) are defined, as managements constantly revise traditional profit-based indicators to reflect factors their operating units can control. For example, as taxes have become less subject to control by local managers, some companies (e.g. Xerox) are putting pretax figures, rather than aftertax, into the numerators of calculations they use to measure ROS and ROA. Other MNCs are changing their indicators to conform to available competitive and industry averages. Perhaps most difficult, companies are struggling to develop criteria to measure such "intangibles" as quality, customer satisfaction and shareholder value.

• **Setting competitive standards of success.** How high to set the standards for successful business-unit performance can perplex companies operating internationally. Differences in accounting and disclosure requirements from country to country can make it almost impossible for firms to compare their criteria with those of their competitors. As a result, many rely primarily on internal unit-to-unit comparisons and analyses of historical data. However, with economic consulting firms developing data bases that overcome language and data availability problems, MNCs will increasingly be able to incorporate competitive and industry data into their planning processes.

• **Adjusting for external factors.** For most performance indicators, companies must find ways to account for environmental factors, especially those totally or partially beyond local managers' control. In addition to taxes, these include foreign exchange fluctuations, inflation and cash flow. For instance, firms whose many financial decisions are centralized need shared accountability for cash flows between headquarters and local management. This is particularly important because securities analysts are scrutinizing cash flows as a measure of shareholder value.

• **Adjusting for management factors.**   Although a majority of companies surveyed now view SBUs as their principal profit centers, the subsidiaries of many of these firms nevertheless retain traditional profit-center attributes. The result, which can be characterized as "profit centeritis," afflicts 78% of the companies in the survey.

To preclude this, MNCs must develop approaches to deal with the human element of management and give people credit for their accomplishments. An equitable sharing of costs and profits on intercorporate sales is one way; some firms use dual transfer prices, one for performance evaluation and another for external reporting. Another technique is pay-for-performance schemes that tie subsidiary incentives to SBU or overall company performance. Finally, matrix management systems may be the solution. These may be formal, such as Dow Chemical's organizational cube structure, or informal, like Ford's cross-functional teams and centers of responsibility.

• **Updating reporting systems.**   Major companies no longer have. the luxury of taking their time to meet competitive challenges. They need to find ways to obtain accurate performance data and organize the information so that business-unit managers can identify areas for improvement—and make the improvements quickly. For MNCs with newly restructured profit centers or new performance measurements, this task can be frustrating. The issue is not one of technology, but of cost-effectiveness and uniformity. As one controller notes, "A reporting system is only as good as its weakest link." His company has found it more cost-effective to continue using a "clunker" of a system for all its operating units, rather than try to adapt a state-of-the-art system to accommodate the special needs of smaller or just-acquired subsidiaries. Moreover, most corporate reporting systems were designed with only external reporting in mind. Some managers say that to expand their existing systems to include new performance measures would be so costly that it makes more sense to design entirely new systems.

74. How to Spot Attractive European Acquisition Candidates

How should companies go about hunting for potential acquisition candidates in Europe? On the following pages, leading investment bankers and fund managers in the UK and on the Continent reveal their views on which companies are attractive targets for acquisition:

- **Companies with strong cash flow and low debt levels.** Unless the acquiring company possesses sizable cash reserves of its own or is prepared to go out and raise new equity capital, acquisitions will necessarily be financed with debt. The resulting interest burden will be easier to bear if the acquired company can contribute a dependable cash stream to service it. At the same time, companies with low debt/equity ratios will not erode the balance sheet of the acquiring company once operations are fully integrated. One UK household products company, for example, enjoys a strong cash flow of about 46 per share, and its negative debt/equity ratio of about −20% would actually bolster the balance sheet of an acquiring firm.

- **Companies with high break-up value.** It is virtually impossible for would-be acquirers to uncover acquisition candidates that mesh perfectly with their own operations; so it is useful if the acquirer can spin off those units of the acquired company that are peripheral to the acquirer's own business. This allows the acquirer to maintain its strategic focus, and the proceeds of the sales can be used to pay down the debt arising from the original acquisition.

  In a surprising number of cases, the sum of an acquired company's parts is worth more than the company as a whole, because those parts can be integrated into a third company's business, creating synergies and economies of scale not previously realizable. Also, certain types of businesses command a higher market multiple than others. For example, the multiples of drug businesses are often twice that of companies in the food or leisure industries.

  The UK household products firm mentioned above is an attractive candidate from this viewpoint as well. According to a London-based analyst with Shearson Lehman, the company's break-up value is about 40% higher than its current market capitalization. This is due to the fact that the company possesses well-recognized brand names as well as valuable nonprescription drug and pharmaceutical businesses. Any one of these operations could be profitably divested on a stand-alone basis.

- **Companies whose shares are loosely held.** Some of the most attractive acquisition candidates in Europe are immune to takeover because another company, a family, or an individual holds a large percentage of the potential acquisition's shares. It is therefore difficult to acquire enough shares on the open market to engineer a general tender offer. Even if such an offer is possible, owners of major blocks of shares are likely to strike hard bargains for the surrender of their holdings.

It therefore makes sense to target firms in which at least a majority of the shares are "free floating." For example, 96% of the shares of one of France's largest manufacturers are loosely held. This, its modest market capitalization and its low price/earnings multiple of six make it an almost irresistible target.

• **Companies with succession problems.**   Exceptions to the above rule do exist, however. A number of family-owned or -controlled European businesses, built up after World War II, now find themselves without a suitable heir to assume the managerial helm. Some families want to realize the gains from their businesses and are looking to sell part of their companies or to cash out completely. There are also other family-owned businesses that do not have the critical mass necessary to succeed in the post-1992 environment and are therefore vulnerable to takeover.

• **Companies with weak management.**   Shareholders are likely to feel less loyalty to a management that they feel has not fully exploited the value of their assets. They are therefore likely to welcome the offer of an acquirer who promises to improve the company's ROA. For example, one UK chemicals firm has a market capitalization of about £250 million without any large protecting shareholdings, and, according to an analyst with Morgan Grenfell in London, "it doesn't have a very clear idea of its strategic future. If there were to be a bid, I don't think investors would flock to the present managers' defense."

• **Companies that stand to gain the most from 1992.**   Companies that already enjoy far-reaching European distribution networks will enjoy a leg up in the post-1992 environment, because so many of the trade barriers associated with cross-border shipping (like product differentiation and administrative red tape) will be eliminated. Other firms will become stronger after 1992, because companies in their industry had previously enjoyed unfair advantages granted them by nationalistic government procurement policies or EC quotas.

Dutch trucking firms, for example, could do a lot more business after 1992, says a European analyst for international money manager Baillie Gifford Overseas. The Netherlands is home to a number of major ports, making Dutch trucking firms natural candidates for providing surface transport throughout Europe. 1992 should see the end of barriers such as permits issued according to quotas that strictly control trucking between European nations. "Dutch transport firms have been losing out in order to protect German trucking firms, among others," says the analyst.

75. Operating in the EC
After 1992

Much has been written about how business strategies of both banks and industrial companies are changing in preparation for 1992. To find out how the chief financial officers and finance directors of companies operating within Europe are responding to the new challenges of 1992, BI, in conjunction with Peat Marwick, Midland Bank and Gotabanken, surveyed the role of finance in 300 EC and non-EC firms. The following are the key findings.

The Role of the CFO

● **An expanding role for the CFO.** As the European and, indeed, global environment become more competitive, it is not surprising that the CFO, as a member of the top management team, is getting more involved in the operating decisions of the company. Among EC respondents, the trend is particularly clear, with 69% of those responding saying that influence over operations has increased. Among non-EC respondents, only 56% agreed with this statement.

● **1992—A big yawn?.** Only 15% of Euro-CFOs ranked the 1992 program itself as a major factor in determining their role, compared with 18% for non-EC CFOs. Instead, the deregulation of many industries and the creation of common standards, especially on the technology side, are the chief factors determining the CFO's role.

● **Information technology is the key.** When asked about the key factor in determining their role, 55% of Euro-CFOs said it was the change in business information needs and technology. The response was particularly high among UK companies, where 66% marked the category. Grouped after this response were three other categories: increasing complexity of financial instruments and markets; needs of the board of directors, audit committees and shareholders, and corporate restructuring.

The EC response contrasts sharply with that of the non-EC CFOs for whom the top two factors shaping their role were globalization of business and financial markets and corporate restructuring. In their case, changes in business information needs was ranked fourth.

One important conclusion is that despite the much touted emergence of US style M&A on the continent, financial executives in Europe are more interested in using technology to sharpen competitiveness than merging with or acquiring other firms.

Enhancing Profitability and Competitiveness

• **People, the number one priority.** As the EC enters the baby-boom years, and as the mobility of European workers grows, 66% of Euro-CFOs chose cultivating a motivated staff as the priority their company should pursue in order to help it achieve overall business goals. In contrast, only 50% of non-EC companies checked this category.

Hard on the heels of staffing for European executives were (1) applying advanced technology, (2) increasing desired expansion route, (3) beating out joint ventures, (4) licensing arrangements and (5) widening distribution and marketing networks.

Financial Management

• **Centralized organization.** For European companies, the financial function is the most highly centralized of all the major corporate activities. Within the financial function, 69% of respondents stated that treasury, both domestic and international, was centralized. Financial planning (61%) and tax (58%) were also mostly centralized. In contrast, international accounting and control (47%) and domestic accounting and control (32%) were both relatively decentralized. In addition to being perceived as generally more efficient, the centralized nature of financial management in international companies is also contributing to the growing influence of the CFO.

• **Profit orientation.** Of the Euro-respondents, 77% indicated that the financial function is taking more of a profit-oriented approach than in the past. But this does not mean that the financial function now has its own P&L. Only 25% of respondents said that they had a P&L. Instead, the financial function is being evaluated according to how it helps operating units achieve their own profit goals (56% responded positively to this category).

• **Back to basics?** Despite the plethora of innovative financial products now offered by virtually every bank, the survey indicates that the corporate appetite for them is relatively weak. A vast majority of European respondents ranked their use of such financing tools as Euro-commercial paper (94%), Euro-equity (100%) and convertibles (93%) as either moderate or rare. On the risk management side, even the vaunted currency option, with its relatively liquid markets and plethora of applications, was used by only 20% of respondents.

Instead, companies in Europe are taking a back-to-basics approach to financial management. Political risk insurance (30%), term loans (25%) and syndicated loans (25%) were the most heavily used financial instruments. In terms of risk management, currency forwards and futures are still the most popular instrument, with 46% of respondents stating heavy use of this tool.

One of the biggest concerns for European financial executives is perhaps the most basic—cash management. After financial planning, Euro-CFOs consider cash management their second highest priority. Cash management services are also the most used tools. The reason is not hard to understand. Perhaps the biggest implication of 1992 for corporate financial managers is the abolition of capital controls among all EC states. Freer movement of capital, coupled with a host of new technologies, means that corporations will have the ability to move their funds in a more efficient manner within Europe than even before.

76. Project Selection: What Local Managers Should Know

The project-selection process can be a source of unnecessary frustration and wasted effort when managers in the field are not made aware of the methodology. As one Connecticut-based controller said, "The new people are out there making deals, trying to build new business. They don't like it when some manager sitting at headquarters simply tells them their project won't provide the required returns."

To help firms evaluate their own systems and communicate their rationale to their field, examples of the basics of project selection as practiced at 10 major MNCs in five different industries follow.

The Basics

All 10 multinationals take the same approach to investment analysis: They first determine a discount rate commensurate with the project's risk and then perform a net present value (NPV) analysis. Typically, the discount or hurdle rate used is the firm's minimum required return for domestic projects, plus a risk premium. This rate is necessarily subjective—more than one executive referred to its determination as an art rather than a science.

However, firms diverge on one key aspect: the types of cash flows considered. In general, firms whose projects feature high start-up costs typically reject cash flows beyond 10 years and completely ignore the potential value of blocked funds. Their rationale is that when significant capital is at risk, the investment analysis must be strict.

Less capital-intensive firms, on the other hand, adopt a longer cash flow horizon in their NPV analysis. Three major consumer goods producers considered cash flows of up to 15 years. These firms also typically included blocked funds, particularly in situations where the new investment was being made in a country where operations already existed. Said one controller, "We're often not concerned whether we can repatriate or not. The capital investment is negligible, so we're able to take a long-term approach."

The most controversial step in the risk-assessment process is the establishment of a hurdle rate. To make this admittedly subjective process more palatable to local managers, firms should develop a consistent approach. "That way, there's at least a perception of methodology," quipped one US firm's controller. For example:

• **Use risk-assessment services as a start.** However, these sources should not be considered the last word.

• **Follow up with local sources.** More often than not, a company is already doing business in the possible investment locale, either through a sales subsidiary or distributor. These can be extremely valuable sources of local information.

• **Set a project-specific hurdle.** The final risk premium should be based on the country but tailored to the project. For example, when a firm offers technology, hard-currency exports or employment valued by the government, its premium should be commensurately lower. One manager uses a hurdle-rate matrix. The process begins with a country's basic risk premium (using a published reference), which is then increased or decreased according to the specific situation.

77. Nine Essentials for
Sound FX Policy

For many of the fastest-growing firms in the US, FX management has become a key issue. To help such firms map their attack plans more effectively, treasury managers around the country put together the following checklist of nine critical foreign exchange strategy points for firms to consider:

(1) Appoint a full-time risk manager. Craig Shular, manager of foreign exchange risk at Union Carbide, contends that risk management is a full-time commitment. "When the market moves, someone has to be there." However, other managers disagree. Says one assistant treasurer, "We just don't have the volume." Says another, "I'd be lucky to get anyone, let alone someone with years of trading experience."

It is true that with the volatility of today's markets, the risk manager needs to stay on top of things. However, where it isn't practical for a firm to devote a single person full time to risk management, then a compromise must be made. In these cases, one person, at the very least, should be designated as the risk manager.

As part of this responsibility, the manager should always be aware of any key announcements or events likely to affect the markets. At the very least, he should be required to monitor the day's occurrences, the firm's outstanding contracts, and net foreign currency positions at least twice daily (in the morning and evening).

(2) ...then give him the ball. Effective risk management cannot be performed by committee. The risk manager must be free to act as the market dictates. A common mistake made by many growing firms is to add excess layers of management control over foreign exchange dealings. If a company isn't comfortable with its choice of forex risk manager, the solution is a new risk manager—not a cumbersome approval process.

(3) Establish clear trading policies. Just as too much control can be detrimental to a hedging program, so is too little. No matter how competent or trustworthy he is, the company must ensure that the risk manager is aware of the parameters within which he is required to work.

To begin with, the risk manager should be shown those specific exposures that the company wants him to manage. He should also be given a specific "open position" tolerance acceptable to the firm's management. Policies should also state the instruments the risk manager is permitted to use, the banks with which he is allowed to deal, even the number of quotes he should solicit on each transaction. Finally, all policies should be made available in a written manual.

(4) Set loss limits. Worth discussing separately from other policies, prudent loss limits are a critical element in any risk management program. While the risk manager should be free to operate, the company should still establish some point at which a losing position must be closed. This could be set as either a percentage of the total position or as a fixed dollar amount. The actual level can be determined by a company's board or finance committee.

While loss limits are essential, they should also be somewhat flexible.

In the volatile world of foreign exchange, short-term aberrations moving counter to long-term trends are commonplace. As a consequence, loss limits are the one place where companies should establish multiple approval levels. If the risk manager can demonstrate just cause as to why a losing position should be kept open, a manager at the next level (say the treasurer) should be empowered to allow the position to run. Firms should set higher loss limits for each successive level of management, with the CFO having the final say.

In tandem with those loss limits, the risk manager must also be shown that it is in fact all right to generate a loss. If the environment is such that the risk manager faces dismissal each time a position loses, he will be tempted to disguise losses—or worse, to play a round of "double-up to catch up."

(5) Keep the banks' interest—don't shop. One way to help the risk manager gain information and expertise is to maintain good relations with supporting banks. A banker convinced that he is building a long-term relationship with a growing firm can be quite helpful. On the other hand, if the bank is given the impression that a risk manager is merely "shopping," any pools of extra assistance will quickly dry up.

"The mistake I made," explains one former risk manager from a West Coast middle-market firm (now a consultant), "is that I bid everything out." The consultant says his error was in doing the right thing with the wrong volume of business. "When you have such a small transaction volume, the bankers are almost doing you a favor." By trying to price his deals too aggressively, the consultant "wound up with a lot of angry, unsympathetic, unhelpful bankers." His advice today? "Keep them honest, but value the relationship more than the price."

(6) For added control, communicate your firm's trading policies to the bank. "We've told our bank traders what our procedures are," explains a Santa Clara-based high-tech firm's assistant treasurer. "If they detect any deviation, and it even hints at foul play, a call goes into our treasurer."

To keep tight control on things, firms should ask for a daily return transmission of all activity with any bank, use recorded lines and consider requiring two signatures for any transaction.

(7) Go slow, be conservative. The last thing a new risk management function needs is to make a critical mistake in the early stages. For this reason, the West Coast consultant recommends that "if at any time you think you are making a mistake, stop. If you do not know what you are doing, stop."

Furthermore, the consultant believes that firms just starting in the area should use the simplest hedges. "You should stick to those exposures accepted by FASB," he says. "Stick with known contracts—don't do forecasted cash flows or proxy hedging."

(8) Use options. One surprising point in Union Carbide's Shular's policy recommendations is his belief that growing firms should get involved with options right from the start. He recommends that firms use options to cover 40-50% of their exposures. "Forward contracts are extremely unforgiving instruments," says Shular. A banking snafu, for example, could hold up a payment from a foreign customer for a week—but the foreign exchange to cover the forward will be deliverable on the specified maturity date, snafu or not.

What firms miss most by sticking to forwards, however, are opportunities to profit from currency movements. For instance, a firm that acquired forward contracts only two months ago at Y134:$1 has accepted a huge opportunity loss—with the yen at Y124:$1. "This will never show up in the financial statements," says Shular, "but it's a loss just the same."

(9) Invest in a solid reporting system. Finally, as much for strategic reasons as for control, Shular believes that management should have ready access to the FX position of the company. "Reports should show exactly what contracts have been opened, what is underlying, what the gains and losses are on the individual positions—and what the risk profile of the entire portfolio looks like." The availability of such information not only assists risk managers in refining or repositioning their portfolio but also "motivates the FX manager to adhere to stated strategy and policies."

78. Professional FX Management: The Pitfalls of Outside Help

Some companies bring in outside professional firms to handle FX management. While FX managers agree that this system suits the needs of some companies, they warn of the pitfalls involved in hiring outside help:

• **Meeting an objective.** The combination of in-house and outside management works only if it meets the MNC's overall objective. "If the goal is to minimize risk, in-house management may be best," says the FX manager of a computer MNC that hired outside help a few years ago. The outside help was dropped when the MNC formalized a risk averse forex strategy and opted for 100% cover when possible. A 100% cover or zero cover were judged less costly and more effective. There was also less of a need to keep an active watch over the markets.

• **Trading room mentality.**   When picking a manager, it is important to pick professional FX management that focuses only on the company's specific needs. Some commercial banks have tried to trade clients' money along with their own. "But the trading desk is not the right place to manage other people's money," warns one banker. "It's a fiduciary rather than a trading responsibility. The trader is basically out there for himself."

• **Losing out on expertise.**   "If 30% or 40% of your revenues are coming from overseas, then it makes sense to keep close watch on the market," says the FX manager at an electronics MNC. MNCs can gain market intelligence and information only by doing their own trading and management. "Bankers know where there's volume to be had and are willing to give you better information. By letting someone else do the active work, you run the risk of becoming dated," he says.

The FX manager of a consumer products MNC agrees: "Our trading is a window into the capital markets. Shutting it means slowing flows of information. You will not build up your own expertise."

• **Meaningful gain.**   Some FX managers argue that giving an outside professional only a small chunk of the business makes little difference. "If you don't give them a big chunk, then the gains are irrelevant," notes one. Adds one manager, "If you're right, you don't have any planning benefits because you weren't planning on being right. You cannot count on profit."

• **Conflicts of interest.**   Splitting your exposure with outside experts may lead to taking opposite positions, fears one FX management consultant. And an MNC also runs the risk of giving money to an institution that is primarily in the business of trading. "They may not make a profit on your position, but, at the same time, they may be writing contracts with themselves and playing against your position," the consultant warns.

79. Putting FX in Its Place: Volvo's Profit-Center Approach

Firms that have organized their currency-trading operations as profit centers generally keep the FX function within corporate treasury. A few of these companies have set trading off as a separate division outside of corporate treasury. But Volvo AB, the Swedish automaker, has taken the profit-center approach to FX management one step further. The firm spun off its foreign exchange management to a newly created, wholly owned financial services subsidiary, Fortos, severing the link between the headquarters and the profit center by creating an independent company.

How It Works

• **Earnings**. Fortos earns most of its profits from two types of operations. First, the firm takes positions for its own account in the foreign exchange markets. "We are the internal bank for all currency dealings within the Volvo group in Sweden," notes an executive. Second, it deals extensively in the money markets, engaging in interest rate arbitrage. It also handles short-term funding needs and short- and long-term cash investment.

• **Control**. Like any subsidiary, Fortos has an annual budget, a balance sheet and an income statement, for all of which Fortos management is fully responsible. Fortos' profit-center status compelled it to adopt stringent control policies to ease management — and auditor — concerns about security. Overall risk limits and strategy are established by Fortos' board of directors, which mainly comprises financial management representatives from other companies within the Volvo group.

On a day-to-day basis, each dealer reports the closing position and the results of the day's trading. Each time a deal is completed, the dealer fills out a slip, which is then entered into a computer system by back-office personnel. The dealers' reported results are then compared against the computer tallies, which are later compared with bank confirmations.

• **Activities**. The separate companies within the Volvo group (Volvo Car Corp, Volvo Truck Corp, etc.) must deal through Fortos. Each company devises its own hedging policy. That policy is then reviewed by Fortos as well as by Volvo's upper management. Ultimate approval of the policy comes from Volvo management. "We cannot tell a company they must hedge," says a Volvo manager. "We can only advise them. We cannot decide."

The individual companies of the Volvo group receive better forex quotes from Fortos than they would if they dealt on their own with outside banks. Fortos obtains thinner spreads for the companies because it nets out the flows from the different companies within the group and pools the resulting transactions, thus ensuring it obtains the best market rate from the banks.

Why a Separate Subsidiary?

Volvo advances seven reasons why it adopted this particular approach to foreign exchange management:

(1) Trading is not a headquarters function.   The main reason for the move was Volvo's organizational philosophy. The view of the company is that headquarters should be devoted to strategic concerns. Trading currencies is not really a strategic function, so it does not belong at headquarters. "Headquarters should be a very slim organization occupied with the overall strategy and care of the Volvo group," says a company financial executive. "The decision whether to sell dollars in the morning or in the afternoon is not a question for the head office."

On the other hand, there are substantial benefits to be had from centralizing the trading operation in terms of netting cash flows and obtaining better pricing. Fortos resolves this dilemma for Volvo.

(2) It builds staff professionalism.   Aside from serving the industrial interests of the Volvo group, the principal objective of Fortos is to enhance the efficiency of its foreign exchange operation and the competence of its operatives. Volvo believes that the only way to build that competence is to be immersed in the market all the time—and that requires Fortos' dealing for its own account. "You cannot really learn the trade and the tricks of the market if you have to wait around for someone in the commercial group to do something and generate an exposure before you can go to work," says an executive at Volvo.

One common criticism of the profit-center approach to FX management is that industrial companies should concentrate on their core products and leave the financial sector to banks and other players. Volvo officials insist, however, that professionalism in the financial area is important for any industrial company.

"It is true that Volvo is a maker of cars and trucks," one says. "But the most important component of the car is money. When we make a car, we get paid for it—and somebody has to handle that. We are involved in finance whether we like it or not. Should we just turn our business over to the banks and let them run it?"

(3) It permits new business opportunities.   The creation of Fortos marked the launching of a whole new business area for Volvo: finance.

Fortos is now the parent company of a Stockholm-based brokerage firm and a finance company in Geneva. As an independent company, Fortos can capitalize on business opportunities within the financial services sector. "We are free to move into new businesses when we see an opportunity," officials say.

(4) It provides hiring flexibility. Fortos' status as a separate company gives it more flexibility in hiring practices. Recruiting FX dealers at higher wage levels than, for example, operational management can cause resentment inside the company. But since Fortos is an independent company, this potential sore spot is eliminated.

This hiring flexibility is especially important in Sweden. Through its independent status, Fortos is released from some of the hiring constraints facing the Volvo group as a whole. Volvo—as part of an employers' organization—negotiates a wage agreement with its unions. Fortos, however, is not bound as tightly by that agreement. "If you were to pay people according to the overall agreement, you would not get any dealers," says one finance executive. "We are not as free as a bank or a broker, and we must consider the way Volvo is handling these questions...but we do have greater flexibility."

(5) It preserves independence from the banks. The Swedish corporate banking market is, to a large extent, divided between the two dominant Swedish banks: Svenska Handelsbanken and Skandinavishka Enskilda Banken. "Volvo has never been a part of either sphere," the company notes. "This independence is something Volvo values very highly. This independent stance requires continuous improvement in our own financial competence."

(6) It allows for better performance evaluation. Fortos stands or falls on its budget results, just like any other area of the company. This approach focuses responsibility for foreign exchange management and makes the costs and the results of the dealing operation easier to track. "Every cent is measured for whatever we do," says a Volvo official. "That information sometimes gets lost in the overall activities of a big company that relegates exchange management and makes the costs and the results of the dealing operation easier to track."

(7) It allows for faster decisionmaking. With the wide hourly swings in today's exchange markets, the ability to capitalize quickly on market opportunities is essential. A profit-center organization allows dealers to act on their own judgment without waiting for official approval, which could hobble dealer performance.

80. Grass-Roots FX: The
Billing Approach of Six Firms

Determining the appropriate currency of denomination to be used for receivables and payables will have a large effect on a company's exposure profile. The rule of thumb is to bill in currencies trading at a premium to the corporation's base currency. Conversely, companies should try to pay in a discount currency.

This is difficult to do in the real world, however. Worse, it may not be the best thing for the company as a whole. A firm that is flexible about the currency in which it bills is often at a distinct competitive disadvantage; and although a company may have more bargaining power as a buyer than as a seller, it may still be forced to accept the supplier's preferred currency of billing if that supplier offers the best materials or the most reliable service.

Six Pointers

Below, FX managers at six major US MNCs reveal six guidelines on how their companies decide on currency of billing.

● **Put marketing considerations first**.   The cardinal rule is to never let exposure considerations get in the way of doing business. According to Craig Shular, manager of foreign exchange risk for Union Carbide, the primary concern is getting the customer to sign the contract. "We will always offer him the opportunity to be billed in his home currency, in the US dollar or in any other currency of his choice." Shular says that a third currency will often fit customer's books. A number of Union Carbide's Soviet customers request billing in Austrian schillings because they have an offsetting receivable in that currency.

A company's bargaining position with regard to currency of billing will also depend on the competitiveness of its particular market. According to David Guthrie of Monsanto, "In a competitive marketplace, there isn't a lot of flexibility to force the customer to take your currency." Business considerations take precedence on the payables side too, even though the company has more power to dictate currency of billing. "Our local and regional purchasing departments get their directives from the worldwide product areas," says John McColley, cash manager for international operations for Texas Instruments. "They must seek out the best source of supply regardless of the currency in which they'll be billed."

● **Build the hedge cost into the price....**   When a firm is forced to bill in a discount currency, it should try to quote a price that reflects the forward points. In that way, its hedging cost is covered by the sale price. "But that is not always possible," says Shular. "If we really want the business, we will often take the exposure onto our foreign exchange book and manage it."

At companies where treasury takes a hands-off approach to currency of billing, however, forward points are not factored into prices by local operations. "It would be gambling on their part to include currency as a benefit in setting prices," reports McColley, "because the number of forward points can change between the time the sale is negotiated and the time it is settled."

● **...but don't forget to look at your own book**. A company's existing portfolio of exposures can open up competitive advantages in terms of currency of billing. If a company can take on a receivable that offsets an existing payable, then it need not build the hedging cost into the quote. That can allow the marketing people to offer a more competitive bid.

"We listen to the customer's desire first," says Union Carbide's Shular. "But if we feel we can be very competitive in a particular currency because of a position on our books, we will bring that to his attention." Similarly, at FMC, the chemicals and equipment manufacturer, treasury is quick to alert the marketing group to currencies in which the firm can offer attractive quotes. "We look at it as a portfolio of exposures, not transaction by transaction," says Foreign Exchange Coordinator Mark Ahn.

Some companies, however, think they are better served by a transaction-by-transaction approach. In that way, the appeal of a particular sale does not depend solely on a foreign exchange play. According to James R. Johnson, director of foreign exchange at SmithKline Beckman, "We prefer that third-party transactions stand on their own economic merit, which does include foreign exchange risk; foreign exchange risk can be managed, though, and is not necessarily a factor if an offsetting position already exists."

● **Don't trade FX risk for credit risk**. Not only does billing in the firm's home currency put the company in a poorer competitive position, "it isn't necessarily the safest thing to do," says Monsanto's Guthrie. "If you are dealing with a small customer in a foreign country, and you try to make him pay in dollars, you aren't necessarily eliminating currency risk. If there is a significant move in the currency, your customer may not be able to pay you, and you have created a credit risk." According to Guthrie, billing in dollars in this case merely disguises the exposure. It does not eliminate it.

• **Try to book in liquid currencies**.   If a company cannot bill entirely in its currency of choice, it should make every effort to bill and be billed in currencies that have liquid forward markets. For instance, at California-based toymaker Mattel, there is very little in the way of imports or exports to third parties. The company has toy-manufacturing companies in the US, Canada and Europe. All intercompany payables and receivables that arise from transactions between the Asian manufacturing subsidiaries and the marketing companies are denominated in US dollars.

Although this exposes the Canadian and European subsidiaries to movements in the US dollar, Assistant Treasurer Bill Stavro feels these exposures are easier to manage than payables denominated in Hong Kong dollars and Malaysian ringgits. Moreover, as long as the Hong Kong dollar is pegged to the US unit, the Hong Kong subsidiary will be relatively immune to US dollar moves. The risk of a significant appreciation of the ringgit against the US dollar is also not great, according to Stavro.

For other companies, life is not so easy. Extensive dealings with third parties mean these companies accumulate exposures in less liquid currencies. FMC, for instance, naturally prefers to quote in the major currencies, but it has often taken on exposures in blocked currencies in order to win business, using countertrade and other techniques to hedge those exposures. "Of course there is a premium attached to quotes in those currencies that reflects the risk we have assumed," says Ahn.

Texas Instruments also often finds itself with receivables in blocked currencies or in units belonging to countries that limit forward market access to domestic companies. In Taiwan, however, the firm is able to deal in the domestic forward market, because the local subsidiary qualifies as a resident firm. In other currencies for which no forward market exists, McColley reports that most multinational banks will structure some product — usually a dollar-indexed investment — that makes it impossible for the company to hedge its risk.

• **Look at financing opportunities**.   When a company does have some choice in its currency of billing, it should look at the comparative costs of financing in the different currencies before making its decision. For instance, Mattel has a manufacturing operation in Italy that invoices its intercompany receivables in ECUs. "The Italy operation can use those export earnings to finance itself in ECUs at a lower interest rate than it can in lira," says Stavro.

81. Measuring Your Exposure to Interest Rate Risk

Major corporations around the world are focusing more intently on interest rate risk management than ever before. As with managing any risk, the first step in hedging interest rates is defining the exposure. In the past, companies have tended to focus on debt ratios—particularly the ratio of floating to fixed-rate debt—as the major factor in determining their risk. They have also focused on their long-term debt portfolio. More sophisticated treasurers, however, are moving to a bottom-line definition of exposure and concentrating on their entire debt portfolio. "Previously, people targeted X% of debt that should be floating or fixed," says Somerset Waters, assistant treasurer at Black & Decker, the worldwide small-appliance and tool manufacturer. "But the percentage of fixed-rate debt does not really tell us anything in terms of the impact on net earnings."

Below are four principal definitions of bottom-line interest rate exposure, garnered from 10 interviews with corporate interest rate hedgers:

• **Future borrowing needs.** According to this limited definition, a firm is exposed between the time it makes the decision to borrow and the time the actual borrowing occurs. For example, one US-based maker of industrial products that is only in the preliminary stages of adopting an interest rate risk management policy makes a distinction between "debt management" and "interest rate management." Debt management concerns the actual decision to borrow and the composition of the corporate debt portfolio in terms of currency, maturity and instrument. The firm constructs a three-year plan and a one-year budget, as well as detailed quarterly forecasts. Each of those documents outlines projected borrowings and interest costs. Interest rate management tries to ensure that the actual cost of borrowing is at or below the planned interest expense.

As with foreign exchange management, the closer future transactions are to occurring, the easier they are to hedge. But if rates dropped significantly in the next six months, says the company's manager of international treasury, "we would take advantage of that to secure borrowing for the next two years. If those rates gave us a good internal rate of return on the projects that had been approved and would be implemented in the next three years, then we would go ahead and do it."

• **Floating-rate liabilities.** This is a slightly broader definition of exposure than the one above. In addition to future borrowing needs, it embraces existing floating-rate liabilities as well. Mattel, the US-based toymaker, has a high degree of seasonal borrowings it knows it will incur each year because of the cyclical nature of its business. However, it also faces a longer-term risk on its outstanding money market preferred shares. The dividend rate on these shares is reset periodically, based on the US CP rate. Mattel uses swaps to hedge that risk. It also has a long portfolio of outstanding fixed-rate bonds that it does not regard as exposed.

- **The gap.** This is the classic financial institution definition of interest rate exposure. The gap is measured as interest-rate-sensitive assets minus interest-rate-sensitive liabilities. Black & Decker includes both short-term and long-term floating-rate debt less any floating-rate deposits it has, split out by currency, in this calculation. It applies a current interest rate to that amount, and multiplies the result by 100% minus the applicable tax rate to get an aftertax amount of interest expense. It then determines how various possible moves in interest rates would affect that amount.

For financial institutions, the gap is relatively easy to measure, since all of their floating-rate assets have predictable lives and well-defined interest rate sensitivities. For an industrial corporation, however, noncash asset life and interest rate sensitivity is necessarily subjective. Northern Telecom Inc, the Canadian telecommunications company's US subsidiary, opts to include not only the financial assets of its captive finance company when it measures the gap, but the assets of its manufacturing company, as well. "We do asset-life and interest-rate-sensitivity analyses of the manufacturing side of the business," explains Greg Grego, director of corporate finance, "but it is rule-of-thumb oriented and not very precise." The company's interest rate exposure stems from the mismatch in asset/liability maturities.

The "fuzziness" in measuring the gap for an industrial corporation has allowed corporate hedgers more latitude to take positions in the market. "The life-of-asset concept is not the sole basis for determining what one's capital structure should be," says Michael Rulle, managing director and cohead of Shearson Lehman's primary capital markets area. Because asset life is a subjective measure, companies will structure their debt portfolio to reflect their individual view of the financial market, as opposed to taking a strict hedging perspective.

- **Opportunity cost.** This is the broadest and most aggressive definition of exposure, because it encompasses a company's fixed-rate as well as floating-rate debt. Companies using opportunity cost calculate their exposure not only as the bottom line impact on interest expense from carrying variable-rate debt in a rising-rate environment, but also as the opportunity cost of carrying fixed-rate debt in a downward environment. "We have $500 million in floating-rate debt and $1 billion in fixed-rate debt," says Dave Bodick, manager of capital markets at Amax, the Connecticut-based mining concern. "As far as I am concerned, I have $500 million to manage in an upward-rate environment and $1 billion to manage in a downward-rate environment."

Since opportunity cost will not show up as a separate item, it becomes more difficult to assess the risk manager's performance. Measured against budgeted interest expense, the manager has an incentive to keep fixed-rate debt in place, and the company could end up paying more than it must for funding. At Amax, one key measure of success is the average effective borrowing cost for the period, which is a combination of actual borrowing rates and hedging gains or losses. If the firm's interest rate view is correct, then its mix of fixed- and floating-rate debt will bring down the average interest cost and the hedging instruments in place will move into the money.

82. Setting Policies for Hedging Interest Rate Risk

The increased attention paid to interest rate risk management has persuaded a number of firms to codify their interest-hedging philosophy into manuals organized along the lines of FX policy manuals. "We have a clearly defined policy of what we want from FX management," says the manager of international treasury at a US manufacturer that is just starting to set up an interest-hedging program, "and we have decided that we want the same thing for interest rates." These policy statements not only define risk, but also determine what hedging instruments are to be used and when, which people are empowered to do the hedging, what position limits should be set for any single instrument and for the overall strategy, and what credit risks are acceptable.

Key Policy Questions

Interviews with 10 corporate interest rate hedgers about hedging policies reveal that while many have not yet written an actual manual, there are five key policy questions that concern all of them.

(1) What is your threshold of pain?   Once the exposure is identified, a hedging policy must be developed. The worldwide tool and small-appliance manufacturer Black & Decker, for instance, reviews its risk monthly but does not have a formal hedging policy at present. "It really takes a humongous amount of net variable-rate debt before you get a significant impact on net earnings," says Assistant Treasurer Somerset Waters. "As opposed to foreign exchange transactions, the principal amount of the transaction here is not at risk—only the net interest expense. We haven't formalized a policy because that risk is not as meaningful as other risks that the company faces."

At Northern Telecom Inc (NTI), the Canadian telecommunications firm's US subsidiary, the consideration of interest risk is different. When the budget plans are submitted, the corporate finance staff determines an absolute dollar level that it regards as an acceptable interest rate hit. How is that number determined? "It's not very scientific," says Director of Corporate Finance Greg Grego. "We ask people what they can live with." The firm's hedging objective is to reduce the amount of volatility in interest expense and to keep deviations from budgeted interest costs within the set parameters without incurring excessive cost. The firm could eliminate the deviation entirely by hedging everything, but it chooses to leave some positions open when the costs for a hedge are deemed excessive or when it makes sense within the context of the whole debt portfolio.

(2) What is the appropriate role for external hedging? As with foreign exchange exposure, there are a number of internal measures firms can take to reduce exposure before they pick up the phone to put on a hedge. With interest rate exposure, this primarily means an ongoing examination of the term structure of the debt and the asset/liability structure of the company. The hedging policies of Amax Inc, the US metals and energy company, focus on the term structure and the mix of its fixed- and floating-rate debt, as well as on external interest hedging instruments. NTI conducts a formal quarterly review of the asset/liability structure of its captive finance company and then considers how it might change its liabilities to match the asset structure more closely. "If it is expensive to rebalance, or if we don't like the market conditions for a new issue, then we use the interest rate hedging tools," says Grego.

Both these companies estimate that they do much more hedging than term-structure management or liability restructuring. David Bodick, manager of capital markets at Amax, for instance, says that his short-term interest rate hedging on a day-to-day basis is 70-80% external instruments and 20-30% term-structure management. "You can do just so much with the term structure," he says. A significant portion of Amax's long-term debt is fixed rate, thus commanding less attention in the upward-rate environment of the last few months. Grego offers a similar 80% estimate for the proportion of external hedging done at NTI. "It is quick and inexpensive to do a hedge, so you can fix a problem right away. That gives you time to put together a deal and launch it when the market is receptive."

The role of external hedges can be limited in foreign markets, a problem that firms will feel more acutely as their debt portfolios become more global. For instance, the portfolio of short-term debt for California-based toymaker Mattel is mixed because foreign operations contract their own local borrowings. Until now, the firm hedged only its US interest rate exposure because of the greater development of the dollar market in forward rate agreements (FRAs). Starting next year, however, it will begin to use FRAs in Hong Kong dollars.

(3) What proportion of the exposure should be hedged? Firms tend to be less cautious with interest rate hedging than they are with FX hedging. As a result, many companies do not have explicit positions on this question, preferring to let their risk managers cover according to their view of the market. The main reason for this, as Black & Decker's Waters points out, is that FX cash flows are usually far larger and more directly linked to a firm's sales and revenues than are interest costs.

Mattel, however, has established a fixed percentage for the interest exposure it wants covered. The company has set an interest-hedging policy for its international treasury department that closely parallels its FX hedging policy. Mattel considers a 50% cover position to be a neutral stance. It covers half of its net FX exposure and half of its US dollar interest rate exposure. The 50% hedge policy has been in place for FX for the past three years, but it was extended to cover interest rate exposure just this year.

(4) What instruments should be used? There are a number of crucial issues to consider when answering this question, including basis risk, liquidity, familiarity and the goals of the hedging policy. Many industrial corporations, for example, do not feel comfortable with the margin calls, exchange requirements and other administrative hassles of interest rate futures. Familiarity developed through the forex hedging markets may also influence the choice of instrument. In its policy, Mattel stresses the similarity between FX and interest rate hedging: It uses currency swaps for long-term FX exposures and interest rate swaps for long-term interest rate exposures. For short-term FX exposures, Mattel uses forward contracts; the counterparts on the interest rate side are FRAs.

The objective of the hedging policy also has a lot to do with Mattel's choice of instruments. "We have used futures and options in the past," says Assistant Treasurer Bill Stavro. "But we feel that our current 50% hedge strategy addresses the objectives that those instruments attempt to address." Mattel feels that a 50% cover leaves the upside open for favorable moves while shielding the company from most of the downside risk, thus emulating most of the effect of an option while avoiding the option premium. Stavro points out that analysts usually compare options with forwards when both are used to cover 100% of an exposure. After running simulations comparing an option strategy with forward cover on only 50% of the exposure, the firm concluded that the latter strategy was more cost-effective and offered roughly the same degree of protection.

Finally, liquidity is a major issue in the choice of instruments. That is why some active interest rate hedgers favor financial futures. A futures hedge can be put on quickly and easily removed. "If you are uncomfortable with futures," says Amax's Bodick, "you will spend more time trying to adjust the term structure." Amax's policy, primarily for liquidity reasons, is to stay away from the more exotic financial engineering offered by financial institutions. "If we don't see a continuing need for the hedge, we lift it," says Bodick. "So we tend to stay with things that have a well-established secondary market."

(5) What are appropriate hedging and trading limits?   Beyond the empowerment and control issues involved with any trading operation, it is crucial that a company establish risk parameters within which the risk manager can operate. Although the default rate on swaps is historically quite low, acceptable counterpart credit risk was catapulted to the forefront of treasury managers' concerns after the 1987 stock market crash. "We are very concerned about credit risk," says Bodick. "On an FRA or a swap, we would do that with a top-tier, high-quality bank."

Some companies also put in policies about the amount of exposure that can be hedged with a particular type of instrument, expressed either as a total dollar amount or in terms of the number of contracts. Those limits change as the magnitude of the exposure changes. At Amax, for instance, the allowable number of outstanding contracts is the primary short-term hedging policy guideline, and it will vary depending on the interest rate outlook and the current mix of fixed- and floating-rate borrowings. Other companies, however, put no restrictions on the amount of exposure that can be hedged with a particular instrument.

83. Tips on Building a Global Shareholder Base

In an effort to build a worldwide shareholder base and gain access to new low-cost funds, MNCs are busy tapping foreign investors. Firms skilled in amassing a pool of global shareholders say success rests on building a solid presence and image in the market. In addition to the all-important factors of timing, share price, profit performance and the balance sheet, executives prescribe a well-developed marketing strategy. Companies cannot simply rely on a "triple-A" credit rating from Moody's or Standard & Poor's to pique the interest of potential foreign investors. Following is a checklist of ingredients to use to build a global shareholder base.

- **Build and maintain a consistent information and advertising campaign.** For Ralph Amborsino and Jerry Hostetter, investor relations experts at GTE Corp and PepsiCo, respectively, one crucial ingredient to success is providing a *steady* stream of information to current and potential shareholders. One of the biggest mistakes companies make is to stage an elaborate dog-and-pony show one or two months prior to an issue, then forget about the investors until the next issue. Remarks Amborsino, "We find it crucial to keep the GTE name in the minds of the foreign investor. We periodically hold presentations, generally making an annual trip to each foreign financial center and perhaps visiting the major foreign markets two or three times a year."

  Another mistake, according to Amborsino and consultant Tim Dawson, director of T.R. Dawson and Co (UK), is that US MNCs often waste time and money by showing off the top brass (a popular ploy on Wall Street) before they distribute the necessary written literature and financial data on the company. Japanese and European investors care less about glitz than about having hard-core facts at their fingertips.

- **Tell the market what it wants to know.** It is important to target the campaign to the specific information needs of investors in each foreign financial center. A consumer food and drink manufacturer (Company A) finds European investors attach great significance to management; hence it devotes considerable attention to the stability of the firm's executive corps. "Conversely, in Japan, we received the best response from the audience when we emphasized the company's strategies and long-term direction."

- **Strengthen investor relations activities.** Amborsino says the role of investor relations is not to "peddle stock" but to accommodate the increasingly complex needs of a global shareholder base. This means the investor relations department must be adept at translating the financial highlights, business strategies and details of the markets in which the firm operates. Complains Company A's treasurer, too many firms beef up their departments with people who cannot even read a balance sheet or satisfy or stimulate investor interest.

- **Consider using local consultants.** MNCs rely on local consultants or financial institutions to a greater or lesser extent (in Japan, it's a must). GTE recommends having a consultant along on visits and meetings so foreign clients know there is a local rep on hand to provide information and to call in case of emergencies. Consultants can also be used to investigate and stimulate investor demand for shares and to target the appropriate audience. For instance, Dawson and Co assisted US-based

PPG Industries in its consideration of London as a source of equity by trying to determine the level of UK interest in PPG stock and whether PPG should list on the London exchange. Some steps taken by Dawson to fulfill PPG's request included analyzing UK investors and institutions that already held the US firm's stock, investigating shareholders in UK competitors such as Pilkington and contacting all analysts who follow the industry. GTE uses Dawson to track shareholdings, compile mailing lists, disseminate information and help in organizing presentations. But like many US MNCs, GTE centralizes responsibility for answering tricky investor queries in the US.

To List or Not to List ...on Local Exchanges

Executives have mixed feelings on the benefits and on the necessity of listing locally. On the plus side, MNCs cite the following attractions:

• **Immediate access to investors.** Company A found its Tokyo Stock Exchange (TSE) listing fruitful. The MNC listed on November 14; by December, it had sold over one million shares.

• **Enhanced name and recognition.** Many companies note that the listing not only is a means of obtaining low-cost equity but also can help a firm secure debt financing at more attractive rates. A US chemicals and plastics manufacturer says that attracting Japanese investors was actually not the major benefit derived from its TSE listing. Says an executive, "We did not list on the Tokyo exchange for capital reasons. Instead, it was a public relations move to boost the name and image of the sub's $1 billion business in the market."

• **Improved government relations.** Several firms reported better access and response to their needs by the Japanese government after listing.

• **Helps local subs attract talented employees.** According to an executive at a US electronics MNC, young Japanese graduates are attracted to foreign companies that demonstrate their commitment to Japan. Listings are viewed as a solid sign of commitment.

On the negative side, many executives charge that the benefits are not worth the expense and administrative headaches. GTE—one of the first foreign companies to list in Japan (1973)—delisted in 1977 because of onerous costs and administrative burdens. Even though a softening of the filing and language requirements in Japan has eased the burden of a TSE listing, many executives still charge that the expense of going to Japan is exorbitant.

According to an executive with another US MNC, the Japanese investment houses "always pestered us to list. So we did, and costs associated with the listing reached well over six figures. Unfortunately, in addition to the expense, we discovered that there was minimal activity on the exchange and we ended up delisting."

Some executives feel it is not necessary to list on the European and Japanese exchanges to attract foreign shareholders. The top four Japanese securities houses and all the major institutional buyers are well established on Wall Street. Thus, the majority of Japanese investment and transactions in US securities are done in New York.

Further, shares issued on the local exchanges in Europe and Japan often do not staff offshore but flow back into the US. Pepsi's Hostetter says the US soft drink and snack food giant is one of the few firms not listed on London because of the ease with which UK investors can purchase Pepsi shares in the US and the tremendous flowback activity between the London and New York markets.

Why Court Foreign Investors?

The driving force behind MNCs' push to develop a global shareholder base is the ability to tap fresh low-cost sources of capital. But executives also cite a number of other advantages.

• Foreign investors add a dose of stability to stock prices since they tend to take a longer-term approach to investments than Wall Street.

• Expanded ownership reduces the risk of having a single or a few investors amass a large equity stake and threaten a takeover.

• Companies can exploit the hefty buying power of investors in foreign financial markets. For instance, London easily follows New York and Boston as one of the world's largest and most active markets. Says Dawson, myopic US companies that restrict their attentions to domestic financial centers, courting smaller US exchanges such as Detroit before London, forfeit the opportunity to satisfy the appetites of foreign investors for US securities.

• Broader demand can boost share prices.

84. Selling Stock in the US: What Every Foreign Firm Needs to Know

For foreign firms building worldwide shareholder bases, the largest capital market is the US, although deciphering Securities and Exchange Commission (SEC) registration rules presents a real challenge. The following examination of the costs and legal and technical issues of tapping Wall Street draws on the expertise of Robert Mangone, partner at the New York law firm Townley & Updike.

The financial advantages of listing a company's stock abroad, whether in the US or some other country, include broadening a firm's financing options, capitalizing on interest rate and currency fluctuations, raising the massive funds needed to implement global strategies and diversifying ownership to fend off takeover bids.

The nonfinancial advantages are less obvious, but can be just as important. Local exchange listings can increase public awareness of products, improve relations with host governments and help subs attract talented employees. The strategic significance of the US market to many foreign MNCs makes it important for them to develop a US presence that goes beyond simply establishing local operations.

Basic Considerations

Foreign firms generally use American Depository Receipts (ADRs). With ADRs, US depository banks maintain custody of deposited foreign securities at their overseas branches and issue receipts as proof of ownership. The receipt is transferable in the US. US investors actually purchase the receipt, rather than the stock itself, and prices are quoted in dollars. In effect, the ADR is an "Americanized" foreign security.

An important consideration for foreign MNCs is registration under either the Securities Act of 1933 or the Securities Exchange Act of 1934, or both. The former is a transactional statute and requires domestic and foreign issuers that want to offer their shares in the US or to US investors to disclose information on their businesses in a registration statement filed with the SEC. Registration of a company's securities under the 1934 Act is required if the firm wants its stock to be listed on an exchange or NASDAQ. The legal requirements and the costs under both acts vary, and depend primarily on corporate intentions. Many foreign MNCs take a conservative approach, starting with a limited commitment and expanding gradually.

Mangone identifies three stages in a typical effort to permit a non-US company's stock to trade in the US:

• **Setting up an ADR program.** Most firms begin by having ADRs issued in the US, on either an unsponsored or sponsored basis. This enables them to test US demand before incurring the significant legal liabilities and costs associated with formal listings or public offerings. An unsponsored program, which costs the foreign corporation almost nothing, is initiated by a US bank with the company's consent. The company does not control this type of ADR program. The terms of the ADRs are determined unilaterally by the depository bank, and other banks are free to issue ADRs as well. A company's consent is critical in order to avoid registration under the 1934 Act. In consenting, the company must agree to furnish the SEC with any documents that it is required to provide under its home country laws. This is the exemption under the US Rule 12g3-2(b). In practical terms, the foreign MNC can satisfy the exemption by simply placing the SEC on its mailing list.

The bank, however, has more obligations. Regardless of whether it is a sponsored or an unsponsored program, the bank must file a registration statement covering the ADRs. The registration statement — Form F6 — provides scant information on the company, but seeks details of the actual ADR program, such as the number of ADRs issued, etc.

A sponsored ADR program entails more corporate involvement and allows the foreign MNC to regulate the terms of its ADRs and to preclude other banks from marketing its ADRs. One advantage: Foreign firms can track ADR ownership and thereby reduce the risk of a hostile takeover. Under a sponsored program, a US bank and a foreign firm enter a "deposit agreement," which details the terms and conditions of the plan and states that the firm will bear the administrative costs and have authority over what voting rights will be granted. The agreement is a fairly standard 20-30 page document that is attached to the F-6 and submitted to the SEC by the bank.

Like an unsponsored program, as long as the foreign firm keeps the SEC on its mailing list, the company is eligible for the exemption under Rule 12g3-2(b). The legal costs of a sponsored ADR program are in the $4,000-5,000 range. Many US banks will agree to absorb the charges in order to expand their ADR businesses.

• **Listing.** Many MNCs permit their ADRs to be traded in the "pink sheets," but Mangone advises listing on NASDAQ or on an exchange from the outset. (The "pink sheets" list quotes for ADRs of nonlisted companies and trade broker-to-broker.) Only sponsored ADRs can be listed. While the listing means higher costs, the increased name recognition as well as the availability of more orderly trading and more widely disseminated price quotations offer significant opportunities for expanding a firm's US shareholder base. When an MNC seeks a listing on NASDAQ, the rule 12g3-2(b) exemption does not apply and it must register the shares and ADRs under the 1934 Act. This entails filing a form 20F with the SEC. This is similar to a prospectus and requires detailed business information, plus financial statements that conform to US Generally Accepted Accounting Principles.

With a NASDAQ listing, it takes about four to six weeks to prepare the 20F, and another six to eight weeks from the date of filing until the SEC declares it effective. Copies are also sent to NASDAQ. The firm and NASDAQ decide on when to begin trading. By registering on a 20F, foreign MNCs also incur an obligation to file periodic records with the SEC, such as an annual report. Legal costs of a NASDAQ listing range from $30,000-60,000.

Some firms elect to list on either the American or New York Stock Exchanges (AMEX or NYSE) rather than NASDAQ. Legally, MNCs face the same requirement—a 20F form—for either an exchange or NASDAQ listing. However, exchange listings are considerably more costly and time consuming. Plus, firms must satisfy other criteria. NYSE listings have two separate standards for domestic and foreign entities. Domestic firms face less stringent requirements and foreign MNCs with 2,000 round-lot (100 shares) US stockholders can qualify. The US standards are: 1.1 million public shares with a market value of $18 million and pretax income of $2.5 million in the current fiscal year and $2 million in the previous three years.

Alternatively, the foreign standards are: 5,000 round-lot shareholders worldwide, 2.5 million shares globally, with a market value of at least $100 million.

AMEX also has two standards and foreign firms with US share ownership of 500,000 shares among 800 US holders, one million shares among 400 holders or 500,000 among 400 holders (where the average trading volume is 2,000 shares or more for the past six months) qualify for the US test. The US standards are: market value of $3 million; minimum price of $3 per share, shareholder equity of $4 million and pretax income of $750,000 for the last fiscal year or for two prior years. Otherwise, foreign standards apply: one million shares held worldwide, 2,000 round-lot holders worldwide, market value of $20 million, shareholder equity of $25 million and cumulative total for pretax income for the last three years of $30 million.

• **Public offerings.** These entail the steepest registration requirements and costs. But offsetting the expense and headache is the potential to raise significant capital to finance operations. In a public offering, the foreign firm turns over its ordinary shares to its depository bank.

The bank then issues ADRs and delivers them to the underwriters for resale and distribution.

Here the SEC requires the foreign firm to file a Form F-1 under the 1933 Securities Act. This involves a complete disclosure of all aspects of the firm's operations. The information requirements under an F-1 can be extremely rigorous and require a concerted three-to-four month effort by the firm's executives, attorneys, accountants and investment bankers. Once the F-1 is submitted to the SEC, it takes another two months for final approval. Legal costs will exceed $100,000.

85. Avoid Problems and Maximize Benefits: Debt-Equity Swaps

A debt-equity conversion is a straightforward transaction: A company buys LDC sovereign foreign debt at a discount in the secondary market and redeems it—as close to par as possible—with the issuing government. The result is local investment capital at anywhere from $0.60 to $0.75 on the dollar.

Several countries, such as Chile, Mexico, Ecuador and the Philippines, have formal programs, while others such as Costa Rica and Brazil are quietly allowing such conversions on an informal basis. Use of the funds is restricted in some countries; in others, it determines the discount. In some programs, firms can also use the funds to retire debt or meet working capital needs.

Points to Watch

Few firms that have used debt-swap financing have been sorry. However, executives who have been through the mill caution others to watch for the following:

• **Be sure you want to invest.** If the funds would be used for investment, as most are, the project has to stand on its own merits. While debt swaps can lower a hurdle rate enough to make a marginally attractive project a go-ahead, they will not rescue a poor proposal.

Experience of many companies has shown that country managers tend to get caught up with the discounts and are anxious to try the debt swaps. While HQ executives should not reject these proposals out of hand, they should be prepared to temper the enthusiasm from the field. One effective—and realistic—way to accomplish this is to ask the local manager whether the proposal would still be recommended if the swap program were canceled halfway through the deal.

• **Be prepared for tight regulation.**   Many companies fail to recognize that debt-swap investments are governed by even stricter rules than investments made at par. For example, to ensure that those buying debt receive no better treatment than the banks who lent the money, repatriation cannot be based on more favorable terms than the bank repayment schedule. There are also restrictions on disposal of the assets purchased. Countries may impose added reporting or other requirements.

Official attitudes are also influenced by the nagging fear that foreigners, given an unfair advantage, will take over the best of the local economy at the expense of nationals. This is an especially important point to bear in mind during negotiations. Although unlikely, a backlash further on could result in rule changes that would put such investment at risk. Some firms are demanding higher hurdle rates as a result.

• **But be prepared to push officials—gently.**   Even fixed redemption discounts can be somewhat flexible. Favorable discount and exchange rates, which are negotiable, can make a big difference in the net benefit. Even if they won't give in on dollar and cents, program administrators may budge on other provisions. Experience shows it doesn't hurt to ask.

• **Choose your intermediaries carefully.**   Be prepared to negotiate hard on the services to be performed, as well as on fees (usually no more than 2% of the deal). Some firms advise setting caps on costs such as legal fees. Others have found that putting the deal out for competitive bidding reduces costs. Remember that the fee should buy you know-how in swap deals, as well as familiarity with local procedures, officials, attorneys and banks.

• **Be realistic about time.**   Even with outside expertise, lots of staff and management time will be required. It is also necessary to allow plenty of time for the bureaucracies to act. Know when to give in on cost issues to keep the project on track. Finally, debt-swap programs are in flux, and some are in danger. If there is a project you think you'd like to do, be prepared to move fast.

86. Dow Chemical's Formula
for Trouble-Free Cost Allocations

For multinational companies that are successful in "globalizing" their worldwide business activities, the price of success is often an outdated system for measuring the performance of their foreign operations. As part of the globalization process, centralized decisionmaking often becomes the norm in key functional areas such as marketing and R&D. Meanwhile, country-specific price-cutting strategies are typically needed to achieve global market share targets.

The inevitable result: General managers of foreign subs find it more difficult to control costs and plan revenues, and corporate HQs find it more difficult to assess local performance with profit-based performance-evaluation techniques such as comparing profit margins among subs or measuring subsidiary profit performance against plan. Following is a discussion of how Dow's internal cost-allocation system compensates for the new norms and ensures the fair and accurate assessment of performance at all levels of the organization.

To stay ahead of the rising tide of corporate globalization, Dow was quick to centralize key functional decisionmaking at the strategic business unit (SBU) level. This allowed the firm to adopt a uniquely global perspective, one that the firm's performance-evaluation system is specifically designed to reinforce. "Instead of viewing each sub as a stand-alone profit center," explains Dow's Corporate Controller Roger Kesseler, "we try to reflect the sub's contribution to overall business-line profitability. We find we can best accomplish this by treating the subs as cost centers, tying local incentive plans to global business-line profits, creating a separate transfer-pricing system for internal reporting and designing the fairest, most equitable system of cost allocation possible."

With over 200 subs engaged in marketing and manufacturing products for up to 16 business lines, Dow quickly came to the conclusion that it couldn't possibly set the bases and rates for every cost to be allocated. Instead, the firm's corporate controller designed a general methodology to be used by every geographic and functional unit when allocating costs to other cost centers or to the SBUs.

"The end result," says Kesseler, "has been a performance-evaluation system that all of our managers find equitable, and a management-reporting system that helps us achieve our long-term goals. Best of all, we can balance the global perspective of our SBUs against the local view of our foreign subs and regional units. We think our system gives us the best of both worlds."

Starting Out: Cost Basics

All of Dow's subs use US Generally Accepted Accounting Principles (GAAP) to record their costs, and almost all of them use the US dollar as the functional currency. The only exceptions are the subs in Germany and in Japan; those subs use the local currency.

"FAS No. 52 lets US companies use a mixture of currencies as functional currencies," explains Kesseler. "We chose to use Deutschemarks and yen as functional currencies for three major reasons: First, our operations in those countries met FAS No. 52's criteria, that is, our financing operations in those countries were large enough; second, we thought the Deutschemark and yen would continue to be strong against the dollar; and third, we wanted to gain some experience in using local currencies, where allowed by US GAAP."

Unlike currency fluctuations, inflationary changes are not reflected in the company's performance-evaluation reports. "For external reporting, we did what was required under FAS No. 33," says Kesseler. "But we never used the results for performance measurement. When FASB dropped its requirement, we stopped trying to account for inflation."

The General Guidelines

Once the costs are properly recorded, Dow's cost-allocation policy establishes a hierarchy of four alternative cost-allocation bases. The guidelines for using those bases are listed below.

(1) Use degree-of-effort allocations whenever possible. The most desirable basis, according to Dow's guidelines, is degree of effort. "Our units are urged," explains Kesseler, "to set standard, predetermined rates, so that the user is responsible only for the number of units consumed and not for the fluctuation in unit rates."

(2) Use homogeneous pools for country-level support services. Costs that cannot be directly allocated—either because no direct measure exists or because the measure is not cost effective—are allocated by what Dow calls "homogeneous pools." These pools include the following:

• **Personnel-related costs.** One commonly used pool is that of personnel—and payroll—related costs. For example, when there are two or more subs within the same country, shared payroll administration costs are grouped into a "personnel related" cost pool and allocated by number of personnel, payroll dollar or number of paychecks.

• **Material-related costs.** These include purchasing or material-handling and storage costs. They are allocated to the units based on the number of purchase orders or dollars of vendor purchases.

• **Capital-related costs.** These include the cost of property taxes, the cost of property and general-liability insurance and the cost of economic evaluation and planning activities. The bases for allocating these costs are direct capital plus service backup, total rolled-up capital, spending for construction in progress or number of authorizations.

• **Sales-related costs.** Product-liability insurance and sales-order entry costs are allocated based on sales dollars, standard cost of sales dollars or number of sales orders.

(3) Use the Massachusetts formula for regional, area or corporate overhead. For costs incurred at the higher levels of the organization benefiting the company or region or area as a whole, the basis for allocation to the units is the Massachusetts formula.

Under that formula, each unit's share is determined by a weighted allocation base calculated as the sum of one third the unit's standard cost of trade sales, one third of its manpower costs and one third of its invested capital. While the exact origin of the term "Massachusetts formula" has long since been forgotten, the formula itself is widely used today, especially for government-reporting purposes by companies that have contracts with the US Department of Defense.

(4) Create a separate category for unrecovered costs. Not all costs are fully allocated at Dow. The residual unrecoverable costs include the cost overruns on degree-of-effort allocations, under which prenegotiated standard unit rates are used to charge out costs. These overruns remain unallocated and are charged to a separate business segment for purposes of performance reporting.

Applying the Guidelines

When these guidelines are applied to Dow's three-dimensional organization matrix (geographic, functional and strategic), the only costs allocated to the foreign subs are those that fall into the first two tiers of the allocation hierarchy (i.e. those allocated on a degree-of-effort basis and those allocated using homogeneous pools). These items include, for example, local administrative support services and the product-development portion of R&D expenses.

Items that fall into the third tier are allocated to the firm's strategic business units (SBUs) but not to specific subs. Examples include forex gains and losses, corporate interest costs and the basic portion of R&D expenses. Items that fall into the fourth tier are not allocated at all. Examples include corporate income taxes.

Dow applies its general cost-allocation guidelines to forex gains and losses, corporate interest charges and centralized R&D expenses as follows:

• **Forex gains and losses.** Forex management is decentralized and conducted at each of Dow's six areas (Europe, Canada, the Pacific area, Latin America, Brazil and the US). The resulting forex gains and losses are allocated to the SBUs by the Massachusetts formula.

• **Corporate interest charges.** The cost of capital on corporate borrowings is charged back to the units using homogeneous pools. First, corporate costs of capital are pooled; next, each unit's share is calculated by inputting interest based on the unit's total capitalization multiplied by the corporate debt/equity ratio; and finally, local interest charges are subtracted from the imputed interest. "The net effect," says Kesseler, "is to bring all units to the corporate debt/equity ratio."

• **Centralized R&D costs.** To allocate R&D costs, the expenses are first broken down into two groups; basic "blue sky " research and "applied" product-development research. Costs for basic research are allocated to the SBUs by the Massachusetts formula. Applied-research costs are allocated by the level-of-effort method.

87. Want to Avoid Government Review of Your Transfer Pricing?

Neither the best textbook in the world nor the most sophisticated linear-regression program will give MNC tax managers the answers they need to solve today's most pressing transfer-pricing problems. That's because there are two answers to every question on taxation: one based on the "official" legal posture of the authorities, the other based on the norm of enforcement.

Discerning differences between the two has never been more important, but managers say it can be an exhausting experience for them, and almost as dangerous for their company as not knowing the answers in the first place. Below are some timely tips for getting the behind-the-scenes story — without paying fees to local tax and accounting firms or tipping off the authorities.

Gauging the Enforcement Norm

In order to learn the answers to transfer-pricing and other tax-reform questions, many MNCs are now arranging itineraries for country-by-country tax-planning tours. As one corporate tax director phrased it, "We find the best way to locate tax-saving opportunities is to be there in person to 'kick the tires' ourselves." Armchair tours are not impossible, but language barriers and distance make it difficult to gain a great deal of useful knowledge from them. In either case, the important thing for the firm's tax officer is to have an investigative procedure prepared in advance. Using the UK as an example, the following steps are suggested:

(1) Look into local sources of competitive data. One of the sources widely used by companies to support an increase in transfer price — and one also used by the Inland Revenue when checking a company's transfer-pricing policy — is the industry-average profit margin. To calculate this average, MNCs need to obtain financial information on other companies operating in the same sector. In the UK, three sources are extremely useful:

• **Annual reports.** All companies registered in the UK are required to submit an annual report to Companies House. This report contains an audited income statement for purely local operations, and it is a reliable guide to a company's profit performance inside the UK. The record kept at Companies House are available to the public at a cost of £1 per company and are supplied inside the UK. The records kept at Companies House are available to the public at a cost of £1 per company and are supplied to researchers on microfiche.

• **Local data bases.** The electronic information company Datastar operates a data base providing information extracted from the annual re-

UK Transfer Pricing

A former Inland Revenue inspector revealed the answers to some commonly asked questions about transfer pricing in the UK.

Q. What initiates an inquiry?

A. Every year a tax inspector will check a company's tax returns. If during the course of his investigations he discovers a marked decline in the profits of the UK subsidiary without a corresponding decrease in turnover, he may inquire into the transfer-pricing policy of the company. Furthermore, if he notices that over a period of years the profitability of a UK subsidiary has slowly declined, he may well suspect the parent company of continually increasing its transfer price; the initiation of a formal inquiry could be the result.

Q. What does a transfer-price inquiry involve?

A. The first thing to remember is that a UK tax inspector is neither an economist nor an accountant. The inspector's goal is to achieve an understanding of the suspect company's operations. This can be a slow process, taking many months. In this initial period he will study tax returns, company accounts and information on imports and exports. The company will not be aware that this is happening.

When the inspector does approach the company, he will ask to see the complete set of accounts for the UK subsidiary. When requesting information the UK tax authorities are usually polite, but it is a very big mistake to assume that this means they aren't interested in the information they are requesting. If they are not furnished with everything they require, the whole process can become more difficult.

Q. How do MNCs generally respond to inquiries?

A. Companies usually provide figures on gross profit margin to validate any increases in transfer price. However, in many cases involving manufacturing, sufficiently detailed figures for specific products are unavailable. Even when detailed product information is available, it is generally more data than the MNC would like to provide. Settlement of inquires generally takes from three to four years, but this depends upon the complexity of the case. The Inland Revenue will not give clearances for transfer-price changes in advance.

Q. What are the penalties if the price is found to be too high?

A. Is a firm's transfer price is found to be too high, then the Inland Revenue will demand interest on taxes back to the time at which the unsuitable transfer-pricing policy was initiated.

ports of many British firms, along with figures on profit margins and return on capital employed.

• **Local publishers.** *Macmillan's Unquoted Companies* contains a limited amount of information extracted from the annual reports of the UK's top 10,000 unquoted firms. A list of the average profit margins of 142 industrial sectors is also included. The data provided can, however, be up to two years out of date.

(2) Conduct your own industrywide survey. Direct contacts with firms operating in your own industry can also prove enlightening. The chief obstacle, of course, is that these companies will naturally tend to worry about confidentiality and "espionage."

One way to overcome this is to agree to share the results of the survey. Another way that works in the UK is to arrange compensation for the participation of other companies. One British firm suggested a "fee" proportional to the time spent and the salary of the person completing the survey form, payable to a predesignated charity.

(3) Compare tax and customs data. In the UK there are two bodies that take an interest in corporate transfer-pricing policy: the Inland Revenue and, to a lesser extent, Her Majesty's Customs and Excise Office. The two have conflicting goals.

The Inland Revenue will challenge a company if it thinks the transfer price is too high, but Customs and Excise will challenge the price if they think that it is too low and that the UK subsidiary is paying too little import duty. Both of these facts must be taken into consideration when setting transfer prices.

To obtain information on customs price standards, MNCs may contact the Customs and Excise Statistical Office, which will supply information on the weight and value of all goods imported to and exported from the UK. Before you contact that office, obtain the current tariff codes of your products. These may be obtained from the EC publication *Harmonized System-Based Tariffs*.

From these figures, it is possible to obtain an average cost per unit weight. If your firm deals in manufactured goods, the cost-per-unit-weight measurement alone is unlikely to persuade the tax inspector of the validity of your case. If it is included as a part of your documentation, however, the figure can only improve your chance of success.

(4) Interview a former tax inspector. The interview above offers insights into the attitudes of the Inland Revenue. The comments and insights are invaluable.

88. Evaluating Treasury Performance: Solutions Prove Elusive

To evaluate treasury performance meaningfully, companies must answer a number of difficult questions. How do you choose performance yardsticks that are not only quantifiable, but encourage managers to meet corporate goals? Accounting information may be objective and accessible, but is it meaningful? How do you evaluate missed opportunities? How do you compare performance from year to year under changing market conditions? How do you measure risk?

To find out how treasury executives view the issue of performance assessment, managers at 20 multinational firms were contacted. However, none of the firms interviewed were satisfied that they had fully resolved the questions above. Their performance-assessment approaches form a continuum from "what if" modeling to the use of benchmarks to the establishment of profit centers.

1 "What if," or hypothetical scenarios.   Many companies utilize hypothetical scenarios as a means of treasury evaluation. Employing microcomputers, they most often look at best-case/worst-case scenarios and try to determine where their actions placed them between the two. Says Ed Bak, director of international treasury at Medtronic, "On the foreign exchange side, we do a running graph of where we placed and removed positions and then we ask 'what if.' If we had been 100% covered, what would it have cost the company now that the dollar has weakened? On the other hand, if we'd been 100% uncovered, what would it have brought the company?"

Few companies, however, use such assessments as part of a structured review. Much of the use of hypothetical scenarios is simply as a learning exercise for the managers themselves, a chance to figure out where mistakes were made and where improvements are necessary. "The question with these analyses is, 'Where do you stop?' " says one treasurer. "If I say I can do a borrowing at 'X' percent today, my boss may say we could have saved 10 basis points if we did that a month ago. I could then say that this deal is maybe better than one we'll get a month down the road. When do you stop measuring?"

(2) External benchmarks.   To add rigor to the assessment process, firms taking the cost-center approach can use external benchmarks. For example:

• **A market rate.**   One company measures its short-term borrowing activity by its ability to reduce its borrowing cost—through the use of options, swaps or prepayment—below an established 30-day market interest rate. "We are constantly fine-tuning our short-term debt structure," explains the assistant treasurer. "We compare our active management against a supposed passive borrower that borrows at the market rate and then just rolls it over month to month."

- **Competitors' reported financials.** Some companies looking for external benchmarks have settled on their competitors' financial statements. SmithKline Beckman, for instance, developed a systematic evaluation of its foreign exchange function through examination of the annual reports of its major competitors.

Competitive analysis can be extended to other areas of treasury as well. "We measure ourselves against other direct issuers of commercial paper," says the treasurer of one large finance company. "We look at their annual reports to see how much they spend to support their short-term debt structure in that field."

For some, however, annual reports can provide only sketchy information about financial management. "They don't tell you enough in annual reports; there's nothing to read," says Apple Computer's treasurer, Bob Saltmarsh. In addition, companies can really make meaningful comparisons with other firms only from their own country because of the widely differing accounting standards that are in use around the world.

- **The company's own financials.** Other managers view their performance as incorporated into the company's bottom line. "All we do is look at income," says Apple's Saltmarsh. "In Apple's case, it's broken up into foreign exchange and [investment] interest income. And we have a pretty easy standard to beat: Come up with more than zero after the cost of any forward contracts or options."

One of the principal problems of relying on financial statements for evaluation is accounting distortion. Some accounting conventions may show a detrimental impact from a transaction that makes good economic sense. Saltmarsh cites an example. "It makes economic sense to buy an option for a year to hedge uncommitted purchases from a supplier. Even though you have purchase orders only for the next six months, you know you're going to buy it from that supplier for the next year. But the accountant would call that a speculative hedge." Such a designation makes gains and losses more visible, thus reducing the incentive to undertake these transactions.

- **Past performance.** Many companies set up internal measures of performance based on their own budgets. Some aspects of cash management, for instance, are easily quantifiable. "You can take a look at the unit costs and get some evaluation in areas like receivables, payables and payroll, " says the treasurer of a US consumer products firm. Every year he assesses as a percentage of sales the total operating cost of the treasury department and write-offs due to bad debts.

One difficulty with this approach is that comparing two different years could be like comparing apples and oranges. The risks and costs associated with certain market conditions can vary enormously from year to year. Says one manager, "Comparative performance from one year to another has to be largely judgmental."

• **Ratings.**   The view of ratings agencies about the balance sheet and the firm's capital structure can also be considered. "There are certain ratios for the assets and liabilities, particularly the long- and short-term debt," says Howard Burdett, Dow Chemical's treasurer for US operations. "The way the rating agencies view the ratios and the rating the company gets are a measure of our success." It becomes necessary, however, to distinguish between the contribution of treasury and that of operations and senior management to a company's rating.

• **Feedback from bankers.**   Explains one treasurer, "If we want information on the pricing of credit lines or something like that, we have to believe what we hear from bankers when they tell us our pricing is pretty sharp. There aren't good ways of determining what others are paying except through this type of methodology, which is not terribly formal."

(3) The profit-center approach.   A profit-center orientation simplifies evaluation considerably, allowing P&L data to become the focus of measurement. But whereas there has been a discernible trend toward turning treasuries into profit centers, many treasury managers remain wary of the increased rate inherent in such an approach.

Although Apple looks at treasury's contribution to the bottom line as a benchmark, it does not take the extra step of imposing a P&L on the function. "We're trying to get rid of the risk," says Saltmarsh. "We have enough risk competing against IBM and the rest of the world, so why add risk to the company?"

Medtronic's Bak agrees. "The feeling here is that the role of treasury is to be active and try to save money, not to be under the pressure of meeting certain expectations. Otherwise you have people doing things which may not be compatible with the corporate risk philosophy."

Finally, some companies question whether profits provide an accurate picture of how well treasury is doing. "We tend to be more interested in measuring and neutralizing exposure," says Assistant Treasurer Irving Levine of NCR. "Therefore, the profitability is irrelevant. We're going to make a profit or loss on the hedge that will offset the profit or loss on the operating exposure. So making us a profit center and showing that we had a profit or loss on the hedge without showing the other side would be unfair and maybe irrelevant measurement."

6
Operations Management

89. Technology-Based Trends That Will Change Manufacturing

BI has identified 13 key trends and developments that will shape manufacturing—and the management of manufacturing—over the coming decades:

- **Ability to turn on a dime.** Computer-based process technologies and information systems have made possible a degree of production flexibility unknown in the past. Techniques like just-in-time inventories, total quality control, material resource planning and process technologies such as computer-integrated manufacturing, flexible manufacturing systems and robotics allow companies to rapidly change production volume, vary the product mix, retool, innovate and develop even more advanced technologies.

- **Continued merging of telecommunications and computing.** More rapid data communication will facilitate flexible manufacturing strategies.

- **Cross-functional linkages.** The increasing use of computer-based information systems permits the integration of manufacturing, marketing, finance and other functions within the organization and facilitates ties to suppliers and customers outside the organization.

- **Obsolescence of today's computers.** Within 10 years, the computer as we know it will have disappeared. Many current mainframes will become, in effect, commoditylike devices, while machines with supercomputing capability will replace them in such functions as mechanical design.

• **Need for new ways to measure success.** Traditional accounting methods cannot properly assess the payback from advanced manufacturing technologies. Many of the advantages of these technologies – increased sourcing and production flexibility, for example – are hard to quantify, as is the cost of falling behind competitors.

• **Demand for upgraded skills.** It has become critical to upgrade the technological competence of both factory workers and managers, particularly in engineering and information systems. It is in the interest of companies, governments and educational institutions alike to help the work force improve its skills.

• **Reorganization of production.** Technology and automation are currently driving the organization of production, but many companies' organization and management systems have not caught up.

• **A new division of labor.** Fewer employees will be required in production, production planning and supervision of labor, while more people will be hired in sales and marketing, R&D, design engineering and information systems.

• **Emergence of microfactories.** Facilities used by several companies on a time-share basis are the wave of the future. They will be continuously reprogrammed to make new and modified products while retaining the economies of scale of dedicated plants. A program sponsored by the Department of Commerce has established several factories in locations throughout the US.

• **Designer materials.** Technological advances in industrial materials will create custom-tailored materials whose properties can be made to fit the precise specifications and cost requirements of a product.

• **Artificial intelligence.** By the year 2000, artificial intelligence will be almost universally used by companies and governments to assimilate data and solve problems.

• **High-tech growth industries.** The leading-edge sectors for the early part of the 21st century will include biotechnology, communications, computers, electronics, industrial materials, space industry, super-conductivity and transport equipment.

90. Factory of the Future: Time-Share Manufacturing

The concept of time-share manufacturing is turning the factory of the future into a service center for a consortium of companies that buy into a flexible computer-integrated manufacturing facility (FCIM), or micro-factory, on a time-share basis to manufacture their products. Some of the benefits are reduced investment risk in high-cost technologies, enhanced market responsiveness, short production runs with the economies of scale of a dedicated plant, just-in-time delivery and flexible global manufacturing.

With the support of the Department of Commerce (DOC) and other US government agencies and universities, microfactories are now being built for use by consortiums of small- to medium-sized US businesses. The essential aspect of an FCIM is that its facilities are shared. A company can buy time in a facility that is equipped to make thousands of products for different companies in different industries through the frequent reprogramming of software. The facility can make one, 10 or 1,000 of a kind — at essentially the cost and economies of scale of a dedicated plant, but it also has the reproducibility and quality control that is needed for a world-class operation.

The Benefits

The following are some of the key benefits of time-share manufacturing:

• Using a common facility reduces individual investment risk in costly automation and provides a higher return on the investment in a flexible facility.

• FCIM factories, designed for continuous reprogramming, will extend the useful life of high-cost manufacturing equipment.

• The factory is built to make new and modified products as the market requires without any downtime for retooling.

• As more and more large companies source parts outside rather than in-house, the microfactory can improve quality, productivity and just-in-time delivery from suppliers.

• The high-entry costs for new product manufacturing can be greatly reduced because a dedicated plant operating at partial capacity is no longer necessary.

• A flexible factory can support new business development and test marketing.

• Once one facility is built, it can be replicated in other locations. A factory can also be reprogrammed from any location.

Because of the ease with which microfactories can be replicated, FCIM facilities should develop into global manufacturing networks through the use of satellite and cable.

• Together with universities, microfactories may be used as teaching facilities and agents of technology transfer.

91. GE Uses FCIM to Sustain Profits in a Mature Market

In 1980, General Electric (GE) proposed a $50 million investment in FCIM for its steam turbine-generator plant in Schenectady, New York, as the best (perhaps only) way to continue to operate profitably in an industry that had once been a company mainstay. For over 70 years, GE had been the leading supplier of large turbines and generators to electric utilities, but by the late 1970s, demand had declined sharply. Annual output at the Schenectady plant was down from a peak of about 40 turbines per year to five. At the same time, new foreign competitors were rapidly gaining strength in the US and overseas. Still, GE saw ample justification for long-term investment: Despite the low demand for new units, the generators provided a lucrative opportunity to sell replacement parts and service.

The substantial investment was worth making. The manufacturing time for small parts dropped dramatically from about 34 weeks to five days, and millions of dollars were saved. But perhaps the best testimony of FCIM's value to General Electric was the closure of a competitor's plant.

Planning for FCIM

GE's FCIM Workhorse

GE's first use of FCIM for an entire operation was in the small-parts shop, where the company invested $5 million in a pilot project. Minicomputers connected to a mainframe data base link all aspects of the business including:

• **Processing orders.** An automated quotation and order entry system allows GE's US and Canadian sales office to give immediate cost information to customers. Each order is transmitted directly to the system's mainframe computer—instantly triggering design and manufacturing.

• **Engineering and design.** Computer-aided design is used extensively. Interactive graphics terminals draw from more than 1,000 parts, design files stored in the mainframe computer.

• **Manufacturing process planning.** Design data is translated into a part recognition code (RC) that defines part characteristics in minute detail. The RC drives an automated process planning system, which determines the order's route through the plant—including timing and selection of machine tools for specific orders, manufacturing instructions for machine operators and estimates for job completion.

• **Factory management system.** Design information is also sent to a numerical control programming system that automatically develops the machining data required to manufacture the part and transmits instructions electronically to the machines. Workers receive job assignments based on computer-calculated delivery requirements. When a job is completed, the time is automatically recorded on the terminal. Finally, the computer network on the factory floor facilitates communications between foreman, quality control and maintenance personnel.

• **Shipment and financial controls.** Data collected by the system is passed back to the business and financial computer systems, which track job completions, inventory status and job costs.

Many experts in the application of advanced manufacturing technologies stress the importance of strategic preinvestment planning for FCIM. The key planning elements on which GE focused are outlined on the following page.

• **Technically oriented task force.** GE's first step was to appoint a task force led by systems experts from engineering, manufacturing and finance to ensure that the final design would reflect long-term objectives. The company avoided the common practice of putting senior managers with little technical experience in charge.

• **Getting a consensus.** Existing procedures for every function related to the manufacturing process were reviewed. Compromises were hammered out to arrive at a system that would address the efficiency concerns of each business function and lay the foundation for an integrated communications network.

• **A focus on strategic goals.** Although GE faced immediate pressures to cut costs, it was more important that FCIM create a factory that would respond to the market for replacement parts, rather than for new units. Reducing manufacturing lead times, therefore, had to be the first priority — no small task given that the production cycle for new equipment was several years, while parts must be turned out in a matter of days. Moreover, parts production demands greater flexibility to accommodate high-volume output of many individual items, some of which are very complex. A typical turbine consists of more than 100,000 parts, some designed in over a thousand configurations.

• **Cost of modernization.** The decision to go with FCIM over less costly efficiency measures was based not only on the strategic value of the initiative, but also on the state of existing equipment. In GE's case, the plant already had installed many numerical control machines and had begun to introduce automation, which reduced the investment needed for FCIM. If extensive plant modernization had been required, much of the benefit could have been wiped out.

• **A 10-year plan.** Based on its review, the task force proposed a plan covering intended capital outlays year-by-year for a decade, plus step-by-step plans for automation and deployment of people. A total investment through 1991 was projected at $50 million (see box page 244).

The Keys to Success

Beyond detailed planning, careful implementation with special attention to several areas was critical. GE used the following guidelines:

• **Maintain support from management.** Since management had committed millions of dollars to FCIM, the project leaders made a consistent effort to supply tangible evidence of progress during the long development period. The first part produced through FCIM, for example, was mounted on a plaque for management – an important symbolic gesture.

• **Update the plan.** Progress is reviewed every two years. After the first progress report, the task force found it was ahead of schedule and was able to move more quickly.

• **Select forward-looking technology.** Instead of settling for existing process planning technology, GE developed its own, the first and only generative process planning system that can plan a part from scratch, rather than having to work from an existing drawing.

• **Ease organizational changes.** FCIM is known for its ability to break down the traditional division between engineering and manufacturing. But the change is not always easy. To facilitate this integration, GE chose a senior engineer to smooth the adjustment to "paperless" design flow and to improve communications.

• **Capture the knowledge of retiring personnel.** GE recognized the value of long-term workers' knowledge of production to the planning for FCIM. It conducted extensive interviews with both shop workers and draftsmen who were generally receptive, even if they were leaving under forced retirement.

92. How Foxboro Became Customer Oriented

After five trying years of record losses, extensive cutbacks and the elimination of entire operations, Foxboro Co. completely transformed itself into a customer-oriented organization, with all its engineering and production capabilities refocused on the marketplace. Foxboro, a major manufacturer of industrial instruments and control systems, is headquartered in Foxboro, Massachusetts. The result of the retrenching was dramatic sales and profit increases.

Besides making sweeping organizational changes to focus the company's resources on the unique needs of customers within specific industries and support all aspects of customer projects from start to finish, Foxboro overhauled its production operations. To survive and thrive, Foxboro believed it would have to make the highest-quality products at the lowest possible costs, with the flexibility to meet customer demands. To do this, management made stem-to-stern changes on the factory floor, drawing on Japanese and other proven methods. Following are some of the most important changes:

• **Multifunctional teams.** Led by production supervisors, groups of production operators, engineers, planners and purchasing managers establish the production process for each product line. Together with plant managers, the teams determine manufacturing objectives and strategies, performance standards and measurements, process controls and work flows. For instance, they reduced throughput time by eliminating several steps between the time a product starts out on the assembly line and the time it is ready to be shipped.

• **Redesigned work stations.** To redefine work stations for dedicated functions, Foxboro brought in operations previously carried out by others outside the area and gave employees greater control over their own operations. Production workers now also select the best tools and equipment for each operation and go to the work stations where they are most needed, rather than wait for the work to come to them. All unnecessary barriers to the flow of production, like shelves, conveyor belts and even walls were removed. In one plant, employees shortened the distance a certain component had to travel from 2,400 to 900 feet.

• **A production system that "pulls."** Foxboro has reversed the traditional manufacturing system so that the final stage in production, shipping, actually initiates the entire process by dictating the flow of products each day. In effect, products are "pulled" by the needs of the market, rather than "pushed" by some abstract production quotas. Shipping determines what must be pulled from testing; testing pulls from final assembly, which in turn pulls from subassemblies, and so on. A daily plan, drawn from a weekly schedule dictates what products need to be produced by each work station each day.

• **Visible signals.** The flow of products from one work station to the next is directed by the content of bins, racks, shelves, forms and pigeonholes throughout the plant. A near-empty bin, for example, informs employees in the preceding area that the item they make needs to be replenished. Supervisors and team leaders no longer have to tell people what to do. "The visible signals tell me whether something needs to be built," explains one worker. "If not, I find something else that needs to be done."

• **Employees as customers.** In the Foxboro system, every production employee is considered the "customer" of those in the previous production area. The onus is on each employee to give the next person in line—his or her customer—a quality product. This means that inspection is no longer separate from production, but is an integral part of the normal production process. Because errors are now caught by employees on the line, fewer bad products are made, and bottlenecks in final testing are less frequent.

• **Just-in-time supplies.** Foxboro extended its system to its major suppliers. "Once our own system was well in place, we started working with our suppliers to help them implement our principles," says Sheila Cody Peterson, a manufacturing staff consultant.

• **Training.** Employees have to be cross-trained to learn all aspects of the jobs they now perform. For the most part, this is done by supervisors. The new work methods do present some problems for employees whose first language is not English. To overcome this obstacle, the company offers a 15-week course in English, which employees attend on company time four hours a week.

As a result of Foxboro's new production system, the company's productivity, quality and delivery improved significantly in a very short time. One plant reduced product defects and throughput time by 90%. The plant now delivers in two weeks, compared to seven or eight weeks previously. In one area, employees have cut overdue orders at any given time from 95 to 10.

Peterson sums up management's view of the new production system: "It is not that individual little things have changed. Many things are still being done the same way. Nor is this just a 'program.' Programs come and go. This is a way of life."

93. Innovation Strategies: Points to Ponder

The quickening pace of technical advance, the globalization of corporate activities, the evolvement of corporate structures and the rise of competitors in newly industrializing countries (NICs) are forcing MNCs to rethink traditional approaches to innovation. Below, BI highlights some significant strategic issues confronting executives involved in the administration of R&D and other elements of innovation strategy.

• **Scope of innovation is widening.** Opportunities exist for invention in all line and process functions, not only in the traditional R&D focus on new product creation. Innovations in these processes, systems and support areas can provide a competitive edge as pivotal as new products. Corporate and industry structures are still being shaken by the microelectronic revolution in information systems.

- **Innovation is a multidimensional process.** Creative work in design, production and marketing may generate more innovations than basic R&D; mutual feedback among these functions is essential for the commercial success of innovations. Contact between R&D staff and personnel in marketing, design and production personnel should be routine.

- **Corporate cultures must encourage innovation, not stifle it.** Clearly stated and appropriately reinforced corporate goals can attract highly motivated personnel. Overly rigid corporate cultures can stifle innovation by impeding learning from sources beyond corporate and industry boundaries.

- **Managing innovation demands flexibility.** Executives can emulate the best features of smaller innovative firms when structuring for innovation. Project teams should be small; interactive learning and competition among multiple approaches should be encouraged. Executives must learn to tolerate mistakes. According to J.B. Quinn, innovative "chaos" can best be guided through reliance on general goals and a few key decision points instead of unwieldy bureaucratic control systems.

- **MNCs are discarding the "not-invented-here" and "not-made-here" syndromes.** Lackluster performances by some high-tech leaders (e.g. Texas Instruments and Intel) show the pitfalls of excessive technological "self-reliance" and isolation from market feedback.

- **Innovation is not a one-way street.** Executives should carefully assess the introduction of new product and process innovations. A new product or process improvement may undermine the innovating firm's own competitive position by upsetting its technical interdependence with buyers or by transforming the structure of its industry.

- **Product life cycles are shorter, but may also be reversible.** The fast pace of technical change and turnaround time puts intense pressure on companies to get new products on the market as fast as possible. However, caution is advised: Product life cycles are not always irreversible. Hasty moves into large-scale production may block exploration of alternative technologies. New advances in production technology (e.g. flexible manufacturing systems) give managers more freedom to devise varied product strategies—and to change them. Moreover, managers should not lightly dismiss "mature" technologies as suitable only for heavy milking; new technical advances may rejuvenate them.

• **The revolution in information technology has eased R&D decentralization.** Perhaps the best option is a "mixed-mode" approach. Central facilities developing proprietary technology can be combined with multiregional, market-oriented innovation efforts, depending on the industry. Global MNCs can thus quickly match product innovations (regardless of origin) with local market opportunities. However, this option presents thorny problems for MNC managers. The rise of local subsidiaries as innovation centers will spark pressures for greater autonomy and higher status.

• **The trend is toward internationalization of R&D.** The rise of high-income societies in Western Europe and Japan offers a wider field for innovation by local and US-based MNCs. A growing number of triad combinations among US, Japanese and European giants are engaging in production and technology sharing.

NIC-based companies are also becoming involved in cross-regional efforts. For example, Hewlett-Packard formed a joint venture with Taiwan's Formosa Plastics Group to develop computer software. State efforts to promote R&D in Japan, Western Europe and leading NICs (e.g. Brazil, South Korea, Taiwan) are intended to upgrade local industry. MNCs can find opportunities to tap local talent for product R&D aimed at regional markets.

• **MNCs should closely examine opportunity costs of technology transfer.** MNCs obtain short-term benefits from licensing or other forms of technology transfer, but these gains may not compensate innovative MNCs for loss of potential gains from direct utilization of new technology through exports or investments in the target market. Moreover, there is evidence that US-based MNCs may be licensing or selling technology in Asia at excessively low rates.

• **Further innovation is the best way to protect technology.** While Washington's efforts at promoting better protection for intellectual property abroad are bearing fruit, the efficacy of patent and copyright protection as barriers to competitors and copiers is limited and probably eroding. The only sure guarantee is to stay ahead in the innovation race.

94. New Approaches to Maximize Payoff From R&D

Many MNCs today are in a classic double bind: They cannot achieve their sales and profit goals in increasingly competitive world markets without a steady stream of new products, but they cannot develop the new products they need without spending an excessively large part of their operating budgets, thereby cutting into earnings. The problem is intensified when companies focus efforts on achieving product breakthroughs, which have a notoriously high failure rate.

Traditionally, the major risk in product development has been that the product that is being nurtured will turn out to be a commercial disappointment or, even worse, a total flop. In recent years, however, the specter of the shrinking product life cycle has come to haunt executives. Simply put, the new worry is that even if a new product meets with success, the success will prove to be too short lived to allow the company to recoup its original investment.

This fear is justified: Product life cycles in many fields, especially those involving advanced technologies, are getting shorter. In a matter of months, nimble imitators can gear up to copy—and improve—new products that may have taken their originators years to develop.

This reality makes it all the more important for companies to get more bang from each R&D buck, since they cannot really opt out of the new product game and remain major factors in their markets. Indeed, despite the double whammy of higher costs and shorter life cycles, most companies interviewed by BI say that they will increase, rather than reduce, their overall R&D expenditures in the coming years. But by attempting to avoid costly failures and to streamline the product development process, they hope to be able to amortize expenses and reap rewards more quickly than in the past.

Improving the Process

To ensure that the process of developing new products is made more rational, consider the following:

• **Take small steps.** Dozens of executives interviewed by BI stress that cost-effective, competitive businesses are characterized by regular, small innovations, rather than by occasional blockbusters. Indeed, some point out that one reason that Japan outperforms the US in some industries is the so-called home-run syndrome that afflicts many US MNCs. These companies pour resources into efforts to develop revolutionary prod-

Minimizing the Likelihood of New Product Failures: New Product Failure Factors and Preemptive Measures

- **Inadequate market research: overoptimistic sales forecasts.** Insist on competent predevelopment research. Check constantly to ascertain if initial research assumptions are still valid and have not been made obsolete by new product entries or by changing buying patterns.

- **Development time and expense substantially over budget.** Consider using a worst-case scenario when allotting time and money for development. From a project's inception, try to anticipate what least cost development alternatives might potentially be used—e.g. commissioned external help, isolated project teams, licensing, etc.

- **Matched or rendered obsolete by the competition sooner than was expected.** Anticipate likely product and pricing moves by competitors and factor these into risk calculations. Focus on what measures might be taken in order to prevent easy copying of the product, particularly by low-cost firms that specialize in product imitations.

- **Inadequate marketing and know-how and/or distribution channels.** Have a clear business plan for the product—not just one that protects sales into the next decade, but rather one that shows step by step what marketing methods and distribution channels will be used to achieve goals and to counter competition. Make sure the product's initial success will come from sales through the firm's normal (familiar) distribution channels.

- **Inability to get production costs down fast enough.** Have a detailed production strategy ready at an early stage of the project. Be prepared to refuse projects that cannot provide a feasible plan for obtaining and maintaining production cost leadership.

- **Product with no real point of superiority in the user's eyes.** Beware spending large R&D sums to develop "me-too" products. Instead, use shortcuts such as licensing or acquisitions. Don't be seduced by illusory product innovations—i.e. those that may have technical merit but will not be perceived by customers as providing real added value.

- **Product developed only for reasons of corporate pride or prestige.** Beware of launching products in difficult segments solely for reasons of pride or prestige. Be sure to avoid attacking entrenched market leaders in such segments without the benefit of a clear competitive edge on several essential fronts—e.g. costs, distribution, design, etc.

ucts and/or breakthrough technologies that they hope will knock the competition out of the market, but that, instead, often fail to live up to their initial promise. In contrast, a majority of Japanese companies are content with the small, but frequent, gains that keep their score steadily climbing.

The best way to counteract the home-run syndrome is to adopt a clearly enunciated policy of incrementalism. This does not mean companies should never invest in visionary ideas. Rather, it means they should be careful to weight their R&D portfolios in favor of step-by-step innovation.

They may even find that this approach is reasonably good at generating breakthroughs, which sometimes result as much from serendipity as from highly structured planning and massive research expenditures.

- **Cover all the bases.** Companies that have good track records in product development point out that it is necessary to evaluate new product ideas from the following four main angles: prospects for sales and profits; capital costs; competitive feasibility; and strategic desirability. Rigorous market research and financial analysis of projected costs and revenues are essential in order to gather information in these four areas. Such efforts, according to an executive of one large company, are aimed at "confirming in the marketplace what our instincts are telling us."

- **Establish immovable standards.** If a new product idea is unlikely to meet a pre-set profitability target within a pre-set time period, the successful MNCs do not undertake it—at least not in its present form.

- **Speed up the development cycle.** The need to conduct adequate research when evaluating proposals does not mean that companies should move slowly in selecting projects. On the contrary, given today's costs and competitive pressures, many executives consider speed in evaluating, testing and rolling out new products absolutely essential to success.

Among the approaches companies are using with varying degrees of success to bring products to market faster are computer-aided design, multidisciplinary project teams and long-range product planning. They are also seeking outside suppliers of technology and/or actual products.

The latter is increasingly important to many major companies such as IBM, Caterpillar, Philips, Thomson, ICL and Kodak. These and many others, including Japanese firms, have all experimented with buying finished products from outside suppliers and marketing them under their own brand names. There can be internal resistance to such a program, but many companies have overcome it.

• **Streamline decisionmaking.** Another way that the process can be speeded up is to reduce the need for elaborate reporting mechanisms and layers of committee approvals. Some executives note that by focusing on low-cost, low-tech, low-risk product-line extensions (e.g. incrementalism), the responsible managers can make more of the operational decisions on their own.

95. Cost of Quality: A New Measure of the Bottom Line

Total quality management (TQM) programs are relatively new for most companies, thus few have successfully quantified the impact on the bottom line. What firms often do highlight is the enormous cost of doing things wrong (on average anywhere from 5% to 30% of total sales). "We believe in Crosby's teaching that in order to get management's attention, you must attach a dollar sign to these things," says Peter Polgar, director of corporate quality at General Instrument Corp (GIC). Below, BI describes how GIC is applying cost of quality (COQ) in the total quality management process.

COQ is the common measure used to quantify the dollar impact of poor quality. It incorporates three elements:

• **The price of conformance—the cost of not making mistakes.** This area includes the prevention of possible errors and defects in design. It also includes quality training, inspection and appraisal.

• **The price of nonconformance—the cost of not meeting customer requirements.** This consists of both internal failure costs (correcting defects before the product is shipped) and external failure costs (correcting errors after delivery to the customer).

• **Lost revenues—from customer defections or failure to connect with potential customers.** Missed phone calls and declining volume order are key indicators.

What Gets Measured Gets Improved

Quality executives say that companies should try to focus on the most important indicators and avoid measurement for measurement's sake. However, some companies new to TQM make the case that a more detailed approach initially can help identify problem areas for improvement. GIC measures COQ both in the divisions and on a corporatewide basis.

At first glance, the number of categories included in GIC's index seems unnecessarily complex. However, because GIC's total quality program is less than a year old, both Polgar and Roger Heffernan, vice president for manufacturing, defend the detail. Recalling a false start with TQM in the early 1980s that glossed over measurement, Heffernan says they have learned that "you can't just wing it." Even taking daily readings in some areas is, in Heffernan's view, necessary at this stage.

GIC does not, however, intend to live with this system forever. Polgar stresses that measurement intensity is good with which to start out. "But in three years, if everything goes right, it will be embedded in the culture," he says.

How GIC Measures Cost of Quality

GIC's two-part COQ report comprises total quality opportunity (TQO) and key quality measures (KQM). The report is reviewed monthly by the headquarters operations committee, chaired by GIC's president.

TQO and KQM are expressed in four categories: total cost of quality (hard), total cost of quality (soft), key quality measures and total quality opportunity, which combines the first two. The hard measures focus on design and manufacturing, while the soft indicators also look at human resources, marketing, distribution and other areas.

● **Cost of quality (hard).**   Four classes of quality costs (prevention, appraisal, internal failure, external failure) are measured in dollars and as a percentage of the cost of sales for the month and year to date. GIC has found that internal and external failure costs tend to be much higher than appraisal and prevention costs: "They truly represent the cost of not doing it right the first time," says Polgar.

● **Cost of quality (soft).**   The following soft measures are expressed in dollars and as a percentage of sales.

(1) **Productivity loss** — total unproductive hours in a month times the fringe benefit rate. Often this serves as an indication of problems beyond the control of the worker, such as recurring part delivery delays.

(2) **Past-due shipments** — orders that are canceled due to missed ship-

ping dates plus 2% per month (the approximate related cost of deferred revenue).

(3) Employee turnover — the sum of three months' salary, fringe benefits and the cost of replacement.

(4) Late introduction of new products. "Speed to market" is one of four priorities established by the CEO in the three-year corporate strategic plan. Improvement in this area sets specific targets for the time it will take a new product to enter the revenue stream.

(5) Engineering change notices. The estimated cost attributed for each notice by a division is $300. (In the defense group it is $1,000.) Numerous nondirect costs are also associated with these changes.

(6) Surplus inventories. This reinforces the connection between just-in-time and quality. "We couldn't possibly have JIT without reducing inventories and you can't reduce inventories without quality," says Polgar. All divisions are charged 2% per month for the excess above plan.

(7) Past-due receivables. The general rule at GIC is that good customers will always pay promptly. If they don't, it is probably because of quality.

(8) Discounts/allowances. This is taken right off the P&L as an ad hoc discount. Asks Polgar: "Why do you have to give a discount at all if the quality is good?"

(9) Unrecovered premium freight — the cost of premium versus regular freight when GIC picks up the tab. "If you are doing things right the first time, you are not going to have to shove something into overnight mail at the last minute," says Polgar.

(10) Customer-service errors — the cost of recording an order number incorrectly, shipping the wrong product, etc.

● **Key quality measures**. KQMs are mostly nondollar measures (percent of total hours, days, numbers). But they also include a few hard and soft COQ measures. KQMs are used to develop strategic planning goals, organize quality improvement activities and benchmark competitors.

(1) Conformance. This combines internal and external failure costs associated with a product.

(2) Relative perceived quality. These measures should reveal how the customer feels about GIC, particularly vs competitors. They overlap with and expand on soft measures. Divisions make extensive use of frequent surveys of key customers who are surveyed on a rotating basis.

● **Total quality opportunity.** Hard and soft TQO are covered in this category—both product and employee performance related measures. Other categories include cycle time and employee involvement.

96. Pitfalls to Avoid When Sharpening Quality Performance

According to a Gallup survey, a majority of US executives believe that to compete internationally, their companies must make further quality improvements over the next few years. Roland Dumas, research manager at Zenger-Miller Inc, an international management consulting and training firm, and Carol Laughlin, market research associate, have conducted extensive analyses of corporate quality programs. Their research yields the following insights into the pitfalls companies encounter when they attempt to make a quality improvement program work.

● **Beware of the obvious solutions.** When senior managers perceive their company has a quality problem, their initial reaction is to assume that worker motivation or skills are at fault. When the first wave of attempts to improve employee performance do not work, or are only partially successful, the spotlight then turns on two other easily identifiable groups: middle managers and suppliers.

   Says Dumas, "The second wave involves tightening management controls and/or pushing the problem upstream to suppliers," who the company now pressures for higher quality. While these methods may sometimes be part of a successful quality plan, they are often done in an ad hoc, fragmented fashion. Instead, management should view quality as an executive leadership issue, recognize that cultural change is inherent in quality improvement and understand that management of quality, like management of sales, is integral to the organization.

● **Executive behavior must guide the quality process.** Many programs fail because top managers do "not really understand the underlying philosophy, much less support, the quality programs they have initiated." They tend to delegate responsibility too quickly and continue to make demands (e.g. unrealistic production quotas) that conflict with new quality standards.

Dumas suggests "starting slowly, small, and in the executive suite." Only when top executives understand the full ramifications of the required changes should the program begin to filter down. He recommends the approach used by the Japanese in the 1950s, where executives shared what they learned only with the management layer directly below them rather than with the overall organization.

A related point is that senior executives should give changes a reasonable chance to work. Consistency is important. Resist the temptation to try every new approach that comes along. Instead, management should work to create a sense of constancy that builds employee trust and a quality ethic that works.

• **Adopt others' successful strategies—but adapt them to your own organization**. The key word here is adapt. Dumas points out that service companies – particularly financial services – often resist using practices first tried in manufacturing, even though the techniques may be generic and directly applicable. For example, statistical process control has been effectively used to measure insurance claims handled and many other white-collar tasks. At the same time, companies must avoid blindly following what some other firm, even in their own industry, is doing.

• **Use in-house talent wherever possible**. If your company has in-house managers with appropriate human-resource or operations management skills, include them in your program right from the start. Too often, quality programs are brought in from the outside with no input from the company's own experts. These are the people, says Laughlin, who can save the company time, energy and money. They know how employees learn, how to evaluate their skills, what training they need to get the quality program off the ground and how to tailor a program to fit the company's specific culture. Perhaps most important, they can provide the outside supplier of a quality system important feedback about what has been successful at the firm. A feeling that employees "own" the process is essential. Dumas cites the risk that, "if everyone attributes success to the consultant and then the consultant goes away, so will the success."

• **Make sure basic know-how keeps pace with new processes.** "Introducing new systems and technologies when people don't have the fundamental skills to use them is a prescription for disaster," remarks Dumas. Laughlin cites as an example a company that taught its workers a new statistical control process and ways to correct technical problems, but did not follow through in making sure that the staff had the communication, leadership and problem-solving skills to make the best use of these new tools. The result: The workers have become "whistleblowers" who can spot a problem, but who don't know how to talk to a boss or coworkers about the trouble, how to identify the cause, and so on. "Once they have these skills, employees will not only do the right things, they will do them effectively," says Laughlin.

Closely related to ensuring that the basic skills are correctly taught is the need to make sure that the cultural and organization changes required to support the new processes are introduced simultaneously.

● **Keep it simple, yet comprehensive**.   First, define quality in a way that is basic, practical and relevant to everyone's job. This means that all quality systems should require the fewest number of steps to complete each task. "No one should feel a quality program is making his job harder," says Dumas.

Next, make sure the new quality-consciousness extends to everyone in the company. Often a quality effort is mounted with those responsible for the final stages of product development in a manufacturing firm or those on the front line in service industries. But the targeted group may not be the source of the problem or it may not be able to solve it. By building a quality perspective into the whole manufacturing or service process (and staff departments, as well), the company can avoid the multiplier effect that occurs later on. Also, quality needs to be seen as a corporate ethic and just as important as the bottom line. Says Dumas: "When held as a higher standard, then there is more buy-in from employees, and the actual financial return will reflect the higher customer approach."

● **Allow for cultural differences when taking a quality program across borders**.   For example, Japanese automobile manufacturers experienced significant difficulties when they tried to establish quality circles in their new US plants, because the process was so unfamiliar to US autoworkers, long accustomed to a more adversarial relationship with management. Dumas notes that a potential area for culture clash between US employees and Japanese management is financial services. As major Japanese financial institutions set up offices in the US and hire large numbers of Americans, the fast-track expectations of young MBAs are likely to bump hard against traditional attitudes of seniority and relatively slow promotions.

He also urges companies not to think of "exporting" a domestic quality improvement program to a foreign subsidiary. Local managers and workers will almost certainly see it as an attempt to shove "something foreign" down their throats. A more productive approach is to tell over-seas operations what its quality standards are. Only if the subsidiary cannot meet the standards on its own should the parent company show it how to do so.

97. Caterpillar's Eight-Point Quality Improvement Plan

A quality pioneer in the US, Caterpillar (CAT) launched its Quality Improvement Program in 1982. Robert C. Dryden, vice president for logistics and quality, describes the eight points in the plan as follows:

• **Creating customer-generated standards.** Customer needs and perceptions should set standards for performance, reliability, serviceability and durability. Increased use of quality function deployment (QFD) techniques is a key initiative in this area.

• **Improving the New-Product Introduction (NPI) system.** Again, customer requirements should govern product design, testing/evaluation, manufacturing planning and process control. The NPI system ensures that customer-generated standards are met. Major goals include reducing engineering changes and cutting time cycles for new-product introductions and updates.

• **Enhancing the manufacturing process.** CAT is establishing an internal quality certification process for manufacturing areas. Other goals include establishing, documenting and improving process control; increasing the use of design for manufacturability techniques; and optimizing the computer's role in manufacturing.

• **Assuring supplier quality.** A continuing area of emphasis has been supplier quality certification. Instituted in 1979, this program requires suppliers to prove control of critical process quality characteristics, to demonstrate product conformance without receiving inspection and to employ a plan for continuous improvement (known at CAT as "annual quality improvement," or AQI; see point 8, on page 261). More than 80% of Caterpillar's worldwide purchases of direct production material are made from certified suppliers. Major goals include supplier participation in design for manufacturability activities and even supplier sharing of warranty expense.

• **Differentiating product support.** A key element of this point is to work with independent Caterpillar dealers to improve parts availability, speed response time and improve the quality of service calls. The goal is 100% end-user (customer) satisfaction, as measured against competitive product support.

• **Capitalizing on field intelligence.** To implement their eight-point plan, the company requires timely and complete information from customers. Thus it has been developing a number of ways to capture customer feedback. One such effort involves mailing customer acceptance surveys to buyers six months after purchase. Another system in use is PREDICT—a method of tracking performance of new products in order to provide early warning of problems.

• **Improving education in quality.** Coordinated by an internal quality institute, this program targets every employee for the quality training his or her job may require. A corporatewide data base assists supervisors in developing personalized training plans according to the tasks assigned to the position.

• **Instituting AQI and reducing cost of waste.** AQI is defined as an "activity which reduces the chronic level of waste or improves the level of process yield to achieve and maintain a new, greater level of performance never before attained." All CAT employees are encouraged to participate in AQI projects and all managers are evaluated on their AQI participation. So far, nearly 3,000 Caterpillar AQI teams have been formed. These have generated more than $450 million in savings and thousands of invaluable quality improvements. The ultimate goal is to achieve a 5% "cost of waste"—including costs of scrap and rework, inspection, internal failure and external failure (such as warranty)—as a percentage of operating income.

Managing the Eight-Point Plan

Responsibility for administering the plan falls to the Total Quality System Committee (TQS), composed of the president, several executive vice presidents, most vice presidents and two directors of the company. For each of the eight points, responsibility for corporate progress is shared by two or three committee members, based on their areas of expertise.

"I *sponsor* point four [assuring supplier quality] because, in addition to quality responsibilities, I am responsible for Logistics and Materials," explains Dryden. "Sponsors" are expected to make frequent progress reports to the president and the TQS committee.

To analyze progress, the sponsors of each point have established criteria for success. This makes it possible to measure progress on each of the points on a common scale of zero to 10. "It's a stepladder, starting at zero — where we have absolutely nothing — and progressing to a level of 10, which is where we want to be in a visionary sense. This helps us see where we are over time, where we want to be and what we need to accomplish in order to get there," Dryden explains.

For point 4, "zero" is "no supplier quality assurance program." The company's ultimate goal is tough. Caterpillar will have reached a "10" on this goal only when "process control of supplied material maintains a rejection level below 0.2% of dollar value," "suppliers participate in all Caterpillar manufacturability teams involved in purchased material," "supplier defects per thousand are less than 10" and "80% of Certified Suppliers participate in warranty expense."

98. Supply-Chain Management: Cooperate for Quality

Supply-Chain Management is gaining increasing acceptance among MNCs. However, there are also obstacles to its adoption ranging from top management indifference to a multiplicity of evaluation programs — to supplier-customer cooperation.

Ways to overcome them may include the following:

• **Secure top management support.**   Revamping supplier policy entails a host of internal reforms, including adoption of "total cost" accounting systems and multifunctional management teams to break down barriers between purchasing and other functions. However, such efforts often face opposition or indifference from executives still attached to traditional adversarial supplier management practices.

There is no substitute for strong initiatives "from the very top." For example in Xerox and Motorola, the CEOs forcefully backed total quality programs and overruled the objections of executives with a price-first fixation. Nevertheless, one purchasing manager pointed out: "How can we convince top management to adopt new thinking about supply chains when they're building defenses against LBOs and corporate raiders?"

• **Build alliances to bring purchasing departments back from corporate Siberias.**   The tendency of just-in-time (JIT) manufacturing programs and SCM principles to shift ownership of the quality function from corporate quality assurance staffers to purchasing or sourcing departments also sparks internal corporate resistance, according to Jack O'Connor, publisher of *Purchasing* magazine. Since their usual role has been "merely" to buy goods required by supposedly more important operations at the lowest price, purchasing sections have often received fewer management and manpower resources and enjoyed less clout in corporate councils. Persuading top management that purchasing departments require parity in resources, as well as compensation, may be one of the steepest barriers to reforming supplier management.

Gary Wojdyla, director of operations for engineering and manufacturing at NCR Ithaca, advises managers to "identify and educate other stakeholders" in their plant's supplier-customer links. Even cosmetic reforms can help: A name change from "purchasing" to "sourcing" can stress its strategic role of obtaining quality resources at low cost.

• **Establish a high-level coordinator for each relationship.** Disputes or miscommunications in partnerships, which often arise from the conventional view of suppliers and customers as adversaries, may require assistance from the top. J.H. Currier, assistant vp for corporate purchasing at NCR Corp, says that his company assigns one top executive to be the contact person for each of NCR's key suppliers. "After all local avenues have been exhausted in trying to settle a dispute, the supplier can turn to his NCR liaison as an ace in the hole."

• **Begin supplier-involvement programs in product and production process design.** Ken Stork, director, materials and purchasing for Motorola, told BI that the structure of as much as 70% of manufacturing costs are determined in the design stage. The early addition of a supplier's technical expertise can lead to improved manufacturing processes, fewer engineering changes, reduced cycle time and lower production costs. Motorola facilitates early supplier involvement by maintaining a data base of its best suppliers. "Designers don't begin work on a project before checking the preferred supplier list," says Stork. Resistance to this trend can be costly. A sales manager for a components firm told BI that a major customer still plays off suppliers against each other for lowest bids and does not involve them in the design of its transportation equipment. "In one project, they've presented us with a series of separate design and engineering changes without advance notice," he said. "We've thus been forced to do the same to our suppliers. Our costs are now higher and the quality—including delivery times—will be impaired."

• **Take the initiative to become a world-class customer.** Stork warns that suppliers who find themselves dealing with a die-hard buyer of the old "line them up and knock them down" school "might search for more appropriate customers." Firms can best avoid this by soliciting supplier evaluations of their own faults and using this input to improve operations.

• **Try to standardize certification criteria.** Several sales managers declared that the proliferation of total quality and supplier certification programs breeds confusion and severely strains administrative capacities. Examples include Motorola's Six Sigma effort and Xerox's "Leadership Through Quality" campaign. Motorola's Stork proposes the adoption of a unified "quality and service rating system" for supplier/customer certification and management. His suggestion: Use the rigorous certification process for application to the annual Malcolm Baldridge National Quality Award.

99. Broadening the Role of Logistics Management

Logistics management at Du Pont, the US-based chemical giant, is no longer merely a matter of seeking the most cost-effective means of moving material. It has now become an integral part of the company's global strategy, with logistics managers involved from the start in such major business decisions as the siting of manufacturing plants or even whether to enter new geographic markets.

"If your logistics plan is not aligned with your corporate strategy, you have a problem," says W. Earl Tatum, Du Pont senior vice president, materials, logistics and services. "This is particularly true as you approach the global marketplace. Tatum reports directly to Du Pont's Chairman and CEO and functions at the highest leadership level of the organization.

Logistics has been integrated with business teams throughout the organization and has been given greatly increased responsibilities. The company has implemented the concept of "total supply chain management," making logistics responsible for the entire supply line — the flow of materials — from raw materials coming in to finished Du Pont products going out. The logistics function is also playing a major role in the company's information technology systems, helping to gather information for both day-to-day operations and strategic decisions.

Early Involvement

When the company plans to locate a manufacturing or other kind of facility anywhere in the world, experienced logistics personnel are among the early company visitors investigating prospective sites. Du Pont's logistics experts undertake the following:

(1) Examine roads and ports, analyze local and regional transport routes, inspect available warehouses and determine if and where new ones would have to be built. If the company will produce hazardous materials at the facility, the logistics specialists consider and select appropriate transport modes, which may differ from those used in the US or other regions.

(2) Determine special packaging and labeling that may be required.

(3) Identify and evaluate prospective suppliers, carriers and other service providers then and there. This thorough approach helps Du Pont avoid building a plant and only then figure out the needed transportation and distribution services.

As Clifford Sayre, vice president and director of materials and logistics, puts it, "Negotiating with prospective vendors, carriers and other services on your knees is very difficult. But that is just the position we would be in if we were not involved in the siting decision from the start."

(4) Determine when and where to use internal transportation and distribution capabilities versus outside carriers and freight forwarders. "We do not feel that we have to do everything ourselves," says Sayre, although he notes that the company has its own transport fleet, which it uses when that is most efficient. And it invariably uses its own skilled drivers when transporting hazardous materials.

Supply Chain Management

The company is currently extending the concept of supply chain management to include its suppliers' facilities as well as those of the suppliers' suppliers, carriers and customers. Strong and substantive relationships with third parties not only improve the flow of material but fosters more cost-efficient systems and procedures of mutual benefit. In Europe especially, it is moving into product development, production planning and scheduling and warehousing as well as overall materials flow. Information management

In the US Du Pont keeps information on every transaction and every shipment. "We are now able to ascertain what quantities or qualities of commodities we are moving in which lanes and what carriers were utilized," says Sayre. "This permits us to get our average shipping costs down and to compare carrier performance."

The company's computer system is also able to determine the cost of servicing specific customers. In some instances it has discovered that the cost of holding an account is unprofitable. "Some of our people find it difficult to yield any sales to the competition," says Sayre, so they pursue sales prospects without considering the cost of servicing them. The financial statements managers receive now contain the cost of transportation and physical distribution right next to earnings. It is not unusual for them to discover that transportation costs equal the price or the profit margin of a product.

By linking up electronically with its suppliers, vendors and freight forwarders, Du Pont has been able to streamline administrative procedures, thereby reducing costs. At one time, for example, it cost about $350 to document each international ocean shipment, and huge stacks of paper were generated. Now, contracts are negotiated and managed electronically: a manager in the pricing office of a railroad, say, and another in Du Pont's procurement office agree upon terms and update tariffs by computer.

100. Singer Cuts Costs With Third-Party Purchasing

The competitive edge gained by offshore sourcing can be eroded by bureaucracy, long value-added chains and distance from supplier markets. To overcome these ills, Singer Furniture Co, the home furnishing subsidiary of US-based SSMC Inc, has replaced most of its international purchasing operations with services provided by an independent overseas procurement agency—the Florida-based IMX Corp. The result is a comprehensive program that promises to significantly trim costs while expanding the range of products Singer can offer North American retailers.

Singer Furniture began offshore sourcing of occasional tables in 1982. Since SSMC's Taiwan office specializes in sewing machines and was not prepared to source furniture, Singer's own in-house buyers, acting through both US- and Taiwan-based trading companies, purchased and shipped finished goods (mostly from Taiwan) to Singer's US warehouses for supply to its retailers. However, by late 1986, management determined that this method was not bringing in product at competitive prices.

Jeff Holmes, president of Singer Furniture, tells BI, "We got caught up in a bureaucratic structure with six layers which burdened the product with excessive overhead." The chain stretched from Singer's own international purchasing arm, through the trading companies, to the Taiwan manufacturer and its subcontractees.

Singer Furniture also bore all the business risk. Says Holmes, "Everyone else was making money off the goods before we received them; no one cared whether or not we moved them out of our warehouse." Finally, despite frequent trips to the Far East and Latin America, Singer's limited corps of buyers were unable to stay on top of market trends.

Early in 1987, Holmes contacted the chairman and CEO of Florida-based IMX Corp, Bill Forester, and asked him for a proposal to revamp Singer's overall sourcing program. Following a successful trial project that sourced bedposts from the Caribbean and which saved Singer 50% off the past buying price in Taiwan, Singer Furniture appointed IMX as its sole and exclusive agent for overseas purchasing.

A Total Sourcing Package

IMX handles all negotiations from consolidated shipments, does all the paper work (e.g. letters of credit, freight, insurance, customs clearance), conducts quality control inspection, and searches for new suppliers in return for a fixed commission based on port of region, free-on-board prices. The program consists of two parts:

• **Manufacturing support.** IMX takes off-shore sourcing of most parts and components for Singer Furniture's US-based plants. These turn out the firm's core lines of home furnishings, ranging from bedroom sets to electronic cabinets.

• **Singer International Merchandise Exchange (SIMX).** The most innovative part of the program involves direct shipment by IMX of 40-foot mixed containers of finished furniture products to Singer retailers from the supplying country. Instead of limiting themselves to occasional tables, retailers are now able to choose their own combinations from 10 product categories (over 400 items) for either port-of-arrival or door-to-door delivery through Singer Furniture's customer service office.

Where Are the Savings?

According to Singer Furniture executives, this program offers several advantages:

• **Buying economies of scale.** By purchasing goods for several clients (including furniture makers other than Singer), IMX is able to consolidate buying power and secure lower purchasing and shipping costs for Singer's finished goods and parts. Forester tells BI that IMX can attain at least 20% savings for Singer Furniture and other clients because of its low overhead and an entrepreneurial approach to global sourcing. "Most MNC overseas purchasing offices have large corporate

overheads, limit themselves to major suppliers and often do not negotiate very hard. Their high profile also encourages local firms to hike
prices. We try to develop smaller firms that have the potential to make
the product, but who may not be as aware of the market price or know
our buyers. We're also willing to put in the extra effort to get the best
price."

• **Sharply reduced management overhead.**   Singer was able to eliminate its international purchasing unit and related corporate charges for
sales, general administration and inventory. It was also able to cut out
the slice paid to local trading companies, further reducing costs. With
IMX acting as Singer Furniture's offshore purchasing arm, the main
Singer involvement is a key member of Holmes's staff who acts as liaison
with IMX. While Singer participates in the selection of and negotiations
for new suppliers, IMX bears most expenses for these functions and for
the administration of the program.

• **Establishment of a fixed cost basis for offshore sourcing.**   IMX is
paid directly by Singer on a commission basis for the manufacturing
support and for the SIMX programs.

• **Lower warehousing costs.**   Under their program, Holmes says that
IMX and local suppliers "don't make money unless we do." For these
added labor-intensive lines, Singer Furniture has become strictly a marketing operation: IMX, its local suppliers and retailers now bear most of
the risk of whether or not these items sell on the US market.

According to Holmes and Forester, the arrangement between Singer
Furniture and IMX contains features that protect against the risks that
would be expected in farming out a function as closely linked to profitability as purchasing:

• **The contract can be canceled at any time.**   "IMX either supplies us
with quality products at a reasonable price or we find someone else. All
I risk is a container shipment," says Holmes.

• **The SIMX program does not directly impinge on Singer's core lines,**
but involves a new program of midrange furniture products for Singer
retailers in the US and, eventually, other markets.

• **Singer and IMX agreed on procedures to ensure quality and open
disclosure of expenses.**   Says Holmes, "We did quality control programs in the supplying plants, which we selected with IMX. We set up

guidelines for overhead structures and applied costs and were involved in the negotiations overseas."

Forester asserts that IMX acts as an extension of Singer Furniture for offshore sourcing, not as an outsider: "We follow a policy of full disclosure with regular computerized reports of all our expenses, from freight costs to our commission. Singer personnel can also participate as much as they want in our activities." Adds Holmes: "I know how much he's going to make; he knows how much I'm going to make."

101. Hewlett Packard Cuts Costs With JIT

Hewlett Packard's implementation of just-in-time (JIT) inventory and manufacturing principles throughout its worldwide operations has enabled the US-based MNC to achieve dramatic savings: Annual inventory costs were slashed by $525 million, and inventory costs as a percent of revenues are down from 20% to 14%. Achieving such results with JIT demands action on a variety of fronts—in organizational behavior, on the factory floor and with supplier relationships. The following illustrates how HP tackled the challenge of changing organizational behavior.

JIT is commonly thought of as an inventory-reduction technique. It is true that with a JIT system a company avoids building up excess inventory by manufacturing only a limited quantity of products at a time, and procuring only the parts and raw materials necessary to produce those items. But this barely begins to explain the whole concept of JIT, according to Richard Holm, manufacturing consultant at the accounting firm of Arthur Young & Co. There are two reasons why companies should approach JIT as a sweeping manufacturing strategy—from product conception to final assembly—and not simply as an inventory-control tool, says the consultant.

First, implementing JIT requires changes in management's approach to a host of issues beyond inventory. Second, the advantages of JIT stretch beyond inventory management. They include lowering overall manufacturing costs, reducing factory space, improving product quality, increasing flexibility and responsiveness to the market, and implanting faster and more accurate communications both internally and with suppliers and customers.

HP is a good example of a company that has taken this holistic approach to JIT. What makes HP's experience particularly instructive is that, like so many MNCs today, it is highly decentralized.

The firm's interest in JIT dates back to the late 1970s when, accord-

When 'Idle' Is Not a Waste of Time

One of the most important effects of JIT is its psychological impact on employees. Explains Harold Edmondson, vice president and director of Hewlett Packard's corporate manufacturing group, "Under JIT, when operators finish a task in the production process, they must sit and wait. They cannot begin work on the next part because this will throw the entire system out of whack. This contradicts decades of telling workers not to be idle."

But employees have a hard time accepting the need to wait, according to Debra Dunn, manager of HP's office of the future. "In fact, production operators have been known to stash work and hold up the line to avoid being idle." It's also difficult for managers to feel comfortable with the idea that their workers must sit around at times.

Even though labor is only 2-3% of total product cost, Hewlett Packard is trying to minimize the impact of idleness on productivity and cost. HP focuses on situations where employees and/or production lines are out of operation for several hours or several days, since there is really not much a company can do about employees' having to be idle for a few minutes. In addition to helping employees adjust psychologically to the idea of periodic slack times, the firm provides employees with opportunities to perfect and develop new skills in their free time. This includes educational materials, seminars on JIT and math classes. The latter are particularly useful, since JIT is based on such disciplines as statistical quality control and materials flow analysis.

ing to Harold Edmondson, vice president and director of corporate manufacturing, a general feeling emerged among HP's 60 divisions that the company needed to protect itself from increasingly aggressive competitors.

Performance analyses by the divisions yielded three broad recommendations for improvement: upgrade product quality, lower manufacturing expenses and reduce inventory costs. To accomplish all three goals, several HP divisions decided to experiment with JIT, a system originated many years ago in the US, but embraced and refined more recently by the Japanese. These divisions' successes caused others to adopt JIT. Today, it is in place in varying degrees at many divisions worldwide.

Edmondson and Dick Love, general manager of HP's computer manufacturing division, emphasize that switching to JIT is a continuing process and not something that occurs overnight. Further, given HP management's solid commitment to decentralization, every division operates as an independent unit and, therefore, has the freedom to design its JIT strategy to suit its own needs. Nevertheless, one of the critical issues that all visions and the overall company must address is accommodating organizational behavior to the demands of a JIT system.

Before a company can install JIT, it must change corporate culture and employee attitudes. Frequently, this means altering their perception of primary responsibilities. For example, it may take a good deal of effort to help employees deal with periodic idleness under JIT (see box on page 270).

To implement JIT successfully, Edmondson and Love recommend working along the following lines:

• **Emphasize total quality control (TQC).** Executives and experts readily agree that JIT and TQC are highly interdependent (some experts claim JIT is a mechanism that enables a company to achieve TQC). For instance, one of the greatest attributes of JIT and its emphasis on manufacturing small quantities of products is that it quickly exposes any problems in the production process. Once a problem is exposed, however, a company must have a mechanism—TQC—to correct the situation, though defining the exact nature of TQC is not easy.

Many multinational companies, such as HP, have embraced the concept of TQC. Yet firms frequently encounter difficulties when it comes to actually developing a methodology and strategy to achieve TQC. One helpful tool for defining and implementing TQC is the eight parameters developed by manufacturing expert and Harvard Business School Prof. John Garvin that test for quality in a product: performance, features, reliability, conformance, durability, serviceability, aesthetics and perceived quality.

Even within HP, TQC has a variety of meanings and can differ from division to division. But underlying them, according to Love, is a view of TQC as a philosophy that must be imbedded in the corporate culture: It is not a one-shot campaign. The TQC approach, which makes achieving high-quality products and total customer satisfaction the top priority for all employees, means a constant tinkering with the manufacturing process. For many HP divisions, TQC entails statistical quality control programs.

• **Develop a preventive maintenance approach.** In a JIT environment, there is no such thing as "putting the fires out." Instead, an employee's first responsibility is to prevent problems from happening.

Since under JIT an entire line shuts down if a problem arises, it is critical to train all workers to use preventive maintenance.

Holm points out that one of the biggest obstacles to this approach, ironically, is often middle management, particularly plant managers who traditionally view their primary responsibility as crisis control.

Shifting mind-sets, Love says, requires some changes in a company's reward and compensation systems. This includes providing incentives for employees who unravel problems before they affect the line. It is also helpful to begin referring to all employees as "problem solvers."

• **Adopt a demand-pull philosophy.** Employees must be conditioned to the JIT philosophy that a firm manufactures only what is needed when it is needed. In other words, says Love, products are pulled, not pushed, through the production process. Holm says if a company receives an order for 20 items, then the purchaser must buy only the raw materials and parts necessary for 20 items and the production operators manufacture only 20.

Manufacturing is driven by market demand. Thus, developing and maintaining close communication between sales and marketing, on the one hand, and manufacturing on the other, is critical. HP's success with demand-pull has been greatly facilitated by decentralization and having a sales and marketing group in each division.

• **Publicize top management's commitment.** Visible displays of top management support can ease employee adoption of JIT. At HP, President and CEO John Young has taken an active role in promoting JIT.

JIT's acceptance by HP divisions has also been helped by the use of "showcase" projects. When a division meets with a high degree of success with JIT, its strategy is lauded by top management and publicized throughout the company. This has a contagious effect as other divisions try to mirror the success of the showcase project.

102.   How Hewlett Packard Combines JIT With Quality Control

For HP's computer terminals division, which combined just-in-time (JIT) principles with a program of total quality control (TQC), the payoff has been substantial. The division has been able to fend off threats from Far East competitors, become the premier low-cost global supplier, reduce factory space by 30%, triple production and increase annual inventory turns from six to 24. TQC has been critical both technically, to alleviate production problems, and strategically, to lay the foundation for JIT.

Quality First, JIT Next

Max Davis, production manager for computer terminals, says, "Operationally, TQC is first needed to eliminate unpredictability in the manufacturing process." Under JIT, products are designed to flow steadily through the process—from procurement of raw materials and components through to final assembly. If this systematic stream is interrupted with any sort of problem, production immediately stops. With such close tolerances built in, a company should apply an intense quality control program such as TQC to the entire production process before attempting JIT manufacturing.

When HP's computer terminal division became interested in JIT, it used its "first pass-turn on" quality standard to determine whether its factories were suitable for JIT. (This is a test to determine if a terminal works the first time it is turned on.) Initial analyses revealed that the "first pass-turn on" rate was just 60%. At this rate, says Davis, "JIT would not have worked. We first needed to improve the rate through TQC." Today, using TQC and JIT, the rate is up to 98-99%.

Identify the Problems

Strategically, explains Davis, TQC "helped us to identify the problems. More importantly, it crystallized what we actually wanted to achieve: to build the lowest-cost, highest-quality terminal by producing more efficiently, using our assets better and increasing dependability in both our manufacturing process and delivery to customers." Once priorities are set, implementing JIT is easier.

TQC and JIT complement each other in a number of other important ways, too. Dick Love, general manager of HP's computer manufacturing division, points to a prime example: JIT's emphasis on creating an uncluttered factory by eliminating excess inventory, work-in process and products awaiting rework is also a key element of successful TQC.

Designing for Manufacturability

Achieving geometric improvements in quality control to smooth the path for JIT requires, of course, some new approaches. Consequently, before applying other JIT elements to manufacturing, simplifying product design is a must, according to Richard Holm, manufacturing consultant for accountants Arthur Young & Co. The reason: "Because it minimizes the risk of error, resulting in higher quality and lower cost." Reducing costs, though always a goal in theory, is especially important for the terminals division because these products have become a commodity item that compete head-on with inexpensive units from Korea, Taiwan and Japan.

As with many other JIT techniques, simplifying the product design is a continuous process. "A company does not achieve a major breakthrough immediately," according to Davis.

HP's computer terminals division has been working on product designs for several years, yet it is only with its most recent generation of terminals that it achieved major new advances. Manufacturing expenses are now significantly lower because the new designs minimize the use of capital equipment and involve few labor-intensive steps. Perhaps the most important cost-cutting move was designing identical assembly steps for all terminals, despite model differences.

In struggling with design simplification, HP finds the following two approaches particularly useful:

• **Encourage team efforts.** Traditionally, product design managers and production engineers work independently. Once the design engineers complete development and make basic decisions on component selection and assembly techniques, they defer to the production engineers, who then iron out myriad technical manufacturing details.

A key JIT principle then is to have the design and production engineers work together; collaboration offers greater opportunities for simplification. "We not only adopted JIT's team approach, we extended the group to include the materials experts, who are responsible for vendor and component selection, and the engineers charged with testing for quality," notes Davis.

• **Involve suppliers.** Suppliers can also play a pivotal role in just-in-time (see box on page 275). According to Davis, "Rather than first finalizing the design and then searching for the supplier with the necessary high-quality, low-cost components, we decided to reverse the process." Based on initial design specs, Hewlett Packard asked various suppliers to submit samples of their highest-quality, lowest-cost components. Only those that had the potential of fitting Hewlett Packard's design needs were considered. The ones that were finally chosen went into the design.

JIT Makes Close Ties With Suppliers Essential

Installing just-in-time (JIT) successfully requires two major commitments from suppliers, according to Dick Love, general manager of Hewlett Packard's computer manufacturing division; (1) guarantee the quality of incoming materials; and (2) make frequent, often daily, deliveries. What's more, flexible planning with suppliers may be needed to overcome environmental and market obstacles to the adoption of JIT. HP's supplier strategies include the following:

• Leveraging corporate purchasing needs. Many HP divisions manufacture similar products and therefore purchase the same raw materials and parts, notes Harold Edmondson, vp and director of corporate manufacturing. In the mid-1980s, management consolidated sourcing at all divisions in a corporate contract to boost efficiencies and reduce costs.

Now each division submits its materials' needs to the central corporate manufacturing group where a team of executives (and purchasing agents from some divisions) then visit potential suppliers to examine their wares, review pricing and discuss required quantities. Suppliers then submit bids and contract terms are settled. Once the contract is signed, the divisions write releases against the corporate contract for materials.

Edmondson finds the use of corporate contracts fits nicely with JIT. He explains, "A supplier is more anxious to accommodate a $9 billion company than a $130 million division. Thus, the supplier more willingly complies with requests for more frequent deliveries and attests to the quality of incoming materials."

• Reducing the number of suppliers. Like many JIT users, HP has switched from using multiple vendors to a single supplier for each component or raw material. In Love's division alone, the number of suppliers has dropped from 75 to 20. Relying on a single supplier offers a number of advantages: It can boost negotiating power on pricing and delivery frequency, as well as foster a closer-knit relationship with the supplier. JIT's reliance on single suppliers entails some obvious risks. Consequently, companies must apply the most stringent criteria to selecting vendors. HP cuts risks by holding in the wings one or two potential back-up vendors. This often means taking the time to conduct evaluations of substitute suppliers.

Other JIT Operating Logistics

The following steps are also essential to making JIT a success in the factory:

• **Streamline the materials flow process.** Harold Edmondson, vice president and director of corporate manufacturing notes that JIT requires careful analysis to isolate the exact quantities of materials needed for a given product and determine when they are needed. "This is central to a company's success in eliminating excess parts and inventory on the factory floor."

Such a study involves attaching a time value to each manufacturing step in order to match all materials and their arrival dates with the production schedule. One helpful tool, developed by HP's applications group, is a standard materials flow software package that helps track planning, purchasing and manufacturing.

• **Reduce lot size.** JIT's emphasis on producing small lots, it turns out, is an excellent quality control tool because it permits production operators to spot defects more quickly. It also offers more flexibility in an environment based on a demand-pull approach (whereby a firm produces just enough to complete an order close to the time it is actually needed).

Under the strictest of JIT systems, the ideal lot size would be a single product, and HP's objective is for divisions to be able to offer this option, even though production schedules and business objectives may actually require larger runs, according to Love.

The computer terminals division is a good example. Says Davis, "Over a two-year period, it achieved the capability of manufacturing one product at a time. However, it is more efficient to gear production to 16 units, since this is the number required to fill one pallet. These pallets are then shipped to our central distribution points in San Jose, California. By focusing on 16 units, or an entire pallet, we avoid the cost of having the distribution center break down and resort a pallet."

• **Minimize set-up times.** Use of small lots is economical only as long as a plant is able to reduce the set-up time. For the terminals division, one of the greatest advantages of standardization of the production step has been a zero, or transparent, set-up time.

103. Cutting Production Costs: Seven Ways to Check

As companies continue to invest heavily in automation to cut production costs in both manufacturing and services, they are coming to recognize that such investments are most effective when made in an already cost-efficient environment. Moreover, automation is a long-term, cost-reducing strategy, given the up-front investment that must be amortized before savings are realized. So for the short and medium terms, the key to cost improvement will be to make more efficient use of existing facilities and resources.

Seven principal ways are used by leading MNCs to achieve durable production savings without resorting to full-scale automation:

- **Improved quality-of-work life.** Many executives say that the single most important factor for low-cost production is the integration of employees, technologies and work sites into systems that encourage high motivation and productivity. Such systems typically embody some of the following concepts: job enrichment, worker flexibility, "multiskilling," teamwork, job rotation, work place humanization, continuous training and incentive pay.

- **More rationalization and standardization.** Rearranging worldwide operations—or even those within a single region or country—with a view toward economies of scale, fewer internal transactions and less duplication yields significant returns. For example, Ferguson, a UK TV maker, recently moved all printed circuit board and subassembly work to one plant, plastic moldings to another and final assembly to a third. The result, says a company manager, is "greater flexibility and a fundamental reduction of our cost base."

- **Improved logistics and work flow.** By carrying out value analysis and various types of work-flow studies, many companies have improved work layouts, speeded up production and reduced materials handling costs.

- **Better purchasing and sourcing.** Outdated supply systems have left many MNCs at a competitive disadvantage in recent years, particularly when compared with Japanese and German firms. Some well-known companies, including Courtaulds, Renault, Chrysler and Caterpillar, credit a major part of their recent turnarounds to total reform of antiquated purchasing practices. These companies have reaped big gains from vertical "dis-integration," outsourcing and more stringent selection of suppliers.

- **Superior inventory control.** The concept of releasing work capital by maintaining lower inventory levels has long since proven its value. Predictably, many Western companies sing the praises of Japan's celebrated just-in-time system of inventory management.

• **General waste reduction.** While some waste is inevitable, an astonishing amount can build up over time. Too much storage or work space is easily spotted and corrected.

Wasted time is the most difficult problem of all — and the hardest to eradicate. (One US human resources consulting firm says the average US worker wastes over four hours per week.)

The best way to reduce waste is through improved management techniques, such as companywide quality improvement programs, more worker education programs and rewards for employees who make waste-reduction suggestions.

• **Quality programs.** Most executives by now are aware of the cost savings produced by carefully constructed quality awareness programs.

104. Why Cost-Cutting Fails:
Six Key Traps

MNCs embarking on — or in the midst of — cost-reduction programs should have no illusions: The chance of failure is high. Often, costs do not end up significantly lower, while operations are disrupted and morale and productivity suffer. The key reason for failure, say executives who have been through the process, is that management often underestimates the dimensions of the undertaking.

Comprehensive cost reduction, especially on a multinational basis, is a complex, long-term proposition. Management must redesign operations, experiment with new processes and systems, make crucial investments and disinvestments, and redeploy personnel. Furthermore, while tackling all these tasks, the firm must continue doing business and defend its markets. With so much going on, it is very easy for the cost-reduction campaign to stumble into one of the following traps blocking the path to cost leadership.

• **Failing to face up to major decisions**. Large cost reductions can be achieved only through major changes, such as production rationalization, work force reduction, investment in new technology and disposal of money-losing or marginal businesses. Making decisions that will affect hundreds or even thousands of people's lives is difficult, and management frequently puts off such moves as long as possible. But this can be disastrous. Research indicates that the most frequent cause of failure in cost-cutting programs is making critical decisions too late.

- **Playing yesterday's game**. MNCs often focus on improving costs relative to their own past performance without first analyzing industry trends and competitors' strategies adequately. Such introspection can be fatal. Substitute products, new technologies, new marketing methods and shifting consumption patterns can quickly transform a firm's entire market. Companies must assume that the future will *not* resemble the past. They have to attempt to plan for the markets of tomorrow.

People Express was a classic recent example of a firm that fell victim to this error. With a lean organization, work force multi-skilling and low wages, the company achieved the lowest operating costs in the US airline industry. But by the mid-1980s, the main determinant of success was no longer low costs. Instead, the criterion had become advanced computerized reservation systems that travel agents could easily access. UAL, American Airlines and others had invested heavily in such systems over the previous decade, and People Express was simply unequipped to compete in the new high-tech game.

- **Putting too much faith in information systems**. A cornerstone of many cost-cutting schemes is state-of-the-art accounting and reporting systems. Better identification of costs together with tighter budgeting and handling of variances is supposed to keep costs down. While improved cost accounting *can* save a great deal of money, some firms err in installing systems that are too elaborate and cost more to maintain and run than they return in value-added. As a management consultant notes, "Some companies are drowning in information...they have everything on computer—every expenditure, every job...but their systems contribute to perpetuating the kind of bureaucracy that low-cost firms try to avoid."

- **Pushing costs from one area to another**. Many companies find they go to great lengths to get costs down in one department, only to find them popping up somewhere else. For example, slashing an apparently bloated employee training budget may dramatically increase the cost of rectifying mistakes caused by poorly trained workers.

Worse is the intentional cost-shuffling sometimes done by managers who are unable to make mandated budget cuts any other way. Intercompany transactions are ripe for this type of abuse. Says one financial manager, "You spend your time figuring out how to get some costs off your books and onto somebody else's."

- **Emphasizing vertical integration**. Although moves toward vertical integration can produce compelling cost advantages, they are risky. The biggest danger is that anticipated cost savings may never materialize, in part because of higher fixed costs and heavier downstream capital requirements. Some companies, such as Chrysler, Courtaulds and Thomson, have found they save more money by reducing integration, rather than increasing it. This is because of the resulting greater flexibility in choosing suppliers and distribution outlets.

Other risks of vertical integration include getting into unfamiliar, hard-to-manage businesses and competing with (and alienating) existing customers and/or suppliers.

● **Not recognizing the limits of cost-reduction.** Even the most carefully planned and executed cost-reduction plan cannot give a durable new lease on life to a business with multiple, sizable problems such as obsolete technology and products or markets in economic decline. In particular, it cannot save an operation whose cost position is grossly and, in essence, permanently out of line with those of strong, innovative competitors.

Executives stress that before it begins a major cost-reduction program, a company should make sure it has a real chance of achieving and maintaining cost-competitiveness over the long haul. If objective analysis indicates otherwise, the company would probably do better to exit the business.

105. Cutting Waste at the Source

For a growing number of companies, the ideal pollution solution is to reduce waste at the source, rather than try to "manage" it later on. The following highlights some of the innovative steps MNCs are taking to minimize their production of waste.

A Stairstep Approach

Many large MNCs are implementing formal waste-elimination programs, which are often given such snappy acronyms as Chevron's SMART (Save Money And Reduce Toxics) and Texaco's WOW (Wipe Out Waste). Most of the programs stress reduction at the source as the first priority, recycling or reuse as the next most desirable approach and incineration or land disposal as the last resort. Some set specific targets, such as Monsanto's pledge to cut air emissions by 90% by the end of 1992. Others simply encourage waste elimination in every possible way and publicly recognize or reward successful suggestions.

Most firms can follow several established routes. The prerequisite is an audit to identify, quantify and prioritize waste streams that may be expensive and time-consuming. Kodak's initial audit took three years. But "the proper evaluation of waste streams is key to any program," says Robert Bringer, vp of environmental engineering and pollution control at 3M, and a formal assessment of problem sources and the feasibility of options are crucial.

● **Good housekeeping.**   Once a company knows the dimensions of its problem, the real work can begin, starting with improved plant housekeeping. "Source reduction is analogous to energy conservation 10 years ago," says David Roe of the Environmental Defense Fund. "Then, the solution started with a simple suggestion to shut the windows. We aren't even at the chemical equivalent of closing the windows yet today."

Housekeeping includes waste-stream segregation, inventory control, operating and maintenance practices and procedures, consolidation of operations, scheduling improvements and spill or leak prevention. Exxon Chemical Americas cut solvent emissions simply by placing floating roofs over solvent tanks, and that action paid for itself in a year. Union Carbide's lab at Tarrytown, New York, has cut wastes by 60% over the past two years with basic inventory measures such as buying in smaller quantities and instituting a computer system to help employees keep track of chemicals already available on the premises.

● **Revised production processes.**   The next step may be to modify production processes by changing equipment or improving process controls. Dow Chemical reduced tar streams by 47% at its herbicides plant in Michigan by changing the heat level and length of the production process. Emerson Electric, a power-tool manufacturer, improved operations by automating its electroplating system. The new process transfers less electroplating solution into rinsing baths, thus reducing hazardous waste.

● **New materials.**   Another approach to waste reduction is finding new raw materials or reformulating the product. Although this is more technically difficult than some other methods, it often provides the biggest payoffs in the long run. "It's the most effective way to go and gets first priority at 3M, because it can completely eliminate whatever is causing the waste problem," says Bringer.

Indeed, 3M's pharmaceutical plant in Northridge, California, has saved $180,000 on pollution control equipment and $15,000 a year in solvent costs by switching from coating medicine tablets with emissions-producing solvents to a water-based coating. And Hoescht's plant in Griesheim, Germany, has cut 8,000 metric tons of zinc oxide wastes a

A Successful Waste-Reduction Program

Any serious corporate waste-minimization campaign must necessarily embody several basic elements:

- **Top management support.** This is the most critical element. Midlevel management may see the problems, but without backing from senior executives, they do not have the authority to do anything. At the same time, line workers must participate. "The largest untrapped resource is the operators running the plant on a daily basis. Getting the line involved and listening when they make suggestions is very important," says Jerry Martin, director of environmental affairs at Dow Chemical. This requires communicating company policies and programs and training employees to look for savings. Many firms successfully couple positive reinforcement with performance evaluations that include a waste-reduction rating.

- **Staying power.** Management must commit to a program for the long haul. "You have to stretch to make long-term goals beyond what you think you can do," says Monsanto's Dennis Redington. Because results come slowly and waste reduction gets more difficult with time, the process can be a test of persistence.

- **Organizational response.** A separate environmental department is often a good idea and it should be a significant player in operations. For example, because 3M's Environmental Engineering and Pollution Control Department has been put on the same plane as other operating units, its decisions have significant effect.

But other departments have to be involved, too. Monsanto responded to a criticism that only environmental specialists were working on the problem by creating a steering committee of representatives from manufacturing, R&D and marketing. This setup involves the waste generators in the decisionmaking.

- **Resource allocation.** Part of a corporation's commitment to waste reduction requires that adequate resources be allocated to carry out programs. At Allied Signal, the Corporate Environmental Department must approve large expenditures before a project is undertaken to ensure that all environmental issues are addressed and necessary financing is included up front.

- **Record keeping.** Careful monitoring and recording of results are essential for comparing performance from year to year. Impressive figures will also motivate employees and garner favorable publicity.

year in making dye intermediates by switching from a zinc granule-based to a catalytic process.

• **Eschewing solvents.** But probably no industry has zeroed in on harmful raw materials to the same extent as the electronics industry. Tired of trying one chlorinated solvent after another only to find new problems with every switch, many firms are looking for ways to avoid using solvents for cleaning semiconductors altogether. Mitsubishi Electric and Taiyo Sanso of Japan have jointly designed a device free of chlorofluorocarbons that uses fine particles of ice and frozen alcohol for washing semiconductors. The device should be on the market next spring, but many other manufacturers, such as AT&T and IBM, are also in the race to find adequate solvent replacements.

• **Reclaim or recycle.** Finally, if the source of the waste cannot be altered, many companies decide to turn to reclaiming or recycling wastes on-site. Chevron, for example, used to dispose of large quantities of slop oil emulsion from its refinery in Port Arthur, Texas. Now it centrifuges the emulsion several times, separating out so much oil that 90% of what once was discarded can be reused in the refinery. In the power industry, the Danish company Haldor Topsoe A/S has developed a catalytic process to remove harmful sulfur and nitrogen oxides from flue gas. It recovers 95% of the sulfur as commercial grade sulfuric acid and reduces more than 90% of the harmful nitrogen oxide to nitrogen, without waste waters, slurries or solid wastes.

106. Environmental Management Gets a High Profile

Faced with tougher regulations and politically charged "green" movements around the globe, many companies are responding with credible progress to reduce the toxic waste by-products of their manufacturing processes. Still, a truly comprehensive environmental management program goes well beyond waste reduction at the plant.

Indeed, most functions in a company today require managers to address environmental protection issues in some way. "Environmental management is not an ancillary function," says William Kelly, manager of international government affairs at Ford Motor Co. "It has become part of the core business."

Corporate Environmental Policies

A corporate code of environmental conduct is the centerpiece of an effective environmental management program. Here are some key issues to consider when setting up a policy:

• **Contents.** At a minimum, a policy statement outlines a company's commitments: to the environmental laws wherever the firm operates, to responsible product design and manufacturing practices, to the provision of a safe workplace for employees and to an effective emergency response in case of an environmental crisis. Several companies also include specific targets for reducing toxic-waste emissions. For example, global warming has inspired IBM to declare its intention to eliminate all ozone-depleting chemicals from its manufacturing processes and products by 1993.

• **Communication to the public.** Though it once may have been sufficient to use these policy statements solely for internal purposes, now it is equally important to spell out corporate commitments publicly. "We formalized a corporate policy in 1977, but did not publicize it to the outside world until this year," says Harold J. Corbett, senior vice president for environmental health and safety at Monsanto.

• **Timeliness.** Although some firms established formal environmental principles over a decade ago, keeping such documents alive means constantly setting new goals. In 1989, Edgar S. Woolard Jr., Du Pont's chairman, announced an environmental program for the 1990s. It has six goals: minimize waste, enhance wildlife habitats, eliminate heavy metal pigments from certain plastics, recycle plastics, involve the community in environmental discussions and link managers' pay to environmental performance.

Organization

Establishing environmental, health and safety management (EH&S) as a separate corporate department (rather than, say, as part of manufacturing) is not a new development. However, the visibility, stature and authority of this group of professionals greatly increased during the 1980s. One important result has been an improvement of organizational frameworks at the corporate and operating levels to ensure that policy is translated into action. Executives say some organizational guidelines they have followed include:

- **Have EH&S report to the top.** The top EH&S executive at many firms in the forefront of environmental management reports directly to the chairman. Executives say the link to the top office is necessary to demonstrate the high priority of environmental issues on the corporate agenda.

- **Be consistent with the corporate organization and culture.** The key is to encourage cooperative networking between people who set environmental policy and those who run the businesses. "There's no magic organizational way to address either compliance or public-policy issues," says Cornelius C. Smith Jr., vice president of community and employee health, safety and environment at Union Carbide. "It is most important, however, for an EH&S organization to be accepted by business management. That means the corporation has to organize the department in the same manner as the businesses are organized."

- **Clearly delineate corporate vs operating roles.** The principal role of the corporate EH&S department should be strategic: to establish and communicate firmwide standards, to keep senior management abreast of important developments in the environmental arena and to guide and assess management compliance (see Auditing, page 286). With the support and guidance of a corporate group, business units can then be encouraged to design their own methods of meeting corporate standards.

  At Union Carbide, Smith heads the EH&S department and reports to the chairman and a special environmental committee of the board of directors. Separate EH&S units exist within each of the three worldwide businesses (chemicals and plastics, carbon products and industrial gases). Each of these units performs a full range of EH&S functions, including training and regulatory monitoring.

  Some companies take a regional approach. Along with its headquarters group, Dow Chemical has a manager of environmental affairs for each of its five regions: the US, Europe, Canada, Latin America and the Pacific.

- **Provide technical support for manufacturing.** Technical personnel on the corporate staff may sometimes be more effective working in the field. "If a plant needs a full-time environmental engineer, put that person on site, not on the corporate staff," says David Barrett, Digital Equipment's director of EH&S.

- **Foster multifunctional communication.** EH&S has worked mainly with manufacturing, but today all functions need to get involved. Several firms, including Digital, have created multifunctional boards that include representatives from EH&S and such other functions as the legal department, engineering and customer service, as well as major business units.

Auditing Options

The corporate EH&S group often oversees the environmental auditing function for the company worldwide, but executives suggest that the most comprehensive audits combine the corporate auditors' evaluations, self-assessments by business and factory managers and reports by outside consultants. Here are two approaches to environmental audits:

• **Team audits.** Digital's corporate EH&S group runs the audit program worldwide, but specific audits are usually carried out by teams of experts from the corporate and regional levels along with site specialists and outside consultants. One consultant evaluates the auditing process itself to ensure objectivity.

• **Manufacturing and management system audits.** Union Carbide administers a worldwide independent corporate compliance auditing program. It also uses a team approach for chemical process safety audits at production sites. In addition, the corporate group regularly reviews line management's EH&S systems. Each year, corporate EH&S selects two or three corporate requirements and assesses how well the business units are implementing them with the EH&S systems they have in place.

Community Involvement

Companies are beginning to encourage input from the public. Conoco, for instance, has launched two new initiatives in this area:

• **Citizen Advisory Councils** will consist of representatives from communities where refineries are located, starting in the US, followed by Europe and eventually extending to all major sites worldwide. The role of these councils will be to help Conoco shape proactive environmental strategies, monitor performance and blow the whistle if the company fails to perform.

• **A yearlong environmental fellowship program** that will give someone from government, an environmental group or academia an opportunity to work inside the firm on environmental issues. The program will also support Conoco personnel who want to work with environmental groups.

Employee Action

Companies are encouraging managers and employees to become more involved in EH&S issues through a variety of programs:

• **Classroom training;**

• **Awareness programs;**

• **Performance-appraisal systems** that tie compensation to participation in environmental-protection programs;

• **Employee volunteer programs.** At Digital's European Services and Supplies Center in the Netherlands, employees started a campaign to reduce the general use of polluting materials. This included a paper and packaging recycling program and efforts to use batteries without mercury. Conoco employees participated in Earth Day this year with tree plantings, beach and highway cleanups and recycling efforts across the US, Europe and the Middle East.

7
Human Resources

107. Ericsson Taps Global Talent Pool

The challenge of recruiting and developing capable managers and deploying them most effectively around the world is formidable—even for companies that have operated globally for many years. Below, BI examines the approach of Swedish electronics giant L.M. Ericsson, the centerpiece of which is an international personnel data base.

With 180 subsidiaries and affiliated companies in 90 countries generating foreign sales worth around 80% of total revenues, Ericsson has long been a leading international supplier of voice, data and text transmissions systems. But in the mid 1980s, competitive pressures intensified dramatically. In the face of rapid technological change, skyrocketing R&D costs and deregulation of telecommunications markets in many countries, Ericsson refocused its strategic objectives. The mission: to strengthen its worldwide position in telecom switching and transmission systems—the firm's most profitable products—while shedding unprofitable lines, notably computers, that had been draining corporate resources.

Managing People to Enhance Strategy

To build a more integrated global business, management paid close attention to the role of human resources. Some of the guidelines Ericsson set to maximize each manager's ability to meet global strategic objectives follow:

• **Tapping talent from an international pool.** "Ten years ago," says Bjorn Carle, manager of international personnel, "Ericsson was a Swedish company doing business abroad," and Swedes dominated the ranks of overseas management. But that policy swiftly proved limiting as the company stepped up its efforts to transfer complex technologies on a global basis. According to Carle, Ericsson's objective now is to find and train the best people in both domestic and foreign operations and to maintain the flexibility to move them to different parts of the world as needs arise.

To meet the high standards set for the global selection process, Ericsson adapted its annual executive compensation survey for foreign managing directors so that it pinpoints personnel with senior management potential. Moreover, according to Gunnar Lennerheim, manager of executive development, one of the key functions of his department is "to be sure that every company in the Ericsson Group has some sort of formal program for identifying candidates with potential." This information is put into the computerized data base Ericsson developed to assist in personnel selection, succession planning, career development and compensation administration (see box, p. 290).

• **International rotations.** Ericsson supports short-term overseas rotations (three to five years) as a grooming process to give managers exposure to operations in different parts of the world. It selects young "corporate high fliers" (both Swedes and foreign nationals) who typically are transferred not only to various foreign subs, but also to new business units and functional areas. Carle says the frequent movement of personnel has not posed any major administrative difficulties or additional expense apart from the considerable costs of relocating expatriates.

• **Tailoring personnel choices to the market.** One challenge in meeting worldwide demand is how to rapidly transfer complex technology. Ericsson's approach is to rely on Swedes familiar with the technology in the early stages of market penetration overseas. The temporary management team then gradually increases the responsibility of locals as the new systems become more established. "The main reason for this approach," says Carle, "is the nature of the product. In order to transfer a very complex technology to a local market most efficiently, it is very important that everything goes right to start with." How the balance of labor between Swedish and local nationals works out depends largely on the nature of the operation and the level of market penetration in the country. Having local nationals run operations generally works best in more mature markets where there is less need for technical support from headquarters.

Ericsson's Computer-Aided Personnel Management

Tightly matching global administration of human resources with the corporate strategic plan at a major MNC requires a complex data base of information on employees, corporate opportunities and operating environments. L. M. Ericsson's approach goes beyond the usual compilation of facts. Working with several other Swedish MNCs (Asea Brown Boveri, SKF and Volvo), Ericsson began to develop a personnel computer-based system, called Eritellus, several years ago.

Initially designed to prepare competitive compensation packages, the current system—in operation since 1986—today offers far-reaching capabilities. Eritellus is a sophisticated tool that Ericsson executives use to orchestrate such areas as succession planning, personnel evaluation, job matching and training program development. The system is used internally by all of the Swedish collaborators, and the firm is now marketing it to other companies. Key features of Eritellus are:

• **Integrated personnel and country data bases.** The personnel data base holds the usual employee background information, along with profiles of important company positions and the names of possible future candidates. It also has a 50-country data base with cost-of-living comparisons, in-country company policies, tax data (allowing salary calculations from gross to net), subsidiary profiles and general country data menus. All information is integrated to cover many types of analyses.

• **Microcomputer network.** The system operates on a group of networked PCs, although it can be installed on a single PC. At present, there are networks online in all human resource areas, at all headquarter business units and at some of the larger subs. "Of course, in a local network, you decide the level of security and it is much more complicated to break into a local network than it is into a mainframe," notes Bjorn Carle, manager of international personnel at Ericsson. To further ensure security, data is coded and password-access restricted.

(Continued)

> • **Collection.** Although most foreign office data is still collected manually, information is increasingly gathered via telecommunications and computer diskettes.
>
> Carle believes that the system has led to "revolutionary" changes in Ericsson's ability to analyze staff needs. For one thing, expatriate administration is now decentralized and therefore more efficient—the task is handled by each business area, leaving corporate executives more time to concentrate on strategic policies. And, Carle says, Eritellus' international overview saves time, produces more accurate data and permits a more uniform worldwide job evaluation system.

For example, in 1987, Ericsson introduced its AXE switching and transmission system in the US and brought in a staff of 175 Swedes to the sub to provide initial technical support. Since then, it has cut this Swedish staff to below 100.

By contrast, Ericsson's 34-year-old Australian sub is described by Carle as a "mini-corporation" that is independent from headquarters. While the current managing director in Australia is a Swede, all other managers are Australians.

• **Training and development.** According to Lennerheim, all personnel receive some form of technical training, but those selected for fast-track career development are exposed to more extensive classroom training in international management. Ericsson devotes major investments of time and money to this training, again with the rationale that effective worldwide marketing of high-tech products requires more than on-the-job experience. Most of this training is conducted in Sweden, but managers may also attend outside programs as well, including Harvard, CEDEP in France and IMEDE in Switzerland. The top talent selected has the option of taking a leave of absence for up to a year for this schooling, or they may complete the program in segments over an 18-month period.

108. Kodak Develops Formula to Hire Top Grads in Japan

Recruitment—one of the stickiest issues facing foreign MNCs in Japan—is probably most difficult for research-based and high-tech firms that compete fiercely for science and engineering graduates. When US-based Kodak opened a new $74 million complex in Japan in October 1988, they found recruiting the necessary scientists and engineers for its R&D center to be one of the company's greatest challenges. By opening day, however, Kodak had landed a staff of 100 scientists, engineers and management executives.

Howell Hammond, vice president and director of R&D for Kodak Japan, offers some pointers to companies competing for top-flight graduates against such heavyweights as Mitsubishi, Sony, NEC and Fujitsu:

• **Concentrate on name recognition first.** In 1985, when Kodak decided to establish an R&D center, Hammond immediately initiated a dialogue with professors and placement officers to strengthen Kodak's name and reputation among the top universities and academics. For two years, Hammond, and later the newly appointed Japanese technical director, regularly visited the universities without ever asking for students. Only in 1987 did Kodak begin to recruit and hire graduating students.

• **Hire seasoned Japanese scientists in key positions.** Recruiting a top-level MITI scientist to serve as technical director ranks as one of Kodak's most important coups, because this individual was instrumental in opening university doors. The former MITI executive assumed responsibility for recruiting and hiring graduates, a task made easier by his solid reputation, contacts and familiarity with the Japanese recruiting system.

• **Forge links with teachers.** Japanese professors — rather than placement officers — have considerable influence on the job choices made by science and engineering students. So it is imperative to forge a strong relationship with respected teachers, even when a company is not actively seeking graduates. Hammond also suggests that at first a company outline its research needs and ask the professor to recommend students, rather than make up-front demands for the top two students. Another technique used by Kodak is inviting professors to R&D and technology symposia, which the company hosts annually to discuss new developments at Kodak and in the industry.

• **Stay ahead of the recruiting game.** Each year, nine academic and 35 industrial/employer associations map out a formal recruiting timetable, which generally runs from May to October. During the May-August period, recruiters may visit schools to meet informally with and leave application forms for students and placement officers. Official job interviews and tests begin in early September. From mid-October, companies may extend job offers for positions that begin the following April.

Although firms must adhere to the schedule—particularly for job offers—Hammond says it is possible to meet casually with students and professors before formal recruiting commences in May. In fact, to overcome the inherent disadvantage of being foreign, firms should invest the time and effort to cultivate professors and students as much as possible outside traditional channels. Visits to operations early in the year are one good alternative. Another reason to establish relationships with promising job candidates quickly is to avoid being shut out by aggressive domestic competitors. There have been instances of Japanese MNCs "kidnapping" the best students during the interview and job-offer period, thus preventing them from meeting with and possibly receiving better offers from other firms.

• **Cultivate ties between staff members and their alma maters.** In Japan, most alumni maintain close contacts with their colleges and former professors, which can help in recruiting future graduates. For Kodak, a unique opportunity presented itself in 1987, when the company hired some graduates even though the R&D center was still under construction. Kodak arranged to have these employees return to the university to begin their research. Since both the university labs and the Kodak researchers were focusing on materials science, both an exchange of ideas and the establishment of valuable interpersonal relationships took place.

• **Advertise in direct-mail magazines.** Ads in these magazines are presented as features, which companies submit and then edit before publication. Four major magazines of this type are issued by such publishers as *Nikkei News*. Kodak cites several advantages in using this vehicle. The company exerts considerable control over what is published, which means it can describe itself in ways that will appeal to the students. These magazines also provide flexibility so that a company can more easily adjust its hiring levels from year to year. Finally, advertising is one of the best ways to communicate with students without violating the official recruiting schedule.

Kodak has relied on direct-mail magazines since 1986 and receives 300 to 500 student responses to each ad. Senior Japanese managers invite the most promising applicants to a tour or technical seminar. At the end of the first meeting, the attendees may fill out a simple questionnaire, which Kodak's senior Japanese executives subsequently screen. Kodak meets with the most promising candidates at least twice more to narrow the field further. By the start of the official recruiting season, Kodak will already have met with several students and identified some of the most attractive candidates.

• **Offer grants and fellowships.** As part of its long-term recruiting strategy, Kodak offers annual scholarships for qualifying students to some of Japan's most prestigious academic institutions. These include the universities of Tokyo, Kyoto, Hiroshima, Hokeido and Osaka, plus the Tokyo Institute of Technology. Included is a stipend of $5,000 per year, English lessons and a trip to the US.

• **Emphasize cross-cultural training.** Internationalization is a buzzword in Japan, and many young Japanese are eager to work in a more global environment. When recruiting, foreign MNCs should emphasize the potentially greater opportunities for training and overseas assignments that they can offer over their Japanese counterparts.

109. Akzo Maximizes Success Using Locals and Expats

Following a buyout of its US affiliate in 1982, the Netherlands' Akzo NV, with sales of over $8 billion worldwide, rapidly carved out profitable niches in the US with a string of acquisitions. Along the way, Akzo consolidated its operations under a wholly owned subsidiary, Akzo America, and integrated its acquired companies into five product divisions. The following are some of the strategies Akzo has applied in the area of human resource management to maximize the benefits of a complex restructuring of its US operations.

A Mix of Locals and Expats

While other firms often downplay the importance of staffing decisions to the ultimate success of their strategies, Akzo has emphasized the effective deployment of people. Here are some of Akzo's guidelines regarding management selection and development for its US operations:

• **Lead with locals.** "The basic philosophy of the company worldwide has been to operate with locals," says Hugh Morrell, vice president, human resources of Akzo America. Also, unlike some foreign firms, which prefer to reserve the top operating positions for expatriates, Akzo takes its "hire locals" policy to the top in the US—it has an American president. The US president also holds a position on the parent company's management committee, which assists a four-man board of management with policymaking for operations worldwide.

The pace at which Akzo has acquired a variety of business cultures has also justified its policy of relying on locals in the US. For example, with the consolidation of Stauffer's specialty chemical activities into the Akzo group, the former president of the Stauffer division was named president of Akzo's American chemicals division.

- **Selective use of expats.**   While the emphasis is on selecting US citizens to run the US business, Morrell cites some important exceptions. First, experts ("technical ex-pats") are brought over to the US for three to five years to help improve product-manufacturing techniques.

Dutch managers also come to the US (the duration depends on the function) for exposure to management techniques and market developments. Morrell suggests that this first-hand view has sharpened their ability to evaluate acquisitions or other business opportunities suggested by US managers.

- **Two-way training.**   Although Akzo promotes the idea of nationals running their foreign operations, the identity of the company is still closely tied to headquarters as the center of a global organization. Thus selected top- and middle-tier managers from overseas subs, including the US, are also given an opportunity to spend time at headquarters through full-term rotations or a four-week management course.

- **A pipeline of talented managers.**   Morrell says that recruiting initially focused on experienced people. Whenever there was an acquisition, most of the talent was retained. In addition, Akzo stepped up its efforts in the US in order to attract people coming out of business schools and undergraduate programs. Akzo also aggressively recruits young high-potential people worldwide "so that we can develop management for the future," says Morrell.

A Phantom Stock Plan

Because of costly and complex SEC regulations, few foreign MNCs include company stock in their benefit packages for US subs. But for foreign firms on the acquisition trail in the US, finding a way around the obstacles to stock plans is critical to an acquisition's success.

Employees at the majority of companies acquired by Akzo "had been used to the investment option in company stock" and were not pleased about losing it when they came into the Akzo fold, says Morrell. As an alternative, Akzo had chosen the phantom-stock route for key executives.

For employees eligible for phantom stock, an allocation account is set up equivalent to the cash value of a predetermined number of shares of parent stock trading on the Amsterdam exchange. After four years, the original share allocation plus any appreciation and dividends is paid out in dollars. However, if the parent-company stock depreciates, the value of the account goes down.

For it to be an effective retention vehicle, Morrell adds, the phantom plan does not permit the employee to cash out before four years. He says, "A typical stock option plan grants a number of shares, and you can exercise a percentage of the after a year and another percentage after that. But ours is all or nothing."

110.   Expats to India: The Pros and Cons

If your company is planning a JV in India, a critical decision is in order, one that will affect costs, management style and strategy: Should you assign one or more parent-company executives to the new affiliate? The following are several compelling reasons for sending in expats, as well as the inherent problems.

Many factors militate against using expats in India. The government is not keen on hosting a large foreign management staff, so it takes time and effort to get expats in. The costs of supporting an expat are very high. Good Indian managers are available at perhaps half the base salary cost. Moreover, families may find living conditions disappointing. Nonetheless, BI believes it is extremely important to have at least one, preferable two, expats in the start-up phase of any JV.

Why Assign an Expat?

The central reason is to establish control. In the early stages of any JV, a large number of decisions are made affecting everything from strategy to market position and costs. While as foreign partner you may have theoretical control over such decisions, it is meaningless unless there is someone on the ground knowledgeable enough to see how the decks are actually stacked.

Although it could be an Indian employee, in practical fact, a new employee generally lacks sufficient confidence in or credibility with the parent to act firmly. Moreover, if he expects to spend most of his working life running the Indian operation, a local manager might be more concerned with establishing his credentials with the Indian partner and may be tempted to rationalize the Indian partner's decisions to the foreign parent. An expatriate's first loyalty will be to the MNC parent; with two or more on-site, they can use each other as sounding boards and better maintain their independence.

Use of Expats Has Other Benefits

• **Corporate culture**. This intangible factor can later decide whether, from an MNC viewpoint, the JV succeeds or fails. It is impossible to set culture long distance; if the fledgling firm doesn't take the imprint of your organization, it will probably take that of your partner's.

• **India expertise**. If your company plans a long-term commitment to India, it is useful to have executives who understand the country. Given India's incredibly complex business environment, on-site experience is crucial.

• **Advocate to the head office**. Working in India's red-tape-ridden environment may require exceptions to rules. Often, only an expat has the clout to sell this at HQ.

• **Better communications**. Local operations often suffer from "corporate neglect" unless an executive with strong ties to headquarters maintains communication.

• **A sense of belonging**. Indian subs frequently feel they need expats in order to be viewed as part of the corporate family and to be guaranteed access to its technical expertise and technology.

• **Impartiality**. India is a complex mosaic of languages, religions, castes, etc. A foreigner can play the role of neutral outsider and can build this kind of impartiality into the corporate culture.

• **Prestige**. Assignment of expats is considered evidence of a stronger MNC commitment than the mere injection of funds and technology. As a result, the MNC is perceived as guarantor of the JV's products and performance, adding to the affiliate's prestige. The presence of a parent-company representative also projects a multinational image that attracts a certain type of clientele.

Long-term players on the Indian scene are divided over whether the expatriate is a necessity. But Japanese trading giant Marubeni believes expats are essential. For its Indian sub to sell effectively and maintain the quality control necessary for long-term customer-supplier relationships, good communications with Japanese counterparts are mandatory. Consequently, it is crucial to have people in India who understand both the parent organization and the Japanese corporate philosophy.

Count the Cost

Still, expats are an expensive proposition. A senior Raychem (US) executive observes that an expatriate executive costs the company 200-300% as much as he would at home. Simon Streatfield, president of Cyanamid India, estimates the total surcharge runs at $100,000 per year over the employee's home country salary and benefits. And, despite generous benefit packages, MNCs find it difficult to recruit candidates, especially if they have families.

One serious mistake some MNCs make is to assign below-average executives who are on slow-growth career tracks and often nearing retirement. Such individuals serve very few of the above-mentioned purposes but realistically may be the only ones who can be persuaded – or spared – to go.

Sending such an expatriate can actually be counterproductive. Instead, try an approach used by other MNCs interviewed by BI: India's tough environment, especially in a start-up venture, is an excellent training ground for high-fliers. This makes it a coveted assignment for younger, fast-track execs.

111. How MNCs Are Developing Global Managers

With more companies seeking profits outside their domestic markets – either through internal expansion or corporate alliances and mergers – international executive development is emerging as an important weapon in the battle for global success. The following are key trends in the development and training of international managers.

A Mix of Expats, TCNs and Locals. Companies are looking more closely at the advantages of hiring local nationals or third-country nationals (TCNs), as well as balancing the mix of their international executive pool to reflect their strategic objectives. The tradition among many US firms, in particular, of relying solely on expats to manage operations abroad is nearly extinct. The emphasis is much more of determining precisely what types of people foreign operations need and then finding them—wherever they are. Whenever possible, many companies opt for local nationals. Although stricter national regulations have, to a certain extent, forced this shift, MNCs of their own accord are becoming more circumspect in their use of expats.

Equal Opportunity. Few companies still limit their search for senior-level executive talent to their home countries. In fact, some human resource executives say their firms no longer recognize any distinction between domestic and foreign operations. Some have granted a form of "equal rights" to foreign-born employees whereby key positions throughout the world are open to anyone, anywhere, who is qualified. Coca-Cola CEO Roberto C. Goizueta, who began his ascent to the top in his native Cuba, and former IBM vice chairman Kaspar Cassani, a Swiss national who rose through the ranks in Europe, are two of the more prominent examples of individuals who made it to the top of companies based outside their home countries.

Such a global approach to deployment and promotion of managers is made possible by the increasingly widespread use of computerized global personnel data bases. These help identify and encourage the best and brightest from around the world.

Overseas Experience a Plus. Firms are placing a greater premium on international experience. Whereas in the past a foreign assignment might have been considered a ticket to nowhere, such a credential has now come to represent the fast track to senior management at a growing number of companies. For example, among his international assignments, Dow Chemical's chairman, Frank Popoff, took charge of Dow Europe as he climbed the executive ladder. At Colgate-Palmolive, CEO Reuben Mark was a general manager in Venezuela and a vice president in Europe. Indeed, Colgate, which today derives over 60% of its total revenue from overseas markets, contends that the more international exposure a person has, the better. Says R. Alicia Whitaker, director of management and organization development, "The career track to the top—and I'm talking about the CEO and his direct reports—requires global experience…Not everyone in the company has to be a global manager, but certainly anyone who is setting strategy does."

The Global Executive. Although there have always been a few expat and TCN executives who have spent the bulk of their careers abroad, international assignments have more often consisted of one or two rotations, each lasting two or three years. Recently, however, the truly "global" executive has emerged—an individual who takes on several consecutive international assignments and eventually assumes a senior management position at headquarters. For example, the chairman of the Netherlands' Philips lighting division is a Norwegian who attained this post after stints in the US, where he was the US subsidiary's chairman, and Brazil, where he was a general manager.

Company Strengths and Weaknesses. The most progressive companies are developing international executive management programs and career pathing strategies that will sustain the commitment of their high-potential people to the international side of the business. BI has found, however, that companies are more successful at attracting internationally skilled executives and providing them with ongoing training than they are at addressing a variety of concerns such employees have. These range from helping families adjust to life overseas to accommodating two-career couples to successfully repatriating the executive at the end of the assignment. Another problem area for companies is recruiting women to work outside the home country.

Fast-Tracking Young Executives.   Some firms actively recruit internationally minded young people out of undergraduate and graduate business schools. In particular, some US-based companies seek out foreign students at US business schools. Wherever they come from, promising young executives increasingly are being sent abroad early in their careers. This may involve either one short assignment or several consecutive postings immediately following entry-level management training.

International Management Curricula.   In addition to regular management development training, companies are offering advanced international management courses to their personnel at home and abroad—from entry level up through the senior echelons. Although the international training needs of those abroad are particularly acute, increasing globalization makes on-going international training as useful to executives at home as it is for those in the field. Some seminars focus on global economic and political issues and their effect on multinational management tactics and others on specific management tactics. Apart from the subject matter, such courses can facilitate contacts among key managers at various subsidiaries.

New Emphasis on Language.   Though most companies do not offer language training that goes much beyond "total immersion" speed-learning techniques, more are making stronger efforts to recruit people who are bi- or multi-lingual. According to Larry Kroh, director of human resources at Coca-Cola, when his department searches its data base for people to fill overseas posts, the first choice is usually for people who speak more than one language.

Family Preparation.   BI's research confirms that the majority of unsuccessful overseas experiences result from spouse or family-adjustment problems. Predeparture preparation and in-country assistance for executives and their families are two kinds of support that can make a positive difference. For example, language training, while not always provided for spouses, is often more critical to them than to the executive, because the spouse typically has to deal with local merchants and bureaucrats as well as household help.

112. How MNCs Hone the Skills of Their Global Managers

The fast pace of change in today's global operating environment for MNCs demands continuous training throughout an executive's career. As a result, in recent years companies have greatly expanded their instructional offerings. Traditional predeparture preparation for overseas assignments and a dollop of cross-cultural training are no longer viewed as sufficient by many MNCs, which are adding substance to their programs.

The latest development on the training front is the creation of intensive international training programs for high-potential employees. Typically, international programs designed for fast trackers are global in scope, designed for several levels of management and include seminars in both "academic" and management subjects. Some require as much as several months of a manager's time, while others are only for a week or two. In many cases these programs are conducted in-house, but universities and outside consultants are also used. A sampling of corporate approaches:

• **IBM** has three types of programs. The first is a two-week advanced management school for newly appointed managers conducted at IBM training locations in the US, Brussels, Tokyo and Sydney. Ideally, approximately 20 managers from different regions are invited to attend. "Part of the value of this training is to have people from different parts of the world spend time with each other," says Don Laidlaw, head of international human resources. The second program is a one-week executive seminar offered at the same locations for managers with at least three years of management experience. Both programs combine sessions on management topics, such as leadership and quality, with discussions of international economics and politics. The third program, the international executive program, is considered one of the most prestigious at IBM. It is run once a year at company headquarters. Senior executives (both country general managers and functional heads) from operations around the world are personally selected by IBM CEO John Akers to spend 10 days in seminars sponsored by the chairman's office.

• **Colgate-Palmolive** has a prestigious global marketing training program specifically designed for high-potential entry-level employees just out of undergraduate and graduate business schools. Training runs for two years, after which the individual takes an overseas assignment.

• **Atlas Copco** runs a five-week international program for mid-career executives in conjunction with the Swedish business school, the Institutet for Foretagsledning. The program is conducted twice a year for 10 participants, executives who have been targeted for key positions as part of the human resource department's succession planning process.

• **Coca-Cola** trains its senior management by concentrating more on strategic business issues and less on teaching concepts. The workshop, Maintaining Competitive Advantage (MCA), deals with strategy development, leadership and managing strategic change. General managers and their direct reports apply these to current business challenges and develop leadership agendas to address local business issues. Begun January 1989, approximately 230 managers completed the workshop. MCA is over. To ensure that the skills in MCA become part of the way Coke does business, MCA Follow-Up sessions are now being conducted.

• **Philips NV** has perhaps one of the most innovative training exercises for young executives, known as the Octagon Program. Each year, 24 individuals (usually in their early 30s) are divided into three groups of eight and given three months to produce a report on a topic related to Philips' operations. Currently, participants are chosen from the firm's European operations, but the program may be expanded to the US and the Far East.

Typical projects might deal with human resources (for example, assessing the future of the position of product manager) or with the business environment (e.g. examining market opportunities in Eastern Europe). Teams are encouraged to find information sources inside and outside the company. Participants are also free to travel anywhere in the world to obtain information, but they must manage their projects within a budget. No time off from regular job responsibilities is allowed.

• **General Motors'** Professional Development Assignment program is designed for US and overseas personnel who are considered to have good potential. Initially, the program was only for foreign employees and involved spending three to six months at a US subsidiary. It now includes US managers, who are sent overseas. Each year, 40 people are selected from a worldwide pool to take part in this highly customized program. Each person defines his/her specific objectives beforehand. For instance, a foreign employee may come to the US to study vehicle painting techniques at several US plants.

GM also runs a Fellowship Training Program for employees of its foreign subsidiaries who come to the US for a year of study at the General Motors Institute in Flint, Michigan.

113. Preparing Expats and TCNs for Foreign Assignments

While MNCs agree that successful overseas tours are the result of thorough planning and preparation, they have different views about how much executive training is really necessary. Some companies provide pre-departure training to all their expats and TCNs, while others skip it unless the executive has never lived abroad or is totally unfamiliar with the region. Not surprisingly, US and Japanese firms place greater emphasis on pre-departure instruction than do European corporations, which operate outside their home markets as a matter of course.

If cost were not an object, probably all companies would prefer to provide extensive training. However, a three-day training program can be expensive. Nonetheless, there are many companies that do place a strong emphasis on pre-departure preparation. Interviews with such firms indicate that, at a minimum, the following elements are included in programs for people going to a country for the first time.

● **Pre-departure family preparation**. This may include family seminars, language training, visits to the country, among other things. AT&T and other US companies use a program developed by consultants Moran, Stall and Voyer (MSV), in which the entire family is sent to MSV's international center in Boulder, Colorado about four weeks before departure. Topics covered there include a general briefing on the country (history, geography, politics, etc.) and information on practical matters, like local customs, culture, schools and so on. According to Nancy Burgess, program director of the AT&T Italtel Management Development Program, the month before leaving is a particularly hectic period for the family, and the Boulder program helps them "set aside time to deal with the move."

• **Language training**.   Many companies encourage, but do not require, language study before going abroad. AT&T may accommodate its executives with private tutoring in their offices or Berlitz classes (which include spouses). Some companies arrange for continuing language instruction once the family is in the new country.

• **Pre-posting site visits**.   Companies usually send the executive and his or her spouse to the country before the employee makes the final decision to accept or decline the post. While not all companies assist the couple in planning an agenda for the trip, those that do find that such assistance makes the visit more productive. General Motor's human resources division takes an active role in helping to identify the things the couple should see and do to learn quickly about living conditions in the country.

• **In-country support**.   IBM, which has large groups of employees in many countries, takes memberships in clubs or organizations like the American Club in Tokyo. At such places, US expats can meet other Americans. Some companies assign well-established expat or TCN families as in-country mentors to newcomers for the first few months of their stay or for the duration of the assignment. GM has an expatriate coordinator who helps a couple during the pre-decision trip to the country and, if they take the assignment, provides assistance after they arrive.

Recently, spouses of several overseas managing directors at AT&T have developed a quarterly global newsletter. It includes articles on their experiences in different countries, along with tips on a wide range of expatriate families' concerns.

114. Putting Retirees to Work: US Firms Are Benefiting

A growing number of companies are developing creative new ways to take advantage of the extensive experience and well-honed skills of retirees, both their own and those who worked for other firms. A company's own retirees are especially prized, because they are a "known quantity," need little or no training, have good work habits (often better than those of younger people) and have demonstrated their loyalty by long years of service to the company. In addition, they are highly motivated, grateful not to have to hunt for jobs at their age, glad to be able to earn extra money and pleased to see their former coworkers regularly.

Employers are confirming what an American Association for Retired Persons (AARP) survey recently revealed: that older people stay with an organization longer than younger people. According to the AARP, the average tenure of new workers aged 20 to 30 is 3.4 years, compared with 15 years for employees aged 50 to 60.

Some companies go to considerable lengths to find retirees with particular skills or experience. Lockheed Missiles and Space Co, a division of Lockheed Corp, and the Avionics Division of Honeywell, to cite two examples, have established computer programs to match badly needed technical skills with available retirees.

More common is the growing use of job banks—pools of retirees set up by a company to fill temporary jobs formerly handled by employment agencies. Often administered by retirees, such banks provide dependable workers without the additional cost of agency fees.

Retiree Job Banks

The Travelers Corp, a major US insurance company, formed a job bank in 1980. Retirees work on a part-time or temporary basis, mainly in clerical or secretarial positions at its headquarters in Hartford, Connecticut. Travelers pays them the midpoint of the range for the jobs they fill (which means they always earn more than the minimum wage) and also splits the agency fee 50-50 with them. The company figures it saves $1 million annually by not having to pay personnel agencies to supply temporary workers.

Travelers actively recruits job-bank candidates from the ranks of employees nearing retirement during a monthlong campaign each year. It also seeks retirees from other companies in the Hartford area. One effective technique is to stage job fairs—called "unretirement parties"—for older people at its headquarters. Prospective workers visit the company's offices, talk to worker-retirees and attend work demonstrations.

At present, some 700 retired people are registered with the Travelers job bank, which is run by two retirees (one of whom is over 80) who work on alternate days, matching workers with job slots. On any given day, they send 80 to 100 retirees to work, meeting about 60% of the company's needs for temporary help. Over the past decade, only one retiree has failed to perform adequately. Travelers recently opened its bank to retirees of other local companies. In a mid-January recruitment campaign, 600 people responded.

Jobs Well Suited to Retirees

The experience of many US corporations suggests that retirees do certain kinds of work particularly well. Among these are the following:

• **Customer relations**. Many older people have developed superior "people skills" over the years, such as patience, courtesy and helpfulness. They often excel in jobs that require substantial contact with the public. A company's retirees also know its business, products and organization inside out. They can therefore handle customer calls and complaints, route them to the right people and avoid giving customers the runaround.

Travelers staffs its consumer-information office entirely with retirees. Sixteen people share four full-time jobs and field 36,000 calls each year. Western Savings and Loan Bank in Phoenix employs 80 people over 65 to staff its "club" for older customers. Cub Foods, a Colorado grocery chain, hires older people to greet and guide older shoppers around its vast supermarkets, helping them find the items they want and assisting in food demonstrations. Days Inns, an Atlanta-based hotel and motel chain, uses retirees in reservations and other departments on reduced schedules. Texas Refinery Corp of Fort Worth employs retirees—some well into their 80s—as sales representatives, even if they do not have selling experience. All work from their homes, and many move from part-time to full-time positions.

The ability of older people to deal well with the public is illustrated by the experience of the First American Bank of Maryland. It reports that even if a younger teller is available, many customers will wait to be served by an older person.

• **Counseling**. The same skills that make mature people good customer-service representatives also give them an aptitude for counseling others. Some companies use them to counsel older workers about retirement. At Levi Strauss, for example, 30 worker-retirees around the US serve as the company's link with its retirees. Known as retiree coordinators, they answer questions about company benefits, assist with medical insurance claims, visit hospital patients and shut-ins and organize community activities for retired Levi Strauss workers. IBM uses retirees who have overcome alcohol problems to work with current employees who are struggling with alcoholism. The retirees provide support that supplements professional help the affected employees get from the company or community self-help organizations.

● **Instructing**. Some companies have started using older people, including retirees, to help younger workers improve everything from basic skills, including reading, writing and arithmetic, to advanced technical skills. A few employers have found that older people are very good at helping recent immigrants adapt to the US work place. Instron, a manufacturer of materials-testing equipment in Canton, Massachusetts, has established a formal "sales emeritus" program, in which older employees and retirees coach younger salespeople.

● **Consulting**. Older professionals and managers, especially those with specialized knowledge or expertise, are proving to be valuable internal consultants. Honeywell's Avionics Division regularly calls in retired accountants, engineers and mid- and senior-level executives to work on consulting assignments. Mead Johnson, a division of Bristol-Myers Squibb, has retained a retired clinical researcher to ensure that university-based studies on the company's pharmaceuticals are done in accordance with FDA regulations.

● **Short-term projects**. Older workers, including retirees, assume a wide variety of tasks for companies that fall short of formal consulting assignments. For example, Con Edison, a public utility in New York City, uses older employees to help prepare for its annual stockholders' meetings. They handle investors' requests for tickets, count proxy votes, help with registration, keep records and serve refreshments. Some companies have used retirees to write corporate histories and employee publications, lead orientation programs for new employees, update job descriptions and personnel manuals, conduct company tours, represent the company at trade shows and register donors at on-site blood drives.

● **Low-skill, low-stress jobs**. Several businesses, faced with a decline in young applicants, are turning to older workers to fill entry-level jobs. Although these jobs typically pay little, some older people are willing to take them to earn extra money or just to stay active. More and more older people are counter clerks in retail stores and stock people and checkers at supermarkets. Minnesota Title Financial Corp in Minneapolis uses retirees as foot messengers to deliver documents to law firms and financial institutions in the city center. And The Washington Post Co now employs nearly 2,000 retirees to deliver papers. The company has found that, unlike the youngsters it previously hired, the older carriers do not mind getting up early in the morning, and they like the job

opportunity a paper route gives them to stay in touch with their neigh-
bors.

115. How Digital Equipment
Turns Multiculturalism Into a
Corporate Advantage

Maximizing the benefits of human diversity—from both personnel and
marketing perspectives—has become an ever-higher priority for MNCs,
particularly those based in the US or with extensive operations there.
Dramatic demographic shifts are taking place in the composition of the
US work force: In 1985, 47% of the US labor force consisted of white
male Americans; by 2000, 85% of new US workers will be Hispanics,
Blacks, Asians, women and immigrants. More broadly, the demographic profile of customers in the US and other countries is changing,
too, requiring greater sensitivity to cultural differences.

Although most companies are only beginning to think about adopting
a more multicultural approach to their business environment,
Massachusetts-based Digital Equipment Corp is one firm aggressively
challenging traditional corporate values and organizational behavior.
"For generations, industry has bent people to fit *its* norm, but now the
norm is becoming diversity," says Donna Taylor, the computer maker's
Valuing Differences manager for manufacturing, engineering and
product marketing.

A New Corporate Function

Digital, like many other US companies, years ago set up Equal Employment Opportunity (EEO) and affirmative action (AA) programs to attract more women and minorities. But Digital soon recognized that such
programs are not enough, particularly because they do not provide
ways for minority employees to communicate with the corporate establishment nor help the organization benefit from alternative perspectives.

To move well beyond the constraints of affirmative action, Digital created Valuing Differences, a continuously evolving management process
that seeks to address any and all dissimilarities that affect the way people communicate and work together. These range from issues of race,
culture and gender in the company's US organization to misunderstandings that routinely arise in a large multinational business—e.g. be-

tween engineers and nonengineers, between people from various countries who speak different languages and so on. Valuing Differences is about moving from a mindset that sees difference as a problem to one that sees difference as competitive advantage," says Taylor.

"Where you are born and raised or what you look like programs you to react in certain ways to people who are similar to you or not," continues Taylor. The essence of Valuing Differences is to get employees at all levels of the organization to examine their own programming and to link it with job skills. Although no one expects personal biases to be eradicated, Valuing Differences provides the opportunity to discover productive ways of dealing with bias to improve effectiveness on the job.

Given the scope as well as the complexity and sensitivity of behavioral issues, Valuing Differences is a very decentralized process. It takes many forms and is led by many different people throughout the organization. Taylor is one of three corporate managers who have full-time responsibility for managing Valuing Differences activities. Other human resources professionals, in management development and EEO/AA, as well as outside consultants, also get involved in supporting the process.

Valuing Differences in Action

Because much of the Valuing Differences process is developed and implemented by employee groups at offices and plants, there is little off-the-shelf training. Similar to other efforts to change corporate culture, such as total quality programs, Valuing Differences encourages learning and skill building through small group discussions and customized applications in specific business contexts or work groups.

According to Taylor, Valuing Differences has a strong bottom-line connection. "It has to do with corporate survival; it isn't just something nice to do in your spare time," she says. Valuing Differences activities include the following:

Core Groups. Groups of eight-10 people (usually a mix of men and women) meet once a month for half a day on company time to focus on issues of diversity (actual differences and stereotypes) that interfere with their ability to work together effectively. A key objective is to help break down misleading assumptions. These core groups have sprung up at sites throughout the company.

Constituency Groups. These represent specific groups — e.g. women, blacks, Hispanics — who join together not just to support one another but also to explore ways to help the company make the best use of the groups' unique abilities. For example, one Hispanic group is looking at how Digital can target its products for Latin American and Hispanic-US markets. Other groups are working on improving internal work environment issues that affect their constituents.

Personal Awareness Workshops. "Understanding the Dynamics of Difference" is a standard workshop initially developed by three human resources professionals in a Digital sales and service group. It brings together 12-20 people for two days to discuss and experience what diversity means and how it affects their working environment. The emphasis is not on solving problems, but on simply recognizing how and why people see things differently. Tools include group discussions, videos and experimental encounters.

Custom Applications. Some plants have established their own multicultural Valuing Differences advisory boards. An engineer in a network communication group has led a project called "Symphony," which brings together employees to examine how they can exploit diversity to improve product design. The name comes from an orchestra's need to blend the talents of many individuals to create beautiful music. Marketing is another function that has used Valuing Differences to examine the increasing diversity of the company's customers and to help spot ways to improve marketing and sales strategies.

Libraries. Valuing Differences libraries of books, articles and videos have been set up in several locations.

Organizational Analysis. Valuing Differences is also generating discussions among managers concerned with organizational policies, infrastructures, the job selection process and other areas that either encourage or suppress heterogeneity.

Global Differences

Digital's European and other international organizations are just beginning to create their own Valuing Differences programs based on the US model. Meanwhile, the US operation has integrated Valuing Differences concepts into its cross-cultural training for executives preparing for international assignments. In addition, it is working to expand the reach of this international training beyond expatriates.

For example, "quick immersion" training capsules might be appropriate for software engineers going on a short trip to Japan or Germany to help out with a particular problem. These short courses provide situational analysis: presenting the obstacles one can expect to find just off the plane as well as helping less-seasoned travelers ask the right questions before they leave the US. More extensive training on cross-cultural issues is given to executives who are not on an international career track but frequently interface with foreign customers or work on projects outside the US.

Then there are the employees who never leave the US. "We do business in 70-plus countries and have lots of people who never physically travel. But they work with people in other countries every day," says Taylor. In particular, she cites Digital's own computer systems people, who sit at their keyboards and communicate with their counterparts in countries they have never visited. "The fact that we are trying to market the advantages of our technology is forcing us to recognize that even words in the same language can mean very different things in different cultures," notes Taylor. By combining the Valuing Differences concept with basic international communications training, people can overcome these cultural gaps.

116. How Firms Are Making Ethics Part of Operating Strategies

In today's intensely competitive environment, it is all too easy for employees to get the impression that, when push comes to shove, they are to take ethical shortcuts. Alluding to that assumption, McDonnell Douglas CEO Sanford N. McDonnell sums up the rationale for his firm's program: "With the tremendous pressure we put on our people to improve the bottom line, we must also exert equal pressure to always take the ethical high road in meeting our goals and objectives." In addition to this impetus for reinforcing ethical guidelines, there is also a growing awareness of the direct impact that high corporate behavior standards can have on matters directly related to profitability, such as heightened consumer awareness of product quality, greater public attention to safety matters and stricter environmental protection regulations.

As these issues test managers' skills in balancing bottom-line objectives with directives on corporate responsibility, companies are finding that a code specifying what cannot be done is no longer enough. They are looking for ways to turn ethics into a proactive management tool for guidance on what should be done.

What Makes an Ethics Program Work?

While few executives would argue with the desirability of institutionalizing ethical standards, getting results is another story. "It is one thing," says David Schmidt, associate director of the Center for Ethics and Corporate Policy in New York, "to have a compliance-oriented set of rules on how to stay out of trouble. It is quite another to turn ethics into something that will enhance performance and competitiveness." BI interviews with a number of firms and their assisting consultants highlight the characteristics of the more effective programs:

• **Create a dynamic code.** According to W. Michael Hoffman, director of the Center for Business Ethics at Bentley College in Waltham, Massachusetts, the risk is that "the code may get tacked on a bulletin board, or simply get passed down through a chain of subordinates." The best way companies can avoid this pitfall, Hoffman suggests, is to get as many employees as possible involved—beginning with the drafting of the code. This view is echoed by Mark Streeter, manager of organizational development at Fluor Daniel Corp. "The fallout from the fadism in participative management is that we finally realized that business is in the hands of the people who produce it not just in the corner office or the executive suite. Therefore, ethics is in their hands." Once the code is in place, employees should be continuously encouraged to provide feedback. In this way, says Hoffman, "they can make the code a living document, not just something that is going to gather dust, but a document that is going to be constantly reviewed and amended."

• **Get strong support from senior management.** Executives unanimously agree that if ethics is to make its mark in a firm, at least one or more individuals with high visibility must champion the cause. At his firm, Sanford McDonnell initiated the creation of a formal code of ethics in 1983 and the development of a substantial ongoing training program. Forty-five thousand employees, from plant form workers to senior managers (including McDonnell), have participated in the program. Although executives acknowledge that it is preferable to have the CEO heading the effort, this is not always necessary or even desirable. At one company, for instance, a senior manager drew up a written code of ethics. His effort had companywide credibility because it stemmed from an actual crisis he confronted within his division.

• **Communicate at every level.** Training is one of the most effective means of communication and one that provides convincing evidence of the company's commitment to ethics. Executives report that participative training, such as ethics workshops and seminars, is a great stimulus to employee awareness of both the content and relevance of ethics codes. Also, such dialogue proves a helpful aid in converting the not-uncommon critics who view corporate codes as an indictment of their own ethical judgment, or simply regard the effort as a public relations exercise.

Most programs include case studies and role playing that highlight dilemmas drawn from situations employees face on a daily basis. At Fluor Daniel, for example, small groups of managers are presented with a series of ethical problems taken from engineering and construction cases. They are then asked to work through these as a group and propose a solution. Situations tend to encourage participants to look to the operating principals of the firm for guidance.

Prior to the launching of ethics workshops at McDonnell Douglas, extensive interviews were conducted with line managers to uncover common issues and get feedback on the degree to which existing ethics guidelines were helping or hindering sound decisionmaking. Workshops are also developed to reflect the specific work setting of the participants. A recent addition to the regular eight-hour seminars for executives is a workshop designed specifically for union employees.

• **Provide an organizational identity.**   While most companies agree that organizational support for ethics is essential to both effective communication and compliance, surprisingly few have established such mechanisms. One of the best-developed examples to date is the system of multilevel ethics committees at McDonnell Douglas. A Board of Directors Ethics Committee, chaired by an outside board member, is charged with a broader spectrum of the corporation's social responsibilities; ethics is only one consideration. An internal corporate committee is led by senior executives, with representatives from the legal, contracts and finance areas. At the component companies, an independent committee reports to the component president. Further down the line, an ombudsman is available to counsel employees who wish to discuss issues in confidence. (Ombudsmen are usually senior managers who are held in high regard and are selected because they are viewed as "approachable individuals.")

• **Monitor at the operating level.**   One of the more innovative approaches to ensuring code compliance has been taken by the Dow Corning Corp. With 20 sales and plant sites across Europe, Asia and Latin America, Dow has taken particular care to develop a system that reaches employees on a global basis. Once a year, a four-member Business Conduct Committee (BCC) conducts "face-to-face" audits at locations around the world. The purpose of these visits, says John Swanson, manager of business communications and a permanent member of the BCC, has been to interview employees to identify problems and find solutions. Swanson concedes that when the program was first launched, area managers were somewhat "intimidated," but he hastens to add that as local managers have become more familiar with the process, they have been more forthcoming.

117. Six Ways to Manage Global Pensions

Given rising pension costs coupled with the sheer magnitude of pension assets and liabilities on their balance sheets, many companies, even those that are decentralized, are finding a degree of global pension co-ordination essential. At a minimum, an MNC should have an explicit worldwide pension policy. This policy should explain how pensions fit into the overall corporate benefits plan and how the company calculates the costs of its pension obligations, finances those obligations, invests pension assets and indexes benefits. The policy should also spell out internal control, reporting and approval procedures relating to pension management.

Pension Control Tips

• Issue a financial guidance letter that outlines the reporting and control procedures for different pension funds.

• In this letter, specify whether control lies with the parent or subsidiary and define procedures for the establishment of a pension board for each fund.

• In most cases, assign an executive from treasury or finance, along with the regional submanager or controller, to the board.

• Issue guidelines on the company's investment philosophy, the different types of investments, the company's permits, any preferred mix of debt instruments (equities, real estate, etc.), freedom of local subsidiary management to approve investment decisions, and which decisions require headquarters' consent.

• Establish procedures to monitor the performance of the investments on a quarterly, semiannual or annual basis.

• Map out general criteria on the selection of investment managers — track record, underlying approach to pension investments, worldwide network, and so on — and suggest how to measure the performance of pension-asset managers.

The following checklist outlines specific steps that can improve the management of MNC pension plans:

• Design your plan around the level of retirement benefits the government will supply. This is the main factor dictating the amount of supplement the employer provides, hence, it is the key determinant of pension plan costs and liabilities, says Roger Atkins, international actuarial consultant with the Wyatt Co. Some countries, such as Sweden, offer such liberal government pensions that some multinational companies do not consider it necessary to establish their own plans.

• Make sure the plan reflects other local laws and practices. Among the most important: benefits typically provided in your industry; common benefit options (e.g. lump sum vs staggered payouts); indexation of pension plans; employer vs employee contributions; availability or popularity of different types of pension programs, such as defined-benefit or defined-contribution packages.

• Conduct an international actuarial valuation to make true costs more obvious. This method of valuation uses a common set of assumptions to analyze and compare the costs of pension plans for all operations and provides management with a more accurate reading of the true costs of its pension plan in a given country than does a valuation using local laws alone. Atkins points out that many governments allow a company to claim a tax deduction for its pension obligations, but then limit the increases in pension liabilities the company can claim. Consequently, calculating liabilities under local laws may not reflect the actual rise in pension costs that a company incurred.

• Select the most cost-saving and tax-saving method of financing pension obligations. Most subsidiaries have several possible ways to fund their retirees' pensions—pay as you go systems, terminal funding, trust funds, book reserves, insurance contracts or multinational insurance pools—although their freedom of choice is frequently constrained by local economic, social and legal considerations.

However, there may be attractive incentives for favoring one approach over another. To foster the growth of domestic capital markets, some countries, such as Spain and Belgium, offer tax sweeteners to companies using trust funds or insurance contracts rather than book reserves. The surge in pension expenses and the rout in the world's stock markets are intensifying the pressure on many MNCs to maximize their pension funds' ROI. The problem is most acute at companies whose pension assets are largely in trust funds or insurance contracts, both

performance-based vehicles. To keep a tighter rein on pension investments worldwide, Atkins offers several suggestions (see box, p. 314).

• Consider multinational insurance pools. In addition to financial advantages, pooling provides companies with an increased flow of information and more control over its own collection of plans. To benefit
most from this financing option, Atkins suggests the following: Use
more than one network, or establish a "small-risk pool." Remove consistent "losers" from the pool. Carefully select the appropriate way to
handle large losses: stop-loss, loss carry-forward or compromise. Place
key retentions and interest credits under tight review. Negotiate premium discounts. Scrutinize annual summaries of pool results.

• Determine the lowest-cost way to provide necessary pension benefit
increases. Companies must from time to time raise benefit levels for
competitive or other reasons. Among the issues to analyze: Are the increases required by law? If not, what is the moral obligation of the company vs the government to provide increases? What is the firm's competitive position in the local environment? What formula should be
used for increases: full or partial CPI? Should (and can) different formulas be used for different groups of employees? How will pension increases be communicated to retirees? Are the increases applied to
vested benefits? What are the tax, financing and investment implications of the pension increase?

118. How to Build, Track and Use a Global Benefits Data Base

For most firms, managing a global benefits program is an enormously
complex task. Simply monitoring diverse foreign plans and the laws
covering them can be extremely difficult. One strategy used by many
MNCs to facilitate monitoring—and management—is to establish and
maintain an international benefits data base at headquarters.

Like most global coordination efforts, creation of a worldwide benefits data base is a massive undertaking. And once the data base exists,
the company must use a variety of techniques to ensure that the data
remains current and benefit packages maintain a competitive edge.
("Benefits" in this discussion refers mainly to retirement plans, but also
includes supplemental benefits, such as life, medical and dental insurance.)

MNCs interviewed by BI cite several advantages to building a country-by-country data base that covers the key components of benefit packages: plan design, funding vehicles and costs. First, the data allows a company to conduct internal and external comparisons to determine whether its overseas benefit packages are competitive with one another and those of other MNCs.

Second, securing information for the data base helps management formulate a consistent philosophy and policy on benefits. For example, when a US-based machinery manufacturer surveyed its global benefit plans, the immediate result was to uncover inconsistencies. But the survey also provided company managers with the basis for a corporate policy that ties an operating unit's retirement plan to its performance.

Third, by highlighting plans of a certain size or type, a data base also shows management which of its overseas benefit packages demand closer attention. For example, Westinghouse's basic strategy is to focus its management resources primarily on plans with assets of more than $500,000, while Eastman Kodak zeroes in on plans other than lump-sum indemnity schemes common to Latin America and Asia.

Building an Information Base

According to experienced benefits executives, a company needs some combination of these three essentials to create a global benefits data base:

• **Survey**. The survey questionnaire should be written simply and targeted to the appropriate executive, usually the general manager or personnel manager. Issues to cover include: legal obligation (or lack of same) for a retirement plan; plan design; benefit formula and payment terms; actuarial assumptions; employee eligibility; number of participants; financial data, namely tax deductibility, annual plan costs, contributions and asset and liability valuations under local and parent-country accounting regulations; and provisions for any non-retirement supplemental benefits.

• **Consultants**. Most MNCs find it useful to retain international actuarial consultants to help set up the system and, later, to analyze the data and ensure that plans comply with local laws and reflect local industry practices. When selecting a consulting firm, look for one with an extensive, sophisticated network, a local presence in 80-100% of the countries where your company operates and good communications among its overseas offices.

• **On-site visits**. At some point in the process — typically, after the questionnaire goes out or after the survey is completed — most firms dis-

patch parent-company benefits managers to each of the overseas affiliates to discuss the corporate benefits policy, how the affiliate's plan fits
in and related issues. If the company is using an actuarial consultant, a
local representative of that firm usually accompanies the headquarters'
executives.

Staying Current

A data base is of little value if a company does not have appropriate
mechanisms to keep it up to date, and if it does not use the data base to
better manage its overseas plans. Here are some of the ways major
MNCs monitor, update and use their data bases.

● **Regular reviews**.   Many MNCs suggest that all elements of a foreign
plan should be assessed, or "audited," and/or revised every two to three
years. Any changes made to plans are immediately entered into the data
base.

At Westinghouse, plan audits are on a three-year cycle, and include
an overview of the plan at headquarters and a follow-up visit to the local
subsidiary. Even with an auditing schedule, however, executives stress
the need for flexibility; changes in local laws or operations often require
spontaneous reviews.

Exxon International, for example, conducts reviews on a "need basis"
rather than on a fixed schedule. When a law changes, an Exxon executive visits the subsidiary to see if adjustments are necessary and to test
whether the revised plan still meets corporate guidelines.

● **Clear control and approval procedures**.   Well-delineated approval
procedures for plan changes (and quick entry of changes into the data
base) keeps home office management abreast of new developments.

A large US-based food company's system of joint parent-subsidiary
responsibility for benefits reporting and control is typical. Subsidiary
management monitors local benefits developments and supplies this information to the operating divisions at parent headquarters. The headquarters, in turn, reports new data to a centralized corporate benefits
staff. This group keeps the data base and shares approval responsibility
with the business units.

Exxon International uses another common approach. It gives its 50
foreign subs considerable freedom to make adjustments to local plans,
provided they inform headquarters. However, major proposals—
changes that would result in a 1% increase in benefit costs or the creation of a new program—do require US consent. But once a proposal is

approved, its specific design and implementation rest with the subsidiary.

● **Corporate polls.** Kodak carries out corporate surveys when it needs to change its plans; the survey results go into the data base, thereby giving the new information a comparative dimension. Kodak's approach works as follows:

Suppose a local pensions law changes, or the data base indicates an affiliate's plan has not been updated in a few years. Headquarters, along with local Kodak benefits manager, conducts an in-person survey of approximately eight other MNCs with operations in that country. The survey, which is coded for confidentiality, covers all key components of the benefits program. Kodak compiles the results to determine how its local plan stacks up against those of the other firms and sends a report to survey participants that spells out any action Kodak is taking and summarizes the survey data.

● **Financial evaluations.** An annual update of overseas plans' financial information is critical if a firm is to properly measure its obligations and review the cost effectiveness of these plans. One computer giant uses its annual evaluation to determine its benefits costs and to ascertain whether each sub has adequately covered both its accumulated pension obligations (the amount an employee is entitled to today, without any future salary increases) and projected benefits, which include salary increases.

119. ESOPs Work by Motivating Employees

Employee stock-ownership plans (ESOPs) make it possible for management and employees to acquire shares in their companies on especially favorable terms. This rewards them for their role in boosting corporate profitability. They further benefit by being able to make a capital gain when shares go up in value. The following gives the benefits of ESOPs to employees and workers.

● **Attitudes improve.** The best reason for employee shareholding is that it releases the pent-up power a company has over the hearts and minds of its employees. George Copeman, recently retired from the management consulting firm of Copeman Paterson, cites the highlights of a 1986 survey, in which 80% of companies with profit-sharing or savings-related schemes stated that their schemes increased employees' understanding of the company's financial position and improved their loyalty and enthusiasm as a work force.

● **Management-employee relationships become more productive.** Employee share ownership tends to improve vastly communications between management and employees, both because the company feels obliged to keep its internal shareholders informed at least as well as outside shareholders and because employees are much more interested in a business in which they not only work but also have a stake.

They watch its profit performance more keenly and feel a link between what they do and the company's results, even though in many cases this link must necessarily be quite indirect. An independent bargaining position is preserved by employees not participating in management, but employee representatives talk to management with a better appreciation of the economic situation and of how to improve their own position.

● **Company performance benefits**. Satisfied and loyal employees can achieve exceedingly high standards of productivity, efficiency and customer service. A 1987 study compared 100 profit-sharing companies (many with employee share plans) with a similar sample that did not practice profit sharing. During an eight-year period (late 1970s to mid 1980s), on all main indicators—return on equity, return on capital employed, earnings per share, growth of profits and dividends per share—the profit-sharing companies demonstrated a better performance. In terms of total investor returns—putting together capital growth and dividend growth—the performance of the profit shares was 78.2% better than the performance on the nonprofit sharers.

Managing International ESOPs

Once a company's management has accepted the case for employee share ownership and understood the tax and regulatory context in the countries where it operates, it needs to implement a plan.

Sometimes, pressure on headquarters to introduce a share plan comes from the subsidiary companies in a foreign country. They tell headquarters what their competitors are doing and what they themselves ought to be doing in the area of human resources policy.

MNCs need policies that in principle treat all employees alike even though different tax relief schemes in many countries will mean difference in practice. Two broad traditions present themselves, that of the US and of the UK, the latter of which is closer in some respects to Continental Europe.

● **The US model**. A US multinational would have a basic pension plan in which all employees participated on the same pro rata basis. But parallel to it would be a voluntary fund to which the employees could subscribe anything from 2% to 16% of their pay. And the company would then match the lower end of this with a minimum of half the employee contribution up to 6%, that is, a minimum 3% match. The company contribution would go into company common stock and the employees would decide what proportion went into a mixed fund equivalent to a unit and trust and what portion was invested in fixed-interest bonds. An employee who can't build up capital through home ownership is likely to concentrate a significant part of his pay on building up resources through this type of fund.

● **The European model**. In European countries, pension legislation has a longer history. Alongside pension relief are home mortgage interest relief and other relief that varies from country to country. As a result major European companies have introduced ESOPs to encourage employees to own shares on their own merits rather than as a means of making provision for retirement.

How ESOPs Favor Workers

The "favorable terms" of an employee share plan cannot instantly be turned to cash because this would be taxable regular income. A holding period lets employees potentially gain on the share value and also triggers capital gains tax relief. In some cases the extent of the relief may depend on the length of time before the shares are sold, thus encouraging employees to continue holding.

The four basic ways of granting favorable terms to an employee follow:

● The company can grant an option to an employee to buy shares in the future, but at today's price. If the share price rises, the shares can still be bought at the option price; by then, of course, they are more valuable. If the share price falls, the option can be allowed to lapse, saving the employee from any loss. This one-way ticket to gain is popular in many countries, particularly for top management.

● The company can sell shares to employees at a fraction of their market price and require them to be held for a period of years. Any tax relief may depend on the length of time the shares are held. This type of arrangement is used in Germany, Scandinavia, the Netherlands and Japan.

• The company can set aside part of its annual profits to acquire shares for employees, and require them to hold the shares for a period of years. The extent of tax relief may depend on the length of time the shares are held. This type of plan is widely used in the UK and the US.

In the US, a special version involves using a company loan or outside financing to acquire a substantial block of the firm's shares. These are placed in a trust on behalf of employees. Thereafter, year by year, part of the company's profits is used to pay off the loan and release the shares for allocation to individual employees.

• The company can lend money to the employee for purchase of shares, perhaps on an interest-free basis, or possibly forgiving any net debt if the shares fall in value below the amount of the loan prior to its repayment. This arrangement is now used mostly in private companies when managers and other key employees are given an opportunity to purchase shares from an existing shareholder.

120. Coping With Indian Labor

Companies in India must come to grips with a new, more assertive generation of workers in India. Compared with their predecessors, who were typically recruited from villages, second- and third-generation industrial workers now coming to the fore are urbanized, better educated and thus more capable of dealing with management. Higher aspirations and needs promote more active participation in trade unions for both material benefits and a sense of power. Workers tend to be more volatile, switching unions if another one offers a better deal or is more militant.

Most Indian firms and many MNC affiliates will have trouble managing the transition, partly owing to attitudes derived from India's entrenched class system. Adversarial relations between management and labor often cause disputes to be seen as zero-sum games: Management either appeases or defeats labor. A serious obstacle faced by Hindustan Cocoa Products Ltd (an affiliate of the UK's Cadbury Schweppes) in its attempt to build cooperative labor-management relations was resistance from managers regarding a more cooperative approach to their workers.

In the quest for labor peace in India, MNC affiliates must avoid a number of pitfalls:

• **Refrain from attempts to buy out labor with above-average remuneration.** Despite high wage levels, Peciso Electronics and Electricals—the Indian affiliate of NV Philips of the Netherlands—has been plagued by labor trouble. Not only do demands subsequently escalate, but higher wage packages provide powerful inducements to stiffen job security demands. Adding welfare-oriented benefits may be better; they are tax-free and promote loyalty.

• **Keep individual plants geographically dispersed.** Avoid heavily industrialized, overwhelmingly unionized areas such as the Bombay-Belapur belt.

• **Don't allow factories to grow too large.** Once the work force reaches a critical mass, problems are more likely to erupt. Avoid overstaffing at all costs.

• **Keeping a pool of temporary workers is just as risky.** Unions have successfully argued with the courts that work done by temporary help is permanent in nature, forcing such workers to be reclassified. Several foreign consumer goods firms have found subcontracting some manufacturing to small-scale units can help avoid this problem.

• **Let unions and their leaders emerge naturally.** It may be tempting to back a leader and have one union emerge as the major negotiating unit. But Peciso found that overt management support undermined the effectiveness of the leader in question.

• **Trying to play unions against each other is even less advisable.** Rival unions will try to one-up each other in taking harder lines with management. Considerable violence—between unions or directed at management—can result.

• **If plant closure becomes inevitable, it may be best to use a preemptive approach** similar to that used in industrialized countries. When shutting down its Calcutta plant, Siemens, India Ltd (51% owned by Siemens AG) offered voluntary retirement to some execs, transferred a few of its 125 workers to another plant in West Bengal and agreed to start another joint venture with the state government. Although the government was dominated by the Communist Party of India (Marxist), it did not block the shutdown, nor was there much union resistance.

121. Controlling Employee Expectations When Companies Merge

In striving to get control of the herd of human problems unleashed by a corporate merger, the first priority is to rein in the burgeoning expectations running wild on both sides. They will appear anyway, and if uncontrolled will give rise to speculation followed by rumor. This will be accompanied by a marked drop in fascination with the company's work, which still needs to be done.

According to M&A veterans and consultants, relatively few companies seem to realize that there are at least two sets of expectations to be dealt with — i.e. those of employees on both sides — and that information given to each must not be contradictory. There are both exciting and motivating expectations as well as the inevitable fears. Most people recommend that the negative actions be gotten over swiftly in order to concentrate on the positive aspects.

As can be seen from the lists below, the hopes and fears typically generated by an acquisition do not necessarily meet the tests of business logic or consistency. They may simply reflect the prevailing climate of uncertainty, fear of change, or the human desire to get to know the new parent and create relationships with the rest of the group. These aspirations can have a positive effect if they are not overlooked.

Information should be provided at a very early stage. It is important that the staff of the company or division that will have most to do with the new acquisition receive the same information.

A Checklist of Hopes and Fears

Negative Expectations. These factors should be neutralized by actions, clarifications and a continuous dialogue as soon as possible:

• Lower compensation

• Change of bonus or perks

• Tighter rein on expense accounts

• Merger to inferior pension scheme

• Redundancies

• Less plush accommodations

- Taken over by a bunch of snobs/philistines

- Removal to another (less salubrious) location

- Lower in the general hierarchy

- Fewer career opportunities

- More bureaucracy

- Less possibility of exercising initiative

- Expected to think too much for oneself

- Too many approvals required

- Possibility of new, unfamiliar boss

- Long period of uncertainty

- Loss of independence

- Need to acquire unfamiliar skills

- New parent doesn't know what it's doing

- Liable to act like a bull in a china shop

Positive Expectations.   These points should be stressed (insofar as they are true), as soon as the negative points have been addressed:

- Part of a bigger/more prestigious company

- Higher compensation

- Better pension scheme

- More comprehensible personnel policies

- Less stingy company

- More dynamic and adventurous company

- Removal of financial uncertainty

- New career opportunities

- Opportunity to broaden experience

- New challenges

- Better working conditions

- Clear future ahead for the company

- Chance to work with fresh, interesting people

- Access to more staff resources

- More chance to exercise initiative

- Chance for more international work

- Less bureaucracy

- More money available for investment

- More stability

122. Organizing and Running an Employee Downsizing Program

Since a large percentage of a company's fixed costs are related to people—wages, benefits, office space, equipment and so on—it is tempting to decide that the quickest and easiest way to cut overhead is to get rid of employees. But while cutting people may be quick, it certainly does not follow that it is easy. Reductions-in-force are difficult, emotional experiences for the manager who does the cutting, for the individual who is cut and for the survivors. They incur large, one-time costs for severance packages and, if handled improperly, may subject the firm to legal expenses. They may also hurt the business. One international manager told BI of a program to cut many full-time employees in Europe and turn that market over to distributors. "This indeed saved money but, more importantly, over time, we dramatically lost market share that will be very difficult to recapture."

Alternatives to Reductions-in-Force

Some companies feel it is wiser (as well as more cost effective) to hold onto their employees rather than dismiss them during downsizing. Looking ahead, they seek the advantage of having a loyal, motivated work force in a future when shortages of workers and managers are expected to occur. Some of their techniques:

• Productivity drive. Tighten up programs aimed at increasing employees' efficiency and productivity.

• Hiring freeze. If people must be added, emphasize employment of part-timers.

• Skills retraining. As task-related or job skills become outdated, retrain workers in whatever new skills are needed by the company. This can be accomplished internally through special company training programs, or externally through tuition-refund plans.

• Job skills bank. Data on each employee's skills are contained in the bank. When a job opens, the individual's skills are matched with job requirements.

• Transfer employees (temporarily or permanently) to other company operations that are healthy.

• Salary freezes, or across-the-board pay cuts (everyone takes a cut of x percent).

• Shorten the workweek (perhaps from 40 hours to 25 hours).

• Job sharing; leaves of absence; voluntary time off. The latter two schemes could be for short or long time periods. The employee's benefit package and seniority status are not affected in either case.

How Not to Do the Job

Many BI readers can undoubtedly recount several horror stories regarding the dehumanizing treatment of individuals who lost their jobs as a direct result of restructuring and downsizing. The following are a few examples that came to BI's attention during corporate interviews: The first two illustrate the virtues of getting a reduction-in-force right the first time, so that it needs to be done just once.

• One company underwent three reductions-in-force in a single year, in July, September and December. A new president and CEO joined this small international professional services firm and saw the need to act quickly to keep it afloat. So he held two all-night sessions with senior management to decide what to do. Parts of the action plan that emerged from these sessions were to eliminate those units that were not cost effective or important to the bottom line, and to downsize all other units by a fixed across-the-board percentage. The plan, drawn up in haste and implemented the next week, proved to be faulty. A second across-the-board cutback was carried out in September, but again it was not sufficient. By the time the third work force reduction took place (the "Christmas Massacre"), the survivors were in shock.

• A major US-owned subsidiary in a European country underwent a significant, well-managed reduction-in-force program. In a series of follow-up meetings and personal messages to employees, the country manager and other senior managers stated: "It is too bad we had to go through this experience, but it is over and behind us. So let's all get back to work. The cuts are finished." Then, just nine months later, a second major reduction-in-force was carried out. Eventually, even two years after the incident, the remaining employees no longer trusted management and harbored negative feelings about the company.

• A multinational US bank decided it was necessary to close a computer facility. Without being given any prior knowledge or warning of the closure, all 150 employees of the facility were told to report to a local movie theater at 9 a.m. one Monday morning. There, someone from the corporate personnel department, whom they had never before seen, informed them that the facility had been closed and locked. Effective immediately, their employment with the company had been severed. He outlined the bank's severance package and said that checks would be mailed.

• Several years ago, a large US consumer products company downsized by eliminating several hundred employees at home and overseas. One of these people was BI's contact in the firm, a manager in the international finance department. On a Thursday afternoon at 4 p.m., he was told to meet with a vice president whom he barely knew, a man whose normal job was in the domestic operating division. The vice president, wasting no time, informed the manager that the company wanted him to consider early retirement. The latter replied that he had no interest in the proposal, explaining that he was 56 years old, enjoyed his work and needed the income. The vice president rejoined: "If you do not agree to early retirement, you will be discharged and your file will be so marked. But if you agree, in addition to the severance payments for which you are eligible, you will receive coverage under the company's major medical insurance plan for the rest of your life. We must have your decision tomorrow."

The entire meeting lasted no more than 10 minutes. After discussing the matter with his wife, the manager accepted early retirement the next day. He informed BI that he found out some time later that the same vice president who had met with him was himself given the same "option" the following month.

Easing the Pain of Employee Downsizing

While there are no easy answers to managing work force reduction programs that minimize human anguish, there are some things that can be done to ease the pain. The checklist below reviews the major steps that should be taken in a corporate reduction-in-force program.

• Before downsizing, communicate the problems to employees. At meetings, explain the financials.

• Simultaneously, undertake a cost-cutting program trimming back office and manufacturing costs, travel, overtime and other expenses in all departments. This will render a reduction-in-force program less of a shock.

• Identify the products, services and functions that must be retained and those that can be eliminated. Once this is finished, it will be possible to determine which jobs should be kept and which cut.

• Create uniform procedures for administering the reduction-in-force program.

• Set procedures for breaking the news to those employees to be severed. This includes guidelines for the conduct of each separation meeting, and the selection and training of those individuals who are to conduct the meetings.

• Create an appeals procedure whereby employees who are to be separated may raise questions about the validity of the factors bearing upon their separation. Some executive(s) involved in the appeals process should have the authority to reverse the decision to separate an individual employee.

• Prepare letters for each individual who is to be separated informing him/her of severance and other relevant allowances, insurance coverage, final date of employment and the availability of assistance for career counseling, resumes and job referrals.

• Establish procedures and responsibilities for notifying individuals and groups outside the company, for example, key customers, local government and the news media.

• Carry out these meetings on the same day with all individuals selected for severance in every location, or at least in each country. Time is everything.

• Each location's senior executive should communicate directly with all employees not affected by the reduction-in-force. This should occur as soon as practicable after the termination meetings (preferably the next day). The manager should outline any organizational changes, explain the separations, address related matters and answer questions.

• The senior executive at each location should report intermittently to employees on progress toward their new goals. If the data are available, he may also provide general updates on the employment status of those who were severed.

• Conduct an employee survey, after several months, as a barometer of attitudes. Run a second similar survey about nine months later. Take the appropriate action at the conclusion of each survey.

123. Giving Bert the Bad News

Telling a worker he or she is about to become unemployed is never an easy job. But it may be an especially unpleasant task if the employee is being let go not because of poor performance, but because of the company's need to downsize. Here are the guidelines distributed by one company to its managers on how to conduct individual meetings with employees to inform them of their termination:

• Treat the individual with dignity and respect. In everything done and said, observe common courtesy.

• Set aside a block of uninterrupted time behind a closed door. Allow no interruptions.

• Get to the main subject early in the meeting. State the message clearly. For example, "Bert, the company's economic crisis has required management to institute a reduction-in-force program. Your job will be eliminated as a part of this program."

• Outline the business reasons for the reduction-in-force program in general, and then for the elimination of the employee's specific job. Frame the remarks in terms of the function and job.

• Be prepared for an unfavorable reaction. The reality of a person's termination almost always comes as a shock. Some people cry. Some just stare. Some get mad. And, be prepared for the unexpected. In one documented instance, an individual said, "I know the company has to cut back, so I'll work for nothing!"

But whatever happens, remain professional. Be understanding and sympathetic, but be professional. Do not bad-mouth the company, fellow workers, or management; and do not encourage the employee to do so. Also, remember that the meeting is not the occasion to give the employee a last chance to save his job; nor is it an appropriate forum to explore what he should do now. Give the employee some time to accept the news and then focus on the future. For example, "Bert, with your education and skills, I am certain that you'll find a suitable position in another company."

• Tell the employee about specific severance terms, benefits, pension and other relevant matters as these relate to him; or provide a memo that details these matters.

• Be prepared to answer questions about continued use of the office and secretarial services, the completion of work in progress, or letters of recommendation and related matters.

• Arrange to collect office keys, calculators, credit cards, passes and other company property.

124. Fuji Xerox's 'New Work Way' Fosters Employee Creativity

Companies operating in Japan face a host of staffing problems that result from a worsening shortage of professional and skilled labor and an increasing desire among Japanese youth for more time for self-development and leisure. Fuji Xerox Co Ltd, the Tokyo-based joint venture (JV) between Xerox Corp and Fuji Photo Film Co Ltd, is addressing both these challenges by revamping its personnel systems and revitalizing its corporate environment through a package of initiatives called the "New Work Way" (NWW).

The Need for Change

According to Kojiro Akiba, associate director and manager of the New Xerox Movement Promotion Office (the office responsible for Fuji Xerox's total quality control activities [TQC]), President Yotaro Kobayashi recognized several years ago that the company was beginning to suffer from "big enterprise disease." Burdened by bureaucracy, employees were becoming passive, while managers all too often favored obedient rather than creative subordinates.

Even the TQC campaign was affected. Since its inception in 1976, the New Xerox Movement had been one of the firm's major strengths. It earned the company Japan's prestigious Deming Prize in 1980. By the late 1980s, however, TQC activities had also become overly formalized. For example, high targets for suggestions and "achievement ratios" tended to erode the value of quality control circles (QCCs) as voluntary problem-solving groups, notably in sales, research and headquarters support functions.

At the same time, however, the company needed to hasten innovation to meet changing market needs. The scope of the copier and office equipment business for Fuji Xerox and its competitors was rapidly expanding, thanks to introduction of color printing and copying, growth of networking among personal computers and other office equipment and emergence of new information-based and educational services.

Building a New Vision

In February 1987, Kobayashi met with a select group of 100 young staff members to mark the 25th anniversary of the JV's founding and discuss its future direction. This "Vision 100 Committee" urged management

to provide a lively and comfortable work environment that would respect and encourage individual thinking and creativity. This concept ultimately formed the basis for the NWW campaign.

Subsequently, senior management held a series of roundtable discussions with various staff levels to generate tangible plans and build consensus. To ensure widespread understanding and acceptance of new initiatives, a "Group-Wide Communications Center" was set up when the
first NWW programs were introduced in early 1988. Besides reforming
Fuji Xerox's TQC systems (see below), most NWW programs have focused on the personnel system in one of two ways. Some initiatives seek
to build an internal business environment that promotes innovation,
whereas others aim to facilitate value-creation by employees.

Toward a Creative Work Life

The NWW offers some concrete benefits to workers — e.g. subsidies for
bullet-train commuting and flextime and half-day holiday schedules.
Less tangible, but ultimately more significant, changes include the
following:

A New Employee Evaluation System.   In place of unilateral evaluation from above, the supervisor and his subordinate are now required
to hold face-to-face discussions about objectives and performance at the
beginning, middle and end of each year. Moreover, the emphasis is now
on rewarding an employee's effort, accomplishments and willingness to
undertake challenges. Previously, evaluations placed a high priority on
conformity and discouraged employees from "risky" undertakings.

Recognition for Special Activities.   Evaluations now give credit
(sometimes leading to bonuses) for activities that contribute to society or
enhance Fuji Xerox's public image. Examples include voluntary social
service, lectures delivered inside or outside the company and the pur-
suit of educational or professional qualifications. Each division manager
can recommend up to 5% of his subordinates for recognition, with a
possible bonus of up to 10% of their basic annual salary.

Job Preference System.   Starting last year, Fuji Xerox employees
were given the right to request jobs from the personnel department,
and more career counseling assistance is now being offered. In the past,
managers frequently wouldn't release employees to take jobs elsewhere,
but now they cannot easily block a subordinate from a new assignment
because the personnel department may intervene.

Flexible Retirement.   Employees nearing retirement age (now set
at 60) are eligible for early retirement and can receive a high percentage
of their retirement bonus in advance. Since this program began in 1989,
fewer than 100 employees have taken this route, but Akiba expects the

number to grow as the average age of Fuji Xerox employees rises and as
more people opt to leave earlier to launch new careers.

Extending the Company's Success

The following NWW programs specifically aim to provide opportunities
for Fuji Xerox employees to create value for the company and society:

"Venture Business Challenge." Initiated in March 1988, this
program provides opportunities for employees to launch new businesses within the Fuji Xerox family. Proposals are accepted annually by
a special committee, which evaluates the feasibility of the suggested venture and considers its potential impact on Fuji Xerox's existing business
lines and image. Only three or four proposals are accepted every year
(about one out of 20 applications).

Among recent new ventures is the Fuji Systems Brain Co, set up in
November 1988 by a 46-year-old section manager to offer consulting on
information processing. Fuji Xerox provided 90% of the Y100 million
capitalization. In December 1990, three employees established the
Ariadne Language Link Co (with Fuji Xerox supplying 85% of the Y20
million capitalization) to offer education-related services to foreign
businesspeople in Japan.

Social Service Leave.   In July 1990, Fuji Xerox became the first
company in Japan to offer a paid volunteer-service leave program
(from six months to two years). Employees with more than three years
of service may apply for the program by submitting a written essay and
undergoing a subsequent interview. Five employees are usually chosen
each year. Eligible activities include volunteer or paid work for recognized international, national or local social welfare or service organizations; religious and political work is excluded.

Theme Leave.   Under this program, employees can apply to take
one- to three-months' leave to do business or scientific research relating
to their work. The first two months of leave are paid, and there are
grants available of Y100,000 to help fund the research. Kobayashi himself took such a leave from late 1990 to early 1991.

Revitalizing TQC Systems

As a key part of the NWW, several changes were made to the TQC program.

(1) The company set up "theme-oriented" QCCs to solve on an ad hoc
basis problems cutting across functional and departmental boundaries.

In the past, because they were set up within single departments, traditional QCCs couldn't readily deal with broader issues and therefore dampened some employees' enthusiasm, particularly in the R&D, marketing and headquarters departments.

(2) Fuji Xerox simplified its "President Diagnosis System"—under which Kobayashi visits individual plants to discuss and develop action plans for quality problems. Previously, plant managers would prepare up to 150 pages of documentation for such visits. Now, plant managers present Kobayashi with only three pages of key data about the plant's operations and its projects. The result is a more direct discussion of the facility's real problems.

8
Management

125. Using Core Competency to Build Competitiveness

The concept of "core competency," though still new, has clearly taken hold at Cambridge, Massachusetts-based Polaroid Corp. By investing in, developing and shaping its operations around its core competence of electronic imaging, the company has been able to differentiate Polaroid's name and products in an intensely competitive global market. It has also provided Polaroid with a strategic platform for innovation.

"Successful companies have always had a way to identify and nurture their strongest skills and technologies—whether or not they knew it," says Peter Kliem, senior vice president and director of electronic imaging. "What's new is the conscious process of making this a cornerstone of your company's philosophy. Core competency for us meant making the intellectual and creative investment in our technology, so Polaroid would keep the leading edge and remain differentiated in a crowded field."

He says firms developing a core competence must continually ask themselves such questions as: What sets us apart as a competitor in the global marketplace? How can we leverage our technology to its maximum level? Where is the market headed? Will it go there with or without us?

Look to the Future

Building on its core competences was a strategic decision for Polaroid, whose management realized about 10 years ago that the company would soon be entering a phase of maturation. The firm's founder, Edwin Land, created Polaroid's initial core competence in the photographic area—instant imaging on paper. As the industry pioneer, the company had either to invent or manufacture everything it needed to get its products to market.

"Fifteen years ago, Land could take the time to improve or develop whatever was required for a Polaroid product," explains Kliem. "Today's global race just doesn't allow for long development cycles. Our competitors would adapt or find a way to utilize the technology that's out there."

Part of the core competency process for Polaroid was to look to the future, decide where it wanted to be and how best to get there. "We realized that electronic imaging required us to include the computer chip in our future," says Kliem. "Certainly, with all the computer expertise around, we did not want to reinvent the wheel. Therefore we are deliberately looking for partners in that industry to help us combine their technology in computers with ours in imaging."

Leverage Your Core Competence

To meet the new competitive challenges, Polaroid has taken several strategic planning steps to leverage its core competences. One of the most visible was the creation of a new organizational structure for electronic imaging activities, designed to focus more sharply on quality and the needs of its customers. This structure is built around the Electronic Imaging group, which embodies all the areas of core competences for Polaroid.

The heart of the company's new structure comprises three market-oriented business units. Each of these has a worldwide focus: Family Imaging, Business Imaging, and Technical and Industrial Imaging. Electronic Imaging is integral to the success of all three of these businesses and feeds directly into them. For example, Kliem observes, Electronic Imaging's research and ideas are shared among the three strategic business units. All the company's electronic imaging initiatives are focused on helping Polaroid achieve its goal of being the leader in high-quality, rapid-access hard copy.

"To accomplish this aim, we must have broad technical competences at various points along the 'electronic signal chain'—from image acquisition to image storage, to image processing, management and display, to image transmission and finally to hard copy output," says Kliem.

Pick and Choose Wisely

Half of Polaroid's R&D dollars are now being spent on electronic imaging activities, which underscores the importance of picking a core competence wisely. "It's expensive to invest so much intellectual and creative capital, and no single strategic business unit can or should have to justify that kind of expense," notes Kliem. "The core competence should be corporate-wide and have corporate sponsorship, since you can't predict what all the fruits of the investment will be—and the entire company should be able to benefit from the outcome."

126. Systems for Smooth Communications With Alliance Partners

Effective and continuous communication is essential to the success of any strategic alliance. While maintaining good communications requires much hard work and planning in any organization, there is considerably more room for misunderstandings and distrust in a bilingual-bicultural relationship between two or more companies with distinct strategic objectives. Below, executives from more than 40 US, European and Japanese MNCs offer several suggestions for building a viable communications infrastructure:

• **Designate clear contact points.**   The foundations for effective communications can be laid by setting up management and technical liaisons within each parent organization. In the alliance between UK-based International Computers Ltd and Japan's Fujitsu Ltd, four different levels of management interface were specified. Steady communication between executives at these four levels is boosted by frequent exchange of technical staff and high speed facsimile machines.

Because of their close working relationship, Xerox and Fiji Xerox have assigned counterparts to work with each other in every function: research, product development, finance, legal, etc. Several joint task forces meet regularly. Each firm also maintains an advisory executive resident at the other's headquarters.

Many European and US MNCs with growing networks of alliances are setting up central liaison units to coordinate creation and management of these relationships; the international departments of Japanese firms often incorporate similar functions. An innovative variation on this theme is Ford Motor Co's establishment of a liaison office in Hiroshima to help coordinate its multiple contacts with its Japanese equity partner, Mazda Motor Corp.

- **Choose the right liaison managers.** Finding the right person to manage the alliance (or to head up liaison points) may determine the success or failure of an alliance. Effective management of a cross-cultural, bilingual relationship imposes high demands. A fairly senior individual who understands the companies and the cultures in which the alliance will operate is required. The alliance manager must be able to both serve as an advocate for his own company's viewpoint and effectively represent the ally's interests within his own company. He must have flexibility, cultural sensitivity and power within his own organization if he hopes to develop trust, respect and influence with the partner.

- **Schedule regular meetings among top executives.** Periodic meetings between the chairmen or CEOs of the partners is strongly recommended by a number of executives to avoid the common and often fatal syndrome of deteriorating senior management involvement after the deal is signed. Even an annual meeting can reinforce personal ties and signal ongoing commitment to the partner organizations. To minimize conflicts and foster better understanding between the two MNCs, the top executives of Ford and Mazda meet semiannually to discuss the basic policies and overall management of their corporate relationship.

- **Encourage cross-fertilization.** No less vital than regular meetings among top executives are contacts between lower-level employees. The links of several decades between Westinghouse and Mitsubishi Electric and between Fuji Xerox and Xerox have been bolstered by programs to exchange staff. Most firms recommend frequent meetings at which operational and technical staff can review whether the venture is on track. Ford and Mazda also hold several levels of meetings, all the way down to monthly working-level reviews of the status and issues of individual projects and priorities. The frequency and variety of these meetings mean a lot of staff travel, but both firms recognize that this is necessary if complex business programs are to progress smoothly without serious misunderstandings.

- **Build systems to overcome language and cultural barriers.** In today's triad joint ventures, language difficulties can create substantial problems, especially between US and European executives and their

Japanese partners. Besides language training programs for employees, selecting the right support staff can help reduce language-based diffi- culties. In Diamond Star Motors (a 50:50 joint venture between US- based Chrysler Corp and Mitsubishi Motor Corp), Chairman G. Glenn Gardner has a bilingual secretary, while President Yoichi Nakane's per- sonal assistant is a Japanese national who has worked for 17 years in the US. Both assistants not only have language capabilities but are also fa- miliar with US and Japanese customs, business practices and industry— abilities that are particularly useful when handling delicate problems.

127. Seven Guidelines for Effective Advisory Boards

Companies deliberating whether—and how—to set up an international advisory board should bear in mind the following ground rules:

• Identify clearly the reasons for setting up such a board. A mere desire to "combat anti-foreign nationalism" is not sufficient. The company should be positively motivated to seek out, and listen to, advice (not all of which will necessarily be flattering) on how to conduct business in foreign markets.

• Select the advisory board's members with great care. Major countries of the company's operations should be represented, but of equal impor- tance to this market coverage is the compatibility of the various mem- bers with each other. A thorough investigation of the backgrounds of all the prospective candidates is essential.

• Identify who from headquarters management should participate in the advisory board meetings. Usually the chairman and several top in- ternational executives are selected.

• Define clearly the duties of the members—and make them attractive. Ideally, this could take a form similar to the charter established by Con- trols Co, and would include a statement that the board has no opera- tional authority but acts solely in an advisory capacity. However, the board members should be fully and continuously informed on the ac- tivities of the corporation and be equipped with a clear set of goals— such as what should the company's global position be 10 years hence, how can the company's image be improved, etc. Without such goals, frustration quickly sets in, and the board ceases to function effectively.

(In this connection, Westinghouse quite often takes visiting board members on a tour of one of the US company's operations, thereby communicating to them the company's clear desire to have the board know as much as possible about the company they are advising.)

• Spell out the relationship to the corporate board and perhaps also to operating management.

• Establish clear agenda and schedule procedures for board meetings. If board members are expected to give presentations at meetings, this should also be stated.

• Work out comprehensive compensation arrangements. Corporate experience indicates that a common procedure is to pay a fee, similar to that paid to outside members of the corporate board. In addition, companies normally pick up expenses incident to the members' attendance at board meetings.

128. Holding International Manager Meetings

Despite the cost in high-level time and in money, companies are increasingly turning to worldwide mangers' meetings as a tool to improve global communications. Bendix International conducted such a meeting in Spain, organized around the concept of a planned dialogue. The firm's experience give rise to 15 pointers:

(1) Holding the meeting at an overseas location can be a definite plus. It allows an overseas affiliate to act as host; it helps other executives learn more about that company's activities; it helps draw parent-company international — and domestic — officers into the field; and it avoids the slightly patronizing aspect of "call the troops into headquarters."

(2) Limited use of outside speakers can prove worthwhile. They widen the horizons of the meeting by presenting outside points of view.

(3) Holding a special international meeting — rather than adding one on as an appendage of a domestic meeting — gives it greater stature. It also avoids the fatigue that would otherwise develop if international executives had to attend a companywide executive meeting first.

(4) The real value of the meeting rests not so much on the program

content as on the opportunity for informal discussions. One executive characterized this key element as the chance to develop "camaraderie."

(5) Worldwide executive meetings should focus on the broad impact and be clearly distinguished from "working" meetings that seek to convey specific technical information or teach the use of a specific management tool or concept.

(6) The use of visual aids may be a mistake because of technical problems, unfamiliar equipment in overseas locations, and the possibility that attention will wander when the lights are turned down.

(7) The sessions should not be too long. One Bendix executive estimates that two and a half hours (including coffee break) per session should be maximum. In addition to not tiring the managers to the point of diminishing returns, short sessions permit greater free time for informal communication among the participants.

(8) Parallel sessions—breaking the group into smaller units—may prove useful.

(9) The program should not be too "tight," and should not try to cover too much factual and detailed information.

(10) The physical arrangements in the conference room need some attention. If an informal atmosphere is desired, it may be better to have executives seated on both the inside and outside of a U-shaped table—thereby cutting down on the size of room needed and increasing the level of meaningful eye interchange.

(11) Early and comprehensive advance planning is essential. Bendix may begin planning its next worldwide meeting as much as one year early. It may have all major presentations reviewed in writing at the head office prior to the meeting, to assure relevance of subject matter and approach. Successive speakers approaching the same topic in different manners can be quite confusing, especially for executives whose native language is not that of the conference.

(12) The worldwide managers' meeting should not be seen as a one-shot affair, but rather as a management technique that needs to be developed and refined from year to year.

(13) The concept of preassigned discussion leaders who follow those making major presentations and who have the specific task of commenting on the previous presentation may be useful. Such a role forces a participating manager to state out loud the presentation's relationship to his own personal experience—which is what the other managers in the room are doing silently.

(14) Participation by key corporate and domestic executives is a plus—and may be essential. The active presence of Bendix President W. Michael Blumenthal was a major factor in the conference.

(15) The length of a worldwide conference should be carefully considered. Too short, and too much gets crammed into a day or two, with perhaps little being accomplished. Too long, and money and time may be wasted. Two or three days may be optimal.

129. Curing Profit-Centeritis

Profit-centeritis is a malady whose symptoms manifest themselves every time line managers take actions that are good for their business units, but not good for the overall company. If not diagnosed in time, the disease can cause serious internal damage. For example, one US firm found its Latin American manufacturing subs buying parts locally at prices lower than they could obtain from the parent company. This generated $1 million more profit each year for the Latin units, but meant $5 million less profit for the company as a whole.

Firms have been especially vulnerable to profit-centeritis in recent years because CEOs have reset priorities and restructured options. At many firms, subtle conflicts have arisen when SBUs and product lines were adopted as principal profit centers for strategy and management decisionmaking, while existing subsidiaries were left as is, with many of their natural profit center attributes intact.

At the core of such corporate conflicts is the innate sense of pride in business unit profit felt by most subsidiary general managers, and the feeling of frustration that inevitably arises when factors—internal or external—threaten to interfere with the subsidiary's autonomy and inhibit its ability to generate profits.

The Cure

Most firms find the best medicine for profit-centeritis to be a healthy dose of company spirit. To apply the antidote, companies use a number of formal and informal techniques. Following are tactics used by some companies that emerged from Business International's research. Most are intended to prevent the disease, but they can be used to cure it as well.

- **Use a matrix management approach.** To encourage a greater understanding of product line objectives among geographic units, some firms (like Dow Chemical) employ a formal matrix management system. Under this system, each geographic unit has a dotted-line reporting responsibility to the heads of the SBUs whose products it carries.

  Other firms, like Ford Motor, use cross-functional teams wherever possible and assign each operating unit responsibility for a product line in which it excels. For example, Ford's European unit has responsibility for small-car (four-cylinder) manufacturing, while a US unit of the company has responsibility for big-car (eight-cylinder) manufacturing.

- **Use educational techniques.** Other techniques that are specifically designed to spread companywide values and to promote teamwork include rotating employees from headquarters to field and from geographic to product units, as well as holding special seminars to explain the direct relationship between business unit decisions and the impact on the parent company. This is especially important in the areas of tax and cash flow, where responsibility is often shared between operating unit managers and financial mangers. Use of the new shareholder value measures has proven especially helpful to Pirelli in spreading companywide values and reviving corporate esprit de corps.

- **Revise incentive plan schemes.** These should be adjusted so that each local manager's compensation is no longer based solely on his own unit's results. One leading US pharmaceutical company now uses a formula based 50% on local unit results, 25% on total corporate results and 25% on subjective factors. This technique is used by another leading US firm that has revised its incentive plan to give special relief to local managers who take actions that improve the total corporate tax picture but hurt their local profits.

- **Revise cost allocations and transfer prices.** Last, to relieve frustration caused by factors that local units cannot control, some firms are revising their cost-allocation systems to reflect actual usage more accurately and to halt the practice of allocating factors not controllable by the local units. At the same time, a new movement toward the use of "see through" profitability and dual transfer-pricing systems (one for performance evaluation purposes and one for external reporting purposes) is reducing frustration by giving local units credit for their true contribution to overall company profits.

130. Checklist for Before, During and After Calamity Strikes

As much as companies would like to believe that industrial accidents and product tamperings won't happen to them, it is important for firms to be prepared for such occurrences. In addition to the potentially calamitous human and environmental consequences of an accident or malicious tampering, a mismanaged crisis can irreparably damage a firm's image with customers, suppliers, governments, the financial community, employees and the general public. Companies can minimize this damage by having a crisis communications and management plan in place. The following checklist offers pointers on how firms can plan in advance for a corporate nightmare and includes a list of dos and don'ts when disaster strikes.

Plan for the Unplanned

• **Have a written plan of action.** Richard Hyde, executive vice president at Hill and Knowlton US, says that firms can avoid many of the blunders that can aggravate crises by keeping a written plan of action on hand. The plan should consist of general guidelines flexible enough to apply to a wide range of problems. It should include a checklist of things to do, key media contacts and names and telephone numbers of decisionmakers in the company and the community. The plan should also outline a strategy for a crisis management team, covering such issues as which functional experts – e.g. legal, medical, technical and public relations – to recruit for the team as well as the role each member will play.

• **Develop a list of worst-case scenarios.** Paul Shrivastava, associate professor of management at New York University and director of the Industrial Crisis Institute, finds that crises can either be managed more effectively or averted altogether if companies identify a worst-case scenario for all products and operations and develop an appropriate action plan for each case. Among issues to consider include an analysis of existing safety and emergency systems at the company's site and within the local community. Some executives suggest working with the local government when formulating action strategies.

• **Watch out for customs.** When firms must maintain some costly emergency equipment at a central facility, management may want to have all the customs paperwork prepared in advance. This way, the equipment can be rushed to an overseas accident without delays. An oil company executive cites a mishap in which systems to clean up an oil spill overseas were detained at customs for over 48 hours, during which time the company lost valuable time to confine the oil slick.

- **Develop in advance a clearance procedure for company statements.** Mapping out this time-consuming procedure in advance is critical to a company's ability to speak and act in unison.

- **Build a safety-conscious culture.** Many industrial disasters are the result of human error, according to Shrivastava. MNCs' top managements can minimize the risk of accidents by treating safety as a strategic issue, not simply an operational task. He offers several techniques by which companies can raise the level of safety awareness among employees: (1) link safety to performance evaluation and career development, (2) offer incentives and rewards to promote safety-conscious employees, (3) develop safety-management training courses and distribute safety information leaflets, (4) establish confidential channels of communication to allow employees to more comfortably act as "whistle blowers" and (5) consider using job rotations for those employees charged with boring tasks where the incidence of error is highest.

- **Update and test crisis-management plans.** Plans may become obsolete unless management regularly incorporates new safety regulations, advances in communications technology and any changes wrought by acquisitions or investments in new products or countries.

- **Be sensitive to early-warning signals.** Firms can avert disasters by learning how to read and effectively respond to early signs of trouble. Few accidents occur "out of the blue." Rather, they are often preceded by early signs of trouble. For example, a memo may cite potential problems in storing hazardous chemicals or suggest treatment for an employee in a critical job who shows signs of alcohol or drug abuse.

When Disaster Strikes

- **"Tell, tell it fast, tell it accurately, is the cardinal rule for crisis management,"** says Hill and Knowlton's Hyde. Once an accident occurs, a firm should work swiftly to uncover the facts and critically analyze the damage. A timely assessment of the problem will help to identify the type of crisis communications and management needed. Further, building the company's response on a foundation of facts will help to avoid a major pitfall in crisis management: over- or underreactions to bad news. An overreaction will fuel hysteria rather than contain the crisis, while an underreaction may bring accusations of insensitivity to an already negative image of a company. Finally, by reporting its own bad news, management can enhance a company's credibility, provide greater control over the situation and minimize speculation and rumors.

- **Target the audience.** Crisis communications is far more effective when the message is tailored to meet the specific information needs of key constituencies—individuals directly affected by the crisis, government officials, the financial community, customers, suppliers, the media and other influential intermediaries, like critic groups. Equally important is the need to ensure that all audiences are covered. For instance, failure to address stockholders could lead to panic share selling, creating ripe conditions for a hostile takeover, as in the acquisition attempt of Union Carbide by the GAF Corp.

- **Keep employees informed.** Failure to explain company actions to employees will hurt morale and promote the spread of rumors. This can undermine management efforts to retain the confidence of creditors, customers and other outside constituencies. Shrivastava notes that Union Carbide's chairman and the managing director of the Indian operation taped and sent out a weekly video on the crisis to all employees. The company also paid special attention to the fears and concerns of employees and the local communities of six other sites where methyl isocyanate, the chemical leaked from the Bhopal plant, was either in production or storage.

- **Remember, time can be your worst enemy.** According to Shrivastava, each crisis has a "window of opportunity" during which perhaps 90% of the damage from a disaster can be avoided if swift remedial action immediately follows the accident. Unfortunately, he adds, at Bhopal the time was less than an hour. But for many other disasters, the time window is longer. For instance, he estimates that in the Alaskan oil spill it was 10 to 12 hours.

- **Identify spokesmen.** Management should appoint executives with strong media and communications skills who can present a positive and proactive image. Shrivastava cautions against allowing lawyers to speak on behalf of the company. Their concentration on liability and insurance issues rather than on the human side of a tragedy can be particularly damaging to a firm's public image.

Some corporations are developing a cadre of media specialists selected not because of their years of experience in company affairs but for their promotional skills and ability to present a creditable image to the viewer.

● **Speak with one voice**.   To maintain control over the distribution of critical information and to ensure that the company's message is clear and consistent, coordination and responsibility for communications should rest firmly with designated spokesmen.

● **Monitor the crisis and provide updates**.   Executives with the GCI Group, the public relations arm of Grey Advertising, emphasize round-the-clock monitoring of the crisis and all media coverage so that an accurate assessment and response can be made. A close scrutiny of media coverage will allow the company to correct errors and address key issues of public concern.

● **Emphasize early CEO visibility**.   The negative backlash and criticism over the delayed public comment and reaction to the Alaskan oil spill by Exxon's chairman illustrates an important guideline in crisis management: An early visit to the accident scene or an initial public statement by the CEO can provide a tremendous boost to a company's image in the public's eye.

A Summary of Don'ts

● **Never attempt to fix blame**.   Companies should focus on action, not point fingers. Communications should focus on what the firm is doing to remedy the situation and provide assistance to any victims. Attempts to lay the burden at someone else's door—however justified—will be negatively received by the public.

● **Avoid "off-the-record" interviews**.   Management runs a high risk of misinterpretations and exaggerations of the facts with off-the-record exchanges. Further, these interviews will confuse and undermine the communications efforts of the official corporate spokesmen.

● **Avoid "no comment" remarks**.   Withholding the facts with a terse "no comment" is likely to be translated either as insensitivity to the tragedy or as something to hide, thereby fueling speculation and hysteria. It also means that later efforts to present the facts will be greeted with skepticism.

● **Do not lie**.   Ethics aside, adhering to a firm policy of telling the truth minimizes the danger of overreacting or underreacting to the situation.

It also makes it easier for companies to correct inaccurate information or challenge biased media statements.

131. Steering the Entrepreneurial Ship

With the proper encouragement from top management, entrepreneurial ventures can help MNCs boost competitiveness. Below are tips on how to spark innovation in complex corporate organizations:

• Pay attention to individual motivation. Give employees who suggest an innovative idea the opportunity to lead—or at least to participate in—the transformation of that idea into a new business venture. Ensure that credit for ideas is widely publicized throughout the company.

• Specify the department or division that will act as sponsor for the venture.

• Consider grouping innovative ventures in a separate division or holding company. Be aware, however, that this approach has its pitfalls—the most important of which is increased isolation.

• Avoid stifling the growth of ventures with traditional reporting and approval procedures. Limit controls to the budgetary essentials.

• Demand strong ties between new projects and relevant technical, marketing or financial expertise in other ventures or in traditional corporate divisions.

• Keep an open mind when evaluating projects. In addition to ventures that fill gaps in product lines or in the company's technological base, consider deals that create new avenues for growth.

• Be flexible over location. Consider locating the venture in a neutral site. Housing the venture at corporate headquarters—where it may have to carry its share of overhead costs or become embedded in corporate bureaucracy—can poison a deal.

• Encourage the venture to develop an identity of its own.

• Allow the venture to develop its own employee compensation program. Do not force the venture to implement existing corporate procedures, such as costly fringe benefits for senior employees, that the venture cannot sustain.

132. Strategies for Profitable Technology Transfers

Seasoned executives find that reaping the full benefits of licensing largely depends on how a company structures, manages and executes the actual technology transfer. Skillful management of a licensing agreement's three key elements—documentation, training and support—ensures the licensee's ability to effectively exploit the technology, minimizes the licenser's costs and maximizes its revenues. Careful attention paid to these points can also plant the seeds for deeper collaboration between the players. Both Fujitsu of Japan and French-based Alcatel have developed tactics that allow them to operate successful licensing programs.

Understand the Licensee

Bernard Gervais, manager for advanced industrial projects of Alcatel's Advanced Manufacturing Technology Center in Brussels, offers an important licensing guideline: The better the licenser knows the licensee, the greater are the chances for success. Even before official negotiations begin, Alcatel—which has successfully licensed its technology in some tough and highly protected telecommunications markets—will visit the licensee to discuss its objectives and motivations for the deal, evaluate its technical talent, components and raw materials, and assess the regulatory environment. Information obtained in this early visit, says Gervais, is instrumental in structuring a well-targeted proposal to win the contract and later tailoring the documentation, training and support operations to suit the licensee's specific needs.

Although particularly useful in LDCs, the precontract visit can also be a good planning tool for cross-licensing arrangements between MNCs in industrialized countries, says Gregory Leonard, director of the advanced products division at Fujitsu Microelectronics. Leonard, who has worked on Fujitsu's cross-licensing arrangements with Ungermann Bass and Sun Microsystems, offers other key operating details to consider when drafting documents or designing training and support:

Documentation

● **Specify language for technical documents**.   Leonard recalls an experience with his former employer. The firm licensed technology to decontaminate nuclear reactors to a French company, but neither party specified the actual language of the technical documents. The arrival of English manuals, which the French firm's engineers could not comprehend, created tension between the partners and delayed implementation of the technology.

- **Avoid literal translations**.   Only a technically astute individual with strong language skills should serve as translator. Leonard recalls another experience: In an intercorporate transfer between an Asian sub and his division, both sides agreed that the documents would be in English. The manuals arrived in literal English translations that were incomprehensible.

- **Emphasize quality, not quantity**. Most documentation in technology transfers tends to be voluminous. A succinct 12- to 15-page summary of the technology and the transfer process will often be more useful than 15 binders.

- **Is that feet or meters?**   Unless licensers, particularly from the UK and the US, clearly specify the measurement system of the technical documentation, this small detail can create scheduling problems. Licensers ideally should agree to provide the technical documentation in both their own and the licensee's measurement systems. "Failure to provide documentation in a form with which the licensee is comfortable can jeopardize the transfer process by making a very difficult task even more difficult," says Leonard. Further, conversions should be prepared early in the process; the potential error rate is much greater when engineers work furiously at the last minute to convert feet to meters and ounces to grams.

- **Timely delivery of documents**. Leonard and Gervais recommend that the delivery of documents coincide with the official launching of the training program. If documents arrive six months before the training team, says Leonard, the material will be stale or forgotten, leading to a less effective training program.

Training

- **Rely on a top-down approach**. Gervais and Leonard are proponents of a top-down approach to technology transfers. The first training sessions should address senior technical and management executives at the licenser's site, showing them the advantages of the technology and an overview of the transfer process. The next phase is a more comprehensive on-the-job training for mid- and lower-level engineers and technicians at the licensee's site.

Leonard points out several advantages to this strategy. The initial seminars help cement strong ties between senior executives and boost the licensee's confidence and commitment to its decision to license technology. They also create in-house "champions" for the deal whose invaluable support makes the challenge of training the engineers and technicians considerably easier for the licenser.

- **Have a training strategy.** Loosely structured training is one of the biggest culprits behind cost overruns and operating bottlenecks. Companies should map out a training package that outlines the structure, focus, format and participants for each session and includes training and testing materials. "The more interactive, hands-on and multimedia the training sessions are," says Leonard, "the more effective will be the transfer." Strict parameters should be set for the official training period to prevent its dragging on endlessly, chipping away at revenues and draining the licenser of critical resources.

- **Pick trainers, not technical gurus.** Not all top-notch engineers are automatically gifted with training skills. Alcatel devotes time and resources to improving the training and communications skills of engineers selected to serve as trainers.

- **Encourage informal information exchanges.** Cultural barriers and communication difficulties can impede even the most well-conceived plan. Fujitsu tries to nurture close ties between the training team and the licensee's engineers by encouraging after-work activities. "Sometimes the best technology transfer is two engineers having a beer together after work," says Leonard.

Support

- **Install telephone "hot lines."** Says Leonard, "Once the documents have been sent and training completed, continued support must be provided to answer innumerable questions and enable the licensee to effectively exploit the technology." This support, however, should be well defined and restricted to specific individuals. Fujitsu assigns staff to telephone "hot lines" to answer requests. Leonard recommends this approach because it "provides a clear channel of communication for the licensee," and it also "funnels queries to defined contact points, thereby releasing other members of the licenser's technical staff from time-consuming support activities."

• **Provide regular updates**. Most agreements stipulate that licensers must provide any changes or improvements to the technology for a limited period of time. Leonard, however, suggests that providing this information on a regular basis not only ensures that the licensee will continue to utilize the technology in the most productive manner, but may also foster opportunities for future collaborative endeavors.

133. Running a Licensing Department: Critical Keys to Success

As R&D costs mount and direct investment restrictions multiply, licensing can be critical to an MNC's bottom line. Whether licensing in or out, two factors are essential to an MNC's success: the way the department is managed and the personality of the man or woman running the show.

Corporations successful at licensing relate that three company styles predominate and that there are three manager personalities that match up with each of these styles. If a company is having a problem with its licensing department, the solution may be as simple as reorganizing to match the manager with the management style. Alternately, companies may opt to completely change the department's setup.

Three Management Styles

• **Profit center**. If the licensing department is a profit center, an "intrapreneur" is needed to head it. Since a profit center is always under pressure to meet income goals, the manager must combine good interpersonal skills with excellent sales ability.

Most companies select someone from marketing to direct this area. Preferably, the person should be well versed in managing divergent cultures. Surprisingly, in a number of cases intrapreneur managers knew nothing about licensing before taking over their functions.

For example, at Company A, the director of licensing came from marketing. The licensing manager, his immediate report, also has marketing experience, but it is supplemented by several years of hands-on licensing management. The licensing manager is responsible for drumming up business, servicing clients and interfacing both inside and outside the company. He is paid on a straight salary basis (no commission). The director believes that this prevents the manager from just signing up companies for the sake of sales, and that this encourages follow-up of existing clients for service problems.

A Licensing Success Story

One firm that has been successful at running the licensing department as a support function is Pfizer Inc. Since it is in the pharmaceutical, chemicals and agricultural industries, among others, the firm constantly needs to be in the mainstream of product development. Pfizer has targeted licensing-in as a source of new products and process technology. The company has become extremely successful at it, and its Licensing and Development Division (LDD) is the largest of its kind in the pharmaceuticals industry, with corporate and world wide responsibilities. The LDD's main role concerns the acquisition of rights to technology.

Pfizer has developed a unique formula for success. The LDD has no line responsibility. It is funded on an annual basis by the businesses it serves in direct proportion to the services provided. The division maintains records of time spent, and allocations are made accordingly. Thus, when compared with the sizable allocation of funds to research, the licensing overhead is minimal and its potential contribution to corporate profits is substantial.

LDD is a separate division of the corporation, and it operates as "support." The vice president reports to the president of the company. (Prior to 1971, licensing was decentralized.) There are nine directors, each responsible for specific areas in the company's key businesses. Each of the directors operates independently with secretarial support only and reports to the division's vice president. All of Pfizer's directors travel extensively.

All directors hold advanced science degrees, and three have MBAs. However, each is a businessman first and a technician second. This is extremely important as the group's success depends on locating technology that can sell. In addition, most of the staff has long seniority with Pfizer. This gives the unit broad knowledge of the company and how it operates and provides each staff member with significant insight into which products will work within the company's organization.

The LDD also finds homes within the company for technology that it believes will be successful, but that doesn't fall within a specific area in the company. Therefore, LDD staff must work with those who support the licensing arrangement and will bolster their position. As one licensing director says, "In order to complete a license, you must have many different people who say 'yes.' A single 'no' has the potential to kill the project."

At another company, however, commissions are part of the compensation package. This firm believes that commissions are important to the successful running of an area that is marketing-slanted. This company has run into no problems regarding quality control because the manager's performance review is tied to meeting established standards.

● **Support function.** In other companies, the licensing department is a support function, not a profit center. This type of department helps divisions plan their licensing strategies to maximize income, with emphasis placed on planning skills and supportive assistance. Team players are highly valued in this type of group. To lend credibility, managers need strong technical backgrounds and long service with the company. Companies with this structure tend to believe that an employee's career path should remain in licensing. The majority pay straight salary only. Pfizer Inc has been extremely successful at licensing through the use of this type of organization (see box on p. 354).

● **Administrative service.** When a department has a combined administrative/service role, managers are expected to manage existing licensing programs and provide service to clients. Uniformly, companies with such departments opt for employees with strong financial and technical backgrounds. As with the support function, the director is expected to have long-time service in the company. Companies attempt to develop career-pathing within licensing, and straight salary compensation is the rule. One twist with this type of department is that individuals from production and operating areas in the company are often rotated in, or else they work part time in the licensing group.

A major consumer goods company has found the administrative service arrangement works best for them. They hired their director from the outside specifically for this job; he has since been with the company for 20 years. The number two spot is filled on a rotation basis with individuals from production. Their primary function is to interface with licensees and coordinate servicing. The third person (permanent) has a technical background and has also been with the company for many years. In other firms, subordinate permanent spots may be filled from finance.

134. How Caterpillar China Handled Obstacles in Licensing Deal

While licensing is commonly utilized by MNCs to enter markets in developing countries, carrying out this tactic in a developing, centrally planned economy such as the PRC introduces special complications. Caterpillar Inc's (CAT) new, comprehensive technology transfer deal for China's construction machinery industry offers some useful pointers on how to package technology for these difficult markets.

According to James Martin, the company's manager of product source planning, Caterpillar started selling equipment to China in 1975 and began receiving requests for technology transfers in the later 1970s. In 1980, Caterpillar management developed a China strategy including sales, product support and technology transfer. It began implementation in 1982 with the establishment of Caterpillar China Ltd in Beijing. Notes Martin, "We decided in 1980 that we had to take preemptive action to build a long-term position ahead of other competitors."

At that point, Caterpillar opted for licensing because it offered more freedom and control—and simultaneously ensured hard-currency income—than did joint ventures in China. (Caterpillar frequently relies on licensing to gain or maintain access to markets, but usually only when actions by local governments or competitors create barriers to further direct sales.) In its licensing program, Martin explains that the company decided to focus on high-volume, medium-sized machinery (such as tractors, wheel-loaders and diesel engines), which China urgently needed for construction projects in agriculture and industrial infrastructure.

China Knocks on the Door

In 1984, Caterpillar signed its first technical license in China for power-shift transmissions with the Ministry of Machine Building Industry (MMBI), the China Machine Building International Corp—the MMBI's trading arm—and two factories in Sichuan. In early 1985, the MMBI suggested that Caterpillar bid for a more comprehensive program covering 10 factories to produce components and complete machinery. The competition quickly narrowed down to CAT and longtime Japanese rival, Komatsu Ltd. According to Martin, CAT secured the contract over Komatsu's lower bid owing primarily to factors other than price. Besides product quality and a strong track record in technology transfer, Caterpillar's sales campaign dealt directly with two critical bottlenecks in contract negotiation:

• **China's chronic foreign exchange shortage.** Caterpillar offered a counter-trade program through the Hong Kong office of Caterpillar World Trade (CWT). CWT will buy manufactured goods from factories under the wing of the State Commission of Machinery Industry (SCMI)which has superseded the MMBI—and turn the forex from overseas sales over to the factories in order to pay for Caterpillar semi-knock-down kits, components and equipment.

• **Contending bureaucratic interests.** Thanks to hints from MMBI officials, Martin was alerted to the increasing role that factory end-users are playing in contract decisions. "At first, we believed that the definite decisionmaking point was in Beijing with the SCMI. However, it soon became clear that the factories had a strong vote. Chinese officials we knew urged us to visit and try to win over some units that may have been leaning toward our competitor. Eventually, we were able to gain support from all 12 factories."

How the Agreement Is Structured

Effective April 1987, the package includes five technology transfer contracts, a countertrade pact and a used equipment sales agreement. The licensing pacts were signed with China Machine Building and the China National Technical Import Corp and cover supply to 10 Chinese factories in nine provinces of the designs and production expertise for specific models of Caterpillar track-type tractors, wheel-loaders, skidders, diesel engines and undercarriages. The package (to which has been added the 1984 power transmission deal) is coordinated by SCMI.

• **Scope of the transfer**. The know-how and countertrade agreements will last for eight years. Although Caterpillar generally prefers longer-term relationships with its licensees, renewal is unlikely as the Chinese prefer to buy, not lease, technology.

Know-how currently used in Caterpillar factories worldwide for these specific models will be featured and updated simultaneously with other Caterpillar plants; any improvements made in China will also be transferred to Caterpillar. The cost for such updating is incorporated into the fees and royalties of the six agreements. The program will include over 100 man-months of training in the US as well as on-site assistance from Caterpillar engineers to get the various factories on line.

• **Structure of compensation**. As with most Chinese licensing pacts, direct compensation is divided into an upfront fee and royalties over the contract's eight-year term all in US dollars. Although Caterpillar officials declined to disclose the amount, it was probably well over the $5 million limit that requires high-level government approval.

• **Unusual pricing formula**. A real concern in structuring the deal was obtaining sufficient and appropriate compensation for its expertise

given China's preference for royalties based on net sales or net value-
added. The US company gained a key concession by securing Chinese
agreement to use a royalty schedule based on per unit output. Martin
said the Chinese side went along with Caterpillar's request partly because this procedure would simplify reporting: Instead of needing to
calculate costs and sales prices in China's complex and often irrational
pricing system, the royalties would be directly proportional to output
figures.

Royalties are thus calculated based on the product of an average percentage of local content over the contract period, the unit output value,
the (undisclosed) royalty percentage and total plant output. The critical
figures for unit output value were negotiated between Caterpillar and
the Chinese side. Caterpillar based its proposals on in-house sales price
and production cost data. Tough bargaining with the Chinese and pressure from Komatsu dropped the actual figures below these benchmarks: "Since many companies are willing to cut prices to get their foot
in the door, the Chinese agencies enjoy a strong bargaining position."
However, Martin adds, "the compensation was within our parameters.
We look to obtain other benefits beyond licensing fees and up-front
payments." Each plant will incur obligations for royalties, but payment
to Caterpillar will ultimately be channeled through China Machine
Building or China National Technical Import.

● **Technology and market protection**.   Caterpillar's designs, factory
production and management techniques are protected by confidentiality clauses for the term of the contract. While acknowledging that "protection is based mostly on trust," Martin believes that "it would not be
easy in any case for the Chinese factories—which are at best 10 years
behind most Western manufacturers—to replicate the sophisticated
know-how we are providing in the short term."

A more pressing issue was discouraging reexports of Caterpillar-
designed equipment, especially since Beijing's technology transfer rules
prohibit any clauses "unreasonably" restricting such exports. Martin admits that this issue was extensively discussed, but contends Caterpillar
will not be threatened. "It will take some time before Chinese factories
attain the quality demanded by overseas markets. Moreover, there is a
tremendous need in China for this equipment. We will also ease the
forex needs through our CT program." Another important point is that
the training program contained in this package is a great deal more extensive than those usually carried out by Caterpillar and will involve far
more people than usual on the Caterpillar side.

135. Setting Transfer Prices:
No Easy Answers

The prices at which units of the same company sell to each other—called transfer prices, or intercompany prices—have a far-reaching effect on the company's success because they affect everything from foreign subsidiary performance to executive compensation to tax obligations. There has never been a single "best" way to set transfer prices for both the parent company and its foreign affiliates (not to mention the tax collectors in all countries concerned). Nor does any system meet all the needs of production, marketing and finance equally well. For this reason, some MNCs use different transfer pricing methods for different purposes, accepting the cost and complexity of maintaining more than one system. Others opt for the simplicity of a single approach, accepting the inevitable deficiencies of whatever system they choose.

Several major transfer pricing alternatives are available to MNCs:

• **Market price.** Prevailing external market prices ("arm's-length" prices) are often viewed as the best transfer-pricing mechanism for external reporting. Because this approach removes internal bias and facilitates validation, it appeals to outside parties, such as tax authorities. From a performance-evaluation perspective, however, market prices may be unfair, because they give the supplying business unit the entire profit on the transaction, including the benefit of any cost reductions due to global efficiencies. To equitably share the advantage of lower costs, transfer prices must be lower than market prices.

• **Modified market price.** Market prices can be adjusted to reflect specific characteristics of the goods or services involved. For example, they may be reduced to reflect lower marketing or distribution costs than occur in external markets. Ordinarily, this will help resolve perceived inequities among supplying and receiving business units. However, a supplying unit that has no excess capacity will still feel unfairly penalized if the lower price cuts into the profits it would otherwise earn on external sales. In such a case, the external profit is a relevant opportunity cost, and it should be factored into the transfer price.

• **Negotiated price.** This price is determined by bargaining between the buying and selling units. Although some MNCs say this technique results in an arm's-length transaction that is just as valid as an external market price, its use in subsidiary performance evaluation has some risks. For instance, negotiators may fail to reach agreement, which could result in counterproductive and expensive procurement of goods and services outside the firm. Another problem is that excessive internal competition can undermine the achievement of congruent goals among business units and result in a serious loss of cooperation.

• **Contract price.** A variation of the negotiated price method is a price agreed upon at the time the firm's business plan is adopted. Such a "contract" price eliminates variances that result from centralized sourcing decisions beyond the control of managers of foreign operations. One drawback is that it does not pass through price hikes in raw materials to marketing units, thereby removing the marketing unit's incentive to recover any inflationary and foreign exchange losses through third-party pricing.

• **Actual cost.** Actual cost, which is sometimes viewed as the absence of a transfer price, can also be used for intercompany transactions if management is willing to bear the cost of maintaining a dual pricing system. Manufacturing facilities are treated as cost centers rather than as profit centers, an approach that resolves many internal disputes over allocation of profits. A disadvantage is that it leaves the cost centers with little inducement to make investments leading to additional efficiencies for the company as a whole. Another problem is that tax authorities generally do not accept this technique, unless some taxable profits are allocated to the supplying business unit.

• **Standard cost.** The use of standard rather than actual costs has the advantage of identifying efficiencies or inefficiencies in the supplying unit. It also facilitates "management by exception" decisionmaking, in which variances from standard cost signal the need for additional investigation and attention by management. A major shortcoming is that standard costs often require making arbitrary assumptions and leaving the company vulnerable to unproductive time spent debating how to set the standards.

• **Modified cost.** This is useful in promoting achievement of strategic objectives. For example, actual or standard costs are sometimes adjusted to encourage more extensive use of certain products or services. Companies that expect to have unused capacity for a time often lower their transfer prices to take advantage of opportunities to provide incremental contributions to the coverage of "sunk" costs. Among the modifications available are variable costs (which use only costs of materials, labor and overhead that vary directly with units produced), incremental costs (which consist of the costs of producing one more unit) and full absorption costs (which include costs that would not change if sales to other business units stopped, e.g. the cost of shared factory overhead).

Picking the Right Pricing Method

Many factors enter into the decision of which transfer price to use and whether to use different prices for external reporting and internal performance reporting. Sometimes one issue is of overriding importance to a company, clearly dictating a particular pricing system. More often, of course, a company's situation is mixed, making the choice a highly complex and probably contentious subject. For most companies, the decision will turn on some combination of the following:

• **Capacity utilization.** MNCs with substantial unused capacity should set transfer prices low enough to encourage additional internal consumption (and use of capacity), but high enough to cover the supplying unit's variable costs.

• **Employee turnover costs.** Like companies with excess capacity, those with periodic production layoffs should consider lowering prices to stimulate increased internal consumption. The long-term benefits of keeping trained workers on the payroll may actually be greater than the immediate cost savings realized from layoffs.

• **Import/export taxes.** An effective transfer pricing system should deal with changes in import/export duties in a way that minimizes these taxes overall. Generally, lower transfer prices mean lower levies.

• **Value-added taxes.** Similarly, keeping transfer prices low can reduce local VAT. These levies tax the value-added within the taxing jurisdiction and are factored into the price at the next sales level.

• **Corporate income taxes.** Shifting profits into lower local tax-rate jurisdictions through transfer pricing normally results in lower overall income taxes. However, higher prices for capital assets increase the depreciation allowances for the business units that receive them. This lowers overall taxes when the assets are transferred from lower- to higher-rate jurisdictions.

• **Local price controls.** Many MNCs have operations in high-inflation markets where consumer prices are controlled by the government. Higher transfer prices on exports of intermediate goods from a parent to a subsidiary in such a market may help support the case for an increase in the price of the final product.

• **Repatriation of foreign funds.**   Lower pricing of sales to a parent reduces the outflow of funds from the home country, while higher pricing of purchases from the parent shifts funds to the home country.

• **Price-cutting.**   In foreign markets where competition is especially keen, a parent company may want to provide extra support to its subsidiaries by decreasing the prices for intermediate and finished goods they import. By having lower costs, the subsidiaries can keep their final prices low.

• **Pressure for wage increases.**   Lower prices for intercorporate sales, or higher prices for intercorporate purchases, by a foreign subsidiary reduce the justification for wage increases at the foreign location by shrinking profits there.

• **Support for fledgling subsidiaries.**   Start-ups often require substantial assistance, which can be provided in the form of lower purchase prices from or higher sales prices to other company units.

• **Forex management.**   Higher transfer prices combined with changes in payment dates can maximize gains and minimize losses on currency transactions.

136. Federal Express: Principles of Communications Excellence

When it comes to quality management, even when top management sets high corporate goals, things can go awry if programs are not carefully communicated down the line. Federal Express puts communication at the top of its management skills list. The company drew up the following list of principles that is used in a general training class. The focus of the class is to look at a manager's communications responsibilities as they relate to employee communications needs.

(1) Know your communication strengths and weaknesses and be committed to becoming an excellent communicator.

(2) Set the example for communication excellence within your work group and take responsibility for your work group's overall communication effectiveness.

(3) Build an open, two-way communication climate to cultivate trust.

(4) Practice active listening to increase your accuracy at understanding others.

(5) Make sure your actions are consistent with your words to protect your communication credibility.

(6) Tailor your communications to the needs, values and beliefs of your audience.

(7) Maintain regular and frequent face-to-face communications with your work group and each employee individually to satisfy the six basic employee communication needs noted above.

(8) Respect the time of others by getting to the point and eliminating nonessential information.

(9) Get feedback on what you communicate to measure how well you are being understood.

(10) Take the risk of disclosing your true thoughts to others to gain the rewards of mutual understanding.

137. Points to Consider for Quality Training

The type of quality training employees should receive, as well as when and how they should receive it, is a subject of vigorous debate among companies. Some emphasize statistics over management concepts; others argue that the balance needs to be equal. Some companies believe there are aspects of quality training that ought to be done the same way for everyone, while other companies have chosen to segment all training on quality by job level.

Nevertheless, there is universal agreement that to succeed with total quality management (TQM), a company must be ready to offer intensive instruction in TQM concepts and techniques and to follow up with general educational support and retraining, if necessary. Quality training usually involves a mix of internal classes led by consultants or company people, off-site sessions with consultants, university courses, and seminars on quality run by professional associations.

Before setting up a quality training program there are several things companies must consider:

• **Education mandates**. Some companies establish firm quality-education requirements in their corporate objectives for the improvement process. At Motorola, for example, managers must invest a minimum of 2.5% of payroll cost in training (quality plus other types of developmental training). A recent company employee development policy mandates that every employee participate in at least 40 hours of training and education each year.

Corning set a goal of 5% of time worked for training in 1991. "Training at Corning, which is basically a condition of employment, has resulted in our creating a training center the size of a small university. Training is frequently on quality methods and techniques, but the real emphasis today is on all skills that help job performance," says David Luther, senior vice president and corporate director of quality.

Johnson & Johnson takes a more flexible approach. For example, top management has extended an open invitation to the management boards of its operating companies to participate in a four-day program on establishing a quality improvement program. The program is run by J&J's own Quality Institute. "It's strictly voluntary because it doesn't work unless they want it to," says Stuart Christie, vice president of operations, technology and development. Adds Gerry Cianfrocca, director of J&J's Quality Institute, "They come to us looking for support. We help them get started, and then we try to guide them along."

• **Start-up training**. Most companies experiment with quality techniques before launching into TQM for the entire organization. Still, executives believe that the best way to engage the whole company is to start with the basics—primarily making people aware of the process and the benefits it will bring to the company and the individual.

The first phase of training in total quality concepts should include the following:

(1) Give everyone instruction—no matter how long it takes—once the commitment to the quality process is made.

(2) Start at the top of the organization and let training flow down.

(3) Establish a common corporate language for quality concepts.

(4) Keep the momentum going with progress reports to all employees.

Starting at the top of the organization and working down has the advantage of promoting management by example as well as ensuring that everyone is starting out with the same basic principles in mind. That is the way Xerox began its quality training process. In January 1983, the top 25 executives collectively formulated the Xerox TQM strategy,

"Leadership Through Quality," and training was developed in-house to support it. A year later, Chairman David Kearns launched the company's quality "training cascade" that has ultimately reached 100,000 employees worldwide.

In the early stages of training, Corning stressed that the basics should be the same for all employees, regardless of organizational differences in responsibilities and tasks. Says Luther, "The shared concept of what quality is all about, along with the common vocabulary for all employees, provided a significant advantage for moving the process forward."

As companies move into more advanced stages of implementation, quality training becomes more closely tailored to specific managerial levels and to the people with specific quality responsibilities (e.g. improvement team leaders, quality circle leaders). In some cases, firms also provide quality training to their suppliers.

● **Use of consultants.** Consultants can be used either in combination with or separate from internal training and play a large role in the development of total quality programs. In general, companies use outsiders to plant the seeds for TQM with senior managers. But once training starts to filter down from the very top echelon, firms are more likely to rely on in-house resources.

● **Internal trainers.** In-house trainers are chosen most often from staff quality professionals and line executives who have demonstrated strong general management skills or some ability to lead a quality improvement project. The main benefit of corporate teachers is their familiarity with the business and the quirks of the organization, which allows them to provide more relevant examples in the classroom. Executives say it is also important to develop internal quality expertise to keep training in place.

● **External options.** Once the awareness stage is complete, companies frequently turn to outside experts who have training programs that focus on a specific aspect of quality management, such as customer service. In addition, some companies enroll their people in university courses, especially in statistical disciplines. They also encourage participation in seminars presented by professional societies, such as the American Society of Quality Control (ASQC) or, in Japan, the Japanese Union of Scientific Engineers (JUSE). Bull SA, the French computer company, is cooperating with schools in Paris and Grenoble to improve quality training at the university level. Explains Pierre-Jean Manegrier, group director of quality, "If companies succeed in improving quality training in the universities, it makes it easier later on to recruit people with state-of-the-art knowledge of the subject."

● **Use of translations**. Most courses taught in the home country are also taught at foreign locations — especially awareness and motivational training. For video materials, the foreign languages are usually dubbed. For written materials, the preferred approach is to get local nationals at the subsidiary to do the translations. "The important thing is to translate the meaning of the concepts, not the words. We have gotten into trouble, as have other people who have done this, by translating literally," says J&J's Cianfrocca.

Given the expense of translation, companies usually select one major language to use for appropriate groups of countries. For example, J&J has used a German-speaking or French-speaking company to process and make improvements on the materials in English and then used French or German translations for the companies whose personnel speak those languages.

● **Quality institutes**. Johnson & Johnson, Corning, Xerox and Caterpillar are among a small group of US corporations that have set up their own training institutes or colleges. Most are dedicated to quality training. Investments in such institutes are costly, but firms that have done it believe that if quality is truly a long-term proposition involving continuous improvement, it must be permanently supported.

Asian Training Strategies

Some quality experts say that Asian firms, especially the Japanese, have a more supportive system for teaching TQM than companies in the US or Europe — particularly in the areas of design and engineering. In many cases, employees receive over 50 hours of technical training. For example:

● Nissan has multiple quality programs developed under the auspices of different functional areas as well as the quality assurance division. A series of programs for technicians (as production workers are referred to in Nissan) and for foremen and plant supervisors has been developed jointly by human resources, engineering and quality assurance. The human resources department is primarily responsible for one management program that looks at quality in different functional contexts. The quality assurance division runs a three-day program on quality in which engineers and nontechnical people participate together.

• Acer Inc, Taiwan's leading maker of personal computers, has its own corporate training center, the Acer Institute of Education. Until recently the institute was used by outside companies as well as Acer's own employees, but it is now devoted solely to Acer. In addition to AIE and other internal training programs, the company pays to have its engineers participate in three months (on weekends) of training by the Chinese Quality Control Council in Taiwan. Managers also participate in training courses in problem-solving and decisionmaking methods.

138. 10 Ways to Keep Your Customer Satisfied

Customer satisfaction has become a dominant competitive issue for companies worldwide. Studies by Forum Corp, a Boston consulting firm that specializes in customer service, reveal that keeping a customer typically costs only one fifth as much as acquiring a new one. Moreover, new customers typically generate less revenue initially than old customers. Finding out what customers want and keeping them pleased is critical. "You have to go for quality," says an experienced marketing task-force manager, "but if you've got the best horse and cart on the street, and nobody's buying horses and carts, you're in trouble." Below is a list of 10 ways to approach this important issue.

(1) Place your customer's interests first, the company's second.

(2) Question customers extensively to be sure you know what they want.

(3) Show commitment: A total quality policy should always include customer satisfaction as the number one priority for every employee.

(4) Internal customers (employees) should perform for each other with the same spirit as for external customers.

(5) Apply measurement techniques to monitor customer satisfaction.

(6) Listen to all your customers—from the distributor, dealer and retailer to the end-user.

(7) Make it easy for the customer to be heard; reduce bureaucracy and make sure management is listening.

(8) Surprise customers with unexpected excellence.

(9) Make your service as good as your product.

(10) Keep in touch with the customers after the product is sold.

9
Legal Matters

139. Guarding Intellectual Property

While intellectual property (IP) protection has improved in a number of problem countries in recent years (e.g. Taiwan, Indonesia and China), piracy is still pervasive and costly. The US's push for inclusion of IP enforcement under the GATT umbrella is subscribed to by most developed countries, but this offers little solace in the short run for many firms marketing products abroad. According to Anthony D. Padgett, Esq, in the Washington office of Thelen, Marrin, Johnson & Bridges, regardless of whether IP eventually falls under GATT, multinational companies have recourse to interim steps to protect their interests:

• **Find out how the country protects IP, if at all.** The key is how IP laws are enforced: Many countries have tough laws, but their enforcement of these laws is lax or inconsistent (e.g. South Korea).

• **Register your copyrights and trademarks in countries in which you do business.** This affords better protection by giving access to the country's legal system (and usually to the police and customs officials as well). Foreign courts seem to accept the concept of trademark more readily than the concept of copyright; hence, trademarks are generally easier to enforce abroad than copyrights.

• **Clearly set out dispute resolution procedures in contracts.** Arbitration often avoids time-consuming foreign court procedures. In contrast to many legal systems, US court procedures appear lightning fast and simple. For example, a US corporation had an IP dispute with a distributor/licensee in Portugal. Because arbitration was not specified in the contract, the case must go to court in Portugal. It will take approximately two years before the case is even heard, much less resolved. Even if the case is settled, the US company can only expect a Pyrrhic victory.

However, companies should be aware that, although arbitration is usually quicker than litigation, it is not necessarily less expensive than going through the courts. The primary advantage of arbitration, of course, is the potential savings in time.

• **Explore entering into licensing contracts with likely problem competitors,** especially in countries without strong IP laws. This is a preemptive strategy based on the premise, "if you can't beat them, join them." Such a strategy at least ensures some financial returns in a high-risk environment.

• **Consider distributing only older material overseas,** especially in countries where the state of technology is somewhat less advanced (e.g. two- or three-year-old software). This will not only provide a market for older products, but better cushion the bottom line against piracy.

• **Establish relations and cooperate with local customs officials and police.** In Japan, Singapore and Hong Kong, tough police actions are possible against pirates. Provided they are given reasonable evidence of piracy, officials will conduct raids on the pirates and destroy the infringing merchandise.

• **Hire a private investigator to gather evidence of piracy and work with local officials.** This proved successful for a prominent US computer manufacturer in Taiwan. When conducting such a proactive IP protection policy, companies may also wish to hire local lawyers familiar with the IP laws and their enforcement.

140. What Apple Does to Catch High-Tech Pirates

With product counterfeiting on the rise, Apple Computer Inc's aggressive war on piracy provides a cogent example of steps MNCs can take to protect their hardware and software. Aside from an organized effort to detect piracy, Apple has filed some 50 lawsuits in more than 15 countries outside the US. Gary Hecker, an attorney with Blakely, Sokoloff,

Taylor & Zafman and a member of Apple's antipiracy team, offers the following suggestions for catching and halting pirates.

Build a Strong Team

• Designate someone within the corporation—either in the legal department or upper management—to head anticounterfeiting efforts. This person should be the key contact for attorneys as well as for others in the corporation.

• Encourage employees to participate in the program. Since signs that pirates are active often show up in obscure newspaper advertisements, direct mail circulars or special promotions at retail outlets, the more eyes and ears you have working on the campaign, the better. Inform employees of how important it is to stop piracy and encourage them to contact the head of the antipiracy team when they learn of suspicious activity. Likewise, a good public-relations campaign that explains the corporation's concerns can yield benefits: More than once, "avid Apple fans" have called to report counterfeit software being offered over computer networks.

• Consider retaining outside investigators to monitor the market. Internal sales figures can often suggest when pirates have entered the market in force, but investigators with good contacts in the domestic and overseas market may be necessary to determine the scope of counterfeiting. Assign someone within the company to run tests on suspected copies the investigators may discover.

• Maintain close contact with customs officials in Washington and the field. Apple lends testing equipment to customs officers at all major US ports, and its attorneys conduct seminars in how to detect pirated software and hardware.

• Make certain your legal staff has the background to understand "hypertechnical" issues. All Apple attorneys working on piracy have engineering degrees.

• Consider turning over evidence of piracy to law-enforcement officials and encouraging them to prosecute. While the bulk of antipiracy actions in the US involve civil suits and exclusion orders, successful criminal prosecution may serve as a deterrent to fly-by-night pirates who will risk having their inventory seized but will not risk even a short jail term.

This advice applies overseas as well. Taiwan recently jailed several persons convicted of piracy.

• Pursue an active lobbying campaign both at home and overseas. Apple and other high tech companies are lobbying hard to strengthen US copyright laws (by raising piracy from a misdemeanor to a felony, for example). Be prepared to testify overseas before commissions that are considering changing existing copyright or patent statutes.

• Don't hesitate to break new ground in court. In the US, software can be copyrighted any time within five years of its creation, but filing early enables firms to act more quickly should pirated copies appear. It normally takes four to six months to copyright software.

• Record the copyright with US customs. This enables customs officers to seize pirate copies when they enter the country. Failure to record the copyright still leaves companies the option of bringing suit in Federal District Court or the International Trade Commission, but these are more costly and time-consuming options.

• Explore all forms of legal protection. Some software may be eligible for a patent as well as copyright protection. Companies should note that the US government keeps such applications confidential while they are pending, ensuring that the software remains secret until the patent is issued. Although much software changes too rapidly and frequently for the lengthy patent process, for programs that provide special graphics or offer novel methods of integration, for example, coverage is much broader than that provided by copyright. The US's Semiconductor Chip Act of 1984 provides a hybrid of patent and copyright protection for chips.

141. Stress on Safety Keeps Litigation Down

The erosion of a negligence-based standard of liability is forcing US MNCs to take drastic action to minimize their exposure to the accompanying surge in multimillion-dollar claims litigation. Following is a discussion on what leading companies are doing to cope with the challenge.

The most basic response has been to raise the price of a product—or to stop producing it entirely. One drug company, for example, has withdrawn from the market for intrauterine contraceptives owing to uncertainties created by high legal costs and adverse publicity. Although the company successfully defended itself in four liability cases, the costs of continued litigation (legal fees in the four trials exceeded $1 million and dozens more are pending) as well as the difficulty in obtaining insurance necessitated a decision to shut down production.

Soaring legal costs are also accelerating the trend toward arbitration and other forms of dispute resolution. Reliance on arbitration leads to quicker settlements and helps reduce the emotional "public interest" factor that often ups the financial ante in jury trials.

Protective Strategies

Without exception, MNCs are placing fresh emphasis on the product safety function. Lawrence O'Neill, an executive at St. Louis-based Monsanto Corp, says, "Firms like ours are forced to concentrate on preventive safety measures because the current liability case load provides no guidelines on how we should respond in a legal sense."

The ultimate goal is to provide management with an early-warning system. MNCs can sometimes correct problems before they reach the attention of regulatory authorities; failing that, at least management has lead time to prepare the public—and itself—for a recall. Some internal initiatives companies are taking include the following:

• **Improving internal accountability.**   To improve the effectiveness of the safety function, some MNCs now penalize units for poor safety records by charging recall and other corrective costs to those that caused them.

• **Making sure legal communicates with engineering.**   One easily corrected pitfall is the tendency for legal staff to receive the bulk of the data on product defects. Technical staff are often the last to hear of a problem even though they are most qualified to solve it.

• **More frequent testing of existing products.**   Monsanto spends over $10 million annually on this function alone.

• **Extensive record keeping** is also becoming more important as a defensive tactic in suits involving products that may have been made decades before they caused injury. In many US states, suits can be filed as long as 30 years after a product is sold. Many companies have created special documentation centers that collect thousands of pieces of paper on every step of a product's development from the initial research to promotion in the marketplace. Staff that work on a product with hazardous potential are often required to review the record and sign it when finished. "If a consumer knows we have a paper trail," says one corporate spokesman, "this tends to decrease his desire to sue."

The Sub Factor

MNCs are advised to take special care to keep a subsidiary's records separate. This can help protect the parent company from liability for defects caused by the foreign unit. Although the trend toward joint liability is clear, why make it easier for the courts?

Labeling and packaging are also receiving more scrutiny. In particular, companies are beginning to cite long-term health threats. Leading manufacturers of paint are changing their labels to emphasize that prolonged use could cause permanent brain damage.

One important conclusion reached by executives familiar with the issue is that internal safety standards must exceed those mandated by government agencies. The argument that a company was observing the full extent of the law and therefore cannot be held negligent is no longer an adequate defense in liability cases. Du Pont Inc suffered a reverse in a liability case after an individual sued management for negligence in failing to inform the Food and Drug Administration (FDA) of adverse reactions to one of the company's drugs. The jury decided Du Pont had a societal obligation to inform the FDA of a move by Canadian regulatory bodies to change the label on stocks of the drug sold in Canada — even if it was not legally required to do so.

142. The EC's Lawmaking Procedures

Tracking EC legislation is extremely important in order to reduce the risk of unwelcome legislative surprises and to gauge the progress that is being made toward the European single market. Companies must also be aware of how the actual decisionmaking process operates in order to effectively lobby for specific laws. The flow chart following illustrates current procedure.

Implementation of a directive begins with a proposal from the Commission to the Council. Under the SEA there are two distinct methods for adoption of a directive: the *consultation* procedure and the *cooperation* procedure. Which procedure is used is dictated by the EC Treaty article upon which a proposal is based.

● **Consultation procedure.** With this method, the Council requests opinions on proposed legislation from the European Parliament (EP)

EC Legislation From Start to Finish
(Directives and Regulations)

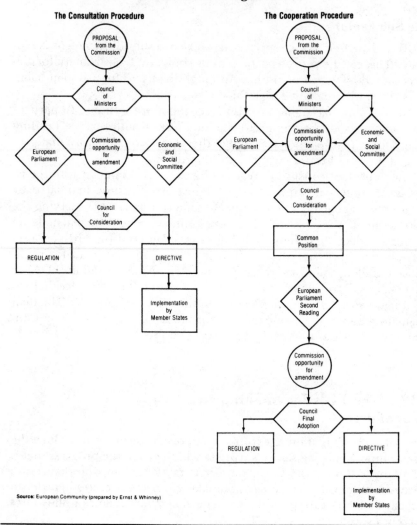

The Consultation Procedure

The Cooperation Procedure

Source: European Community (prepared by Ernst & Whinney)

and, in most cases, the Economic and Social Committee (ESC). The Council can then adopt it as proposed, incorporate suggested changes or leave it "on the table" for future consideration.

• **Cooperation procedure.** Under this form, the Council also requests opinions from the EP and ESC. After these opinions are received, the

Council adopts a *common position* (CP). (If no agreement is reached, the proposal will most likely remain "on the table.") Once a CP is achieved, it is transmitted to the EP, which has three months to accept, reject or propose amendments on its *second reading*. At this stage, the Council may again amend the proposal if it so chooses. The proposal is then returned to the Council, which has three months in which to make a final decision. In the event that no decision is reached, the proposal will lapse.

Adopting the Proposal

Whether the Council can adopt a proposal by a *qualified majority* or has to reach a *unanimous decision* depends in the first instance upon which article of the treaty the measure is based. Situations requiring unanimity include the following:

• To introduce amendments of its own initiative to a proposal;

• To adopt amendments proposed by the EP that are not accepted by the Commission;

• To adopt a measure when the EP has rejected the Council CP under the cooperation procedure.

In general, the most effective lobbying takes place while the Commission is still drafting measures and certainly prior to their first reading in the EP; thereafter, amendments are harder to introduce.

143. How to Cope With EC Competition Laws

In response to the EC's competition laws and the heavy fines for noncompliance, many MNCs are establishing internal programs to ensure that their business practices meet the terms of the law. Not only do such programs minimize the possibility of unanticipated litigation, but they are also useful in instructing all levels of personnel on what to do when investigators descend in a "dawn raid." Lynda Martin, a London-based lawyer with Baker and McKenzie and an expert on compliance programs, points out that "a carefully developed compliance program will reduce fines, even if a violation should occur either by an isolated breach of the policy or because of an unexpected Commission interpretation of the rules."

In a speech at a BI conference in Madrid, Martin listed three key rules to follow in establishing a compliance program:

(1) A tailor-made approach is essential. Do not adopt other firms' programs assuming "one size fits all."

(2) A program should be flexible enough to fit the company's present business objectives and accommodate future changes.

(3) Care should be taken to ensure that compliance efforts are not too aggressive but are implemented carefully on the basis of a thorough knowledge of risk management.

A mastery of detail is essential to successful implementation of the program. Lawyers helping a company prepare must have a full understanding of the firm's business, including data regarding both formal agreements and informal behavior. Here is an outline of what they need to know:

• The company's products/services, geographic area of operation and turnover;

• The markets in which the company operates and its respective market shares;

• Extent of participation in trade associations;

• Names of all suppliers and the terms of contractual arrangements with them;

• Customer and dealer selection policy;

• Pricing and discount policy;

• Patent, know-how, trademark and copyright ownership; and

• Joint ventures and other cooperation agreements.

According to Martin, once the information is collected, the company must face the following issues:

• Is the firm dominant in any markets in the EC?

• What kinds of relations are maintained with competitors? Are ties more extensive than participation in industry trade associations?

• Do dealer and distribution practices comply with existing block exemptions or court decisions? What about pricing and discount practices, intellectual-property-right agreements and joint ventures?

What to Do When the EC Shows Up

The bottom line in all compliance programs is making sure that employees are aware of the procedures. Once a program has been drafted, training sessions will be needed to increase the effectiveness of the procedures; the issuance of manuals or guidelines is not enough. Compliance with the policies must be monitored on a regular basis.

Just as important in making compliance programs effective is ensuring that all employees know what to do in the case of an EC investigation or "dawn raid," which generally occurs without prior warning. As a result, Martin suggests that a company have "a nominee at each location with special instructions on how to deal with the situation until the company's legal representatives arrive" and that "a legal rep should always be present." During the inspection, these procedures must be observed:

• The scope of the authorized inquiry should be identified;

• All questions and responses should be recorded by the company's representatives;

• Only questions relating to documents handed over should be answered;

• All documents should be copied in at least two sets, so the company has a permanent record of the information supplied to the commission and;

• Privileged correspondence with the company's lawyers should not be divulged to the Commission.

10
Public Policy

144. Monsanto Decentralizes Without Losing Public Affairs

In 1985, Monsanto directed its strategic focus away from petrochemical commodities and concentrated instead on high-value-added products in biotechnology, specialty chemicals, pharmaceuticals, nutrition chemicals and sweeteners. Besides a significant reduction in personnel, the restructuring entailed a shift from a fairly centralized corporate management structure to one featuring six highly autonomous major operating groups. In the ensuing reorganization of staff functions, the corporate public affairs (PA) division presented special problems. "After 1985, the idea of having a large, centralized public affairs unit in a decentralized company didn't make much sense. Our diverse operating groups had their own individual communications needs," according to Thomas Slocum, Monsanto's director of public affairs.

For a year after the restructuring, Monsanto CEO Richard J. Mahoney examined how certain public affairs functions could be operated by outside agencies but still be available on demand, without Monsanto's having to carry the full expense of dedicated staff. This concern became a critical issue as the firm's global communications needs grew. According to John Hussey, then Monsanto's vice president for public affairs and now a senior vice president with Hill & Knowlton (H&K), "Mahoney knew that Monsanto could not afford to maintain highly qualified public affairs officials in each of its target countries."

Conversations between Mahoney and H&K CEO Robert Dilenschneider in 1986 led to the present experiment. According to Hussey, Dilenschneider took the initiative as part of his effort to explore new ways of building closer linkages between public affairs agencies and their major clients. Monsanto was a natural target for his efforts, as the St. Louis-based firm had been a major H&K client for over 20 years. Mahoney prized H&K because it already had offices in 56 countries, including the key markets where Monsanto already has or plans operations. The two sides entered concrete negotiations in December 1986. By mid-February 1987, the new arrangement was up and running.

What Going Outside Entails

• H&K executes most Monsanto corporate public affairs functions on a global basis. H&K provides support for Monsanto's efforts in government relations (in the US and abroad), biotechnology public affairs, corporate communications, environmental communications, issues research and employee communications. Monsanto can access H&K staffers to perform particular tasks (e.g. speechwriting, drafting annual reports, media monitoring) for the time needed for completion.

Monsanto staffers are primarily involved in directing and coordinating programs and projects carried out by H&K employees, besides carrying out activities that can be handled only by Monsanto personnel. In Washington, for example, daily monitoring of the US congressional, executive and judicial branches, and various lobbying activities are being done for Monsanto by H&K's large office. However, official Monsanto staffers still work directly with the US federal Environmental Protection Agency and other congressional and regulatory offices on specific regulatory matters that affect Monsanto chemicals, herbicides or pharmaceuticals.

• Monsanto's corporate public affairs staff operations were downsized. In place of the previous 25-person corporate public affairs department, Slocum now heads a 13-person unit. He told BI that the new partnership only changed the structure, not the content or quality, of Monsanto's existing corporate public affairs programs. These continue to be focused on a narrow range of critical issues that affect the Monsanto group as a whole.

• Key Monsanto staffers were shifted to H&K. The most unique feature of the deal was the incorporation of several Monsanto PA staffers into H&K and their recomposition (with some added H&K personnel) into a dedicated account team that can utilize H&K's resources for Monsanto's benefit. In all, nine Monsanto executives accepted offers of employment at H&K. They include Monsanto's former directors for policy analysis and communications, public relations, corporate publications, and media relations. This arrangement allowed Monsanto to halve its corporate public affairs staff, while preserving the continuity of these operations. Moreover, the move greatly enhances H&K's ability to understand and service Monsanto's needs. The benefit programs for all nine executives were immediately picked up by H&K, and each individual received monetary incentive to make the transfer.

• H&K charges Monsanto a set monthly fee for its services. This arrangement of a monthly set fee encourages economy on H&K's part and provides a useful yardstick by which to measure savings.

Making the Experiment Work

Communication and coordination have proven to be the keys to success in making this arrangement work. The steps being taken to ensure this include:

• Coordination by a two-man, Monsanto-H&K team. Hussey and Slocum "direct and guide" the working relationship on a daily basis. Slocum works with top Monsanto executives and with Hussey to set his firm's public affairs objectives. Slocum communicates daily with former Monsanto executive Frank Stokes, now H&K's director of policy analysis in St. Louis, to set priorities and monitor the work flow and quality of assignments.

• Developing links between Monsanto and H&K offices. The pact allows overseas Monsanto offices — including existing PA staff in Brussels, Sao Paulo and Asia — to get additional support from H&K, or make use of their personnel areas without Monsanto PA representatives. Thus, local Monsanto management in Japan, for example, can work with an account executive at H&K's Tokyo office. That executive keeps Hussey closely informed as to both the issues raised by the Monsanto side and his own suggestions, while the Monsanto person relays his concerns to St. Louis. Hussey and Slocum are then able to more cohesively build program recommendations.

The arrangement also opened the way for better coordination in transnational public affairs campaigns. An example is the biotechnology public policy program developed by the two firms for the US and Europe. According to Hussey, "Without this relationship, Monsanto's management in Europe might have hired two or three other PR firms, which would first have needed training. More importantly, it would have been difficult to ensure that the agencies in Europe were saying the same things that we were in the US. Since members of my team sat on the Monsanto internal biotech committee, we knew the thinking behind the program and could ensure that our messages were consistent."

The Challenge of Communication

According to Slocum, one of the best challenges to Monsanto in making the experiment work was learning how to use the H&K organization. "The added value for us is the access to this worldwide organization, but it took time to step out of a mode of operation suitable for a centralized structure and then learn how to tap into H&K's 1,800 professionals."

According to Monsanto and H&K executives, the only major problems that have occurred have involved communications. Even though the key H&K executives handling Monsanto's account were originally from Monsanto, "a degree of sensitivity was lost because we were no longer down the hall, but across the town or the country." An H&K executive also notes that "the only glitches in performance have occurred when communications between the two sides have not been fully open."

To cope with this issue, Slocum and Hussey work to strengthen lines of communications between the two corporations. Weekly staff meetings are held between Monsanto and H&K staffers in St. Louis, and telephone conferences take place daily between each of the New York City, Washington and St. Louis offices. Moreover, the two firms have established permanently linked computer and telephone connections. Relates Hussey, "When the phone rings at the Monsanto PA department, it actually rings at H&K's St. Louis office. Thanks to the interconnections between our IBM computers, we can now put a document on the desk of any Monsanto executive by pushing a few buttons."

145. How Amoco Canada Rescued Poor Start on Dome Takeover

When Amoco Corp's Canadian unit launched a $5.2 billion offer for Calgary's Dome Petroleum Ltd in the spring of 1987, it did not anticipate the intensity of political and public scrutiny that would follow the largest takeover attempt in Canada's history. The offer became the subject of parliamentary debates and national opinion polls, and has provided ammunition for anti-free-trade groups.

Amoco Canada underestimated the level of public pressure that could be exerted on a government beset by wandering popularity. It also misread the degree to which Canadian ownership would become an issue, even though the Brian Mulroney administration clearly did not want to interfere. As a result, the company was less prepared than it should have been in meeting public challenges to the takeover. But observers agree that once the firm launched its public relations campaign, much of that criticism was diffused.

Getting Off on the Wrong Foot...

Immediately preceding the offer, Amoco Canada's President T. Don Stacy briefed Energy Minister Marcel Masse and Finance Minister Michael Wilson. This successfully deflected official criticism and won firm official support that will endure beyond the conclusion of the deal. But Amoco Canada was not so direct in its dealings with the press. Between April 18, 1987 (when the offer was made) and May 14 of that year (when the details were given), it left most media dealings in the hands of Dome. This created a serious credibility and public relations void—interpreted by many as the arrogance of a US MNC.

According to an Amoco Canada spokesperson, the company faced a difficult decision at that time. While the takeover announcement represented an agreement by both companies to enter into negotiations, the groups most affected by the proposal were Dome's creditors and shareholders. Under the circumstances, management felt the company had to keep a low profile—even if doing so was not the best strategic move. The negative impact of the silence was exacerbated by the fact that the company name was little known outside the oil and gas industry.

...And Quickly Correcting

In the week following the May 14 explanation of the terms of the merger, Amoco continued to maintain a low profile. But as its image problems worsened, a two-prong offensive was launched, with support at the highest level of the company. The lead was taken by Stacy, who was tireless in selling the merits of the deal to the central Canadian financial press, business and government leaders and other public figures. According to Ian Doig, publisher of *Doig's Digest*, a leading energy industry publication in Canada, "it was the legal department that won the initial battle for Amoco Canada, while the public relations department was slow to come to grips with the problem." However, says Doig, "once Amoco got into the situation about mid-May, they did a superb job." The public relations strategy stressed two major areas:

• **Emphasize the positive.** Rather than try to answer nationalist critics, Stacy's efforts focused on the benefits of the takeover: The merger would eliminate Dome's drag on the Alberta oil industry, no jobs would be lost and the synergistic effect of the merger would help stimulate the Alberta economy. This same public relations awakening helped Amoco neutralize the strong nationalistic response to the fact that the acquisition would reduce Canadian ownership in the industry. Amoco also worked well with the press. Stacy, according to an observer, went "across this country from one editorial board to another," and in the process established a strong rapport with the press and the public.

• **Sweeten the pot.** Following discussions with Investment Canada, Amoco announced that it would issue equity in the merged company in Canada. The issue will eventually cost Amoco several million dollars in lost US tax benefits, but management believed the decision to have been a very effective countermove. It virtually halted the arguments put forth by TransCanada Pipelines Ltd, the only Canadian bidder and a rejected suitor for Dome. Even more importantly, it gave Canadians a valuable extra reason to support the growth of the venture.

Amoco's most persistent obstacle was its dealings with creditors. Three Canadian banks, owed more than $2 billion by Dome, were the most vocal critics. They felt they were not given the same consideration shown the government and were particularly angry that in between the time the offer was announced and May 14 they were not brought into the picture. Further, they were outraged that Dome continued to negotiate a rescheduling of its debt at the time it discussed the sale. The company's response was to hang tough, weathering the attacks by sticking firmly to its original terms.

The approach here, too, was to up the ante. Secured creditors were offered an average $0.88 on the dollar and unsecured, $0.35. Amoco made some adjustments within the terms of its deal that gave the secured bank creditors more money.

The Message for Other Companies

The lessons from the Amoco Canada experience have a common theme important for investors in many other countries as well: Although the foreign investment context has changed — perhaps even dramatically — an MNC should still use the same public affairs primer that was valid in the 1980s. The basic pointers are:

• **Don't underestimate nationalist sentiment.** Amoco went into the takeover arena with the blessing of Energy Minister Marcel Masse. He said he would not stand in the way of foreign takeovers of ailing energy firms. But, according to an experienced Canadian political observer, "While the government had no problem with the acquisition of an un-

healthy company, nationalists—inside and outside the government—
still saw the opportunity to draw attention to it." The fact that the government softened its stance does not necessarily mean that the
underlying support for a restrictive policy disappeared.

• **Symbols still matter.**   Dome was once a symbol of Canadian efforts
to regain domestic control of oil and gas resources. In fact, in the late
1970s, Dome was the prime example of a national energy policy that
encouraged Canadian investment as a stepping stone to growth.
Heightening this sensitivity was the fact that the energy industry itself
carried much symbolic clout. Although some industry analysts say that
energy no longer leads Canada's public agenda, others believe that Canadians still feel domestic ownership is important in the energy sector
and US ownership is already too high.

• **Don't overlook the external context.**   The timing of Amoco's offer
coincided with the Canada-US free trade talks, and this intensified public scrutiny of the move. With pressure from the Canadian negotiators
to raise Canadian equity participation and job creation requirements,
which were at the center of the foreign investment debate, the Amoco
bid not surprisingly attracted more than the usual interest in a transaction of this kind.

146. Guidelines for Corporate Giving

Experts in the philanthropy field have suggested several guidelines for
companies to follow in setting up a successful program:

• **Assess needs.**   Companies should meet with community leaders to find
out the most important causes. In addition, internal surveys among employees are useful to determine issues that are important to the work force.

• **Be strategic.**   After needs have been determined, the firm should
decide which ones it is best suited to address and how doing this fits in
with overall corporate strategy. A strong focus is especially important
for companies with limited funds. However, the program should be
flexible to allow responses to changing needs.

• **Target related areas.**   Pursuing projects that attack connected issues
not only makes administration and public relations easier for the firm,
but also ensures a greater effect.

- **Involve all levels of the company.** Commitment by top management is crucial for success of the program, and participation by key executives is the fastest way to create a positive public image. Community involvement by other employees is necessary to provide greatly needed human resources for various causes and to boost the firm's visibility and familiarity within the community.

- **Encourage volunteerism.** Volunteering can be one of the most effective contributions a company can make: Volunteer activity appears more sincere than a cash donation, and it is often more useful than throwing money at a problem. It also serves as an excellent way for a new firm in town to get involved and become known within the community.

  "Volunteering humanizes the leaders of the company," says Alan Parter, president of Parter International, a firm which assists companies investing in the US with their community, public and government public relations efforts. "It is also a way to make business contacts, and it gets the support of the employees, which is a very important part of philanthropy."

- **Consider setting up a foundation.** Foundations not only signal long-term commitment, but also provide stability for giving programs, because they are shielded from the business cycle. Foundations may be more efficient in distributing funds than the parent company, which must make charitable donations from repatriated profits. Finally, foundations create distance between the company and the beneficiary so the firm doesn't appear overly self-serving, e.g. when funding research efforts at a university.

- **Make sure your foundation and/or direct-giving program has enough resources.** One quick route to failure is to leave charitable work to the CEO to perform a few hours each week. Practitioners estimate that, for a nationwide direct-giving program, a company must commit at least one professional, one secretary and at least $1 million a year for donations. On the other hand, if a company wants to spend less than $100,000, it could have an impact, but only in a very small local community.

- **Corporate foundations must be careful when establishing by-laws.** Administrators suggest that funding guidelines, while necessary to provide guidance, should not be overly restrictive. They need to be changeable as community needs change. Executives who establish foundations must also remember to keep the investment strategy broad and independent. One foundation's endowment is unnecessarily shaky because it is heavily invested in stocks related to the company's industry, which is not doing well.

• **Direct-giving programs should start out small.**   Begin with a local-level project to become familiar with community leaders and the process of giving. Any national program must allow for local/regional differences. Companies need to give local units enough autonomy and voice in the giving program so the company can respond to local needs. Every community has its own requirements; local residents and workers know them best. Many companies ask local committees in each facility to decide where a portion of the company's resources will be allocated. For example, Hitachi provides matching funds for designated organizations and projects nominated by employees through Community Action Committees.

• **If you choose to advertise, prepare the ground first.**   Harlan Flint, director of external affairs for BP America, recommends that, as part of getting acquainted with the community, a new CEO till the soil in advance of any specific "good works" announcement. For example, the CEO may want to meet with the editorial board of the local paper(s) and talk about the company's philanthropic programs and goals in general. "It's easy to ignore a press release,"says Flint. This way, the CEO has established the necessary relationship base first. The CEO may also want to check whether any public or opinion leaders are members of an organization to which he or she belongs.

• **Tread lightly in the arena of cause-related marketing.**   This is a tricky area. Companies can go over the edge, and aspects of their efforts that are self-serving can rebound to create bad PR. Much depends on having a product or service that lends itself to a cause. For example, Scott Paper has a fall promotion called "Learning Tools for Schools." Apple seals are applied to Scott's entire consumer-product line. PTAs, students and school associations can sponsor seal-collection drives, enabling the local school to redeem them for books, computers or other equipment.

But while some companies can make cause-related marketing tasteful and effective, this is not always the case. For example, many considered the contributions to the restoration of the Statue of Liberty and the Olympics based on product purchases as self-serving media scams. Notes a leading expert in the field. "It is all about name and logo recognition...Finding something that promotes huge visibility."

147. A-RACE: Community-Relations Program

Created by the Center for Corporate Community Relations at Boston College, A-RACE is a model for developing an effective community-relations program. It consists of five stages: Assessment, Research, Action Planning, Communication and Evaluation.

Assessment

The purpose of the Assessment phase of the A-RACE model is to help identify a program focus. The program focus is established through an information-gathering process.

- **Step I: Know your company**

- What is your company currently doing in the community?

- What are other divisions of the company doing in their communities?

- What has your company done in the past?

- In what organizations are your employees currently involved?

- What is the perception among key leaders of what your company has done in the community?

- **Step II: Know what other companies are doing**

- What are the other companies in your community doing? List their major projects and contributions activities. Relate corporate gifts to some standard (e.g., corporate gifts divided by total number of employees or sales or deposits).

- **Step III: Know your community and its needs**

- What are the characteristics of your community—population, ethnic composition, age distribution, housing conditions, transportation? (This information is usually available from your community's planning agency.)

- What changes in the characteristics of your community are expected during the next five to 10 years? (Again, this information is usually available from your community's planning agency.)

- What are the current needs in your community as determined by:

(a) Your needs assessment activities;
(b) Needs assessments conducted by other agencies in your community, including United Way, Area Agency on Aging, Department of Human or Social Services, community planning agency;
(c) Employee needs assessment (what do your employees see as community needs?); and
(d) National and local business memberships.

Once the assessment phase is completed, the next task is to develop programs for the issues area. There are three types of programs:

• **Internal programs.** Programs within the company that have a community relations focus, such as volunteer programs and contributions programs.

• **External existing community programs** that provide corporate support for an existing organization in the community, or engage in a collaborative corporate venture.

• **New external community program** to develop an entirely new program to meet an unmet need in the community.

This is where the RACE formula is valuable. In each instance it is necessary to conduct Research, develop an Action plan, Communicate the plan and Evaluate it, in order to develop a successful program.

Research

• **Step I: Determine issue area based on results of assessment**
• **Step II: Conduct an external resource analysis**

• List the organizations and agencies in the community offering services in the selected issue area.

• Find out which employees of the company are currently participating in these organizations and agencies.

• Interview the directors of the agencies to determine the scope of the agency's services.

• **Step III: Conduct an internal resource analysis**

• What leading unique resources does your company have that can assist you in developing a focused program?

- What in your company's mission statement or product line can be used to focus in on the type of program you want to develop?

- Interview employees in the company who have leadership positions in the agencies in the issue area.

- **Step IV: Investigate similar programs developed by other companies**

Action Plan

- **Step I: Establish a program goal**

- What do you intend to accomplish? (Determine feasibility of establishing an advisory committee composed of key company employees to help plan and support the program.)

- **Step II: Set objectives**

- This is a critical step. Objectives form the basis for determining what activities should be performed, and also help establish criteria for evaluating how well they are being performed.

- **Step III: Prepare action steps**

- What steps will be needed to achieve each objective? (Include time schedule, and costs and fix accountability for each step.)

- **Step IV: Establish control**

- Who will be assigned responsibility for the program?

Communicating the Plan

- **Step I: Develop an external communications program**

- News releases to local newspapers.

- Special events that can publicize the company's participation in the program.

**Step II: Develop an Internal
Communications Program**

- Inform key staff about the program.

- Run stories on the program in your company publications: in-house newsletter, magazines, publications to stockholders.

• If an advisory committee has been established, use it to publicize the project within your company.

Evaluating the Program Results
• **Step I: Determine ways to measure results**

• Satisfaction surveys from among program consumers.

• Informal surveys of community organizations about the program.

• Focus groups.

• Social responsibility audits.

148. Dos and Don'ts of Lobbying in the US

Washington has become a changed playing field for corporate lobbyists. The old-boy network has broken down, and issue expertise has become much more important. Jeffrey Trammell, a former congressional staffer and now senior vice president-legislative affairs group for Hill and Knowlton Public Affairs Worldwide, notes that "part of the problem here is one of perception, not reality. In the past it was seen as influence peddling, not providing information. Congress has become more sophisticated, larger, with many points of contact. Today a lobbyist must rely on good information and relate it in a timely fashion. Lobbying has become an information-providing activity rather than relying on who knows whom." Trammell says "lobbyist" is not a dirty word and thinks a company should not shy away from such activities. "Any interest that has a legitimate story should tell it. Most members of Congress rely on timely and accurate information."

Below is a list of important points for running a corporate government affairs program.

• **DO know what you are talking about.**   "You are only as effective as how much you know," remarks Isabel Hyde, Washington representative for Goodyear Tire & Rubber.

• **DO tell the truth.**   "Your word is your bond," says Hyde. This sentiment is echoed by many other corporate representatives: "If you don't provide information or your word is not good, you will lack credibility the next time around." Trammell is blunt: "You have an obligation not to mislead."

- **DO be judicious in when and how you approach members of Congress.** "Know the members you are dealing with and what their agenda is," urges Steve Walker, director of government relations for Reynolds Metal. Walker believes his penchant for trivia helps him in developing relations with members and planning his strategy. "Know when it is time to ask for help and when not to. Don't expect someone to commit political suicide for you," he adds. Lobbyists should be aware that the political composition of a district or state as well as the individual's ideology may mean that the representative or senator cannot support the company's position 100% of the time.

- **DO look for the local angle on a position.** "A congressman or senator always will give first priority to the interests of his own district. A foreign interest should constantly look for ways to point out its business interests in the US, to give its arguments a 'local angle,'" notes Trammell. For example, Trammell was involved in planning a campaign for the Airbus consortium to deflect complaints that US companies were buying aircraft from Europeans rather than US manufacturers. Hill and Knowlton compiled a list of US suppliers to Airbus and matched them to congressional districts, approaching those representatives. Similarly, Walker says he has cultivated relationships with the 20 senators and 30 members of the House in which Reynolds Metal has facilities.

- **DON'T use the same approach with every congressional committee.** What works for Commerce and Tax doesn't for Armed Services and Foreign Relations. Trammell elaborates: "You have to know how each committee sees itself. Each committee has a personality, depending on its chairman, its members and its historic role." Trammell advises looking at the jurisdiction of a committee in deciding how to approach it. For example, the members of the Armed Services Committee will view the world from a defense perspective and ask what a particular bill would do to national security, while the Finance Committee might be more concerned with its effect on the balance of trade, and the Commerce Committee, with transfer of technology. In lobbying, "you have to be prepared to address the specific areas of interest of each committee," says Trammell.

- **DON'T go it alone.** Build coalitions. Goodyear's Hyde estimates that one third of her time is spent in this way. The breadth and depth of coalitions matter much more than in the past. Hyde says that today creating an all-business coalition "won't get you anywhere." It has to be much broader. For example, work she did on corporate takeover reform built a coalition that included state attorneys general, governors, the Association of State Legislators and consumer groups.

• **DON'T waste the time of members of Congress or their staff.** "People get too involved in minutiae. Members of Congress and their staff are incredibly busy people. Your issue is not necessarily their priority. Understand their time constraints and the pressures on the Hill. Staff appreciate this. Some executives drone on and on about their favorite subject because they have the senator captive. That's not the purpose for being there," cautions Trammell.

• **DO prepare written corporate position papers.** "Have good written materials. Make sure they are concise. In the press of time, staff may have to review your position. It is very important to have accurate materials" to leave with them, adds Trammell.

149. How to Choose a Public Relations Firm

A particular company's need for outside public relations (PR) assistance varies with its size, industry and internal capacities (staff size and expertise, quantity of funds available and in-house equipment). Interviews with PR executives of six foreign-owned companies in the US produced the following recommendations for selecting the appropriate firm:

• Choose a company on the basis of its general reputation, its expertise and its longevity in the business.

• Be sure the firm has prior experience with the objectives or tactics for which you are hiring it.

• Be sure the firm understands your business.

• Check with the prospective PR firm's other clients, other companies in your industry and personal contacts for their experience and recommendations.

• Know the people who will actually handle your business on a day-today basis. Do not hire a firm solely on the basis of the top executives you meet at lunch.

150. Importance of PR for Foreign Firms Acquiring US Companies

Not all foreign investors realize that their first communications and public-affairs challenge arises even before they have made the investment. In fact, this may be one of the most crucial opportunities to position the company and foster its long-run health. PR executives agree with Harlan Flint, director of external affairs for BP America, who says, "You can't begin too early" to develop good public relations. "You are creating a presence in a particular region and will be affected for a long time to come by how you initially enter." Stan Sauerhaft, vice chairman of Burson-Marstellar, makes the key point here: "Communications should be part of the whole strategic plan, not an afterthought."

Although all foreign investors face a higher public acceptance hurdle than US companies would, public resistance is usually even stronger if the means of investment is acquisition. Below, BI outlines a two-phase plan for foreign firms who find themselves in such a situation.

Phase I

Environment. "Quite often there is a feeling among people, if a foreigner buys something it can't be good, or it would have been better if a US company" had purchased the business, says David Duffy of Adams & Rinehart, a major corporate PR firm based in New York. Duffy speaks for most when he warns, "This issue will become increasingly visible and heated as we go forward."

A foreign company making a hostile takeover bid has a far greater and more serious PR problem. The US takeover object will have the advantage in knowing public opinion and shaping it as well as in calling upon state and local officials to aid in its defense. If the takeover is friendly, the requirements for a company to explain itself are still there, but obviously the task is much easier to perform.

Message. Stress the benefits of the deal, what it will mean to employees, the community and consumers. Be prepared to address hostile reactions in the case of an unfriendly takeover attempt. Negative local reactions can be softened or diverted if local community leaders can be convinced of such benefits as:

• The company is financially strengthened by the acquisition or mergers;

• The product or service will be improved and will be more competitive in the world market;

• The acquirer or partner will make a technological transfer;

• Jobs will be created, or at least saved; and/or

• The foreign company has a history of leaving key management in place.

If a company cannot rely on its reputation in previous acquisitions, then handling community relations will obviously be even more difficult. "If you've done a deal in a nasty way, you will have three times more problems the next time," Sauerhaft points out. However, the company may still succeed in putting a positive face on the current acquisition. Sauerhaft suggests that the acquiring firm "face up to the nasty things it has done" and see if it can make one or more of the following arguments:

• The previous management was not producing adequately.

• A particular plant or facility would have gone under without the acquisition.

• "We made a difficult decision the previous management could not."

• "Sure there were 2,000 employees in the past and now only 1,100 jobs. The alternative could have been zero."

Strategy. "The biggest single mistake by an acquirer is the presumption that it is a purely financial transaction, that money speaks. Most acquirers make that mistake most of the time. It is the one from which all the others [mistakes] tend to derive," says Gershon Kekst, president of Kekst & Co., a leading New York-based public relations firm. Foreign acquirers must pay attention to how management feels and the feelings of all the other constituent stakeholders, as well. "You must pass the public scrutiny test" for your deal to succeed, he adds. The following suggestions will help smooth the way:

(1) Do your homework. Alan Parter, President of Parter International, a firm which assists companies investing in the US with their community, public and government public relations efforts, notes that companies spend tremendous time and resources in analyzing the financial and marketing aspects of the deal, but too little on communications. "The company to be acquired or with which you are entering into a joint venture already has an image in the community. It has strengths and weaknesses in its own communications," he says. Parter recommends that the acquiring firm not only find out what the community's perception of the deal is, but also perform a communications audit on the takeover target's standing in the community, its capabilities and perceptions (internal and external).

(2) Identify all the affected stakeholders. They can include employees, stockholders, customers, suppliers/vendors and various organizations with which the company has regular interaction (e.g. government bodies, regulatory authorities, unions, community groups). The stakeholder scope and the complexity of the communications effort will vary a great deal depending on the size of the acquisition as well as whether it is friendly or hostile. Parter points out that for small and medium-sized companies, the issues will be much more localized. The strategy will also be affected by the type of business the two companies engage in. Acquisitions made in the defense or banking industries, for example, will always run into more difficulty because they are more circumscribed by regulations if not also public opinion.

(3) Set priorities. Regardless of the size of the deal, Parter cautions: "Know that you can't necessarily win with all the various groups involved. There is a plethora of communications issues that need to be dealt with. Preparation alone doesn't mean that you can solve all of them. There may be countervailing interests. What may be attractive about the deal to consumers may not be to employees, for example. Know what the choices are and what your priorities will be." This research and analysis process should yield clear results as to the various risks involved in the deal. Management can then decide whether proceeding is worthwhile.

(4) Address the stakeholders. Kekst explains that the acquiring company must explain how each group's stake will be affected. "The acquiring company must show it understands the historic stake, respects it and will not breach it. It just cannot stand up and say this." The acquirer must rely on its own history to explain to the various groups who it is and verify that its intentions are reliable. In addition, it must explain why it chose the target company, adds Kekst. The takeover target has a similar obligation to explain the same issues to all the stakeholders, i.e. why it is selling itself to another company and why that particular one. Kekst emphasizes that the acquirer must deliver the message "with conviction and understanding that you are making a commitment."

How to handle shareholders will depend on how large the company is and how friendly the deal is. Duffy notes that, in his experience, "the average company is somewhere between one half and three fourths held by institutional investors. Institutions are much less likely to give consideration if the acquirer is foreign or domestic. They will look at the financials more, such as the premium. To the extent that they do think about this, they may wonder, 'Does the fact of the foreign acquisition make the deal any less likely to happen?' Patriotic issues are not likely to enter."

Neil Call, executive vice president of D.F. King, a New York-based company that specializes in investor relations, proxy solicitation and public relations, suggests that foreign investors prepare to answer such commonly asked questions about the deal as:

- Is the price right? What is the total value of the transaction?
- Is the financing in place or reasonably so? How will it be handled?
- Has a fairness opinion been obtained? From whom?

(5) Pay attention to timing.   Timing communications, public, government and community relations efforts around an acquisition is crucial and should be done as soon as possible. However, it will vary according to the particular situation, the most obvious example being whether the takeover is friendly or not. First, the acquirer should talk with management of the target about all these various issues. If this is not possible before the deal is announced, because of legal or other reasons, then it should be done immediately once the information becomes public.

Executives should contact government officials simultaneously with or as soon as possible following the public announcement of the deal. Duffy provides details: "Let's say a company announced on Friday morning its intention to acquire a company in Cincinnati. The first thing that morning, we would hand deliver a letter to the mayor, the governor and the elected representatives in Washington saying, 'Here's what we are doing and why. We would like to meet with you to discuss this at your earliest convenience.'" Duffy points out that it is difficult for politicians to complain about the deal without having talked to the buyer first. Besides, " 'foreign acquirers' sounds ominous and nebulous. If you have a person who represents that foreign acquirer," the task consequently becomes humanized and easier, he goes on.

Phase II

How to continue to develop the image of the company will depend on many factors. All companies to a certain degree will need to cultivate good relations with most if not all of the stakeholders.

For customers, the PR strategy will depend on such factors as:

• How competitive is the market in which the company operates?

• What kind of product or service is being sold? If sales are being conducted business-to-business, then the outreach may include brochures, sales materials, trade shows, etc., notes Parter. If it is a consumer product, maybe an occasional splashy event will be staged.

For employees, these PR factors are important:

• Size of company;

• Nature of labor force (e.g. union/nonunion/mixture; part time/full time; professional/clerical/blue-collar; centralized locations/highly scattered locations);

Here the company may sponsor newsletters, seminars and other events, community and philanthropic activities and/or parties for employees.

In any event, a company needs to ensure that its postacquisition communications continue to be strong and that it is prepared for any contingency that might arise. Company K tells how it was unprepared for an unsolicited tender offer. The director of public relations heard about it on a Sunday afternoon, just a few hours before the store appeared in the local press. On Monday, the company was confronted by full-page advertisements in *The Wall Street Journal*, announcing the acquirer's interest in buying shares. As employees first heard about the offer through the news rather than from their employers, the PR Department issued a short press release on that Monday for employees and the news media, saying the offer was being reviewed by the board and no specific comment was available. The company transmitted this to all branches via telex. No internal briefings were scheduled because they would violate federal securities law dealing with insider trading. The PR Department could not adequately deal with employees' concerns because there was not time to do so. Staff time was devoted to arranging all the board meetings. Finally when the board rejected the offer, the PR office sent a press release to employees and the media saying so.

151. How to Deal With Demands for Information

Public scrutiny of individual MNCs is rapidly becoming more organized—a trend that could threaten overseas operations and that should be met with corporate action. Public interest groups are compiling detailed files, reports and in-depth studies on specific firms and are increasingly asking companies themselves for information and cooperation.

MNCs must also prepare to be investigated on a wider range of subjects from now on, from consumer, environmental and energy issues to other upcoming areas. New groups are emerging, with labor unions, churches and shareholders becoming more active along with international institutions and local government agencies. In handling their requests, firms should consider these points:

• **Know with whom you are dealing.** Some groups are well established and respected, with proven records of fair reporting and respect for confidentiality. Others are less experienced or may be local chapters acting without the knowledge of parent organizations. Determine each group's reliability based on its merits, as well as its mandate to seek corporate information.

• **Assign specific responsibility.** Many companies have found that requests from organized public groups often require a different approach from routine media relations, which can be handled by public affair departments. It may be useful to charge overall responsibility to a single executive or line employee. If responsibility is scattered, cooperation among departments and especially with overseas subsidiaries is essential to minimize confusion and develop compatible answers.

• **Differentiate among requests.** Major research projects that seek interviews with executives and managers deserve careful consideration. Modest requests for basic data or official company positions can be handled more simply. Avoid a casual attitude toward any requests.

• **Decide what to divulge.** Find out to whom the information will go and how it will be used (e.g.in stockholder resolutions). Keep up to date on disclosures required by law. Not all local or state agencies, or even legislative committees, have subpoena powers. Remember that groups can often collect information from other sources, including data already in the public domain or available under local laws such as the US's Freedom of Information Act, but that much of it may be incomplete, outdated or inaccurate.

• **Cooperate whenever possible.** Many groups will repay candid and substantive cooperation with reports that reflect favorably on firms. If companies work closely with investigators, some of whom may not have expert knowledge of their subject, more opportunities will arise for firms to make them aware of wider issues and complexities, and final reports are more likely to be objective. Also, be sure to review report drafts for factual inaccuracies and to make further suggestions or comments.

• **Consider setting disclosure guidelines.**   Some companies, including banks and auto manufacturers, have adopted specific guidelines in the form of manuals to define their own disclosure policies beyond the legal requirements. Firms using guidelines to coordinate policy should also review them regularly as conditions change.

• **Publish annual "social reports."** More MNCs find that annual reports describing how they meet their corporate responsibilities can go far toward satisfying public demands for such information. To do so, reports should consist of more than a simple list of charitable donations.

Index